D1596810

Self-Consciousness and Self-Determination

Studies in Contemporary German Social Thought
Thomas McCarthy, General Editor

Self-Consciousness and Self-Determination

Ernst Tugendhat
translated by Paul Stern

The MIT Press, Cambridge, Massachusetts, and London, England

This book was set in Baskerville by The MIT Press Computergraphics Department and was printed and bound by Halliday Lithograph in the United States of America.

Library of Congress Cataloging-in-Publication Data

Tugendhat, Ernst.
  Self-consciousness and self-determination.

  (Studies in contemporary German social thought)
  Translation of: Selbstbewusstsein und Selbstbestimmung.

  Bibliography: p.
  Includes index.
  1. Self (Philosophy)—History—Addresses, essays, lectures. 2. Self-consciousness—History—Addresses, essays, lectures. I. Title. II. Series.
BD450.T8813 1986   126   85-31235
ISBN 0-262-20056-2

Contents

Translator's Introduction

In *Self-Consciousness and Self-Determination* Ernst Tugendhat takes up a set of problems that have been a central preoccupation of the modern philosophical tradition from Descartes onward, namely, the special nature of self-consciousness, self-knowledge, and self-relation.[1] In addressing these topics Tugendhat wrestles with a number of difficulties that are quite familiar within this tradition, such as the problems posed by the incorrigibility of first-person reports of conscious states, by the epistemic asymmetry between first- and third-person ascriptions of conscious states, and by the puzzles concerning the possibility of third-person access to the experiences, intentions, and beliefs of others. But he also takes into account a wider conception of self-consciousness and self-relation that has been neglected by much of the modern tradition—that is, the sense of self-consciousness and self-relation that is involved in an agent's *practical* self-understanding in his activities and in his life as a whole. This is the sense of self-consciousness that may be ascribed to an agent when we say, for example, that he really knows 'who' he is or what he is doing with his life; it is a sense of self-consciousness that we might want to ascribe to someone as a virtue (or as a vice, if he is conspicuously self-deceived in his intentions), and hence it is closely related to the form of self-knowledge that is demanded in the Delphic motto *gnothi seauton* (Know thyself).

From Descartes to Kant it was assumed that in the structure of self-consciousness—in knowledge of one's experiences or of oneself—philosophy had discovered the basis for a secure, fully justified form of theoretical knowledge. Fichte and Hegel extended the foundational status of the principle of self-consciousness from theoretical to practical philosophy, seeking the basis for a rational, autonomous form of life in the fully developed concept of a practical relation of oneself to oneself. Nevertheless, in Tugendhat's view, the modern philosophical tradition did not succeed, in its accounts either of theoretical or of practical self-consciousness, in identifying the relevant structures that could serve to elucidate the phenomena in question. Hence, if we hope to clarify the precise nature of self-consciousness in its theoretical and practical sense, we must critically examine the conceptual models by which the entire modern tradition was oriented in characterizing the phenomena and try to develop an alternative conceptual framework that more adequately captures their constitutive structures.

This is precisely the task that Tugendhat sets himself in *Self-Consciousness and Self-Determination*. He is quite clear about the sources of confusion that have misled the modern tradition in its construal of the self-consciousness relation. There are basically two models that have exercised crucial importance here. The first, which Tugendhat calls the subject-object model, treats consciousness essentially as a relation to an object; from this perspective, self-consciousness is understood as that peculiar relation to an object in which the object is identical with consciousness itself, that is, one has oneself 'before' oneself. The second misleading model is epistemological, involving the idea that in self-consciousness one gains a special access to oneself through a kind of inner perception, a turning of one's observing gaze from outer objects to one's inner self.

How have these two models led the modern tradition astray in its understanding of the self-consciousness relation? They jointly contribute to the picture of self-consciousness as a reflexive relation in which the subject turns back upon himself, directs his glance upon a private, inner sphere and thereby directly apprehends himself qua object. In Tugendhat's view, this picture is misguided in at least three crucial respects. First, it fails to recognize that the object that one is aware of in self-consciousness is not an object in the ordinary sense, but a propositional object. In expressing an awareness of a feeling of sharp pain, for example, it would be senseless to say "I know I" or "I know pain"; rather, one's awareness is expressed in sentences of the form "I know *that* I am in pain." Similarly, in practically relating to oneself as a human agent, one does not relate to something inside oneself, a core of one's personality or subjectivity that one somehow 'sees';

rather, one relates to oneself practically in relating to (i.e., in deliberating about) the issue of how one is going to live—what sort of activities, relations, and so on one is going to engage in. It follows that the states of mind to which the phenomena of self-consciousness refer are propositional attitudes, and hence that the attempt to grasp the latter in terms of a reflexive relation is deeply misdirected.

Second, the epistemological orientation of traditional theories of self-consciousness toward the model of inner observation misleadingly reduces first-person self-ascription of conscious states to third-person ascription of perceptible predicates to material objects, which takes place essentially from the perspective of an observer. It is thereby implied that in ascribing conscious states to ourselves we first identify something 'inside' ourselves (an I or an ego), to which we then ascertain that a certain predicate, standing for a conscious state, attaches. As Tugendhat shows, this analogy breaks down on closer examination if one attends to the actual function of the singular term "I" in identification and to the rules of use governing the first-person self-ascription of predicates standing for conscious states. If one brings this reflexive model of inner seeing or observing to bear in trying to understand how we relate practically to ourselves as agents, the consequences are even more disastrous. For precisely what is inconceivable on this model is the sense in which our relation to ourselves as agents is constituted not in a contemplative perception of our inner self or personality, but in a volitional choice of what we are going to do with our lives and hence 'who' we are going to be.

Finally, the third misleading implication of the traditional picture of self-consciousness is that it is an essentially solipsistic relation that the individual enjoys merely by reflecting back upon a private inner sphere to which he alone has privileged access. In Tugendhat's view, self-consciousness in its theoretical and its practical sense is essentially linked to the rules of intersubjective speech and to the norms of the social community in which the agent defines those activities central to his life. Any attempt to make sense either of the first-person self-ascription of conscious states or of the practical self-relation outside of this intersubjective framework will necessarily fail to account for the conditions of meaning presupposed in each of these modes of relating to oneself.

Tugendhat develops his alternative model of self-consciousness through an interpretation of three philosophers who stand in a critical relation to the prejudices of the tradition: Wittgenstein, Heidegger, and Mead. He turns to these philosophers because they are conceptual innovators. Each sought in his own way to disengage himself from the categorical assumptions of the tradition and to understand the phenomena of self-consciousness on a new basis. This is especially true of Wittgenstein and Heidegger. They both attempted to break away from the traditional notion of consciousness as a domain in which the subject 'represents' an object and in which one's self is encountered through inner observation or perception. In Wittgenstein's case, the repudiation of the model of inner 'seeing' led to an entirely new understanding of those sentences in which knowledge of one's conscious states is articulated: They are to be understood as expressive and not as cognitive. In Heidegger's case, the rejection of the contemplative model of self-consciousness led to the discovery (or recovery, if one considers Aristotle) of an entirely new dimension of self-relation neglected by the modern tradition: A self-relation constituted not in reflexively apprehending something inside oneself, but in adopting a practical, volitional stance toward the unavoidable question of how one is going to live.

It is only in this connection—that is, of the practical relation to oneself—that the originality of Mead's account of the self can be properly appreciated. What Mead demonstrates, according to Tugendhat, is that one's practical relation to oneself is not an individual, private affair; it is only articulated in an inner conversation with oneself that rests on an internalization of social norms and the possibility of conversing with others. It follows that one's conception of oneself as a practical agent is constituted socially in both a genetic and structural sense, and that the prospect of a rational or reflective self-relation can only be understood in terms of achieving a possible consensus with other rational interlocutors about matters pertaining to the good life.

It should already be apparent from these preliminary remarks that, contrary to the tradition, Tugendhat does not regard the topic of self-consciousness as a unitary one. Rather, it involves two distinct sets of phenomena, each of which requires its own separate philosophical elucidation. The first set of phenomena has to do with first-person knowledge of one's own conscious states and is characterized by Tugendhat as immediate epistemic self-consciousness; it is expressed in sentences of the form "I know that I ϕ," where ϕ stands for a conscious state. The second set of phenomena does not refer to an epistemic or theoretical consciousness of oneself at all, but to a practical relation to oneself that each human agent necessarily adopts in deciding how to live his life, in addressing the inescapable choice of what to do and 'who' to be.

Accordingly, Tugendhat's discussion of self-consciousness falls into two main parts. The first deals with immediate epistemic self-consciousness. He begins by subjecting a recent, traditionally conceived account of this relation—that of Dieter Henrich—to a devastating "language-analytic" critique, and he then turns to Wittgenstein's treatment of this problem in the *Philosophical Investigations* and in the "Notes for Lectures" in order to reconstruct an alternative view that avoids the absurdities of the old model. In the second part of the book he develops his account of the practical relation of oneself to oneself and of the higher-level reflective or autonomous self-relation through an interpretation of Heidegger and Mead, and he concludes by contrasting this higher-level conception of autonomy to a corresponding traditional conception, namely, the Hegelian view of freedom as expounded in the theory of ethical life (*Sittlichkeit*).

While Tugendhat's analysis of immediate epistemic self-consciousness contains several points of prime philosophical importance — including a perspicuous defense of Wittgenstein's private language argument and an interesting attempt to reconcile the expressive and assertoric status of the "I ϕ" sentences — I shall devote the remainder of this introduction to his concept of the practical relation to oneself and of self-determination. I have two reasons for doing this. First, there is a substantial body of secondary literature already available in English on the later Wittgenstein and on the problem of the "I ϕ" sentences. Second, and more importantly, Tugendhat's conception of the practical self-relation and of self-determination breaks new philosophical ground and reorients areas of inquiry that have only recently attracted the attention of contemporary Anglo-American philosophers. It has a direct bearing, for instance, upon current discussions of such topics as the nature of human agency, the connection between the concept of a person and the idea of responsibility, and the significance of our capacity to engage in reflective, second-order evaluation of our wants and desires. His achievement here consists in disclosing the relevance of the concept of autonomy, in the specific sense of rational *self*-determination, for our notions of agency, responsibility for self, and ultimately even the good life. He manages to show how this concept—whose significance, partly owing to the influence of the Kantian tradition, is commonly restricted to the moral and political spheres narrowly conceived—is crucially linked to the standards of evaluation we apply to agents in deciding how they shall live, who they are, and what they take to be the good life.

My remarks will fall into two parts. First, I shall try briefly to locate Tugendhat's conception of self-determination in relation to the characteristic views on autonomy elaborated by Kant and Heidegger. I shall argue that Tugendhat's idea of self-determination can profitably be situated somewhere between the Kantian idea of the autonomy of reason and the Heideggerean idea of authenticity, and in this respect can be understood as suitably remedying the excesses of both. Second, I shall consider some more recent debates concerning the concepts of human agency, responsibility, and reflective self-evaluation and try to indicate how Tugendhat's account significantly advances the argument.

What does it mean to relate to oneself, and in what sense can this be regarded as definitive of what it is to be a human agent? The central idea is roughly this: It is characteristic of human beings that they do not merely exist in a factual sense, subject to certain wants and desires, but rather always exist in such a way that they must assume a relation (either implicit or explicit) to their existence. This relation, moreover, cannot be understood as theoretical or contemplative, but must be grasped as volitional and practical. At the most basic level it involves adopting a stance of either affirmation or negation toward one's existence, that is, facing the unavoidable choice of either continuing with one's life or bringing it to an end. Of course, human beings do not face this situation of choice without further qualification: The question of being or not-being is always simultaneously the question of being or not-being in such and such a way, under such and such circumstances, and hence it brings one up against the issue of how one intends to live one's life and what sort of a person one wants to be. This implies that in relating to their impending future life human beings necessarily relate to a series of fundamental, practical questions (which need not be explicitly posed) concerning who they are, what they want, and what kinds of activities they intend to engage in. Tugendhat's thesis is that in (either implicitly or explicitly) confronting and answering this spectrum of questions, human beings are involved in a relation to themselves in which they are required to define their identity; they do so in deciding which among a range of possible ways to live they want to make constitutive of their "existence."

Tugendhat is not merely interested in clarifying the general sense in which human agents relate to themselves in adopting those intentions and purposes that define their life-activities and hence their identity. He also wants to elucidate a second, more eminent sense in which an agent can be said to relate practically to himself—that is, in the mode of autonomy or self-determination. The notion of self-determination that comes into play here is one that would incline us to say, for example, that someone has really settled for himself what he is doing with his life, what he wants, and 'who' he is; his preferences, standards of evaluation, and view of the good life are not determined by forces alien to him, such as the social expectations of others, but are decided by the agent himself. Tugendhat refers to this higher form of the practical relation to oneself in which one decides "for oneself" who one is and what kind of life one wants to lead as a reflective self-relation; it is characterized by a stance of self-questioning toward one's wants and volitions and a concern for assessing the truth of those factual and normative beliefs that are implied in one's preferences and actions.

In developing his concept of the reflective self-relation, Tugendhat seeks to find a middle ground on the question of autonomy between Kantian rationalism and Heideggerean decisionism. Self-determination, properly conceived, can be understood neither as the pure autonomy of reason nor as the resoluteness of an exclusively individual, authentic choice. In one sense Tugendhat firmly endorses the revision of the idea of autonomy introduced by the tradition extending from Kierkegaard to Heidegger: The concept of self-determination has practical relevance only as the self-determination of the person as an individual person, and not as the universal self-determination of reason. This means that the problem of self-determination arises principally in connection with what Tugendhat calls the fundamental practical question, namely, Who am I and what do I want to do with my life? This question reaches beyond the de facto characterization of the subject by his desires, goals, and purposes; the agent here poses the de jure question to himself: Am I living the kind of life that I really want, am I the sort of person that I ought to be? It is precisely because human beings have the capacity to step back from their wants, purposes, roles, and activities and raise the question "Who am I in these manifold relations and what do I really want?" that the issue of self-determination acquires genuine significance. To be self-determining in this context implies that in raising this question the agent is in a position to decide for himself what types of activities he wants to engage in and what sort of person he wants to be; he does not find his choice 'determined' by his own immediate desires, by the expectations of others, or by the conventionally accepted norms of his community.

What does it mean exactly to decide for oneself who one wants to be and how one wants to live? Tugendhat argues that one can be self-determining only insofar as one poses the practical question in its fundamental sense—that is, with reference to what one intends to do with one's life as such. One cannot, of course, envision an agent who does not pose practical questions at some level, even if it is merely to deliberate about which means are most suitable for achieving a set of predetermined purposes or ends. The point is, however, that the significance of such questions can be either narrow or comprehensive. They have narrow significance if one's purposes are not placed in question but only the means, or if one assesses immediate purposes in light of unquestioned long-range purposes or accepted social norms and values. In contrast, they have fundamental significance if one places one's purposes, goals, and normative commitments into question without presupposing any further fixed (personal or social) points of reference that are not subject to question. According to Tugendhat, in raising this kind of practical question one is placing one's life as a whole into question, because one is raising the issue of who one wants to be, that is, how one ought to understand oneself as an agent who desires and acts. Furthermore, the possibility of attaining (or approximating) self-determination in one's decisions hinges on one's willingness to raise the practical question in this comprehensive sense, for it is only on this basis that one can explicitly exercise a choice with regard to one's fundamental life-possibilities.

In explicating the concepts of self-determination and of choosing for oneself in terms of our willingness to raise the fundamental practical question, Tugendhat stands close to Heidegger's treatment of autonomy in terms of the idea of authenticity. For what is characteristic of inauthentic existence is precisely that it involves *Dasein*'s failure explicitly to confront its own practical possibilities; rather, it allows itself to be guided by what is conventionally regarded as good (by the "they-self") and thereby evades the question (and fundamental choice) of who it wants to be. Contrariwise, authentic existence involves *Dasein*'s resolve not to conceal the range of practical possibilities that are open to it, but to address the question of what it is doing with its life independently of the fixed, conventional normative standpoints that prevail in the social community.

Tugendhat's conception of self-determination diverges dramatically from Heidegger's model, however, in its assessment of the role of reason in guiding the way that one answers the fundamental practical question. In Tugendhat's view, the principal failing of Heidegger's account of self-determination is that it neglects the importance of the question of truth and rational justification as a constitutive feature of fully responsible, autonomous choice. It is for this reason that Tugendhat insists that self-determination is realized only in a *reflective* self-relation; reflective here means deliberative, that is, directed to an objectively justifiable choice of what is good. The point is that in raising the fundamental practical question one's concern is not merely to decide for oneself what one wants, but also to decide what it is best for oneself to want, that is, what sort of life and identity would actually be best for oneself among the possible alternatives.

Since the fundamental practical question is directed to the issue of what is good, better, and best, the answer at which it aims cannot be decided merely on the basis of the agent's arbitrary subjective preferences. Rather, the answer that is sought is an objectively justifiable choice, a choice of what is actually (in truth) good for the agent. This implies that there are objective reasons for preferring one set of practical alternatives to another, that there are objective standards of evaluation whose relevance should not be ignored, and that the advice and counsel of others may be solicited in trying to ascertain what is objectively preferable. It is in this sense that Tugendhat argues that an autonomous self-relation must be directed to the question of truth and to a rationally justifiable choice; contrary to Heidegger, it cannot be understood merely as choosing independently and resolutely *if* this necessary relation to reason and to truth is overlooked.

Tugendhat specifies at least three distinct ways in which the question of truth is relevant in answering the practical question regarding one's own good. First, one must have (or strive for, as a regulative ideal) knowledge of oneself, of one's underlying dispositions to volition and to action, in trying to decide what it is that one really wants to do and to be. For obviously one cannot intelligently decide what it would be best to want unless one has well-grounded knowledge of what one has already been inclined to want and to do and what the consequences of this have been; thus, it would be important to know, for example, that one has a talent for engaging in certain forms of activity, that the performance of a certain class of actions enhances one's sense of well-being, or that one has a proclivity to engage in certain types of social relations that prove unpleasant or destructive in the long run. Second, one must assess whether one's knowledge of the available possibilities of action is well-grounded; for ultimately the choice of what to do is a choice between distinct possibilities of action, and if one's factual beliefs concerning one's situation of action are false, one's choice will be misguided. Third, one must assess the truth of a range of normative and evaluative assumptions regarding one's own well-being and the welfare of others that are ordinarily implied in any decision about how one wants to live. For it is inconceivable that one can face the question of who to be or how to live without making normative and evaluative judgments concerning what is good or bad to do in light of (1) the legitimate interests of others (i.e., 'moral' judgments) and (2) a concern for one's own well-being or flourishing. Since these normative and evaluative assumptions are not merely expressions of the agent's arbitrary preferences but involve a claim to truth, they must be accepted or rejected on the basis of their fulfillment of this claim if the agent's choice of his own good (based in part upon these assumptions) is to be regarded as self-determining or autonomous.

While Tugendhat devotes considerable critical attention to elucidating the necessary role of rational justification in the process of autonomously deciding how one should live, he emphatically denies that one's choice of one's own good can be determined entirely on objective, rational grounds. There is a point in the process of adducing grounds or reasons for one's life-choices at which one must stop and simply appeal to the fact that one wants to live in such and such a way; in other words, there is an irreducibly individualizing, volitional component to one's choice of one's own personal good in which the only thing that makes the object of one's choice part of one's good is the fact that one has chosen it. Thus, autonomous or self-determining choice involves de-ciding for oneself in accordance (as far as possible) with rational, ob-jectively justifiable standards.

It should now be clear how Tugendhat's conception of the reflective self-relation represents a middle position between the Kantian idea of the autonomy of reason and the Heideggerean account of authentic choice. In his view, autonomous choice requires that one decide in the mode of *rational volition*. This means that the agent's choice of how he wants to live must be governed by rational considerations insofar as these are relevant to the determination of his true good, but it must also reflect a distinctly individual exercise of preference for which the agent must bear sole responsibility. From this perspective, an agent can fail to be autonomous in two ways: (a) by refusing to submit his decision to rational justification as far as is possible, and (b) by failing to act at all because he cannot find a complete justification for a prospective choice. In this way, Heidegger's idea that self-determination requires deciding for oneself is preserved, but it is linked to the question of truth and rational justification, which are conspicuously absent in his account of authenticity. On the other hand, the fundamental Kantian intuition that autonomy can be attained only by means of a relation to reason and truth is sustained, but the standards of reason and truth are no longer severed from the irreducibly individual context of choice within which we decide how we want to live.[2]

I shall now shift my ground slightly and consider Tugendhat's conception of the practical self-relation from a rather different perspective—that is, in light of current debates concerning the concepts of human agency, reflective self-evaluation, and responsibility for self. For this purpose I shall examine three recent contributions to these related topics by Harry Frankfurt, Gary Watson, and Charles Taylor and try to indicate how Tugendhat's account bears directly on several key issues raised in this discussion.[3]

In his influential paper "Freedom of the Will and the Concept of a Person," Harry Frankfurt presents an account of what he regards as the essential feature of "the concept of a person," and he claims that this feature provides a clue to a proper understanding of what is commonly meant by "freedom of the will." According to Frankfurt, the peculiar characteristic that defines the concept of a person is neither that such a creature is motivated by wants and desires, nor that he makes choices and engages in deliberation, nor even that he possesses reason. Rather, the essential difference between persons and other creatures who may have all the capacities mentioned above is that a person may also want to have (or not to have) certain desires or motives. Persons, in other words, are capable of forming what he calls "second-order desires" in which they express a preference for for the sort of desires, motives, and purposes they want to move them to action. It follows that persons are capable of wanting to be different, in their motives and purposes, from the way they actually are. As Frankfurt puts it, persons have "the capacity for reflective self-evaluation that is manifested in the formation of second-order desires";[4] this means that persons are concerned about which among the desires and motives that they have will lead them to act, and in this sense they care about the sort of will that they have.

In clarifying the significance of this capacity to form second-order desires or volitions, Frankfurt presents us with an important contrast, namely, an agent who lacks this reflective capacity but who still has first-order desires and hence is moved to do certain things by his wants and desires. Frankfurt calls such an agent a *wanton*, and he imagines that a wanton may even have the capacity to deliberate about the course of action most conducive to the satisfaction of his wants and desires. The point about wantons, then, is not that they do not use reason in deciding how to satisfy their wants, but that they are not concerned with the quality of their wants, that is, which desires motivate them to action. They pursue whatever course of action they are most strongly inclined to pursue, and they are indifferent to the question of which of their inclinations will turn out to be the strongest. Frankfurt points out that all nonhuman animals that have desires belong to the class of wantons, as do young children. The contrast provided by the wanton is instructive because it makes Frankfurt's claims about the essential importance of our capacity for reflective self-evaluation more intuitively plausible; agents who can reason only about how to get what they desire but who cannot consider and hence cannot care about the desirability of the desires themselves appear to be missing something that is quite fundamental to our conception of human agency.

How does Frankfurt's notion of second-order desiring shed light on the problem of freedom of the will? In most cases an agent who forms a second-order desire does not merely want to enjoy the experience of having a certain first-order desire; he also wants this desire to function as one of his effective motives to action. In Frankfurt's terms, he wants this desire to constitute part of his *will*, and in this respect his second-order desires are referred to as "second-order volitions." According to Frankfurt, it is only because human agents form second-order volitions that freedom of the will may be a problem for them. He understands freedom of the will as the freedom to want what one wants to want. In other words, an agent who enjoys a free will is in a position to determine which of his first-order desires will be effective by means of his second-order volition, so that he can actually have the will (i.e., the effective first-order desires) that he wants to have (at the second-order). To enjoy freedom of the will, then, is to secure the conformity of one's will to one's second-order volitions, and to lack freedom of the will is to be unable to do so. Frankfurt's example of someone who lacks freedom of the will is the *unwilling* drug addict: While he has a second-order volition affirming his first-order desire to refrain from taking an addictive drug, this second-order volition is ineffective; his first-order desire to continue taking the drug proves too powerful, and hence he ends up taking the drug against his own 'will,' that is, in violation of that first-order desire (to refrain) with which he has identified himself through his second-order volition.

It should already be clear that the essential importance that Frankfurt ascribes to our capacity for reflective self-evaluation bears a strong resemblance to Tugendhat's assessment of the definitive status of the practical self-relation. The key idea in Tugendhat's account is that human beings do not merely exist in a factual sense, subject to wants and desires, but always exist in such a way that they must adopt a practical relation to their existence (affirmative or negative) in which they evince an understanding of who they are and what they are doing with their lives. This relation to one's existence corresponds closely to what Frankfurt means by "second-order" volition: What is at issue is not an immediate wanting or desiring, but the (implicit or explicit) adoption of a life-conception in terms of which one assumes a position on the question of whether and how to live. This adoption of a life-conception ultimately entails an assessment of which of one's first-order desires one wants to be effective, since in deciding how one wants to live one obviously must also choose which of one's desires one wants to issue in action. In this sense, Tugendhat's conception of the practical self-relation represents a more comprehensive structure of reflective self-evaluation than Frankfurt's notion of second-order volition: It includes not only an evaluation of the desirability of one's desires, but also (and more primarily) an evaluation of the desirability

of the alternative forms of life or possibilities of action between which
one must choose in deciding how to live.

Tugendhat also provides an analysis of the concept of freedom that
stands in close proximity to Frankfurt's account of freedom of the
will. In Frankfurt's view, an agent enjoys freedom of the will if he
has effective second-order volitions. This means that if his second-
order volitions had been otherwise, the first-order desires that moved
him to action would have been correspondingly different; in other
words, he is free to constitute his will (his effective first-order desires)
as he wants (in second-order volition). Tugendhat offers a similar analysis of the sense in which one expresses one's freedom of volition in
sentences such as "I can now perform action X *if* I want to," as in "I
can now break off this lecture if I want to." He notes that in such
sentences the agent draws attention to the fact that whether the action
is performed or not depends exclusively on his volition—that is, on
whether he *wants* to or not. But he further points out that this wanting
to which one refers in expressing one's freedom of choice—"I can if
I want to"—is not an immediate wanting or desiring, but a reflective
second-order wanting that stands in the domain of deliberation. One
is not saying here, for example, that one can break off the lecture if
one is overtaken by an immediate desire to do so, for the type of
freedom thereby expressed would apply no less to unhindered animals
and young children; rather, one is saying that whether or not one
breaks off the lecture depends on one's own deliberative, second-
order choice of what one really wants to do, which is made at one
remove from one's immediate wants and inclinations.

Tugendhat designates the agent's capacity not to be directly moved
by immediate wants and inclinations, but to deliberate and thereby
effectively to decide what he really wants to do as the formal concept
of freedom; he regards this concept as roughly coextensive with the
idea of moral accountability.[5] As we have already seen, however,
Tugendhat does not think that this concept of formal freedom provides
an adequate purchase on a significant part of what we ordinarily mean
in ascribing freedom to human agents. In particular, the concept of
formal freedom does not address the issue of whether the agent's
second-order volitions are themselves freely or autonomously chosen;
in Tugendhat's terms, it fails to consider the higher-level practical
relation to oneself in the mode of self-determination. In making the
distinction between the formal concept of freedom and the higher-

level concept of the practical self-relation in the mode of autonomy, Tugendhat takes his analysis of freedom and human agency beyond the limits of Frankfurt's conception. For Frankfurt's view construes freedom of the will exclusively in terms of the effectiveness of one's second-order volitions in determining first-order desires, and it thereby neglects the problem of whether the agent's adoption of these second-order volitions is itself free or the product of 'forces' alien to him.

If one considers the paradigm cases around which Frankfurt develops his model of freedom of the will, it is apparent that his distinctions are well-suited to explain the sense in which an agent who suffers from compulsive desires (e.g., the unwilling addict) has an unfree will. Such an agent fails to have the will that he wants to have, and he is thereby motivated by 'alien' desires with which he does not 'identify.' The shortcoming of this conception, however, lies in its positive conception of freedom: It merely involves the will's self-instituted harmony or agreement with itself, the determination of one's effective first-order desires by second-order volitions. As Frankfurt clearly remarks, "Suppose that [someone] enjoys both freedom of action and freedom of the will. Then he is not only free to do what he wants to do; he is also free to want what he wants to want. It seems to me that he has, in that case, all the freedom it is possible to desire or to conceive . . . there is nothing in the way of freedom that he lacks."[6]

Consider the case of an agent who is free to want what he wants to want, but who has not decided for himself what it is that he wants to want. Perhaps he has merely borrowed his standards of evaluation from his society or his social class without questioning them, perhaps he has an inarticulate wish to fulfill the values and aspirations of his parents, or perhaps he has unknowingly been subject to brainwashing or indocrination of some sort. In all these cases the agent has effective second-order volitions; he has the kind of will he wants to have, and hence on Frankfurt's analysis he enjoys freedom of the will. But surely we want to reserve a sense in which such agents are not free, or significantly less free than agents with similar second-order volitions who have adopted their standards of evaluation through a process of critical self-questioning and discussion with other rational interlocutors. The point is that the agent's volitional freedom is not merely a function of the effective conformity of his will to his second-order volitions, but is crucially affected by the mode of adoption or genesis of these second-order volitions themselves. It will not do here to introduce a further higher-order volition and insist that the agent must be free to want to want what he wants to want to want. For it is quite conceivable that at least some (if not all) of the agents cited in the counterexamples above would meet this requirement of having effective third-order volitions, and in any case the same problem may be posed at each higher level without any prospect of avoiding an endless regress.[7]

The agent's freedom with respect to his second-order volitions, then, does not appear to have to do with their conformity to volitions of a higher order; rather, it has to do with how the volitions themselves are adopted. As Tugendhat suggests, the key issue here is whether the agent has adopted these second-order volitions by choice, or whether he has relinquished this choice to other agents or to forces lying outside the context of his own deliberation. Tugendhat offers two hints concerning how we might determine whether an agent has chosen his second-order volitions for himself, that is, in the mode of self-determination. First, we can ask whether he has raised the practical question—What do I really want and how do I intend to live?—in a fundamental sense, or whether he has always presupposed certain fixed or conventional points of view in raising this question. Second, we can ask whether his adoption of second-order volitions has been guided by rational considerations, whether he considers them revisable in light of the outcome of rational discussion and argument, and whether he can provide a rational justification of them as far as is possible.

What is at stake in raising these two questions is the extent to which, in Frankfurt's terms, the agent has realized his capacity for reflective self-evaluation in adopting his second-order volitions. In this sense, freedom of the will is not something that the agent either enjoys or lacks, but is a graded achievement that is correlated with the agent's employment of his reflective capacities in developing his practical conception of himself, his life, and his possibilities of action. The presumption is that agents who realize this capacity more fully make choices that can be more properly characterized as "their own," and hence in this respect they can be judged to be freer or more autonomous.

This points to a second, related difficulty with Frankfurt's analysis of second-order volition that further discloses the relevance of Tugendhat's account of the practical self-relation. This difficulty has been explored by Gary Watson in his paper "Free Agency." According to

Frankfurt, there are no "essential restrictions on the kind of basis" upon which one can form second-order volitions; they may be formed "capriciously and irresponsibly," without any serious thought of what is involved, and still provide the grounds for an agent's identification with certain first-order desires as his own.[8] Frankfurt's admission appears tantamount to claiming that one can be a wanton, so to speak, with respect to one's second-order desires and volitions without any loss of freedom of the will; if one adopts a second-order volition capriciously and thoughtlessly, then surely one does not have any stake in what one's second-order volitions turn out to be. As Watson points out, however, in this case it becomes unclear why second-order volitions should have the special status accorded them by Frankfurt in determining which desires we regard as truly our 'own.'[9] After all, second-order volitions themselves are merely desires, and if one does not care about what one's own second-order volitions are, why should they have any special relationship to 'oneself' or determine which among one's first-order desires are truly one's 'own'?

It might be tempting to suggest, following Frankfurt, that what gives second-order volitions their special status in relation to 'oneself' is that they have one's own desires as their intentional objects, whereas other desires refer to objects or actions outside oneself. But to endorse this suggestion would be to ignore the fact that there is an important class of preferences that an agent exercises for things 'outside' himself— preferences of the first order[10]—that themselves entail second-order volitions. What I have in mind here are preferences for courses of action, particularly courses of action that are constitutive of an agent's conception of the good life. If someone decides that he wants to become a Trappist monk or that it is essential that he devote his life to combating social injustice and alleviating suffering, this clearly implies that he wants certain attitudes and motives to be effective (e.g., those involving piety and contemplation or rectitude and altruism) and contrary motives to be ineffective. It is arguable that it is deliberation about these sorts of preferences—that is, about courses of action that are constitutive of one's conception of how one should live—that forms the framework within which one assesses the desirability of one's desires. As we have already seen, Tugendhat's structural account of the practical self-relation makes it evident why deliberating about these sorts of first-order preferences has a special primacy in reflective self-evaluation. For the fundamental question that an agent must face

in deliberation is whether and how to live, and it is only within the
context of answering this question that he must adopt a position
toward his first-order desires and inclinations.

A similar point is developed by Watson, who revises Frankfurt's
distinction between higher and lower orders of desire in order to
provide a more adequate account of the primacy of our reflective
evaluations in establishing which desires we regard as our 'own.' He
claims that the fundamental dichotomy here is not between two different orders of desire, but between two different kinds of motivation:
desiring and valuing. In valuing a state of affairs, we express a preference for it that rests upon a judgment that it is good for us; hence
valuing something provides us with a motive for action that is based
upon a reason. An agent's values are here understood as those principles
and ends he would reflectively articulate as definitive of a good, fulfilling
life. In contrast, in desiring a state of affairs we express a preference
for it that is not necessarily based on a judgment of its worth or
goodness at all; we can desire things quite independently of whether
we value them (e.g., those desires engendered by our bodily appetites),
and hence it is possible to desire things that we regard as worthless
or even evil. Now Watson construes the problem of freedom as one
that concerns the relation between what we value and the desires that
motivate us to action. If we are motivated to act by what we value
and hence judge as good for us, we enjoy free agency, while if we
are motivated to act by desires that do not conform to our values,
our actions are unfree and our effective desires are in some sense not
our 'own.'

What does Watson gain by reformulating Frankfurt' conception in
terms of the opposition between desiring and valuing? First, his model
demonstrates why our reflective evaluations have a special primacy
in identifying certain desires as our 'own' without risking the prospect
of an endless regress that is threatened by the appeal to higher orders
of desire. We are inclined to identify those desires as our 'own' that
are desires for what we have judged on sober reflection to be constitutive
of the good life for us. Second, Watson's conception makes it clear
that our reflective evaluations are not merely higher-order preferences,
but are based on practical judgments regarding what constitutes a
good way to live; it is for this reason that argument and rational
justification are possible in this domain. Third, Watson's view entails
that our reflective evaluations are not related exclusively (or even

primarily) to our desires, but to courses of action. For the initial practical
question in deliberation is not which of one's desires should be effective,
but which course of action is the worthiest or the best to pursue in
light of our overall conception of our good.

In revising Frankfurt's model, Watson sketches an account that is
in some respects remarkably close to Tugendhat's conception of the
practical self-relation. As we saw earlier, the fundamental practical
question for Tugendhat is also how one intends to live, and it is always
raised from the standpoint of deciding what is the best way to live;
hence one's answer to this question (if explicitly formulated) must
assume the form of a practical judgment about the good life for which
rational justification is at least possible. Nonetheless, there is one important sense in which Watson's view is subject to the same limitation
as Frankfurt's: It does not go beyond the formal concept of freedom
to deal with the problem of what it means to adopt one's standards
of reflective evaluation responsibly or autonomously. For Watson, no
less than for Frankfurt, freedom means only willing in a self-instituted
harmony with oneself; one enjoys free agency to the extent that one
effectively desires what one values. What is missing from his analysis
is an account of the conditions relevant for assessing the agent's relative
freedom or autonomy in adopting his system of values.

In his paper "What Is Human Agency?" Charles Taylor addresses
just this question of how agents can be regarded as responsible to
greater and lesser extents for their standards of reflective evaluation.
He makes a number of interesting points, two of which bear directly
on our discussion. First, he argues that our self-evaluations of who we
are and what we are doing with our lives must be understood not as
descriptions of a fully independent object (i.e., our desires) that is left
unaltered by the description, but rather as *articulations* of something
that is initially inchoate, confused, and partially unformed. Hence, to
adopt a certain characterization (articulation) of what one is doing as
an agent is to shape what it is that we desire and hold important. In
this sense, an altered description of one's motivations can significantly
change the motivations themselves.

Although our self-interpretations in this respect shape or constitute
our experience of ourselves as agents, it does not follow that they are
arbitrary or that "anything goes" in this domain. Precisely because
they represent an attempt to articulate who we really are and what
we take to be of decisive importance for our lives, they can be more

or less adequate, more or less self-clairvoyant, more or less truthful in expressing who we are and what we really want. At the same time, it is important to recognize that what these interpretations try to do justice to is not something independent; in adopting one or another self-interpretation, we tend to become different from what we were before and hence accessible or inaccessible to further self-evaluation in new ways.

Taylor's second point has to do with the relevance of the concept of responsibility. In his view, the issue of responsibility arises here because it is always within our capacity to reevaluate our fundamental interpretations of ourselves and our lives in light of their adequacy to our own experience and the experience of others. Our evaluations are always open to challenge for two reasons: first, because they are articulations of a sense of oneself that is partial and inchoate rather than descriptions of an independent object, and second, because they are often distorted by imperfections of our character that need to be identified and reassessed. In Taylor's view, we reevaluate our fundamental self-interpretations by raising the following sort of question: Have I really understood what is essential to my identity? Have I truly determined what I take to be the highest form of life? Taylor claims that this kind of reevaluation is radical in the sense that none of the terms of one's own self-understanding is considered immune to revision; hence I cannot evaluate some of my intentions, purposes, or values in light of other ideals or aspirations that I presuppose as fixed, but must submit the most basic formulations by means of which I describe myself and my life to critical scrutiny.

Taylor compares this kind of radical reevaluation of oneself to those forms of philosophical inquiry in which one proceeds from a sense that there is something wrong with the traditional, conventionally accepted distinctions (e.g., analytic-synthetic, mental-physical, materialism-idealism), but does not yet have an adequate language at one's disposal to formulate an alternative view. One hopes that struggling with the initial question will reveal a new way of looking at the problem, a new set of categories and terms that will illuminate an area of experience that was entirely obscured by the traditional conceptions. Similarly, in radically reevaluating ourselves, we must try not to adhere to our old, favored terms of self-description, but to adopt a stance of openness to new ways of understanding ourselves (and our activities, purposes, and values) that might emerge from a renewed process of self-questioning. In this process there is no fixed yardstick, since all the previously employed, 'traditional' terms of one's self-evaluation are open to question. One can only attempt to open oneself to those aspects of one's own experience and the experience of others that somehow do not 'fit' with one's present evaluations of oneself and one's life and that can therefore point beyond the limits of one's present conceptions.

Taylor suggests, then, that there is an important sense in which agents can be regarded as more or less responsible or autonomous in determining their fundamental self-evaluations and hence in settling the question of 'who' they are. This is a function of the extent to which they actually engage in the process of radical self-questioning. In this way they are able to define for themselves their standards of evaluation and hence their motives for action by explicitly raising the question of their identity. Since we all have the capacity to engage in this reflective process, and since it is up to us whether we do so or not, it is also reasonable to conclude that all agents can be regarded as responsible for 'themselves' in this specific sense, whether they undertake radical self-evaluation or not.

It should be apparent that there is a sharp convergence between Taylor's conception of responsibility for self and Tugendhat's account of the practical self-relation in the mode of autonomy. As we saw earlier, a key criterion for autonomous choice on Tugendhat's analysis involves raising the practical question in its comprehensive sense; this implies that the agent addresses the issue of how he should understand himself with respect to his fundamental purposes and intentions without presupposing any fixed points of reference, either with regard to himself or with regard to conventionally accepted social norms and values. This idea closely approximates Taylor's concept of radical self-reflection: What makes this reevaluation of oneself radical is precisely that none of the terms in which one characterizes one's purposes and identity is immune to challenge, and hence one cannot appeal to a fixed yardstick or standard.

Nonetheless, there is another sense in which Taylor's and Tugendhat's views appear to diverge significantly. This concerns their understanding of the status of what is placed in question in radically reevaluating one's identity. For Taylor, one's fundamental evaluations must be understood as articulations of one's desires and motives; these articulations are not construed simply as descriptions, since they do not characterize an independent object but shape it in important respects. In contrast, for Tugendhat the relevant terms of self-characterization are to be understood as answers to the practical question of whether and how I shall live, and hence they are to be regarded as expressions of intention rather than as descriptive assertions about one's conscious states or behavioral dispositions. One important consequence of this difference is that for Tugendhat the crucial question in radical reevaluation is to decide, in light of one's ongoing intentions, how one really wants to be, that is, what sorts of activities and relations one really wants to engage in. On the other hand, for Taylor the question appears to have a more descriptive cast, namely, whether my articulations of who I am and what I take to be important are faithful to my largely inchoate sense of myself and of those things that are worth caring about.

On closer examination, however, Taylor's and Tugendhat's views are less divergent than they initially appear. As indicated earlier, on Tugendhat's model one can only rationally decide what one really wants if one's decision is informed by a descriptive knowledge of one's own dispositions to action and volition (the sort of knowledge demanded in *gnothi seauton*). Hence Taylor's notion that one's articulations must be more or less adequate or faithful to one's inchoate sense of oneself is mirrored by Tugendhat's assumption that one can only make a rational decision about what one really wants if one knows the sorts of things one is generally inclined to want. In neither case, however, are the authors sufficiently explicit about what is involved in these relations of self-clairvoyant articulation or choice informed by self-knowledge.

Tugendhat makes one very provocative suggestion about the meaning of rational justification as it concerns evaluating our decisions about how we shall live. Following the lead of Aristotle and Mead, he claims that justification in this domain is related to the possibility of attaining a consensus of a very specific sort, namely, a consensus of those who "are most experienced in the matter," that is, those who have practical wisdom. On this view, the criterion of correctness in evaluating an agent's decisions regarding his own life is whether his decisions would meet with the approval of those who are experienced in these matters. Tugendhat is careful to point out that this does not imply that there is only one ideal possibility for human life or that someone can simply take on an ideal conception as his own; he continues to insist that

"every path of self-discovery and self-determination must be an individual one." Nonetheless, in deciding how we shall live, we implicitly
make a value judgment that we have chosen the best way to live that
is possible for us, and this judgment is subject to the constraints of
objective justification. Tugendhat's thesis is that the only justification
conceivable here is that we have the capability to convince "properly
experienced" others of the merits of our life-choices.

Tugendhat is well aware that his thesis is sustainable only if he can
offer an account of what makes someone properly experienced in
matters pertaining to the question of how we shall live, and he provides
at best a tentative solution to this problem. What is interesting about
his proposal is the direction in which it points in clarifying our understanding of the framework in which one raises and answers questions
concerning one's true good. As I see it, his proposal points to the fact
that the framework in which we formulate and justify decisions concerning how we shall live must inevitably assume a *narrative* form.
For, if one considers what goes on when we justify our life-choices to
someone else (or to ourselves), it immediately becomes apparent that
we must set these decisions in a story, a narrative context within
which they can appear as intelligible, reasonable, practical responses
to the experiences and background that have shaped us as agents.
Similarly, if one considers the formulations in which we define our
identities as agents (as answers to 'who' we are), it becomes apparent
that they must be understood as ways of making sense (both retrospectively and prospectively) of what we have done and what we intend
to do; in this respect, their function or point can only become evident
if they are set in a narrative life-history (which may also include a
history of the relevant practices and communities to which the agent
belongs).

Thus if one wants (with Taylor) to refer to our own terms of self-
characterization as articulations or self-interpretations, it is arguable
that what they articulate is not so much one's inchoate sense of oneself
as the sense that is embedded in one's past and present activities,
concerns, and relations. It is perhaps for this reason that the literary
form best suited to a reflective consideration of the different possibilities
of defining one's good is not the philosophical treatise, but the novel
and the biography. If this kind of problem is to receive philosophical
illumination at all, it can only be achieved by reconstructing the reciprocal interplay beween our narrative self-understanding and our

practical experience in the context of an individual life-history—a task that Hegel, for example, sets for himself in the introduction to the *Phenomenology of Spirit*.[11]

The framework of a narrative life-history provides not only the definitive context of justification for our practical self-understanding and choice, but also the background within which the posing of the practical question itself is warranted. It is clear that individuals who raise this question continually, who are persistently concerned with the issue of 'who' they are and how they want to live, do not thereby attain a greater degree of self-determination; they are more likely to be regarded as suffering from a typically modern neurosis. The point here is that there are some occasions in one's life when it is suitable to engage in the kind of radical self-reflection envisioned by Taylor and Tugendhat, and other contexts in which it does not serve to advance one's self-understanding or prospects for autonomous choice. But it is only possible to identify such occasions or contexts under a specific narrative description of one's life as a whole, and hence such a description must play a crucial role in assessing when and whether such radical self-questioning can promote the agent's aspiration to autonomy.

The preceding remarks on the importance of the framework of a narrative life-history are intended only as a suggestion of the direction in which Tugendhat's views might lead in clarifying what it means to face one's life and oneself responsibly. In this respect his position exhibits important affinities with recent work that has explored the significance of narrative self-understanding in one's quest for the true good.[12] But whether one agrees or disagrees with Tugendhat on this point, his analysis of the structure of human agency, rational choice and responsibility represents a distinguished addition to our contemporary philosophical understanding of these topics.

Notes

I want to thank Georgia Warnke, Tom McCarthy, and Ernst Tugendhat for their help in preparing this translation.

1. Tugendhat's most important earlier works include: *Ti kata tinos. Eine Untersuchung zu Struktur und Ursprung aristotelischer Grundbegriffe* (Freiburg, 1968); *Der Wahrheitsbegriff bei Husserl und Heidegger* (Berlin, 1970); *Vorlesungen zur Einführung in die sprachanalytische Philosophie* (Frankfurt, 1976; English

translation: *Traditional and Analytical Philosophy: Lectures on the Philosophy of Language*, trans. P. A. Gorner, Cambridge, 1982).

2. To be sure, the specific structure of practical reasoning on Tugendhat's account appears far more Aristotelian than Kantian: Deliberation is directed primarily to ascertaining the best possible course of action in view of a rationally justifiable conception of the good life. Nonetheless, the inspiration for his fundamental idea that free or autonomous choice must be governed by standards of reason and truth is Kantian.

3. The papers I shall draw upon are Frankfurt's "Freedom of the Will and the Concept of a Person" (*Journal of Philosophy*, vol. 68, no. 1, January 1971), Watson's "Free Agency" (*Journal of Philosophy*, vol. 72, no. 8, April 1975), and Taylor's "What Is Human Agency?" (*Philosophical Papers*, vol. 1, Cambridge, 1985). The papers of Frankfurt and Watson and a shorter version of Taylor's paper entitled "Responsibility for Self" are collected in an anthology entitled *Free Will* that is edited by Gary Watson (Oxford, 1982).

4. Watson, ed., *Free Will*, p. 83.

5. It should be noted that Harry Frankfurt does not think that the concept of moral responsibility is coextensive with that of having a free will. His argument here is based on a distinction between having a free will and doing something of one's own free will. In his view, the latter is a necessary condition for moral responsibility, while the former is not. His point seems to be that one may be regarded as morally responsible for actions performed from first-order desires that could not have been otherwise *if* one affirms these first-order desires in second-order volition. In such cases the agent does not have a free will, because his will (his effective first-order desire) is outside his control. Nonetheless, by affirming his first-order desires at the second order, he makes this will his own and hence may be said to perform the action of his own free will. Frankfurt's example of such an agent is the willing drug addict, who is physiologically addicted and cannot do otherwise than take the drug but who may still be regarded as morally responsible for taking it insofar as he affirms his desire for it in second-order volition. On this point see *Free Will*, pp. 94–95.

6. *Free Will*, pp. 92–93.

7. Frankfurt takes up this problem again in a later article, "Identification and Externality" (in *The Identity of Persons*, ed. A. O. Rorty, Berkeley, 1976, pp. 239–251).

8. *Free Will*, p. 89n.

9. On this point cf. *Free Will*, pp. 108–109.

10. I am using "first-order preference" in this paragraph to refer not to a volition that is immediate or unreflective, but only to one whose object is something 'outside' oneself rather than one's own desires or motives.

11. My claim for the relevance of Hegel's philosophical method here may appear surprising in view of the rather critical treatment it receives at Tugendhat's hands in the last two chapters of the present book. However, there is a point in the last chapter in which Tugendhat accords a kind of subsidiary validity to the dialectical method of the *Phenomenology* insofar as it restricts itself to a reconstruction of the reciprocal interplay between consciousness's conception of itself and its effective experience of the 'truth' of this conception.

12. See, for example, chapter 15 of Alasdair MacIntyre's *After Virtue* (Notre Dame, 1981).

Author's Preface

In my *Traditional and Analytical Philosophy: Lectures on the Philosophy of Language*, the use of the lecture form was really only a literary fiction. In contrast, I actually gave the lectures presented here in fourteen two-hour sessions in the winter semester of 1974–1975 in Heidelberg. The text has been extensively revised, of course, and in several parts (particularly lectures 7 through 12) thoroughly rewritten.

Traditional and Analytical Philosophy sketched a language-analytical concept of philosophy in the sense of a formal fundamental discipline. Its thesis was that the traditional idea of such a fundamental discipline could only be realized in the idea of formal semantics. The limits of such a conception of philosophy, however, could not be ignored (pp. 74ff., 93ff.). I distinguished this systematic conception of a language-analytical fundamental discipline from a "methodological concept of language-analytical philosophy" (93), which consists solely in the view that concepts can be clarified only by examining the rules of use of the corresponding words. This methodological concept of linguistic analysis raises a claim that extends beyond the limited conception of formal semantics and applies to all conceptions of philosophy, however they may be defined, assuming only that philosophy has to deal with the clarification of concepts. The view that the language-analytical method is in this respect the only genuine philosophical method implies the thesis that this method is also the only adequate method of interpreting all previous philosophy. This thesis is put to the test in the present book in relation to one particular sphere of problems of traditional philosophy that seems to be far removed from the analysis of language. My hope (certainly only a hope) is that I can succeed in making the meaning and possibilities of a constructive language-analytical critique so evident that the reader will ascribe the deficiencies of the interpretations only to the author and not to the method as such.

E.T.
Starnberg, February 1979

Self-Consciousness and Self-Determination

Lecture 1

Introduction I: Preliminary Clarifications

Why a course of lectures on the topic of self-consciousness, you will want to ask. This word no longer has a special ring to it. But this was not always the case, so we must ask ourselves whether it has lost its former significance justifiably and what relevance this term can still have, or perhaps must have, for us.

Modern philosophy from Descartes to Hegel thought that in the concept of self-consciousness it had discovered not only the decisive methodological principle of philosophy but also the foundation for an enlightened, autonomous existence. At the point within his *History of Philosophy* at which he turns to the treatment of Descartes, Hegel writes:

> Actually we now first come to the philosophy of the modern world, and we begin this with Descartes. With him we truly enter upon an independent philosophy, which knows that it emerges independently out of reason. . . . Here, we may say, we are at home, and like the mariner after a long voyage over the tempestuous sea, we can finally call out, "Land!". . . In this new period the essential principle is that of thought, which proceeds solely from itself. . . . The universal principle is now to grasp the inner sphere as such, and to set aside the claims of dead externality and authority; the latter is to be viewed as out of place here.[1]

In repudiating all authority and all traditionally held assumptions, Descartes thought that with self-consciousness—with knowledge of oneself—he had found a secure foundation for a well-grounded form of knowledge. Fichte grasped the relationship of oneself to oneself simultaneously as self-determination, and he thereby made self-consciousness the principle not only of theoretical but also of practical philosophy. Self-consciousness was conceived as the principle of a form of life (*Praxis*) grounded upon reason.* Hegel began with this principle, but he also superseded it. He demonstrated that a relationship to oneself only exists in the process of recognizing and being recognized by another self-consciousness. In Hegel's formulation, the 'truth' of self-consciousness is 'spirit.' Thus, the concept of self-consciousness lost its position as the supreme practical principle as a result of Hegel's deeper understanding of it. After Hegel and up to the present day, the issue of self-consciousness has been relegated to the status of a special theoretical problem, just as it has always been handled within the tradition of English empiricism. Within this context the question is merely how to grasp the precise structure of knowledge of oneself. The most advanced position in this tradition is currently represented in Heidelberg by Dieter Henrich, his student Ulrich Pothast, and Konrad Cramer.[2] One might speak here of a Heidelberg school in the theory of self-consciousness. Its representatives have tried to demonstrate that all previous attempts to make the structure of knowledge of oneself intelligible result in paradoxes.

How should we assess this decline of the problem after Hegel? Perhaps it is justified. It may well be that we can no longer ground the conception of a rational form of life upon the concept of self-consciousness, or even upon its deepened Hegelian version. But if this is the case, we must have an alternative. This question cannot be unimportant to us, assuming that we have an interest in a form of life that is governed by reason. You might suggest that the concept of reason can provide just such an alternative. But it is questionable whether the concept of reason can be understood as practically relevant unless it is considered in connection with the concept of the relationship of oneself to oneself. In Hegel's case as well the concept of reason formed the bridge between the concept of self-consciousness and that of spirit. It may be, nevertheless, that while Hegel correctly traced Fichte's concept of self-consciousness back to its social-interactive structure, he carried out this inquiry on the basis of a concept of reason that covered up the phenomenon of a rational relationship of oneself to oneself; thus, he led the entire problem into an impasse. In any case, a standard appears to be established with Hegel, below which one should not fall, even if it may no longer prove to be valid. If it is in fact no longer valid, this must be demonstrated. Even so, I

---

*In this context Tugendhat prefers "form of life" rather than "practice" for the German *"Praxis"* (Trans.).

certainly have no intention of beginning immediately with a critical discussion of Hegel. For we first need to develop the proper points of view before proceeding to such a critical discussion; otherwise, we will remain mired in an immanent interpretation, as is customary in the Hegel literature. But where can we find the relevant points of view?

A direct return to Hegel or Fichte is out of the question for a second reason: We cannot simply overlook the thesis of the Heidelberg school that all attempts to make the structure of self-consciousness intelligible have led to paradoxes. Henrich explicitly demonstrated these paradoxes in connection with his analysis of Fichte. Therefore, we must first critically examine this structural question before we can consider the dimension of the problem that is practically relevant. The Heidelberg school itself has not indicated any path leading out of these paradoxes. Hence, we must attempt to question the conceptual framework within which the phenomenon of self-consciousness is described throughout the entire modern tradition, and which was adopted by the Heidelberg school as self-evident. For there are no paradoxical phenomena. When paradoxes arise in describing a phenomenon, we must assume that the description proceeds from inappropriate premises, that is, it employs inadequate categorial means. Once again the question arises: How can we discover the appropriate points of view from which to question the premises of this tradition? It is natural to suppose that such points of view can be found among modern philosophers who have been concerned with the same problem, but have disengaged themselves from this tradition. It is for this reason that I will discuss Wittgenstein, Heidegger, and G. H. Mead in the central part of these lectures. In the writings of Wittgenstein and Heidegger the term *self-consciousness* is admittedly not to be found at all. But as we shall see, this is only a consequence of the fact that they conceptualize the phenomenon with new categorial means. In order to make it clear why I hope to gain a new access to the problem from these particular authors, I will first try to provide a preliminary account of the phenomenon or phenomena that are designated by the expressions *self-consciousness* and *relationship of oneself to oneself.*

I can now properly begin the introduction of the topic of these lectures. There are, in particular, four questions to be answered: (1) Which phenomenon or phenomena are designated by the expressions *self-consciousness* and *relation of oneself to oneself*, and what sort of problems do these phenomena present? (2) Which methodological means are available to tackle the questions that arise? Which ontological and epistemological models traditionally stand at one's disposal? It is only on the basis of the answer to this second question that (3) I will be able to clarify why I hope to gain a new access to the problems under consideration from the philosophers I have mentioned; in this context I can also provide a preview of the general line of argument of the lectures. Finally, (4) I must return to the question of practical relevance. So far the assumption that this topic has practical relevance has been based solely upon a review of past philosophical history. The question of whether this assumption is justified can only be answered through the elucidation of the phenomenon that I am now about to develop. Today I will begin by addressing the first question, and I reserve consideration of the other three questions for the next lecture.

What is meant by the expressions *self-consciousness* and *relation of oneself to oneself?* We must anticipate that the two expressions do not designate the same phenomenon. Let us begin with the word *self-consciousness*. Is is immediately striking that there is no equivalent in ordinary colloquial usage that captures the meaning of this word as employed in philosophical terminology—namely, as designating the consciousness that someone has of himself. In colloquial speech the words *self-conscious, selbstbewusst* have a much more limited meaning, and this meaning is not even the same in the various modern European languages. In German we call someone *selbstbewusst* if he has a positive sense of self-worth and consequently displays a confident bearing. On the other hand, there is no genuine equivalent in German for the English *self-conscious*. In the English usage a self-conscious person is one who reflects upon his own behavior in his conduct with others to such an extent that he is inhibited, and thereby acts with uncertainty. In both languages the expression concerns forms of relating oneself to oneself that affect one's conduct with others, though they are forms that are directly contrary to one another. At the outset I would like to set aside the meanings that the word *self-conscious* has in ordinary language. They designate forms of relating oneself to oneself, and precisely for this reason they are not forms of mere consciousness of oneself.

Thus, *self-consciousness* in the sense of "consciousness of oneself" is a technical philosophical term. We will later address the question of why it has no equivalent in colloquial speech. Whereas the meaning of words such as *self-conscious* and *selbstbewusst* in ordinary language can be inferred only from their modes of use, the meaning of the word *self-consciousness* in the philosophical sense appears to follow from the meaning of its component parts: consciousness of oneself.

We must obviously first ask, then, what the term *conscious* signifies within the larger term *consciousness*. In Freud's *New Introductory Lectures on Psychoanalysis* we find the astounding sentence: "We do not need to discuss what is meant by "conscious," since it is clear beyond all doubt."[3] In the next sentence he says: "We call a psychical process *unconscious* whose existence we must assume because we infer it from its effects, although we know nothing of it." If we simply attend to this concept of an unconscious psychical process without even analyzing it more closely, we can reconstruct what Freud means here when he calls a process or state conscious.

Freud expresses himself somewhat imprecisely: He insists that we have no knowledge of the unconscious psychical process though we can infer its existence. But it is clear that one can also know something that one infers; Freud does not mean that we cannot have knowledge of the unconscious process, but only that we cannot have direct, immediate knowledge of it. This implies conversely that a psychological state is conscious if the person whose state it is has an immediate knowledge of it. This is indeed a substantive thesis, and we can let rest Freud's declaration that the meaning of the term *conscious* is clear beyond all doubt. This thesis concerning the meaning of the term *conscious* emerges not only through recourse to this Freudian definition of the unconscious; it obviously corresponds to a widespread conception. Husserl, for example, has two different concepts of consciousness, which he distinguishes at the beginning of the fifth *Logical Investigation*, but the concept that roughly corresponds to our sense here is the one to which he accords primary status: consciousness as the unity of experience. What Husserl calls experiences corresponds to what Freud terms conscious psychical processes, and the experiences are similarly defined for Husserl by the fact that they are objects of a possible immediate knowledge; Husserl conceives of this knowledge as inner perception, which poses an additional problem that I do not want to consider at present. If we return to the definition that I extrapolated from Freud, we can clearly eliminate the presumption, with reference to conscious beings, that our subject matter necessarily pertains to a psychical domain; this presumption was required only for an account of the unconscious psychical dimension. We then arrive at the following definition: Those states of a being are conscious of which this being has an immediate knowledge. This definition is certainly not unproblematic. Nevertheless, I am satisfied at the present stage of introductory reflections with a provisional plausibility.

Let me now remind you that I began this examination of what we mean by the term *conscious* in order to be able to apply the result to the case of someone who is conscious of himself, that is, who has a consciousness of himself. Now unexpectedly, something quite different has resulted. On the one hand, it is not clear without further progress how we can apply the concept of consciousness just elaborated to the analysis of consciousness of oneself, because the concept of consciousness developed so far is still not conceived as necessarily involving a consciousness *of something*. On the other hand, we find that a certain concept of self-consciousness is implied in the concept of consciousness that was just presented. We saw that a state is conscious if the being whose state it is has or can have an immediate knowledge of it. Thus, we can now ask, Isn't this immediate knowledge that we have of states of ourselves what is meant by self-consciousness or, to express myself more cautiously, one of the meanings that the word *self-consciousness* can have? *Self-consciousness* in this sense would not be just any kind of consciousness of oneself, but a form of knowledge. You may object, perhaps, that the knowledge that someone has of his states is still not a consciousness of *himself*.

I will come back to this objection later, and first pursue the other difficulty to which I alluded a moment ago. This difficulty is that the concept of consciousness developed so far is not adequate to subsume the concept of self-consciousness because self-consciousness clearly is consciousness *of something*, irrespective of whether or not we have to conceive it (as was just suggested) as *knowledge* of something. Accordingly, the following procedure seems to be indicated. In contrast to the preceding concept of consciousness, we need a narrower concept through which consciousness is understood essentially as consciousness of something. We would then have a basis on which to elucidate the concept of self-consciousness by replacing the variable *something* in the expression *consciousness of something* with *oneself*.

Let's see whether this strategy works. At first everything seems quite simple. For the desired distinction between a narrower concept of consciousness of the required type and the wider concept of consciousness just elaborated already exists in the philosophical literature. It has been worked out with great clarity by Husserl at the point just mentioned, at the beginning of the fifth *Logical Investigation*. Within the class of experiences in general—or, as we can also say, within the class of conscious states in the sense defined so far—Husserl distinguishes a class of experiences that he designates as intentional experiences. Following Franz Brentano, he characterizes this class of experiences by virtue of the fact that they are directed toward objects. The experiences of perceiving, knowing, loving, desiring, wishing, and intending are given as examples. When we perceive, we perceive something; when we desire, we desire something; when we intend, we intend something; when we know, we know this or that. But the reference here to the central role of transitive verbs, which are to be completed in a sentence by an accusative object, signifies only that these experiences are relational. How is the relation that is supposed to exist between consciousness and its object to be distinguished from other relations between two objects?

Husserl speaks of a state of being-directed toward the object, but this talk of a state of being-directed is obviously a metaphor that yields nothing on closer inspection. The older philosophical tradition of the modern period does not offer much insight here either. In this context the Latin term *repraesentatio* was employed, which is translated in German by the term *Vorstellung*. Consciousness, or rather conscious being, is supposed to represent objects. But what does this mean? The naive conception was that in consciousness proxies or representatives of the object are present; consciousness was envisioned as a receptacle in a kind of analogy to the brain, in which small images are to be found that are then grasped as representatives for the object by the subject, who is conceived on the analogy of the rear wall of a *camera obscura*. Although conceptions of this type persist in the trivial philosophy of our century, it has been recognized within the serious philosophical tradition at least since Kant that conscious beings do not relate to the objects of their consciousness through proxies but directly. But how is this relationship to be understood? The language of representation was retained in spite of the critique of the proxy theory, but in such a context, it lost all intelligible sense. A fashionable mode of discourse that arose particularly within German Idealism was that of the subject-object relationship; it is similarly entirely empty, since the question is obviously, How is this relationship constituted? We will later see that it is not only empty but misleading, and that it had especially devastating consequences for the understanding of the phenomenon of self-consciousness. In German Idealism the attempt was also made to grasp the distinctive character of the consciousness relation through a kind of activization of general ontological concepts. In this connection a special role was granted to the concepts of identity and difference. Since the subject is to be understood somehow as acting, it was argued, one can grasp the subject-object relation by viewing it dynamically. The subject *is* not only distinguished from the object but also distinguishes himself from it; he posits the object as something distinct from him. I will examine these conceptions later and demonstrate that they have no meaning, or in any case that they do not possess the meaning they are purported to have. It may already be clear without much reflection that one cannot apprehend something like the consciousness relation by elevating ontological relations such as those of identity and difference to the status of alleged activities.

In contrast to these attempts to construct the fact of consciousness of something out of spurious concepts, Husserl's simple and undeniably metaphorical characterization of this relation as a state of being-directed is still preferable. And perhaps you might claim that we must be content to acknowledge 'representation' as something ultimate, since we simply cannot insist upon interrogating the foundation of everything. We certainly cannot inquire into the foundation of everything, but to use Wittgenstein's phrase, Have we really already arrived at hard rock, which bends our spade back? In what sense? You will say, If you reflect upon yourself, if you look into yourself, surely you see that your consciousness is directed toward something. But here I would answer, First, what do you mean by the suggestion that I should look into myself? Is this also supposed to be a kind of self-consciousness? Just try to look into yourself. Isn't this also an inappropriate metaphor— namely, that we may turn our glance, which is directed outward, inward through a so-called act of reflection? For my part I can see nothing at all there. And if you say—and you thereby find yourself in good philosophical company—that you did not intend your suggestion in such a way that one should look inward with one's eyes, but rather it concerns a quasi inner eye, an inner sense, doesn't the expression *quasi inner eye* already indicate that you are once again only using metaphors? Indeed, I have to say, As long as you cannot translate the metaphor to me, I have no guidance as to how I should follow your demand. Second, you insist that one can simply see the way in which consciousness of something is a state of being-directed. Is this the case? In which sense of being-directed? A gun barrel or a signpost can be directed toward something. Perhaps if we consider the glance that is directed toward something, we will come closer to the point at issue. This certainly has a clear sense, and if I glance toward something I have a consciousness of it. Yet the fact that we speak of being-directed in the case of visual perception merely rests upon the distinctive character of this type of perception, namely, that it is directed from a particular standpoint into three-dimensional space. If we take away the spatiality of this state of being-directed, nothing more remains left of the attribute of directedness. This reflection again indicates the extent to which we are inclined to interpret the talk of consciousness of something metaphorically in accordance with the model of seeing, a tendency to which the entire European philosophical tradition from Parmenides to Husserl has fallen victim.

I cannot hope to have convinced you from these scant remarks that the conception of consciousness-of as a quasi seeing and the talk of inner looking are fictions. Nor is it my intention that you now accept whatever views I have presented, but only that you more or less understand me and are now prepared to follow me further—with all the necessary *reservatio mentalis*.

In addressing the question of how the consciousness relation is constituted, I think we must thoroughly abandon the idea of taking our bearing from any sort of inner perception. If we now attend closely to the point on which Husserl actually focused in his account of intentional experiences, we find that it lies in the way we speak about these phenomena. Indeed, he said we establish that when we think or desire, for example, we always think something or desire something; and if we now consider how we make this discovery, it is obvious that it emerges from the way we speak. The characteristic feature of the verbs to which Husserl brought attention is at least *prima facie* a semantic one. And here I would like to interject the general observation that this insight did not occur to Husserl merely by accident. Rather, the types and modes in which all these phenomena, such as consciousness, self-consciousness, consciousness of something, and I, are initially given is precisely a linguistic one, and this is actually true for all objects of philosophical reflection. In the final analysis this implies no more than the triviality that the words *consciousness*, *self-consciousness*, and so on are just words, and a clarification can begin in no way other than as an inquiry into their meaning. No serious person can doubt that this is the only way to begin. The paths first begin to diverge at the point at which we think we discern the meaning of words by intuiting something with a spiritual eye.

Let us leave this issue undecided, and attempt to pursue the semantic-grammatical connection to which Husserl alluded a step further than he did. Perhaps in this way we will be able to find the desired criterion for distinguishing the consciousness relation from other relations. Can anything further of a semantic-structural character be said about the grammatical object of these verbs other than that it is the grammatical object? At least in most cases, yes. If we look at consciousness relations such as wishing, believing, intending, knowing, and fearing, we find that their grammatical object is never an expression that designates an ordinary object, that is, a spatiotemporal object; rather, their grammatical object is always a nominalized sentence. One cannot wish or know spatiotemporal objects; if one wishes something, one always wishes that something is or would be the case. The expression *I know* (*Ich weiss*) is not to be completed by expressions such as *the chair*, *Mr. X*, and so on, but rather we find "I know that it is raining today," or "that this chair is brown," or "that a chair stands here."*

If we take any assertoric sentence "p" such as "it is raining today," we can always objectify what is expressed by reformulating it through nominalization as "that p," for example, "that it is raining today." The objects that are designated by expressions such as "that p" are not spatiotemporal objects. The chair indeed stands here now, but the fact that it now stands here does not itself have a determinate position in space and time. The ontological status of these objects is controversial, and this is not the place to examine it. It must suffice to note that the objects of most intentional experiences are objects of this kind. Different technical expressions have been adopted in order to refer to objects of this sort: Husserl speaks of states of affairs, and English philosophy uses the expression *proposition*; thus, in English philosophy those intentional experiences whose objects are propositions are called *propositional attitudes*, that is, attitudes toward propositions

---

*In German there are two different verbs that are both translated in English as "to know": *wissen* and *kennen*. *Wissen* refers to knowing in the sense of having knowledge about something, while *kennen* refers to knowing in the sense of being acquainted with something or someone. Tugendhat is using "know" here in the sense of *wissen* rather than *kennen*. (Trans.)

or states of affairs. Now it is my view that even those intentional experiences that are related not to propositions but to ordinary objects are founded upon a conscious relation to a proposition—in other words, upon a propositional consciousness. I have substantiated this thesis extensively in an earlier lecture course,[4] and therefore I would like merely to sketch the argument here. The matter is somewhat complicated because there are different groups of nonpropositional verbs, and the affair is a bit different in each case. In all cases, however, the concept of existence plays a decisive role. In this context I proceed from a characteristic of intentionality to which Brentano called attention. He pointed out that in intentional relations the second member of the relation does not have to exist. I will now employ the symbol "N" to stand for an arbitrary name of a spatiotemporal object. What Brentano meant was that someone can fear, love, desire N, although N does not exist. In contrast to this, nonintentional relations are not possible unless both members of the relation exist. If N does not exist, it is not possible for someone to hit N, or to devour him, or to stand next to him.

How is this special feature of intentional relations to be understood? Should we say that in an intentional relation the object is, so to speak, in the mind of the person concerned, and for this reason the relation is possible even if the object does not exist in reality? But by this account, an object or its representative is located in consciousness, and we would once again be committed to the absurd proxy theory. How can we provide a clear sense to what was meant above? Indeed, we can do so if we say, He who fears, loves, admires, N must at least believe that N exists. I can fear the devil even if he does not exist, but I cannot do so without believing that he exists. Hence, the point to which Brentano called attention—namely, that the object of an intentional mode of consciousness does not have to exist—is primarily a consequence of the fact that one can relate consciously to an object only insofar as one believes that it exists. Of course, the claim that an object exists is a proposition; and believing that it exists is a propositional consciousness. You might perhaps say that our capacity to believe in the existence of an object presupposes the simple intention or representation of the object as such, and in the latter case we would have an intentional consciousness that does not imply a propositional consciousness. Nevertheless, this view that one can refer to an object without believing that it exists, or without at least imagining that it exists in the mode of fantasy, is wrong; I have shown this elsewhere, and summarizing it now would lead us too far astray.[5]

Thus, if all intentional consciousness is either directly propositional or implies propositional consciousness, we can lay down the following universal principle: All intentional consciousness is propositional. *Intentional consciousness* designates a relation that is distinguished from other relations in the following way: It is a relation of a spatiotemporal entity—a person—to a proposition, or implies such a relation.

Does this mean all intentional consciousness is necessarily linguistic? This view is strongly suggested, because a proposition is an object that cannot be identified spatiotemporally. If we ask *what* it is that he is afraid of or that he aims at or that he believes, we identify the proposition at issue by means of the linguistic expression "that p" ("he fears, believes, that it will rain"); and "that p" refers back to the simple expression "p," that is, to a declarative sentence. Still, the question of whether we actually *can* identify propositions only by means of language is unsettled. If it were answered affirmatively, one would have to say that when we ascribe fears, beliefs, and so on to animals or to children who cannot yet speak, we are using these words figuratively or, in any event, with a different meaning as a result of the fact that what these words refer to could not be grasped as a *propositional attitude*. I want merely to draw attention to this question today without offering a solution. At present the important point is simply this: The thesis that all intentional consciousness is propositional does not imply the wider thesis that all intentional consciousness is expressible only in sentences.

It is more significant for our purposes that intentional consciousness is not only not necessarily linguistic but also, obviously, not necessarily conscious in the sense of the concept of consciousness elucidated earlier. As we have learned from Freud, we can fear, believe, or intend something without having an immediate knowledge that we are in this state. Thus, the real meaning of intentional consciousness—as consciousness of something—which has now been defined as a relation to a proposition, does not correspond to a narrower concept of consciousness, as Husserl believed; rather, the two concepts of consciousness overlap one another: There are experiences that are not intentional, and there are intentional relations that are not experienced.

What are the implications of all this for self-consciousness? I suggested that we should first make the general structure of consciousness of something clear; on this basis we were to acquire a concept of what consciousness of oneself means by replacing the variable "something" accordingly. It has now become evident that though the expression *something* in the talk of consciousness of something is not in itself wrong, it clearly leads to an underdetermination of the structure at issue; this underdetermination finds expression in the prevalent talk of the "subject-object" relationship. As we have just seen, consciousness of something is propositional. It is not related to objects in the ordinary sense of this word, but to propositions. It has or implies the structure *consciousness that p*. And since in the case of self-consciousness knowledge is supposed to be involved, we can set aside the weaker possibility that consciousness that p is only implied. Knowledge does not merely imply, but possesses the structure *knowledge that p*.

If we apply this result to self-consciousness, an important consequence follows. When we found in connection with Freud and Husserl that conscious states are those of which there is or can be an immediate knowledge, it might have looked as if the objects of this knowledge are precisely those conscious states and experiences. But we cannot put this into the form "knowledge that p." One cannot know a state or an experience; this would be an ungrammatical, meaningless expression. One can only know that something is in such and such a state. The expression that supplements the word *knowledge* in the sentence I just formulated has the form "that p." In the case of the immediate knowledge of conscious states this implies that this sentence must have the form "he knows that he is in such and such a state." The person involved himself obviously expresses this by using the word *I*. His immediate knowledge of his conscious states is expressed in statements of the form "I know that I. . ." and any predicate may follow that expresses the possession of a state of consciousness. Thus, for example, we have the sentences "I know that I am bored," "I know that I no longer intend to attend this lecture," and so on.

This result is certainly not suggested by either Freud's or Husserl's terminology. Freud refers to a psychical process in the passage that I cited earlier, and Husserl refers to an experience. In both cases, therefore, the conscious state is converted into an object on its own account. Freud and Husserl thereby stand in the misguided tradition of English empiricism, which I will deal with later. The outcome of our discussion is not only the result of the conceptual analysis of intentional consciousness; it also corresponds to the actual facts regarding the way we express the immediate knowledge that we have of ourselves. It is expressed in sentences of the form "I know that I. . . ." Indeed, it also follows that as false as the assumption of knowledge of isolated states is in the empiricist tradition, the assumption made in the Idealist tradition since Fichte—namely, that there is self-consciousness in the sense of knowledge of an isolated self or, as is so nicely said, of an ego—is no less false. Here the unitary character of the phenomenon is ruptured from the other side, that is, from the side of the subject. If someone believes that there is such a type of knowledge, I would have to ask him, Where do you find knowledge of this kind, that is, how is it expressed? What we find, of course, are not sentences of the form "I know me"; this would again be an ungrammatical, meaningless sentence.

Now you might concede that our examination of self-consciousness must proceed from the form just elaborated. But you might object that precisely because we intelligibly formulate a sentence such as "I know that I am in such and such a state," it is presupposed in knowing the proposition at issue that I relate myself somehow to the object designated by the subject of the subordinate clause; that is, I relate myself to myself, to the subject of my states, and this must be analyzed further. Now, of course, this must be examined more closely. The only thing I want you to concede for the moment is that self-consciousness, in the sense of the immediate knowledge that one has of oneself, is a type of knowledge that is expressed in the specified sentence form; thus, we have to elucidate this type of knowledge in addressing the question of self-consciousness in this primary sense. Indeed, I do not maintain that the phenomenon under consideration has already been elucidated merely by demonstrating that it is expressed in the specified sentences. On the contrary, only now can we pose the questions that must be posed here.

First, who is this subject of states of consciousness? I can immediately cite two answers that we find in philosophical literature. The first and older conception is that something is involved that is exclusively the subject of states of consciousness; for this reason it is also assumed that only the subject himself has access to himself. This subject has been designated in philosophy by expressions that are not to be found in ordinary language, but arise through the formation of substantives from expressions occurring in ordinary language; thus, one speaks of *the* consciousness, and in particular of *the* ego (*das Ich*), or also of *the* self. The second possible conception is one that is suggested by the manner in which we speak, and in philosophy it was first elaborated by Wittgenstein. It consists in the claim that when I say "I am sad," I refer by the word *I* in this sentence to the same thing to which you refer when you say "Mr. Tugendhat is sad." There is no doubt that this is the way we speak, and hence it is clear that the conception that refers to an ego and the like amounts to a reform of language; we will later have to see whether or not there are good or only unsatisfactory reasons for it. If the person to whom I refer by *I* is the same as the one to whom you refer by the name Tugendhat, this obviously implies that the subject of my states of consciousness is not *merely* the subject of my states of consciousness, for otherwise you could not know anything about this subject. It must therefore be a corporeal, spatiotemporal being who is intersubjectively identifiable. Nevertheless, a problem still remains here. Do I have to know that my name is Tugendhat in order to use the word *I* in those sentences in which an immediate knowledge of my own states is expressed? One calls expressions by which we refer to individual objects singular terms. One can obviously refer to one and the same object with different singular terms, and each of these terms may involve different criteria for identifying the object. For example, the same person whose name is Ernst Tugendhat also can be identified as the person who lives on the top floor of Hausackerweg 28, and someone who knows me as the person who lives there does not need to know my name. Besides this same person also can be denoted by the word *I*, although only by myself. Now I obviously can meaningfully use the word *I* in sentences like "I know that I have anxiety," even if I have forgotten what my name is and where I live. This fact does not justify the assumption of a special noncorporeal object called the ego; but it leads to the following question: How can the particular reference that is made by means of the word *I* be distinguished from other references to the same person that are made by means of proper names or distinguishing characteristics? This raises the question of which particular criterion of identification governs the use of the word *I*; and this means nothing other than this: What is the meaning of the word *I*?

The second question that is indispensable for the elucidation of knowledge of one's own states concerns the foundation of this knowledge. Earlier I objected in passing to the doctrine of inner perception or inner seeing. But now the question becomes even more urgent: How is the talk of immediate knowledge that I am in such and such a state to be understood if not in this way?

A difficulty emerges in connection with this second question, which we can already answer provisionally in light of our account of intentional consciousness. It concerns the problem that self-consciousness seems to imply an infinite regress. If the knowledge that I am in such and such a conscious state is itself a conscious state, it appears to follow that I also must know that I know that I am in such and such a conscious state, and so on. In order to avoid this regress, I have cautiously stated so far that a state is conscious if he who has it has *or can have* immediate knowledge of the fact that he is in this state. This weak formulation that consciousness merely implies the *possibility* of self-consciousness corresponds to Husserl's conception, but in his case this simply followed from his view that this knowledge takes place in a peculiar act of self-perception. This conception appears to be phenomenologically false. If someone has a toothache, he not only has the possibility to know that he has it, but indeed he knows it. Then, the regress appears to arise. It does not arise, however, if we now remind ourselves that intentional relations do not have to be conscious. Admittedly one will not be able to say that self-consciousness is unconscious in the pychoanalytical sense; it might, however, be preconscious in Freudian terms. I am now merely interested in demonstrating formally that the phenomenon does not imply a regress. We will only be able to clarify how this state of affairs is to be understood more precisely by answering the question of how such an immediate type of knowledge is to be understood in general.

We can also now understand why the word *self-consciousness* does not have this meaning in ordinary speech. There are two reasons why there is no need for such a word in ordinary language. First, as we have just seen, self-consciousness is expressed in individual cases in sentences of the form "I know that I . . ." And if someone wants to say *in general* that he has self-consciousness, it suffices to say on the basis of the connection between consciousness and self-consciousness that he has conscious states, that is, that he is 'conscious.' In Latin this connection is well expressed by the term *conscientia*.

Finally, I would like to mention the following difficulty: The concept of consciousness, as I have introduced it here in connection with Freud and Husserl, implies that insofar as a being is conscious, it also has self-consciousness. Can this be assumed for animals and small children? It seems initially plausible to ascribe self-consciousness to someone only if he can use the word *I* and can formulate sentences such as "I know that I. . . ." But this would constitute a narrower concept of self-consciousness. Since self-consciousness can be preconscious, it also does not need to be articulated linguistically. And perhaps one can also say self-consciousness, like all other knowledge, becomes a conscious state only if it is expressed linguistically. Then no problem arises in granting animals and small children self-consciousness in the same sense that one grants them consciousness: They cannot express either linguistically. This is admittedly only a negative explanation, and it remains unclear which criterion we must invoke in order to ascribe consciousness to a being that cannot express itself linguistically. This is one of the questions that I do *not* intend to answer in this course of lectures.

Lecture 2

Introduction II: Formulation of the Problem and Program

I still have not finished answering the first of the four introductory questions, namely, the question of which phenomena are designated by the expresssions *self-consciousness* and *relation of oneself to oneself.* In the first lecture I developed a provisional concept of self-consciousness: the immediate knowledge that one has of oneself, of one's own conscious states. Further, we have seen that one must take both of these aspects together: I can know neither myself (or 'my ego') nor my states taken by themselves, but only that I have such and such states. In order to demarcate this phenomenon from other modes of relating oneself to oneself that are not theoretical, one can characterize it either as epistemic self-consciousness (from Greek *episteme* "to know") or as theoretical self-consciousness, because in this mode a person relates himself to himself solely assertorically.

More precisely, we must use the term *immediate* epistemic self-consciousness in order to distinguish our present concept from a wider concept of epistemic self-consciousness that includes all knowledge that is expressed in sentences of the form "I know that I. . . ." For naturally there are sentences of this form in which the predicate does not stand for a conscious state, that is, for a state of which the person concerned has an immediate knowledge. Such sentences may pertain to my physical properties — for example, "I know that I was born in Berlin," or "I know that I am six feet tall" — as well as to my character and modes of behavior, for example, "I know that I am a coward," "I know that I tend to react to situations of such and such a type in such and such a way," or "I know that I love Elizabeth." The characteristic feature of all these modes of nonimmediate knowledge of oneself is that such knowledge is in principle accessible to others in the same way it is to me, and in some cases it may even be more readily accessible to others. My mother knows better than I whether I was born in Berlin. I do not have any immediate knowledge of whether I am a coward or not; this can only be disclosed in my actions. I know immediately whether I am *in love* with someone, but somebody else can know whether I love someone just as well or perhaps even more easily than I do because this again can be demonstrated only in my behavior. Therein lies the humor of the remark "I love you" when understood as a communication, because it is thereby supposed that one is communicating something to the other person that is directly accessible to oneself and only indirectly accessible to the other; such a presumption involves a confusion of a mode of behavior with a conscious state.

The form of epistemic self-consciousness considered by modern philosophy is exclusively immediate epistemic self-consciousness. The narrow extent of this concept of epistemic self-consciousness (which focuses on the contents of consciousness) becomes evident if one considers that it is not immediate epistemic self-consciousness that is demanded by the Delphic motto *gnothi seauton*: "know thyself!" Immediate epistemic self-consciousness cannot be demanded at all, because one simply has it; on the other hand, one must strive for the self-knowledge intended in the motto. In contrast to immediate epistemic self-consciousness, it is meaningful in this case of self-knowledge to refer to a false and a true self-consciousness. Self-consciousness here is not knowledge in the strict sense, but it consists in beliefs that at best approximate a kind of knowledge. Knowledge here is only a regulative idea, that is, the idea of self-transparency in relation to who (what kind of person) one is.

It appears convenient to distinguish a more specific concept of mediate epistemic self-consciousness in the following way: It corresponds not to that form of self-consciousness *demanded* by the motto *gnothi seauton* but to that form of self-consciousness to which the motto refers; for we need a unitary concept here that comprehends both true and false self-consciousness, the knowledge of oneself as well as the lack of knowledge of oneself. Of course, not all mediate epistemic self-consciousness is pertinent here. The motto *gnothi seauton* does not concern my physical properties, but exclusively my dispositions to action and volition; knowledge of my biography is involved only insofar as it is relevant for my dispositions. The epistemic self-consciousness that is related to the motto *gnothi seauton* is distinguished both from immediate and from other types of epistemic self-consciousness by virtue of the fact that it is practically relevant. It is not itself a practical relation of oneself to oneself, but still quite theoretical; nevertheless, it is a theoretical relation that is relevant for the practical relation of oneself to oneself because it has to do with one's own dispositions to action and volition.

What sort of phenomenon is involved in the talk of the relation of oneself to oneself? We are now dealing with a phenomenon that must be distinguished from the different forms of epistemic self-consciousness and, in particular, from the phenomenon of immediate epistemic self-consciousness; it is a phenomenon that is no longer epistemic, that is, theoretical. I will restrict myself in the preliminary clarification of this phenomenon to a few general remarks. We will understand it in a structurally adequate form only later through the interpretation of Heidegger and Mead. In contrast, it was necessary to provide a structural clarification of immediate epistemic self-consciousness in the Introduction because we need it for the critical examination of the Heidelberg school from which my interpretations will proceed.

I can now begin with the meaning of the word *self-consciousness* in ordinary language. We have already seen that in German the word is used in the following way: We call someone self-conscious if he has a positive sense of self-worth in contrast to someone who has an inferiority complex. If we want to develop a philosophically relevant concept of the relation of oneself to oneself by proceeding from this meaning of self-consciousness in colloquial speech, we must try to identify the general structure that functions as the basis of this particular form of the relation of oneself to oneself. If we consider the status of this self, who is either highly regarded or held of little account, it is not at all evident that it involves the person in the same sense as that previously indicated in referring to a subject of states. Contrary to what was suggested by the schema of epistemic self-consciousness examined earlier, persons are not merely substances with inner and outer states; rather, they are beings who act. It is characteristic of agents, first, that their actions take place in a framework of intersubjective relations and, second, that they have the possibility of self-determination within these relations. As agents we are what we do and want; in this sense we already have a relation to ourselves that is different from the epistemic one. At the outset it is entirely unclear how this relation to ourselves is to be understood.

The relation in which we speak of self-determination appears somehow to be founded as a higher level upon this relation to ourselves that we have in doing and wanting something. We have the possibility to disengage ourselves from what we do and want and from the intersubjective roles in which we function, and to ask ourselves, Who am I in all of this? And this means, of course, What do I myself want? What does the talk of "I" and "self" signify here? It obviously has something to do with the autonomy and self-determination of the agent; and this autonomy and self-determination stand opposed to the expectations of others, to existing intersubjective norms and to one's own instinctual drives, that is, those desires that immediately assert themselves. As you can see, I am thereby addressing a set of problems that is examined in psychoanalysis under the title "ego strength" or "ego identity." Ego psychology, however, is thoroughly naive in its conceptual account of the structure of this phenomenon. It entirely neglects an elucidation of the sense in which one can speak here of a relation to oneself. And then, of course, the question arises as to which resources are to be attributed to this so-called ego in order for it to be capable of self-determination and hence to be free from both its contingent roles and its contingent desires.

We can attain an initial or preliminary perspective in understanding this practical relation of oneself to oneself on the two levels that I indicated if we attend to the following: We have the possibility of relating ourselves to the desires and beliefs of our fellow men in such a way that we adopt a position toward them, and we also have the possibility of adopting a position toward our own desires and beliefs. The fundamental words by which the adoption of a position is expressed are *no* and *yes*. It indeed seems plausible to understand the primary constitution of the autonomy of the agent in light of his capacity to say no; what is involved here is not the saying of no and yes to statements, but to imperatives. As someone who has the capacity to say no and yes to imperatives, a being constitutes itself as free in a formal sense. He then even learns to say yes and no to his own intentions, just as he has done to the imperatives of others. All human action is an explicit or implicit choosing. How the agent thereby relates himself to himself, and what this can mean in general, has admittedly not yet become intelligible; we must keep it in mind as an open question.

On this first level of free action the adoption of a position still lacks a standard. The situation becomes different when we adopt a position not simply toward desires or intentions but also toward beliefs, because beliefs raise the claim to be true, a claim that is contested if one says no to them. Now our actions and intentions are also determined by beliefs; one acts in a certain way because one believes that such and such is the case and that such and such is good, whether for oneself or in general. One can therefore adopt a position toward actions and intentions by assuming a position both toward the beliefs about facts and toward the conceptions of value or the norms that the actions imply. And in this way one can adopt a position in particular toward one's own actions and volitions; this adoption obviously contains not only the possibility of denial, that is, the possibility of contesting a truth claim but also the possibility of raising a question.

If one relates oneself to one's own actions and volitions by questioning them, one can speak of a *reflective self-relation*. The word *reflection* stands in close affiliation with the theme of self-consciousness in the philosophical tradition, but it is obviously ambiguous in this connection. On the one hand, it is used in the sense of epistemic self-consciousness; on the other hand, one can understand it as standing for the question of truth insofar as this question relates to the presuppositions of one's own actions. It is natural to suppose that the second form of the practical self-relation, which can be called self-determination, is connected to or identical with this reflective self-relation in which the presuppositions of one's own action are placed in question. This concept of a reflective self-relation also seems to be connected with the second meaning that the Latin *conscientia* has, aside from "consciousness" and "self-consciousness," namely, "conscience." It appears evident that the concept of the reflective self-relation as described above possesses the structure that is generally ascribed to an autonomous (independent as opposed to heteronomous) conscience. Finally, it is obvious that we have reached the point in the practical self-relation at which the form of epistemic self-consciousness demanded by the motto *gnothi seauton* becomes relevant. It would indeed be an error to assume that the question of truth pertaining to the reflective self-relation is identical with the question of who I truly am. Even though the question raised by *gnothi seauton* merely concerns one's own dispositions to actions and volitions, it also serves as a component part of the overall question concerning the truth of the beliefs that are implied in one's actions and volitions. At present we must leave unsettled the problem of how this component question is related to the more comprehensive one, that is, how practically relevant epistemic self-consciousness plays a role in the reflective self-relation.

We can now conclude our treatment of the first introductory question, namely, the question of the range of phenomena to which the words *self-consciousness, conscientia, relation of oneself to oneself,* and *reflection* refer. An important outcome of this initial attempt at clarification is that these terms do not refer to a unitary phenomenon. There are two phenomena—epistemic self-consciousness and the practical relation of oneself to oneself—and they do not fall under a unitary species. Epistemic self-consciousness is expressed in sentences of the form "I know that I. . . ." I have not specified a definite sentence form for the relation of oneself to oneself; but it is natural here to think, first, of sentences expressing intentions ("I will do X") and, second, of sentences of the form "I can do X or Y." These sentence forms belong together; the sentence in the first-person future is a sentence expressing intention only if the second sentence form is possible in which the *can* expresses freedom. Finally, the interrogative form in which practical reflection is expressed corresponds to the "can" sentence, that is, as "should I do X or Y?" (here "should I" signifies the same thing as "is it advisable"). Again I must leave open the question about how in all these sentence forms a relation to *oneself* finds expression.

In the case of both epistemic self-consciousness and the practical relation of oneself to oneself, additional subdivisions emerged; in the case of epistemic self-consciousness, we noted the distinction between the immediate and the mediate. I will begin the interpretations with immediate epistemic self-consciousness because this was almost the exclusive preoccupation of the traditional philosophical treatment of the problem of self-consciousness. Within mediate epistemic self-con-sciousness, we identified the domain pertaining to the motto *gnothi seauton* as an important nucleus that could be characterized as practically relevant. In the case of the practical relation of oneself to oneself different subspecies did not arise, but different levels did: the immediate and the reflective relation of oneself to oneself. The only connection that has been disclosed so far between the epistemic and practical self-relation consists in the fact that the mediate epistemic self-consciousness demanded by *gnothi seauton* is relevant for the reflective relation of oneself to oneself, and plays a part as a component of the latter. On the other hand, a formal correspondence exists between immediate self-consciousness and the practical relation of oneself to oneself: In both cases something is involved that only is what it is from the perspective of the person concerned; this means that the sentences in the first person are not symmetrical with the corresponding sentences in the third person. In contrast, mediate epistemic self-consciousness is a type of knowledge that is not to be distinguished from the same type of knowledge that proceeds from the perspective of the third person. Mediate epistemic knowledge of oneself is only a particular case of knowledge of person X by person Y (i.e., the case where X = Y); therefore, it does not present a set of problems pertaining specifically to self-consciousness, except in the way in which it enters into the reflective self-relation. For this reason these lectures will be divided into two main parts: The first half will deal with immediate epistemic self-consciousness, and the second half will deal with the practical relation of oneself to oneself on both of its levels.

Now let us proceed to the second introductory question posed in the first lecture: Which methodological means, which ontological and epistemological models in the philosophical tradition, are at our disposal for the analysis of self-consciousness and self-relation? There are three models of primary importance upon which the traditional theory of self-consciousness has been based.

The first is the ontological model of a substance and its states, a model that has characterized the tradition since Aristotle and, moreover, is deeply rooted in the fundamental structure of our speech, that is, in the subject-predicate structure. The second model is the so-called subject-object relation. It is presupposed as self-evident that consciousness involves having something before oneself, the 'representation' of an object. Hence, it is presumed that it consists in a peculiar relationship between the subject and an object: One has something before oneself. This has led to the conception of self-consciousness and the relation of oneself to oneself in general as a relationship between the subject and himself qua object: One has oneself before oneself. The third model is based on the epistemological presupposition that all immediate empirical knowledge must rest upon perception. This presupposition has led to understanding even knowledge of oneself and the relation of oneself to oneself as a kind of inner perception. The entire traditional theory of self-consciousness, the German as well as the English, evolved within the framework of these three models. Many philosophers have rejected one or the other of these models but have failed to offer another positive conception in its place.

In the traditional theory of self-consciousness the first model has been most subject to question, although in reality it is the most harmless. It was first rejected by Hume; and in the Humean tradition, in the work of William James and Husserl, we find the conception of a stream of consciousness, an immanent connection of conscious experiences, taking the place of an entity to which conscious states belong. It appears very disputable, however, whether this model really must be abandoned for epistemic self-consciousness; it is tempting to suggest that it was rejected by the tradition originating with Hume only because the subject was conceived as something inner rather than as the material person.

The second model, the idea of a subject-object relation, has remained decisive at least in the German tradition up to the present day, and this means up to the present Heidelberg school.

Finally, the third model, the epistemological orientation toward seeing, can be traced back to the origins of Greek philosophy. It has been presupposed by the entire English as well as German theory of self-consciousness, except in those cases in which the second model was supposed to suffice and the mode of the relationship was left unspecified.

If we now recall our preliminary elucidation of the phenomena, it is already clear at first glance that all three models are hopelessly misguided for the purpose of understanding the practical relation of oneself to oneself. The situation is somewhat more promising for immediate epistemic self-consciousness. The first model appears to be appropriate here, although it cannot contribute much toward clarifying the phenomenon. On the other hand, we have already seen— though we will deepen this understanding in the critical examination of the Heidelberg school—that the second model is misguided. The decisive question in elucidating immediate self-consciousness is how the so-called inner sphere is accessible to us, and this is the question for which the third model offers a direct answer. I have already expressed my doubts about the idea of inner perception. In any case, it is not evident at first glance that this model is misleading. This will have to be shown later. And of course we can demonstrate that this model is wrong only if we can offer an alternative explanation of how the so-called inner sphere is accessible to us.

These comments upon the second introductory question lead directly to the answer to the third introductory question, namely, why I hope to elucidate the phenomena of self-consciousness by means of an interpretation of Wittgenstein, Heidegger, and Mead. If the ontological and epistemological models employed by the traditional theory of self-consciousness prove to be untenable, we obviously must begin with those modern philosophers who have tried to break through this traditional categorial apparatus, that is, the focus on the representation of objects and the correlative subject-object relation, and the focus on seeing and perceiving. In different ways Heidegger and Wittgenstein have attempted to accomplish precisely this. What the efforts of both philosophers are directed against can be identically characterized in the negative: It is the traditional conception of understanding—or, to use Heidegger's term, of disclosure (*Erschlossenheit*)—as a relationship to objects and the traditional conception of disclosure as a seeing and an observing. Certainly, in their positive conceptions both the points of departure and the methods of the two philosophers are entirely different, and for this reason we will have to make use of both.

Wittgenstein was traditionally oriented in his selection of problems, but he is the real and sole methodological innovator, whereas Heidegger remained methodologically naive. As much as he rejected the model of seeing in grasping the thematic objects of philosophy—such as understanding and 'disclosure'—he remained entrapped by the Husserlian model of the intuition of essences in his conception of philosophical method. One somehow has 'to see' the phenomena to be described, so he believed. Of course, this was meant metaphorically; but what is the metaphor a metaphor for? Wittgenstein had only the traditional problem of self-consciousness in mind as a topic, that is, immediate epistemic self-consciousness, but he strove to disentangle this phenomenon from its metaphorical distortions. On the other hand, Heidegger overlooked this phenomenon from the start, relinquished it to the conceptualization that was rooted in traditional models, and focused directly upon the practical self-relation. He is the only philosopher to clarify this relation structurally in such a way as to render intelligible what I had to leave earlier as an unsettled question, namely, how this phenomenon involves a mode of relating oneself to oneself.

The starting point of both philosophers was also entirely different. In sharp contrast to Wittgenstein, Heidegger proceeded directly from the problem of self-relation. This was not yet subordinated to the general question of being in Heidegger's earliest work—for example, in his review of Jaspers—although even here Heidegger already understood this problem as an ontological one. He asked, How is "I am" to be distinguished from "it is"?[1] This was a novelty in the history of ontology; it is now not merely a question of distinguishing different meanings of *being* and *is*, as is done in the Aristotelian tradition by treating *am* simply as a grammatical variant of *is*; rather, in the statement "I am" being is supposed to have another sense than it has in "it is." According to Heidegger, I am not related to my being in the "I am" statement 'aesthetically,' that is, in the mode of looking or contemplating. I do not describe my being as something present-at-hand (*Vorhandenes*), but I relate myself to it in the mode of 'self-concern' (*Selbstbekümmerung*);[2] this being thereby does not have the sense of being-present-at-hand, but I relate myself to my being as something that I, as he says in *Being and Time*, have "to be."[3] Heidegger confers the title "existence" on this to-be. He rebukes Jaspers on the grounds that he still has only grasped existence 'aesthetically,' in the mode of contemplation.[4]

What Heidegger means by this to-be can be made evident most simply by recalling Hamlet's question: "To be or not to be—that is the question." It is a question that is obviously not theoretical. Someone who poses it is not asking whether something can be asserted, that is, whether it (he himself) is or is not, or more precisely, will or will not be. On the contrary, this question concerns the issue of whether the questioner says yes or no in a practical sense to the being that impends at every moment; and this means he either wants to prepare an end to this being or he is willing to continue with it. We are beings, according to Heidegger, who only are insofar as they relate themselves to this being—to the accomplishment of life that impends at any given time. This relating of oneself to this being is indeed not a representing, and it also cannot be understood as a consciousness of something; rather, this relation consists in the fact that we can say yes or no to our to-be, or, more accurately, we always have to say yes or no to it. Persons are beings who do not simply exist in a factual sense, but exist in such a way that they take an implicitly affirmative or negative position toward their existence. In this context we encounter the adop-

tion of a position of yes or no on a level more fundamental than the
one that appeared in my first provisional interpretation of the relation
of oneself to oneself. For this adoption of a position is not only not a
theoretical assumption of a stance toward beliefs but volitional and
practical; it is also obviously more fundamental than the volitional
assumption of a position toward any imperative. But Heidegger can
now incorporate all practical adoptions of yes/no positions (and this
means all intentions) within this adoption of a yes/no position toward
one's own to-be for the following reason: In relating ourselves to our
to-be we also relate ourselves to it in such and such a way; that is,
we say yes or no to being such and such, and this means to acting
in such and such a way.[5] Thus, Heidegger attempts to incorporate the
actions and intentions of a human being as well as his temperaments
(Befindlichkeiten) and moods (Stimmungen) within the structure of his
relation to his to-be.

For the present preliminary account it is important only to recognize
that Heidegger breaks through all three previously cited traditional
models by means of this conception, although formally he is guided
by a structure that was well known in the tradition, namely, the
structure that allows for a distinction between something—a being—
and its being, that is, its existence. Admittedly this structure does not
actually contradict the substance model, though Heidegger himself
believed that it did; in any case, he brings something different into
consideration by using the structure of substance-existence that is not
implied by the structure of substance-states. It is clear that the relation
of oneself to one's own being contradicts the third model, since the
idea that the impending to-be is something that we could inwardly
perceive, or in some other way quasi see, is absurd from the outset.
But, the most important point is that the subject-object model is
undermined here in a way that is much more radical than the one I
developed in the preceding lecture; I objected to this model merely
by pointing out that all intentional consciousness is related to propositional objects or implies a propositional consciousness. This objection
does not deny the claim that the subject relates to objects, but only
stresses that it relates to objects of a special type; on this basis it is
clear that self-consciousness cannot be understood in such a way that
something is simply related to itself, that the subject itself becomes
the object. In contrast, we are now dealing with a self-relation that
is not a consciousness of an object but a relation of oneself to one's

own to-be. While it was assumed in German Idealism that the relation of oneself to oneself necessarily has the structure of a relation of something to itself and thus must appear as a kind of self-mirroring, Heidegger presents the following alternative model: The human being relates himself to *himself* in relating himself to his existence—to his life as it is impending at any given time. He thereby sketches an answer to the question that I had to leave unsettled in my provisional characterization of the relation of oneself to oneself, namely, how someone relates himself to *himself* in his practical adoptions of the yes/no position—in his "I can. . . ." His answer reads as follows: The subject relates himself to himself, not by becoming the object, but by relating himself to his existence.

We find a completely different point of departure in Wittgenstein. The late Wittgenstein—and we will have to deal only with him— initiates a new line of reflection upon the nature of the meaning of our linguistic expressions, and hence upon what it means to understand a linguistic expression. And Wittgenstein's rejection of the second and third models must be understood in this connection. Apart from names and pronouns, linguistic expressions do not stand for objects. Therefore, the form of disclosure (*Erschlossenheit*), in Heidegger's terms, that is involved in understanding linguistic expressions is not consciousness of an object, that is, not intentional consciousness; thus, the subject-object model is again rejected in a radical manner. Above all, Wittgenstein is unremitting in opposing the view that conceives of the meaning of linguistic expressions as mental pictures, which we somehow have before us in a mental seeing. This critical rupture of the traditional model of understanding linguistic expressions also makes it possible for Wittgenstein to regard a person's knowledge of his own inner sphere in such a way that it is not construed as inner seeing.

In contrast to Heidegger, Wittgenstein remains quite traditional in the range of topics he addresses under the problem of self-consciousness, although he is methodologically more radical; his method provides a necessary tool that will be indispensable in separating the meaningful from the absurd in Heidegger's own conceptions. This radicality in method admittedly consists in something very trivial: Namely, in the requirement that in philosophy, as in all discourse directed toward attaining an understanding, we are not allowed to employ metaphors if we cannot provide an intersubjective account of their meaning. According to Wittgenstein, providing an intersubjective account of the meaning of a word means indicating how the word is used. If you want to know what a word means, says Wittgenstein, I do not refer you to something that you see—there is nothing there to be seen, and even if there were something, it would be of no service to you in attaining intersubjective understanding—rather, I show you how the word is used. This insistence upon the mode of use is certainly not the end of all philosophical wisdom, but it is surely its beginning. I do not see how anyone can deny this, assuming that he wants to do philosophy in such a way that others understand him and he understands others.

Hence, what is at issue is the elimination of a metaphorical mode of speaking in philosophy, and above all the removal of the metaphor of seeing that dominates all traditional thinking, since this is the fundamental metaphor to which one can appeal in using any other metaphor. One employs a word, for example, and then expects that others will somehow see what one means. Through suggestion one eventually convinces them that they see something. In resisting this, one can do no more than assume a stance of naiveté in the face of each philosophical use of words or confess to a lack of understanding. According to Socrates, the beginning of all philosophical inquiry lies in this confession of ignorance.

Many people fear that this Wittgensteinian method leads to a curtailment of philosophy, but the opposite is the case. According to Wittgenstein, traditional thinking essentially consists in assimilating the unlike and in leveling differences; thus, one assimilates all the other words of language to names, the knowledge of the inner domain to knowledge of the external world, and thinking and understanding to seeing. We can find an adequate conceptual framework for phenomena that have not been understood until now because they have been assimilated to others, or treated metaphorically, only if we clarify the way we talk about these phenomena. Of course, one always hears the following objection: "But we want to get to the things themselves, and not remain caught up in words." If someone replies to me in this way, I must ask him: "Are you speaking as an empirical scientist or as a philosopher? If you are speaking as an empirical scientist, you are completely right, since in this case the clarification of words is only a preliminary stage and the empirical investigation must follow. If, however, someone believes he can proceed the same way in philosophy, he must have some kind of counterpart in mind that fulfills the role experience serves in the empirical sciences." Does one therefore believe in a quasi experience of some kind of essences? This is the way Husserl envisaged it. But in this case we again encounter the model of mental seeing. This recourse to a fictitious world of mental seeing is the alternative to the analysis of the use of linguistic expressions, or else one constructs supposedly logical-structural connections, as in Hegel's *Logic*; but these logical connections can be established only in a system-immanent fashion, and in this sense they are not related to our ordinary understanding of words, which at least must provide our starting point.

There are two reasons why I begin my analysis with Wittgenstein and only subsequently turn to Heidegger: First, Wittgenstein deals solely with immediate epistemic self-consciousness, while Heidegger tries to elaborate the structure of the practical relation of oneself to oneself; second, through our interpretation of Wittgenstein we can acquire a method that will remain fundamental for everything that follows. If my reflections on Wittgenstein's method are correct, our decision regarding whether to proceed by means of linguistic analysis in this broad sense of the term is not a matter of discretion. Rather, the recourse to the modes of use of words is fundamental for all philosophical inquiry; therefore, all my interpretations, even those of the nonanalytic philosophers, will necessarily assume a language-analytical form.

G. H. Mead did not carry out a critical examination of traditional philosophy as fundamental as that of Wittgenstein or Heidegger. To a greater extent his contributions have the character of suggestions, which he—as a social anthropologist doing philosophy—did not formulate with the conceptual precision we expect from a philosopher. Nonetheless, his conception is equally revolutionary, and it is only on its basis that it becomes possible to understand the structure of that self-relation which I have designated as reflective. According to Mead, the phenomenon that is designated by terms such as *self*, *self-consciousness*, and *reflection* is constituted in speaking with oneself, and this mode of speaking with oneself is constituted socially, that is, in the internalization of speaking with others. This internalization of speaking with others runs through several levels, of which two are particularly important; on the first level the others are those of the concrete group, while on the second level they include anyone who can speak at all, hence all rational beings. Thus, the conception of a self-relation emerges in which one speaks with oneself in the same way that one would speak with any partner. It is not sufficiently clear in Mead what the structure of this speaking with others and with oneself is. Nevertheless, it can hardly be anything else than that of the yes or no adoption of a position, and if what is involved is a discourse with oneself that is like discourse with anyone else, this reflection can only have the sense of raising the question of truth. Admittedly it remains unclear in Mead's work to what extent this talking to oneself is a relation to oneself; one can understand this only by connecting Mead's insights concerning the relation of oneself to oneself with those of Heidegger. These philosophers complement each other.

It is only with Mead that we will attain the level of Hegel's concept of self-consciousness and spirit, that is, as the conception of a practical self-relation that is constituted in interaction with others and is at the same time understood in light of the relation to truth. Hence, after the interpretation of Heidegger and Mead we will be prepared for a critical confrontation with Hegel's conception, that breaks away from the traditional models that still guided him; further, this criticism can be developed from the perspective of a position that still considers centrally important the connection between self-consciousness and a life grounded in reason. For Hegel as for Mead, the higher level of self-consciousness (which Hegel calls spirit) is constituted in the relation to universality, but for Hegel the unity of self-relation and the relation to universality is not that of the adoption of a position in discourse. Rather, the self is constituted as a being-for-itself in distinguishing itself from others, and it acquires its "truth" insofar as it knows itself in this being-for-itself as simultaneously identical with universality; this is "the 'I' that is 'We' and the 'We' that is 'I,' " as Hegel says at the point in the *Phenomenology of Spirit* at which he first introduces spirit as the truth of self-consciousness.

Our interpretation here will have two tasks. First, we will have to disentangle what Hegel means from the inadequate formal-ontological conceptual scheme in which it is presented by subjecting his views to linguistic analysis. In the previous lecture I already noted that German Idealism attempted to grasp the structure of self-consciousness by raising the ontological 'relations' of difference and identity to the status of alleged activities; Hegel employed this strategy in developing his sociopractical concept of self-consciousness and spirit in the same way he had used it earlier in reconstructing epistemic self-consciousness.

Of course, I know that many of you here in Heidelberg think that this talk of distinguishing oneself from others and identifying oneself with others is quite unproblematic. It remains to be seen, nevertheless, whether and how one can clarify the way in which these expressions are used.

Thus, we will have to ask what it is to which Hegel is actually referring when he speaks of the identity of what is different and the restoration of unity out of the nonidentical, and so on. It is obvious that he is referring to socioanthropological structures, not ontological ones. But it is not initially clear how these phenomena are to be grasped in a structurally adequate way. The only thing that is relatively clear is the experience that provided Hegel's starting point, which he himself described at the beginning of his early work, *The Difference between Fichte's and Schelling's System of Philosophy*, as an experience characteristic of his time—namely, the experience of the individual's separation or alienation from his natural and social environment. The problem of alienation and its overcoming was taken over by Marx, admittedly with essential modifications. In posing this problem a specific conception of the good or true life is presupposed; it is assumed that the individual finds his self-fulfillment in relating himself to another, and particularly to a group of others. Nonetheless, one cannot clarify this view by taking the subject-object schema in hand and claiming that the issue here is a subject-object unity, or an identity-in-difference and the like.

Thus, our first task of interpretation will be to disentangle what is involved here from the distorted and misunderstood formal-ontological concepts that obscure it. Our second task will be to oppose the significant conception that remains to Mead's conception, or, better said, to the conception that emerges from the interpretation of Mead and Heidegger. One might characterize the Hegelian conception in the following slightly pedestrian fashion: The good or true life consists in an affirmative relationship of the individual to his environment, his fellow human beings, and so on, a relationship that does not deprive him of his autonomy. This conception entails a specific, substantive answer to the question of the right form of life as posed in the reflective self-relation. On the other hand, Mead's conception involves something quite different; for it describes a structure of self-relation and of intersubjectivity that does not represent a specific *answer* to the question of the right form of life, but reflects the structure of this *question*. In

Hegel the question of truth still plays a role in a certain sense in philosophy, but it is no longer an essential constituent of the activity of men as described in this philosophy. On Hegel's model a definite conception of the true and good life is dictated to man or to society, as it were, by philosophy, and the requirement that each individual pose the question of truth himself in concert with everyone else does not figure as an essential feature of this true and good life. In contrast, the conception that will emerge through our analysis of Mead—of an intersubjective domain of subjects reciprocally criticizing themselves and one another with regard to truth—implies nothing specific in terms of content, aside from the presupposition that there never can be a truly good life if the members of society are not themselves free to raise in common the question of the truly good life. This suggests that in Hegel we find a closed relation to truth, whereas in Mead the relation to truth that is relevant for the problem of self-relation is an open one. Thus, the strength of Mead's conception becomes more evident in demonstrating its superiority to the Hegelian view.

I have now reached the point at which I can explain how I want to organize the course of lectures. In the first part I will consider the structure of immediate epistemic self-consciousness; I will begin by demolishing the way that the problem is traditionally posed by the Heidelberg school, and then interpret the Wittgensteinian conception, which is itself beset by serious difficulties. In the second part I will analyze the problem of the practical self-relation, and it should be clear from my preceding remarks why I will here deal successively with Heidegger, Mead, and Hegel. Thus, I will put the innovators Wittgenstein, Heidegger, and Mead at the center of my interpretations, and support these interpretations by setting them at both the beginning and the end within the framework of a critical attack upon a corresponding traditional position.

I can now finally address the fourth introductory question, posed in lecture 1, concerning the relevance of the problem of self-consciousness. One can judge the relevance of a philosophical topic from two standpoints—first, in light of its immanent philosophical interest and, second, in light of its interest apart from philosophy. In the early modern period the topic of self-consciousness was regarded as fundamentally relevant in both respects. But in view of the elucidation of the phenomena that I have presented, we can no longer assume that there is such a unitary topic; Fichte improperly conflated immediate epistemic self-consciousness and the practical self-relation.

For both Descartes and Kant (though in wholly different ways) immediate epistemic self-consciousness appeared as the foundation of what they aimed at in theoretical philosophy. In Descartes' case this involved securing the foundation of an absolutely certain form of knowledge, whereas in Kant's case it involved clarifying the condition of objective experience. Knowledge of oneself seemed to Descartes to be the most certain, indubitable form of cognition, and as such paradigmatic and the basis for all secure knowledge. The unity of self-consciousness appeared to Kant as the foundation and guarantee of the objective unity of experience. Today hardly anyone would conceive of the task of theoretical philosophy in the way in which Descartes or Kant did. It would lead us too far astray here to justify this view, and hence I can only uphold as a thesis the claim that today one must assume that the task of theoretical philosophy is elucidating the implicit presuppositions of our understanding.[6] Understanding, however, is always unavoidably intersubjective. All knowledge and all objective cognition presupposes understanding. Thus, even if one wanted to set the topic of theoretical philosophy as narrowly as Descartes or Kant did, it is not obvious that one could ground this conception by appealing one-sidedly to a putative pre-intersubjective self-consciousness. As far as Descartes is concerned, we will see in elucidating immediate epistemic self-consciousness that it cannot be understood in any sense as solipsistic. And Kant himself already recognized that the unity of real ('empirical') epistemic self-consciousness does not require any corresponding objective counterpart, and hence he postulated a special 'transcendental' self-consciousness for this function, whose value ultimately remained unclear.[7] Furthermore, it is questionable whether something like objectivity can ever be grounded in self-consciousness; it seems rather to be grounded only in intersubjective speech.

The outcome of this extremely condensed summary, which is more of a thesis than a justified conclusion, is that theoretical self-consciousness does not have the philosophical relevance assigned to it by Descartes and Kant. Does this imply that immediate epistemic self-consciousness has no immanent philosophical relevance at all? I do not think so. If the task of theoretical philosophy is elucidating the implicit presuppositions of our understanding, then every philosophical topic is relevant that can lead to an extensive revision of prejudices concerning the models we use in tackling the phenomena of consciousness and understanding. If the fundamental traditional models prove to be inadequate for understanding theoretical self-consciousness and if this topic therefore requires a new categorial framework (i.e., new models), its immanent philosophical relevance is thereby confirmed. There are, of course, also other philosophical topics whose elucidation has repercussions for philosophical conceptualization in general. The topic of self-consciousness has immanent philosophical relevance in this sense, but it does not have the primary importance that Descartes or Kant attributed to it.

Is immediate epistemic self-consciousness also relevant in a sense that extends beyond philosophy? Someone held a lecture here not long ago on self-consciousness in the traditional sense, that is, on immediate epistemic self-consciousness, and in order to underline the importance of the topic he appealed to the relevance of the question, Who am I? Now this question is ambiguous. Nevertheless, it is only relevant if it is meant in the sense of *gnothi seauton*, and immediate self-consciousness contributes nothing to this sense, at least if we understand it in the traditional sense as I have characterized it up to this point. The immediate knowledge of ourselves that we have under all circumstances cannot be practically relevant. One could claim practical relevance for this type of self-consciousness only if it became evident that it also stands in a tension between not knowing oneself and knowing oneself. At present I have to leave this issue unsettled.

What is the situation in the case of the practical self-relation? We relate ourselves to our own to-be in such a way that it somehow 'concerns' us.[8] Heidegger originally described this phenomenon as self-concern, and he later replaced this word by the term *care (Sorge)*.[9] Hence, if one's own being is the ultimate object of concern or interest for each person, one might say that the philosophical question of the practical self-relation centers on the structure of what is ultimately relevant to anyone at any given time. But is it true for everyone that one's own being is the ultimate—and that should doubtless also mean the single ultimate—object of one's concern? In reply to someone who raises such a question, we must obviously ask, What else could or should a person be concerned about?

Three answers are conceivable: One should not (only) be concerned about oneself, but about God; one should not (only) be concerned about oneself, but about being; one should not (only) be concerned about oneself, but about others, society, or mankind. The modern recourse to self-consciousness has been criticized from each of these three perspectives. The critique from the theological perspective is accurate in a historical sense in any case, because the recourse to self-consciousness can be understood at least in Descartes as a movement that suspends the constraints of faith. This critique and this interpretation are advanced in the essay by Gerhard Krüger entitled "The Origin of Philosophical Self-Consciousness." The claim that the recourse to self-consciousness represents a fall, not from God, but from being—from 'the' being—is a thesis of the late Heidegger, which I mention only as a curiosity. Irrespective of the question of the *genesis* of the problem of self-consciousness, the only perspective from which we are disposed to question the relevance of the practical self-relation today is undeniably the social one. Indeed, from this perspective the entire topic of self-consciousness today may easily appear to be obsolete in a practical sense.

Nonetheless, it is questionable whether such an opposition between self-concern and social engagement is justified. I do not intend to deal with this question in general terms, but to consider it in light of the two concepts of the practical self-relation that emerged earlier and whose contrast will guide our exposition. In this context it is significant that for both Hegel and Mead the practical relation of oneself to oneself is a relation of oneself to others.

Let us begin with Hegel. The social objection can no longer be raised in the face of his conception of the overcoming of self-consciousness in Spirit—that is, in view of a conception based upon the well-being of the community, which is constituted by the well-being of individuals who understand themselves in terms of their being within the community. One might rather be inclined here to ask whether self-consciousness has been "overcome" to such an extent that a self-relation is no longer really involved. I do not want to examine this question now, but instead to pursue a slightly different problem. While the social objection admittedly can no longer be raised against this Hegelian conception, this does not prove that his conception represents the true good or the ultimate object of an interest guided by reason, which is also the ultimate reference point for all questions of relevance. If we do not want to affirm or deny something dogmatically as the true good, we must provide grounds to justify what we affirm and to refute what we deny. In other words, one must raise the question of truth.

Now someone who raises the question of truth regarding what is ultimately relevant already puts himself in the context of the inter-subjective self-relation that emerged from our consideration of Mead, which I have designated as a reflective self-relation. Hence, the recourse to the reflective self-relation does not by itself signify a prejudice in favor of an egocentric position, but simply represents the condition of the possibility that questions of relevance on the whole can be posed rationally at all. This reveals the connection between the idea of a practice guided by reason and the properly understood idea of self-consciousness (in the sense of a reflective self-relation that is understood intersubjectively), which even at present cannot be abandoned. Thus, the answer to the question of the relevance of the topic of the practical self-relation is that it concerns the general condition of the possibility of rationally posing ultimate questions of relevance.

Is the relevance of this philosophical problem for life beyond philosophy actually confirmed in this way? Someone could raise the following objection: The philosophical clarification of the formal structure of rational questions of relevance is neither a sufficient nor a necessary condition for concretely posing rational questions of relevance. In other words, the philosophical theory of the reflective self-relation still does not lead to a reflective self-relation, and a reflective self-relation does not require such a theory. This is correct. Nonetheless, a connection appears to exist. If something is structurally analyzed or neglected in the philosophy of a period, the probability exists that it is also concretely practiced or neglected in this period.

Lecture 3

The Traditional Theory of Self-Consciousness at an Impasse

I will begin today with immediate epistemic self-consciousness. (For the sake of simplicity I will henceforth omit the word *immediate* when the reference is clear.) I already developed an initial, preliminary clarification of the structure of epistemic self-consciousness in the first lecture. It has the form "I know: I ϕ," where "ϕ" is a predicate that designates a state of consciousness. This clarification, which is still completely formal, raised two crucial questions: (1) What constitutes the particular mode of identification of a person by means of the word *I*, and (2) On what is the knowledge of epistemic self-consciousness based? If we can properly answer these two questions, we will have succeeded in clarifying epistemic self-consciousness. For this involves knowledge of a state of affairs that is expressed in a predicative sentence ("I ϕ"). Now it is generally the case that one knows a state of affairs that is expressed in a sentence of this form if and only if (1) one knows which object is identified by means of the singular term of this sentence, and (2) one knows that the predicate of this sentence pertains to this object. If one applies these two conditions to the sentence "I know that I ϕ," the two questions indicated above follow.

I will attempt to answer these questions through an interpretation of Wittgenstein. It is presupposed by Wittgenstein as self-evident that epistemic self-consciousness has the structure "(I know:) I ϕ." Before turning to his position, I want to confirm the correctness of this structural approach by critically examining the traditional theory of self-consciousness, which proceeds quite differently. I will restrict myself here to the consideration of a single position, namely, that of the Heidelberg school. There are two reasons why I have chosen to analyze this position exclusively—one is subjective and context bound, the other is objective.

The subjective or accidental reason concerns the fact that I am holding this lecture before a public here in Heidelberg; I can assume that most of you who have already thought about this topic at all will view it within the horizon of the Heidelberg school's outlook.

The objective reason is that the Heidelberg school seems to me to represent the most advanced position within the traditional theory of self-consciousness, and perhaps it even marks a discernible end point of this tradition. In order to make this clear, I must first provide a general characterization of the traditional theories of self-consciousness and offer a schematic account of their various forms.

The reliance upon the subject-object model can be regarded as a characteristic feature that runs through all traditional theories of self-consciousness. On the other hand, a reliance upon what I referred to as the third model, namely, that of seeing or perceiving, can be regarded as universal only if one also includes the weaker term *representing* (*Vorstellen*) within it; in any case, we can regard the expression *representing* as the most inclusive, since all the more specific conceptions of the subject-object relationship can be subsumed under it. Thus we can characterize the following structure as the most universal schema for traditional theories of self-consciousness: z represents x. From this perspective, the various traditional theories can be distinguished according to (1) whether or not x was regarded as identical with z, and (2) what x and z were regarded as designating.

Let me first address the second point. The traditional theory of self-consciousness is divided into two camps on this issue. After the subject-object model had obscured the complex propositional structure (I ϕ) of the objective side of knowledge of oneself, two possibilities existed for reducing the complex unitary phenomenon to one or the other side; that is, it was possible to regard x and, relative to it, z either as "the ego" or as the "ϕ" states. In order to understand this development one must return to Descartes, who did not yet make this reduction but provided an additional motive for it—aside from the subject-object model—in his belief that it was necessary to grasp the subject whom everyone addresses by *I* as an immaterial substance. This led to the rejection of the reference to a subject altogether by Hume and the empiricist tradition following him, since an immaterial substance is not to be found in the inner sphere. This tradition must be understood in view of its decisive reliance upon the third model; this elicits the conclusion that there is nothing perceivable to which the inner states belong. The representatives of this tradition did not consider the possibility that the inner states or experiences are inwardly perceivable to perhaps as little an extent as an immaterial substance. On the other side, the tradition of transcendental idealism beginning with Kant shared this repudiation of an immaterial substance, but correctly believed that it was not permissible to dispense with the concept of the subject of inner states. But since it also accepted the Cartesian thesis that this subject cannot be the same as one whom we designate by *I* in ordinary language, namely, the respective person, it had to assume the existence of a special "transcendental" subject, which was referred to as the ego. I do not want to go into the special obscurities that are bound up with the talk of "transcendental" in this context.

Thus, the two candidates for x and z in the schema z represents x are on the one hand the ego and on the other hand the conscious states or experiences. And now I can return to the first point, to the question of whether or not x is regarded as identical with z in this schema. Let us first consider the less tempting alternative that they are not to be regarded as identical. In light of the second point it is clear that there are exactly two possibilities, and both of these have been represented historically. One possibility is that the ego and the conscious states are divided between the two sides z and x. Of course, the only way this is conceivable is by assuming that the ego represents the conscious states. This was roughly Kant's conception. He also split up the unitary phenomenon I ϕ, but he did so in such a way that both fragments are preserved in the distinction between the transcendental subject and inner sense. They are now distributed on the two sides of the subject-object relation: The expression "I know that I ϕ" became "the ego represents ϕ." Kant recognized the difficulty that 'the ego' must also somehow be given, but he regarded it as insoluble.[1] The second possibility of x $\neq$ z is elaborated in Husserl's doctrine of inner perception as presented in the extreme, uncontaminated form characteristic of the first edition of his *Logical Investigations*.[2] It is assumed there that both x and z are experiences, but different ones. Every experience can be represented by a second simultaneous experience, an act of inner perception. The weakness of this conception is readily evident. According to it, an experience a represents another experience b; but in what sense can this experience be identified as self-consciousness?

The Heidelberg school has exhibited the untenability of theories that assume that $x \neq z$,[3] and is committed from the outset to theories that assume that $x = z$. In the schema x represents x either 'the ego' or the conscious states can be substituted for x. The second conception has been advanced by Franz Brentano.[4] The most significant representative of the first conception is Fichte.

The Heidelberg school proceeded from the tradition originating with Fichte in Henrich's essay *Fichtes ursprüngliche Einsicht*. I can now briefly indicate how he formulated and developed the problem. In the essay on Fichte, Henrich exposes two fundamental difficulties that arise for a conception of self-consciousness that conforms to a Fichtean model. In this essay he still believes that Fichte himself came close to their solution. In his second essay, *Selbstbewusstsein*, the difficulties seem to him insoluble. They hold to the same extent for a conception such as that of Brentano.[5] But if this is the case, there is no available solution within the framework of traditional theories of self-consciousness.

Instead of questioning the traditional models themselves, Henrich adheres to the traditional conception of self-relation as a kind of 'being-acquainted' ('*Bekanntsein*') with oneself, but he believes that it is necessary to transfer this from self-consciousness into a phenomenon of consciousness, which no longer expresses itself as an "I." Pothast takes a basically similar step, although he argues differently on points of detail. Of course, the following question arises: Can one ascribe a self-relation to a form of consciousness for which a connection with self-consciousness is no longer supposed to be constitutive? Henrich seems to waver here. On the one hand he would like to adhere to this position, but on the other hand he recognizes that if he does the two difficulties he identified for self-consciousness must reemerge.[6] Pothast adopts the more decisive position; he draws the consequence that consciousness can no longer be grasped as a self-relation, and also does not imply one: "Consciousness is accordingly to be thought of as a completely 'objective' process, in the sense that no aspect of a knowing self-relation enters into it" (p. 76).

Thus, it appears that the internal consistency with which the Heidelberg school pursues the implications of the traditional theory of self-consciousness leads to the disappearance of the phenomenon to be explained—namely, self-consciousness. In the theory of the Hei-delberg school, then, the traditional theory of self-consciousness seems to lead by itself to an absurd result. For this reason I think that the Heidelberg school marks a discernible end point in the traditional theory of self-consciousness.

In critically assessing the Heidelberg school, I will certainly take note of this dynamic aspect, which finally leads it to abandon the phenomenon to be explained; but I will not make it central. Such an immanent critique would be unproductive. This result can be only a secondary indication for us that the phenomenon is already misun-derstood in the basic assumptions. The burden of my argument will rest, first, upon a critical analysis of the method and mode in which Henrich grasps the phenomenon to be explained and, second, upon an examination of the two fundamental difficulties to which he brings attention. Here I will have to ask whether the difficulties disappear, or are in any event resolvable, within a language-analytical conception; by a language-analytical conception of epistemic self-consciousness I mean one that is based on the way this self-consciousness is expressed in language rather than on an appeal to inner evidence.

In his first essay Henrich is intent upon exhibiting the two fun-damental difficulties from the outset, and this stands in the way of elucidating the phenomenon of self-consciousness. The structure of the phenomenon itself seems to him to be self-evident. He describes it in this way: "Self-consciousness is distinguished from other forms of knowledge by the fact that the same state of affairs enters into it in a twofold position" (p. 12). By "in a twofold position" he means, "In the single case of self-consciousness, thinking and what is thought, having and what is had, Noesis and Noema are not differentiated from one another. Where the I is, both are present, namely, the subject and this subject as its object" (11). Thus, Henrich makes an explicit and unambiguous appeal to the subject-object model: The subject is itself object to itself. And from the sentence just cited it follows that a being who has this structure is designated as an I. Thus, the word *I* is not employed as a personal pronoun, as in ordinary speech; rather, as Pothast correctly observes (p. 37), it is employed as *conceptus communis* or, more precisely, as a substance-predicate, so that one can refer to *an* I in the same grammatical sense that one can refer, for example, to a man or an apple. We designate something as a such and such if it has a specific structure, and in the case of the I this is supposed to be the structure of the identity of subject and object, of thinking and what is thought. Since Henrich also understands the relationship more precisely as one of knowledge, one can also say that it involves the identity of knowing and what is known. On the one hand, the relationship is one of knowledge; but since an identity between knowing and what is known is supposed to exist and since this identity is in turn supposed to be known, the relationship is also designated as an identity: "Self-consciousness exists in the identity of its relata" (13). Hence, one arrives at the formula I = I, which was first introduced historically by Fichte. Nevertheless, Henrich employs it, not merely for the purpose of interpreting Fichte, but as the formula that apparently expresses the fact of self-consciousness adequately (though not sufficiently). It is not sufficient because the identity sign by itself does not express the fact that the identity relation is supposed simultaneously to be a relation of knowledge.

If we now ask how Henrich arrives at this remarkable phenomenon, which he designates as self-consciousness and the I, and if we set aside the merely historical connections, we find the following answer on page 14: The described state of affairs is one "that we all perceive insofar as we have knowledge of ourselves and recognize ourselves through the expression *I*." Hence, Henrich appeals to intuitive evidence that is supposed to present itself "insofar as we have knowledge of ourselves."

If we focus first upon the second part of this clause beginning with *insofar*, the suggestion is that we encounter the described phenomenon by attending to what is disclosed when we use the word *I*. I have already noted that Henrich—and in general the tradition in which he stands—does not understand the word *I* as a personal pronoun and so-called index word, which is the way it is used in ordinary language. Henrich even writes that if one understands this word as an index word, "the problem is eliminated" (p. 49).

The fact that a philosophical tradition employs a word differently from the way it is used in ordinary language, and the fact that the problem that it raises would be eliminated if one returned to the ordinary use of the word, is in itself harmless and quite normal; indeed, it would be a misunderstanding to think that a language analyst must promptly feign deafness whenever a word is used in a way that diverges from ordinary language. From a language-analytical viewpoint, the philosopher is obviously free, for example, to use the word *I* differently from the way it is used in ordinary language; but in this case he must explain how he is using it. There is also no reason to insinuate that Henrich has evaded this demand. It is satisfied if we interpret the clause beginning with *insofar* in such a way that its first part is an explication for the second. As we have already seen, the meaning of the word *I* in the special philosophical sense is to be a being who has the structure of knowledge of itself.

Thus, the question of how we arrive at the phenomenon described by Henrich refers us back to the first part of the *insofar* clause. The thesis is apparently: We discover the described phenomenon by attending to the way we have knowledge of ourselves. Let us, therefore, make the attempt and attend to how we have knowledge of ourselves! How should we go about doing this? There are, to be sure, only two possibilities. The first is the intuitive one: One insists that one *sees* how one has knowledge of oneself, evidently in a spiritual sense of seeing. On this assumption, Henrich also would have to claim that one sees that this knowledge of oneself has the structure specified by him. The other possibility is that one takes note of the fact that "to know of oneself" is a linguistic expression, and therefore one examines how we use this expression. If we adopt the first, intuitive proposal, it becomes difficult to see how we can make ourselves understood intersubjectively, assuming that we see something there at all. On the other hand, if we adopt the second proposal, we in fact encounter a phenomenon, namely, the knowledge that is expressed in sentences of the form "I know that I ϕ." This knowledge, however, does not have the form of a self-relation of a subject to himself as claimed by Henrich; and one surely also cannot claim here that an identity exists between knowing and what is known, since what is known is obviously a proposition.

At this point Henrich could retreat to the intuitive position. It is indeed conceivable that a phenomenon exists here that is not directly accessible through language, to which one can linguistically refer only in some indirect way. In order to deny Henrich this line of retreat, I would like to go a step further in the critique and advance the following thesis: The phenomenon described by Henrich—and, as I must always add, by the tradition in which he stands—is not only not actually given in language but also not possible; one can say *a priori* on conceptual grounds that it is impossible. This is, of course, a strong assertion. One has no means of proof here to convince someone who wants to adhere to Henrich's position at all costs; for he always has the option of replying that the words are to be understood differently in this particular case, so that even what is impossible for the normal understanding of words becomes possible.

The phenomenon described by Henrich seems to me to be impossible because it contradicts our understanding both of knowledge and of identity. We already saw in the first lecture that knowledge is essentially propositional. Hence it follows that a structure of the form "I know myself" is one that is in itself impossible, since it contradicts the meaning of *knowledge*. One could raise the following objection: Just as consciousness of oneself is not comparable to any other form of consciousness, so also the meaning of *knowledge* involved here is of a different type. But it does not suffice to assert something so abstractly; one would have to explain this other meaning that the word *knowledge* is now alleged to have, and I know of no such explanation. It is conceivable that Henrich later sensed this difficulty himself, since in the second essay he speaks mainly of an "acquaintance (*Kenntnis*) with oneself" (cf. pp. 277ff.); of course, he also does this because he now needs a concept that is primarily applicable, not to the consciousness of an I, but rather to consciousness as such. But the term *to be acquainted* (*kennen*) is in reality also always propositional: Being acquainted with something or with oneself always means being acquainted with it or oneself as a such and such. In contrast to "I know myself," "I am acquainted with myself" is a meaningful but manifestly elliptical expression. If someone says this, he obviously invites an answer like this one: "So? What is it, then, that you know about yourself?"

The second absurdity in the model of self-consciousness that Henrich inherited from Fichte lies in the method and manner in which the relation of knowledge and the relation of identity are conflated with each other. We will later have to examine whether and in what connection a knowledge of identity is part of epistemic self-consciousness. It is doubtless true that sentences like "I know that I = Ernst Tugendhat" are meaningful. This sentence can even be false (I take it for very unlikely, but it is logically possible; it may be that I only imagine myself to have this name, or to be the person designated by this name). The sentence "I know that I = I" is also meaningful, although it is as trivial as the sentence "I know that this = this" (when I point both times to the same object while saying "this"); it is trivial because it cannot be false. But in the sentence "I = I" it is completely absurd to say that the equal sign has the force of knowledge. The equal sign can belong only to the propositional content of what is known by someone; knowledge cannot itself crawl, so to speak, inside this relation.

I already know what the Fichteans and Hegelians among you will reply: I am entitled to adhere to the ordinary meaning of identity to just as little an extent as to the ordinary meaning of knowledge; and if I complain that absurdities result, I must realize that a unique phenomenon is involved that must lead to paradoxes precisely insofar as one tries to apprehend it by using expressions of ordinary language. The view to which I refer here is not that of Henrich; as an analyst one can fruitfully come to terms with the writings of the members of the Heidelberg school because they forgo the recourse to paradox and dialectical argumentation. Nonetheless, to those who argue in this way I would propose the following compromise: It may be dogmatic to want to exclude the possibility at the outset that there are paradoxical phenomena; but the recourse to paradox should in any case only be thought of as a last resort, when all means to avoid it have failed. It appears to me impermissible to proceed in any other way on the assumption that the phenomena must be paradoxical because otherwise they would appear too trivial. It seems to me that the phenomena are hard enough to understand when one wants to see them clearly; indeed, it is only then that they are hard to understand.

After trying to demonstrate that the phenomenon described by Henrich under the title "I" is neither actually given nor possible, we still might question whether there is not something to be retained from his analysis even if one admits that epistemic self-consciousness has the structure "I know that I ϕ." In this way, a point of departure could emerge for our later positive analyses and our critical examination would not remain merely negative. The following reflection may already have occurred to you: Granted, the propositional content of epistemic self-consciousness is the entire sentence "I ϕ"; but isn't it presupposed that the knower, the I, must know that he is identical with the subject of the "I ϕ" sentence in order to know that this sentence is true? And isn't this knowledge that both occurrences of the word *I*, which are found in the full sentence "I know that I ϕ," stand for the same person roughly what Henrich is referring to?

Two points must be noted in this connection. First, this problem of identity as presented here has meaning only in the context of the question of how I can know that a "ϕ" predicate applies to me. Second, the suggested reflection has the status of a supposition or a hypothesis, and does not rest on a claim to self-evidence. The question of whether such a supposition is necessary can be answered only by elucidating the conditions of knowledge of "I ϕ" sentences. Since the suggested reflection merely describes a possibility and is not based on self-evidence, we can obviously exclude from the outset every explanation of this allegedly presupposed identity sentence that contains absurdities. In particular, we can exclude the possibility that an identity sentence is presupposed that has the form "I know myself."

It is important to be clear at the outset about the sort of answers that can be countenanced here, so that we do not once again become lost in the traditional vagaries. The additional knowledge that is expressed in an identity sentence is necessary if and only if my knowledge of the application of a "ϕ" predicate to myself is achieved in two steps: first, in knowing that something is "ϕ" and, second, in establishing that this something is identical with myself. Actually, there are sentences of the form "I know that I such and such" whose truth is established in this two-step procedure, for example, "I know that I was born in Brno." How do I know this? I know (through hearsay) that E.T. was born in Brno, and I know that I = E.T. But this sentence is surely not an example that is analogous to an "I ϕ" sentence. Hence, it appears that this two-step procedure pertains to knowledge that is characteristic of mediate epistemic self-consciousness, because in this case a predicate is involved whose applicability can be known only insofar as I am the so-and-so; therefore, the additional question can always arise here as to whether I = the so-and-so. But if this is correct, we must regard the claim that this schema may also apply to immediate epistemic self-consciousness as a very improbable hypothesis.

An adherent of the traditional theory of self-consciousness might reply: "You are completely right that in the case of immediate epistemic self-consciousness one does not know first that a being is 'ϕ,' and then that I am this being; on the contrary, I know immediately that I am identical with the being who knows that he is 'ϕ.' This, however, is precisely the identity to which Henrich refers in his description of the phenomenon, that is, an immediate identity of myself with myself. Hence, this is the identity that is expressed in the sentence 'I am I'; and the knowledge of this immediate identity serves as the presupposition of my capability to know that I ϕ."

This argument rests on a confusion. The talk of an immediate identification is meaningless if it is supposed to represent an achievement of knowledge. Either the identity that is involved is one that first must be ascertained, in which case we have a sentence of the form "I = a"; and here the two-step procedure described above results: first characterization, then identification. Or, in contrast, the identity is not one that first must be ascertained, in which case it is tautological. Of course, anyone who uses the word *I* in the same sentence twice can also say in a trivial sense "I = I"; but in so doing he expresses only a tautology and not knowledge.

We will pursue this problem further in connection with the second fundamental difficulty that Henrich brings to light. In any case, it seems to me that the foregoing argument closes off the last remaining option for those who persist in defending Henrich's account of the phenomenon. For we can now not only assess and criticize this account of the phenomenon as a historical curiosity but also (although to my knowledge this has never historically happened) retrace step by step how one could move from the genuine phenomenon of immediate epistemic self-consciousness to the construction of this curiosity. The steps are these. (1) One correctly notes that the subject-expression "I" has a function of identification; but this is not investigated more closely (its elucidation would constitute the answer to the first question raised at the beginning of today's lecture). (2) One establishes that there are sentences of the form "I know that I such and such" in which this knowledge presupposes the knowledge of an identity sentence "I = a." (3) One concedes that in the case of immediate epistemic self-consciousness no sentences of this type have to be known. And now (4) one makes the mistake of claiming that at least knowledge of the truth of the sentence "I = I" is presupposed, and one understands this as an achievement of knowledge on the basis of a false analogy to "I = a." (5) It also cannot suffice to say "I know that I = I," analogously to "I know that I = a," since the problem repeats itself for the first *I*; for this reason such formulations as "I know myself" and the conflation of the knowledge and the identity relation ensue.

We can now move on to the two difficulties that, according to Henrich, must arise for any theory that attempts to understand the phenomenon as characterized. In his first essay Henrich initially considers a theory of self-consciousness that he calls the theory of reflection (*Reflexionstheorie*), which does not do justice to these difficulties; he then presents Fichte's theory as an attempt to resolve these problems. In his second essay Henrich no longer believes that Fichte's approach can resolve these difficulties. Therefore, he refers only to the theory of reflection, and since the two difficulties are insurmountable for this theory, he concludes that self-consciousness is unintelligible on its own terms and that one must return to consciousness. What is astonishing about Henrich's procedure is that these difficulties never provoke him to doubt whether the phenomenon of self-consciousness has been correctly described in the first instance. For Cramer, we are confronted with "an incontestable state of affairs," and only its "explanation" leads to difficulties that "appear close to insurmountable" (564). After just having seen the absurdities that are associated with the traditional framework that the Heidelberg school accepts, we can only regard it as probable, if not self-evident, that this framework must lead to insurmountable difficulties. Nonetheless, it is worth looking at them in detail.

Let us consider the first difficulty. What does Henrich mean by the phrase *theory of reflection?* The talk of reflection involves the use of the spatial metaphor of turning back upon oneself (*Sichzurückwenden*); the subject, who (according to the theory) "is primordially related to objects, turns back upon himself" (p. 11). And now Henrich can directly formulate the difficulty. Self-consciousness is supposed to be consciousness of an I (*Ichbewusstsein*). But as indicated, something is an I only if it has the structure of the identity of knowing and what is known. But if, according to the theory of reflection, self-consciousness is supposed to be effected by turning back upon oneself, the identity of knowing and what is known is established only in the act of this turning backward. On the other hand, the subject to which the act turns back is already assumed to be an I. Thus, on the one hand the act of turning back is supposed to yield awareness of the I, and on the other hand it is only in this act that the I is constituted in accordance with its concept. Hence, as Henrich demonstrates, a circle emerges. In assuming an already existent subject, the theory of reflection presupposes what is actually supposed to be constituted only in the relationship to itself.

Henrich then demonstrates how Fichte's theory of the I (*Ichtheorie*) must be understood as an attempt to avoid this circle. Fichte begins with the assumption that a subject cannot be presupposed who is prior to the act of self-consciousness; rather, he assumes "that the subject himself emerges only in conjunction with the entire consciousness

I = I. . . . When Fichte talks about the self-positing of the I, he is thereby referring to this immediacy, in which the whole I comes to the fore at once" (18). A quote from Fichte may provide further elucidation: "The I posits itself absolutely, that is, without any mediation. It is at the same time subject and object. The I only comes into being through its self-positing—it is not an already preexistent substance; rather, its essence in positing is to posit itself, it is one and the same thing; consequently, it is immediately conscious of itself."[7]

If this proposal by Fichte is to have any value, it must be possible to ascribe a clear meaning to the talk of "positing" and "self-positing." Henrich draws attention to the fact that Fichte never defined his talk of "positing" (18). He himself attempts to elucidate it by stating "that something simply emerges without previous existence, and in emerging it stands in a relationship to knowledge" (19ff.).

I suspect that two ideas were combined in the concept of positing. The first idea concerns the affirmative character of judgment or, more precisely, of the being that is asserted in judgment. In this sense Kant could say, "The concept of affirmation or positing is completely simple and generally the same as that of being."[8] Here the word *positing* is understood in the passive or middle voice. When Fichte attributes an active meaning to it and speaks of an act of positing, this implies that what is posited on Kant's account because it is now is grasped as something *being* posited in its being. It is obvious here that positing has a second sense—namely, that of creation. Thus an originally theological notion of being as the emergence of something made or produced is now linked with the logical-ontological notion of being as posited-being. Fichte, in particular, requires this second aspect in order to be able to assert that something comes into being only in an act.

Can the talk of positing, nevertheless, be made intelligible by means of such an explanation? The reference to its theological origin provides little help unless one assumes that the theological notion of a *creatio ex nihilo* is itself intelligible. In any case, one must be aware of how dubious it is to secularize this theological concept by applying it to our self and world understanding, as is done in German Idealism; for this notion was itself based only upon analogies and metaphors.

An additional difficulty arises, of course, when one speaks not merely of positing but also of self-positing. Is such a notion of the self's creation of itself out of nothing capable of reconstruction? If not, Fichte's attempt to overcome the difficulty of the theory of reflection specified by

Henrich must be regarded as a failure. The Heidelberg school itself finally came to this conclusion. According to Fichte, the I is supposed to come into existence only insofar as self-positing takes place, and the existence of this act of self-positing is supposed to be the product of just this positing. In this connection Pothast asks, "How can it be alleged to take place if it does not yet exist?" (71). And Henrich too remarks in his second essay, "The circle in the concept of this self-related knowledge is not removed by bestowing the quality of immediacy upon it" (268).

The problem with the theory of reflection that Henrich identifies (and from which Fichte proceeded) rests on the assumption that we are analyzing something whose essence consists in the identity of knowing and what is known. For someone who does not acknowledge that the phenomenon of self-consciousness has or presupposes this structure, the difficulty does not exist. The difficulty, which is in fact insoluble, is only an outcome of the absurdity of the basic approach.

In my view the situation is different in the case of the second difficulty identified by Henrich. While the first problem disappears as soon as one no longer speaks of 'the I' (and associates this with that nonsensical structure), the second problem can be formulated even with reference to the use of the pronoun *I*. To be sure, this difficulty can also be resolved, but only in connection with an elucidation of the use of the word *I*. For this reason I would like to defer the discussion of Henrich's second difficulty to the next lecture, since we can move directly from there to the language-analytical clarification of self-consciousness and to Wittgenstein. Today I merely want to look at the conclusions Henrich draws in his second essay from the fact that the attempt to understand self-consciousness is supposed to lead to a dead end in light of the two specified difficulties. In so doing I will conclude my critical analysis of the Heidelberg school today, reserving only the examination of Henrich's second difficulty for the next lecture.

As a result of the difficulties that emerge for "egological" theories (263), Henrich locates his problem in his second essay in the wider context of a theory not only of self-consciousness but also of consciousness. But what does *consciousness* mean? Henrich provides no answer to this question. And Pothast even explicitly states that he cannot answer it. It concerns a "predicate that is not further analyzable, which belongs to all the parts of psychic life with which we are acquainted" (79). This explanation might recall the definition of *con-*

sciousness that I provided in the first lecture, assuming one understands *acquaintance* in the sense of immediate knowledge.[9] But for Henrich and Pothast this can no longer serve as the *definiens* because they no longer want to define *consciousness* by recourse to self-consciousness.

Instead of offering an explanation of the meaning of the term *consciousness*, Henrich is content to employ examples; he refers in particular to "the situation of awakening," which he describes in this way: "Suddenly a complex of sense impressions, pictures, and dull bodily feelings is present, often filled with symbolic and affective significance, a world out of nothing, which is associated with the past only through recollection and recognition" (260). "Suddenly something is present"— but for whom? For itself, or for the person who awakens? If the latter, then we already have self-consciousness: The person is himself conscious of this. For human consciousness this seems to be generally characteristic. Since Henrich attempts to abstract from this and offers no other conceptual criterion for consciousness, he once again remains dependent upon an indeterminate intuition. Of course, it is difficult to envision from the outset how a rational dispute is possible concerning a phenomenon for which we can provide no verbal account.

Henrich's thesis now is that one can better elucidate "acquaintance with oneself" (277, 8) if one removes it from self-consciousness back into consciousness. This appears at first to refer back to the empiricist tradition, which left a subject out of consideration and focused one-sidedly upon the conscious states. As is to be expected, Henrich's discussion of the theories of this tradition, which is developed in the second section of his essay, has a negative result. In the third section he examines the "egological theories of consciousness" (263), by which he means essentially the Fichtean tradition. These theories now appear to Henrich to be hopeless because of the two fundamental difficulties.

Henrich summarizes, "The problem of a theory of consciousness is only now disclosed in its full difficulty." The second fundamental difficulty of the theory of self-consciousness "applies in just the same way to any theory of consciousness that renounces all egological means but nonetheless wants to account for the egoless consciousness as a self-relation, ultimately in accordance with a model that is based upon reflection" (268). This statement shows, first, that all of the theories of self-relation that Henrich considers are constructed according to the simple subject-object model ("reflection"), which he elaborated at the beginning of the Fichte essay. Second, it indicates that Henrich feels compelled to repudiate the phenomenon of self-relation in general. One obviously wonders, In this case can one still talk about an "acquaintance with oneself" at all? Pothast replies to this question in the negative, and he comes to the conclusion that consciousness is a "completely 'objective' process" (76). In this way the phenomenon that was supposed to be explained is abandoned.

In contrast, Henrich attempts in the fifth section to sketch a new theory of consciousness, which does not understand the term *consciousness* as "self-relation" but interprets it in such a way that it "remains acknowledged that we are immediately acquainted with consciousness" (275). Consciousness must be understood as a "dimension," but it is "a dimension . . . in which an acquaintance with itself is included" (277).

Doesn't Henrich thereby concede that consciousness has a self-relation? For this reason he notes on the next page that "careful qualifications are in order." "Without conscious acquaintance with the fact that consciousness is there, there would not be any consciousness at all. Nevertheless, neither this event nor the dimension that contains it has a relationship to itself." This appears to mean that there is an acquaintance with the fact that consciousness lies before one, but this awareness cannot be ascribed to consciousness and it obviously also cannot be ascribed to a subject. Here one indeed encounters the limits of intelligibility.

In conclusion Henrich offers the following explanation: "If one could abandon the statement that consciousness includes an acquaintance with itself, then it would be easier to be convinced that such circles do not again arise" (278). To be sure, in this case such circles would no longer arise. But then the phenomenon that was to be made intelligible would also be abandoned—as is obvious in Pothast's case. But it was precisely Henrich's thesis that consciousness includes an awareness of itself. On the other hand, those circles *must* arise, according to Henrich's own account, as long as one has no model for understanding "acquaintance with oneself" other than that of reflection. It is worth noting that at the point at which he brings the traditional model under the most extreme pressure, Henrich would prefer abandoning the phenomenon of "acquaintance with oneself" rather than severing this phenomenon from the traditional model. To be sure, the crucial concept of acquaintance with oneself is negatively contrasted with the self-relation that is based on the model of reflection; but in its positive meaning this concept remains thoroughly unelucidated to the same extent as the concept of consciousness. In order to acquire a meaningful elucidation of the expression *acquaintance with oneself*, it would seem plausible to return to the level of self-consciousness and thereby abandon the traditional model rather than the phenomenon. In this sense, one may conclude that the traditional theory of self-consciousness ineluctably points beyond itself in the final phase of its development.

Lecture 4

Descending from the I to "I"

In the essay on Fichte, Henrich deals only briefly with the second difficulty, which in his view arises for all theories of self-consciousness (13ff.). He presents it more extensively in the later essay (266ff.), and here he deems it the crucial and insurmountable difficulty for all theories of the I. He describes it in this way: "The I must in every case apprehend *itself* in self-consciousness. Since this apprehension is supposed to have the character that is proper to a knowing apprehension, the I must have some conception that the thing that it is aware of is it itself. . . . It must . . . in every case be capable of stating with certainty that it is acquainted with itself in self-consciousness. . . . As is well-known, this certainty is infallible, instantaneous, and indubitable to such an extent that even the question 'whether the you with whom you seem to be acquainted as yourself is really you yourself or perhaps someone entirely different or something else' appears absurd." The "question 'Is this I of which I am aware really mine?' " is always "already answered. . . . Rather, an answer to it that was not a yes" would be "absolutely absurd, and hence the question also becomes meaningless" (266).

To begin with, it is surprising that on the one hand Henrich regards the positive answer to this question—rightly I believe—as indubitable, and on the other hand he treats it as an insoluble problem. On the one hand, he takes even the question—rightly I believe—to be meaningless, but on the other hand he thinks that its positive answer is still in need of justification. Can the meaning of Henrich's question as to how I know that I am myself and not someone else be understood at all? Isn't this just as meaningless as the question of how do I know that this thing that I just pointed to now is really this thing and not something else? We must suspect that a question of identity is being raised here without sufficiently providing an account in advance of how questions of identity can be meaningful. Naturally I can raise a meaningful question of identity with reference to this thing over there if I already conceive of it as the such and such; that is, I can ask whether it really is the such and such, for example, whether this person I am pointing to really is Mr. Theunissen. Thus, it is meaningful to ask how I can know that this $=$ A; on the other hand, the answer to the question of how I know that this $=$ this is that it is a tautology, and the truth of a tautology is *a priori* certain. In a completely analogical way it appears meaningful to ask whether I $=$ the father of this girl, or even whether I $=$ E.T.; but in the question of whether I $=$ I there is nothing to ascertain because it is a tautology.

It is conceivable that Henrich would contest this assertion of an analogy between the statements "I $=$ I" and "this $=$ this." He might say the following: In the case of "this" only an identification is involved, but in the case of "I" a self-identification is at issue. To which I would reply, this admittedly is the difference between "this" and "I," but what difference does this make for the tautological character of both identities? It is just as logically necessary that I $=$ I as it is that this $=$ this. If Henrich were to object that the problem is indeed not that I $=$ I, but how I *know* myself as myself, I would ask in return, What does "as myself" mean? What is meant here by *myself* and *I*? Evidently it is no longer the structure of the I from which Henrich began; the talk is no longer of 'an I,' but of myself as an individual, of 'my I.' In this expression—*my I*—the technical philosophical term *an I*, which is supposed to designate an object for which the equation "subject $=$ object" is valid, is now combined with the expression *mine* deriving from ordinary language, which refers back to the singular term *I*. Since Henrich formulates his difficulty in this way (Is this I of which I am aware really mine?), we must first ask whether the difficulty arises if one remains within the framework of the traditional theory of self-consciousness and adheres to the subject-object model and the talk of "an I." Second, since it is apparent (a) that one no longer speaks here merely of 'the I,' and (b) that on the contrary this second difficulty is not even capable of formulation without the ordinary word *I*, the mode of use of this word must now be investigated. For we can decide whether or not the parallel to "this" is justifiable only by clarifying the meaning of this word.

Let's begin with the first point. Henrich explains his difficulty in this way: "In order to arrive at an identification with himself, the subject, of course, must already know under what conditions he can ascribe something that he encounters or is acquainted with to himself" (266ff.).[1] Thus Henrich proceeds from the following presupposition: The subject represents objects; it 'encounters' the latter. How is it ever to know that the particular object that is it itself, that is, the subject, is in fact it itself, the subject? And this question indeed appears unanswerable. Hence, while the difficulty Henrich indicates did not emerge at all as long as the question was formulated in ordinary language—namely, as how I know when I refer to myself that the thing to which I refer is identical with the person who does the referring—it arises immediately when the problem is formulated in the conceptual terms of the subject-object model. And we can also immediately see why it does. Henrich describes the problem in this way: How can I know that I am something that I encounter? For purposes of clarity, let us assign the symbol "A" to the something that I encounter here. Now the question is whether the object = the subject, whether A = I. But the question now no longer concerns the state of affairs characterized by Henrich as indubitable. It is now clear why Henrich on the one hand regards the positive answer to the question as indubitable, and on the other hand treats it as an insoluble problem. It is indubitable insofar as Henrich relies on the formulation characteristic of ordinary language, in which the question is merely whether I = I; it is insoluble insofar as Henrich immediately interprets this question in terms of the subject-object model, and here it really has the form of whether I = A. Can we also assume here, as in the case of Henrich's first difficulty, that the problem is resolved as soon as one no longer relies on the subject-object model?

But, you will surely ask, what takes the place of this model? It no longer appears to suffice to refer to the tautology "I = I"; on the contrary, the question is, If I do not refer to myself by knowing that something I encounter is identical with myself, then how shall we positively understand the reference to oneself? I believe that the only way we can pursue this question is by investigating the mode of use of the word *I*. By this means we will gain access to the language-analytical conception of epistemic self-consciousness. We can already find a first step in this direction in the Heidelberg school in Pothast's account. In contrast to Henrich, Pothast holds the view that only the first of the two difficulties disclosed by Henrich is fatal for the theory of self-consciousness, while he regards the question, Am I really in possession of myself in the object that I call I?, as resolvable through a "consideration of linguistic usage" (32).

Thus, in examining the question of the mode of use of the word *I* we can proceed by considering the corresponding account by Pothast (23–32). This point of departure, however, entails a limitation on the posing of the question. For the general approach of the traditional theory of self-consciousness leads Pothast to confine his attention to the isolated word *I* in his analysis of ordinary usage. Now we already saw in the preceding lecture that it is very important for the question of self-identification whether or not the predicate that follows *I* is a "ϕ" predicate. And it will become clear that the mode of use of the word *I* cannot be elucidated at all without examining the special function of this word in the "I ϕ" sentences. Nevertheless, following Pothast, we can first see how far we can go without considering whole sentences, especially the "I ϕ" sentences.

Pothast correctly assigns the word *I* to the class of expressions that one calls index words or deictic expressions. First, the demonstrative pronouns *this, that*, and so on belong to this class of expressions; second, there are the personal pronouns, and third one finds the adverbs of location and time such as *here, there, now, then*, and *today*. The class of indexical expressions as a whole comprises a subclass of those expressions that are called singular terms. A *singular term* is an expression whose function is to refer to an individual object. More precisely, the function of a singular term consists in its use by the speaker to specify which object among all objects he is referring to; that is, he specifies the particular object among all objects to which the predicate expression is to apply that complements the singular term in a sentence. For example, when someone says "Peter is ill," he specifies by means of the singular term *Peter* which object he now intends to describe as being ill.

The indexical expressions are distinguished from the other singular terms by virtue of the fact that the object that is referred to by them depends upon the speech situation. For example, the word *this* does not stand for a specific object on its own, but when someone uses it and at the same time points to something, he is thereby referring to the thing at which he points. The fact that these expressions do not stand for an object on their own does not mean that they do not have a unitary meaning on their own. The meaning of an expression is what one explains in explaining its mode of use. And all these expressions, of course, have a mode of use that admits of uniform explanation. This is explained by indicating how the reference of these words to objects is a specific function of the speech situation. For example, one explains the word *this* by noting that it is used to refer to the object at which one is pointing.

Perhaps you may find it peculiar that I also designate adverbs of location and time as singular terms, and thus imply that places and times are objects. This does not correspond to the ordinary use of the word *object*; and if one says that personal pronouns stand for objects, this also fails to correspond to the ordinary mode of use of this word, since normally we do not characterize persons as objects. I already mentioned earlier that language analysts sometimes use words in ways that deviate from their ordinary usage. If one does this in philosophy (when it is done in a responsible way), it generally means that one wants to underscore a specific similarity that one regards as essential. If it has been customary in analytical philosophy since Frege to designate persons, times, and places as objects as well, this is because they share a key feature with those things that one ordinarily calls objects— namely, they are individuals to which plurality and identity pertain. By *plurality* I mean that one can speak of several persons, places, and times and that one can count them; and it is thereby implied that one must be able to determine whether a place or person is different from, or identical to, another. And when we have such pluralities, we must have the verbal means that enable a speaker to specify which individual of such a plurality he is referring to. These verbal means are precisely the singular terms. Quine once coined the motto No Entity without Identity, and to this one might add, No Identity without Entity; whenever we speak of identity we are dealing with objects. Of course, the word *object* is itself of no consequence to me. A technical term like *entity* would perhaps be preferable.

If we now consider the particular indexical expression *I*, it can easily be seen that its rule of use is that by means of this expression the respective speaker refers to himself. This explanation readily harmonizes with the general explanation of indexical expressions that I have given. The meaning of the word *I* is a unitary one, but it implies that the expression stands for a different object, or to put it somewhat more agreeably, for a different person depending on who uses it.

The explanation of the meaning of the word *I* that I have just given can also be found in Pothast (24). Certain characteristic features follow from this meaning, and on this basis the use of *I* can be distinguished from that of the other indexical expressions. Pothast relies partly on Castañeda in this connection, but does not go as far as he does.[2]

The characteristic feature to which Pothast gives special prominence is that "the word *I* in contrast to others of its kind always designates one and the same individual for him who uses it" (24). This peculiar feature is surely not especially interesting, since one can formulate corresponding characteristic features *mutatis mutandis* for other indexical expressions as well; for example, the word *here* has the peculiar characteristic that at the location in which it is used the same place is always designated.

Far more important than this aspect are its complementary sides, which are ordinarily not noticed: first, the fact that the same place that is designated at this location by *here* can be designated from another place by *there*, and second, that from this place the other places can be designated by *there* ("there, so and so far and in such and such a direction from here"). The indexical expressions generally form correlated groups of this sort—here-there, now-then-before, I-you-he—and the use of an expression from a group is connected in a systematic way with the use of other expressions in the same group.

Indeed, it is clear, for example, that someone still does not know the meaning of the word *here* if he consistently designates the place at which he finds himself by *here* but does not know, first, that *here* is to be replaced by *there* when one designates the same place from another position and, second, that by *here* an individual place is singled out from the plurality of places as the one directly referred to (from which the others are seen as "there and there"). The reason this systematic connection with the use of *there* is part of the meaning of *here* is that without this connection *here* could not function as a singular term, that is, it would not designate an object in the previously described sense; for in this case the word would not pick an individual out of a plurality, and there would be no possibility of grasping what is designated as identical in an altered speech situation. Here an additional fundamental weakness of the subject-object model comes to the fore: It is a simplification to think that there could be an isolated reference to only *one* object ('the object'); rather, it is constitutive for the reference to an object that as an individual it is picked out of a plurality. Every reference to an object always already stands in a field of multiplicity. (In the philosophical tradition only Kant recognized this, although he had a different concept of an object.)

What I have just demonstrated with reference to the example of *here* is, of course, equally valid for the other groups of indexical expressions, in particular for *I*. And this means it is constitutive for the use of *I* that someone who says *I* knows, first, that this same person can be addressed as "you" and can be designated as "she" or "he" by other speakers, and, second, that he thereby picks out an individual person among others whom he can designate as "they." If this connection did not exist, *I* would not be capable of designating an entity. It therefore also pertains necessarily to the use of the word *I* that everyone who employs it knows that others can refer to the same entity he refers to as "I" as "he" or "she" or by means of a name, because this follows from the word's definition; for by means of *I* each respective speaker designates himself. This account implies a plurality of speakers, and therefore it also implies that the speakers can reciprocally refer to one another. Thus, in examining a feature that Pothast regards as characteristic of the use of *I* we have encountered a fundamental structure of all indexical expressions, which is certainly also important for the correct understanding of the word *I*.

Now let us turn to the characteristic features that distinguish the use of *I* from *this*, *here*, and *now*. A characteristic to which Castañeda has called attention, and which is overlooked by Pothast, is that when the word *I* is used significantly it is not possible that the entity referred to does not exist.[3] This is not true for the word *this*, or, more precisely, for the combination "this so-and-so," for example, "this beetle." If I say "This beetle that I have in my hand is red," it is possible that the expression *this beetle* does not refer to an object. You may look and say, "But there is nothing there," or "There is no beetle there." On the other hand, if someone says "I. . . " it is indeed conceivable that these sounds were uttered by a machine, but if *I* was used significantly by a speaker, it is inconceivable that the entity referred to by the expression does not exist. Castañeda has correctly noted that this characteristic of *I* also applies to *here* and *now*. It may be false that a beetle is now here at the place to which I am pointing, but it is not possible that the place is not there. What is the reason for this difference between *I*, *here*, and *now* on the one hand and *this* on the other hand?

Let us first attend to another characteristic that is brought out by Castañeda and only mentioned in passing by Pothast, namely, that the use of *I* cannot be reduced to the other demonstrative expressions.[4] The reduction of the expression *I* to *this speaker* has been attempted, but this reduction miscarries by virtue of the fact that the word *this* for its part can only be explained through a reference to the respective speaker. The reference to the respective speaker is obviously also fundamental for understanding the words *here* and *now*.

If we now want not only to register but also to understand these two characteristic features, we must go a step further in the understanding of indexical expressions and singular terms in general. The peculiarities that have been mentioned indicate that there are also specific dependencies between the different groups of indexical expressions; and I must now add that such dependencies—in part reciprocal, in part one-sided—also exist between the different overall classes of singular terms. I have extensively discussed these connections in an earlier course of lectures, and therefore I can simply present some points here as theses with the aid of examples.[5] We have already seen that the function of singular terms is to enable a speaker to specify which object among all objects he is referring to. I will now designate this function, following Strawson, as the *identification* of the object of reference.

How can spatiotemporal objects—and persons are also spatiotemporal objects—be indentified? They can never by identified in the final analysis with a proper name. It is one of the simplifications of the earlier, pre-Fregean philosophical tradition to believe that proper names are those singular terms by which we can somehow 'directly' refer to an object. For example, when I speak of Michael Theunissen, this proper name does not furnish a criterion by which to identify the person referred to. One can ask in response, "Michael Theunissen— who is that?" On the other hand, those singular terms that one calls characterizations or definite descriptions—an expression of the form "the so-and-so"—can identify an object only in a specific context, and not 'definitively.'[6] If I replied to the question of who Michael Theunissen is by saying he is the youngest professor of philosophy at this university, you could once more ask, "And who is *that?*" And in a reverse sense, if one is talking about the youngest professor, for example, it appears more informative to answer the question of who that is by saying it is Mr. Theunissen. We would advance a step further if Mr. Theunissen entered here; I could then point to him and say, "Mr. Theunissen—that is this person here." This would be an identification by means of an indexical expression. But would you thereby have a criterion by which to distinguish this person from all others? In a certain sense, yes. For one would remember the face, and human physiognomies are distinguishable to a relatively high degree. But in the case of a snail, for example, it would surely be much more difficult for us. And even people change their appearance over the years, aside from the fact that there are identical twins, and so on. Moreover, even in the case of an object that does not change its position in space (e.g., a mountain), we must account for the fact that we ourselves change our position in space but are still capable of coming to an agreement, with other partners located at different places, about the object as something identical; and this happens because we can replace the indexical expression by an expression that assigns the object a place in the spatiotemporal system. For example, Mount Everest is understood as the mountain that has such and such spatial relations to other geographical facts, or, more precisely, that is at such and such a degree of latitude and longitude. In the case of a mobile material object such as a snail, the criterion that decides if this snail here is identical with the one we saw there yesterday is whether or not we could have followed its path from one place to the other in perception. This holds true to the same extent for persons. Although normally speaking it is pragmatically simpler to recognize a person on the basis of his appearance, that is, to rely on his appearance as something constant, we still regard only spatiotemporal continuity as the ultimate criterion of whether the person here is actually identical with the person of the same countenance who we recently saw there.

If we did not know in what spatiotemporal relation our here and now stood to the objective reference points of the spatiotemporal system (e.g., Greenwich, and the birth of Christ), however, the spatiotemporal coordinates by means of which we identify objects would become meaningless for us and would lose their identifying function. Hence, although (as previously indicated) an object cannot be identified solely by means of indexical expressions, the indexical expressions still remain fundamental for all identification, particularly the expressions *here*, *now*, and *I*. The respective speaker is the ultimate reference point for himself of all spatiotemporal identification, although he could not identify anything at all by this alone, that is, without objective reference points.

The system of identification of spatiotemporal objects has now been sufficiently described to allow us to discern the basis for the two characteristic features cited above—that is, for the special position, first, of *I* and, second, of *here* and *now*. The irreducibility of *I* that was noted as the second characteristic feature follows from the fact just indicated, namely, that the respective speaker is the ultimate reference point for himself of all spatiotemporal identification. This irreducibility is only a partial and negative aspect of the fundamental fact (which follows from the train of thought just advanced) that the capacity to use the word *I* is the condition of the possibility of referring to objects. (One might object that children already refer to objects before they have the use of the word *I* at their disposal. But one must be very cautious in speaking of a reference to objects. There probably are preliminary forms that can be empirically identified; this would be a matter for genetic investigation. If one understands by reference the type of identification that I have just described, it implies the understanding of "is identical with" as well as the systematic cross-references of different classes of singular terms, which children scarcely have at their disposal prior to the capacity to say *I*. I admit, however, that I have not investigated this empirically.)

Further, we can now understand the distinctiveness of *here* and *now* in contrast to *this*, which was brought to light in discussing the first characteristic feature.[7] It is based upon the fact that we identify objects—material objects or events—*in* space and time by noting their position in the spatiotemporal system. Although spatiotemporal positions for their part are only identifiable through concrete points of reference—material objects and events—it is still the spatiotemporal positions, and not the material objects and events, that stand in a unified and continuous connection. Hence, we identify the material objects by citing their existence in space during a specific period of time, and we identify an event by noting that it happened at such and such a time in such and such a place; it is therefore always questionable whether or not such an object really existed at the identified spatiotemporal position. On the other hand, one cannot speak of the existence or nonexistence of any given identifiable spatiotemporal position once the spatiotemporal system is constituted, because existence signifies the presence of an object in space-time and is consequently not applicable to this space-time itself. We can now see that the issue here does not merely concern the special distinctiveness of the words *here* and *now*, but relates to all expressions that identify a spatial or temporal position.

For this reason it is also clear that a proper analogy does not exist between *here* and *now* on the one hand and *I* on the other hand. In the first place the distinctiveness of *I* does not extend to the other expressions by which persons are identified. And, second, when it is significantly employed, *I* in contrast to *here* and *now* stands without exception for an entity existing in space and time. Moreover, since I cannot doubt in my own case that I employ the word *I* significantly, the self-evidence from which Descartes proceeded arises—*cogito (loquor) ergo sum*—though certainly not as an immaterial, nonspatial existence.

We can now return to the starting point of our discussion and try to see how this elucidation of the use of the word *I* can contribute to resolving Henrich's second difficulty. Let us first look at how Pothast addresses this problem. Pothast did not consider the role of the word *I* in the context of the problem of identification and the referential connections between different groups of singular terms; he restricted himself to the explanation that by the word *I* someone . . . designates himself' (24). He adds the following reflection to this account: "If one translates the phrase used up to now 'by *I* someone designates himself' into the first person, it reads: 'By *I* I designate myself.' . . . This indicates that the resulting reformulation can specify what is designated by *I* only by once again employing the sign in a covert form. . . . The regress that one . . . encountered in the attempt to know oneself as oneself thus corresponds to a definitional regress in the attempt to say what the sign really means" (24ff.).

I do not find it very easy to understand his reflection, but this much appears to me clear: Pothast is mistaken if he thinks that one can translate the explanation of the meaning of the word *I* into the first person. The sentence "by *I* I designate myself" is false. It no longer expresses the meaning of the word *I*, for if this account were correct then no one else besides me could designate himself by means of this word. The word *I* would no longer be an indexical expression, but a special kind of name, a nickname, that is used for me and only by me.

The characteristic feature of an indexical expression is that its reference to an object is a function of its meaning and of the speech situation. In the case of *I* this means it is a function of the speaker and is therefore variable; it is this aspect that is lost in Pothast's so-called translation into the first person. In this connection it is also clear that the well-known fact that children understand and learn to use the word *I* relatively late is ordinarily interpreted incorrectly. From the standpoint of the traditional theory of the I, it has been assumed that this difficulty to learn the word *I* arises because the special accomplishment the child must perform is that of the so-called reflection. The difficulty that children have in understanding the use of the word *I*, however, is in reality exhibited prior to their own use of the word. The difficulty that the child has is to understand how *others* use the word. He is involved with persons a, b, c, and he is accustomed to associating a name with each person, for example, the names a, b, c. And now his difficulty consists in understanding that when a speaks about himself he says "I," and that when b speaks about himself this is again true, but when a speaks about b he says "b," and when b speaks about a he says "a." Hence, the difficulty consists in the fact that the word *I* is used by the *respective* speaker in order to speak about himself. The difficulty does not consist in the fact that a speaks about a: As long as the child generally understands subject-predicate sentences, he does not have the slightest difficulty in understanding when Mama says "Mama is coming right away." Thus, it is not the so-called reflection of the speaker that is difficult for the child to understand, but the fact that the word *I* is used by the *respective* speaker in order to speak about himself. And as soon as little Hans has understood this detachability of the word *I* from a specific speaker—that is, as soon as he has understood how others use the word—he can do so himself, speaking about himself as "I" instead of as Hans without thereby attaining a new level of understanding. Admittedly *I* is not an equivalent for the name Hans when Hans speaks about himself, just as *I* was also not an equivalent for the name A when A spoke about himself. For *I*, of course, has a different meaning from that of Hans or A (assuming that one can speak of a meaning for proper names at all). Every singular term designates the object for which it stands from a certain viewpoint (Frege said: mode of givenness), which depends upon its meaning and is different from other viewpoints from which the same object is designated by other singular terms. When the child learns the word *I*, he does not simply learn an equivalent, but a new point of view from which one can refer to an object. This also holds correspondingly for the other indexical expressions. The phrase *this girl* is an equivalent for the name Petra to just as little an extent as *I* is for Hans. "This girl is Petra" is a synthetic statement in the same sense as "I am Hans."

Pothast apparently believes that Henrich's second difficulty arises from the translation of the rule of use of the word *I* into the first person. I have not succeeded in fully understanding the intricate reflections on the pages that follow (25–32). Still, Pothast appears to believe roughly the following. (1) He takes the translation into the first person to be, not false, but unnecessary. (2) In his view this drives one to question whether one associates "the correct object with the word" (31). But (3) the answer that is given to this question in the sentence "by *I* I designate myself" remains circular, tautological (31ff.). Pothast reaches the conclusion: "The question 'Do I really have myself in the object that I call I?' cannot be regarded as meaningful as long as nothing more than tautological criteria are specified for answering it" (32). This sentence is just as ambivalent as the preceding statements. Does Pothast believe that this question is really meaningless, or is the restriction "as long as" to be understood so that it is meaningless only "as long as nothing more than tautological criteria" are provided? But nothing more than tautological criteria *can* be given for answering the *question as formulated.* And if Pothast thinks that this question or one analogous to it is not meaningless if nontautological criteria are provided, why doesn't he indicate what form this question assumes in this case? The reason for this seems to me to be that Pothast has not investigated the mode of use of *I* far enough, and in particular that he has not taken the problem of identification into account.

Hence, we get no further with Pothast. We must instead begin with the relations of identification that have emerged from our analysis. We have seen that every "ultimate" identification of something spatiotemporal has a subjective and an objective component. By the *objective component* I mean that we identify (distinguish from all others as the one referred to) an object by specifying its spatiotemporal relations to other objects; and by the *subjective component* I mean that this specification has a meaning for us only if we know in what spatiotemporal relation the reference points used in this specification stand to our own here and now. A spatial position and a point in time are not yet identified by the words *here* and *now* alone. Nevertheless, the spatio-temporal position that they designate constitutes the ultimate reference point of all spatiotemporal identification. Further, these words are used in such a way that the spatiotemporal position that they designate is indeed not identified, but is referred to as identifiable; for one knows that from another position the here is regarded as a there.

Let us take an example. Two people in the mountains have lost their way in the fog; they sit down somewhere, and one says, "It is terribly cold here." Has he specified where it is terribly cold by saying *here*? Perhaps the two have brought a radio set with them, and they report to the valley "Here, where we are, it is terribly cold." Of course, the natural response would be, "But where are you after all?" If the two now radioed back, "We are here," would they then have specified where they were? Yes, insofar as *here* is formally a possible answer to the question "where?" And, of course, no, because by *here* the position at which one speaks is not identified. It is a different matter if a search party is in the area and calls out "Where are you?" and those who are being sought reply "Here." In this case this *here* enables the position of the speaker to be identified from the perspective of the search party as a there, which stands in a certain direction and at a certain distance from the here of the search party. If the search party knows its own position relative to the village in the valley, or relative to any other objectively identified position, it can inform those who are lost where they are, that is, what their position (which they designate by *here*) is within the objective coordinate system.

A similar situation occurs in the use of the word *this*. For example, I point to a man and ask who he is. If one answers "he is this man," the man is thereby identified to just as little an extent as the place was identified by the answer "we are here." If, on the other hand, one answers "he (this man) is Mr. Theunissen," this constitutes an identification because it is implied that the name is associated with distinguishing characteristics and even criteria on whose basis the relevant person can be reidentified within the spatiotemporal system.

Now this also applies analogously for *I*. If I call someone on the telephone and he asks "who is speaking?" it is obviously absurd to answer "I," unless I assume that the other person knows my voice. I certainly refer to a single identifiable person by *I*, just as I refer to a single identifiable place by *here*; but I identify this person when I say "I" to just as little an extent as I identify this place when I say "here." The word *I* is not merely an insufficient answer to the question of who I am, it is no answer at all.

Now we can understand how Henrich's second difficulty could arise, since it resulted not only from a reliance upon the subject-object model but also from a reliance upon the ordinary use of language; it rests on the misunderstanding that because a single, identifiable person is in fact referred to by the word *I*, this person is also in some (or even in a special) way already *identified* by it. What Henrich took to be irresolvable was why a mistaken identification is not possible in referring to oneself. The solution is that in a case in which nothing is identified, there is also no possibility of a false identification. False identification is possible only in those cases in which I provide a nonempty answer to the question of who I am, and thereby identify myself. When I say "this man," for instance, I can be asked who that is, and I can then answer that "this is Theunissen, and Theunissen is the one who was born in such and such a place," and it may turn out that this is an error, that this man is not Theunissen at all. In just the same way, when I am asked who I am, I can reply that I am Ernst Tugendhat, and that I was born in such and such a place, and that my path of life in space and time, on whose basis I can be identified, is such and such; and here it also may turn out that this is an error, that I am not Ernst Tugendhat at all and that I only imagine myself to be this person.

Nonetheless, the two cases described are not entirely analogous. We have already seen that the use of *I* is closer in a certain way to that of *here* and *now* than to that of *this*. We just noted that the word *here*, when used in a specific context, can serve to identify the place of the speaker from the perspective of another speaker. There is also something analogous to this for *I*. When somebody in a group of people says something, one can ask in response "who said that?" and the relevant person can identify himself for the others by saying "I." He does not have to say "I"; he may also simply raise his arm. But when he says "I" he has thereby given a sign that can be replaced by "he" or "this (that) person" in the same way that "here" in the other example was replaced by "there." And we have seen that it is an essential part of the mode of use of *I* that someone who employs it does so under the following assumption: Someone else can respond to this expression in such a way that the same person to whom he refers as "I" is referred to by the other person as "he." Now, the word *he* is an equivalent for *this (that) person. He* and *this person* therefore have the same position relative to *I* that *there* has to *here*. Thus, in contrast to the use of *I*, in the use of *this person* (and obviously to the same extent in the use of every expression of the form "this such and such") a first level of identification can already be found. By "this such and such" I specify which such and such I am referring to among the many in my surroundings, and I do so by pointing to a specific place in my surroundings. It is certainly merely a first level of identification, since the object referred to is identified only within my immediate surroundings. The essential difference between *I* and *this person* (or in general *this such and such*) is that by *this* one refers to an object on the basis of an observation, while in contrast by *I* one does not. This does not imply, of course, that by *I* reference is made to a nonobservable, immaterial object. Rather, just as we had to conclude earlier that the entity is not identified but is referred to as identifiable, so now we must advance the following thesis: In referring to the entity by saying "I" it is certainly not observed or perceived, but it is referred to as observable or perceivable.

We have now reached a point in our exposition that leads beyond the restriction that was imposed by focusing on the Heidelberg school's account, namely, the restriction of our analysis to the isolated "I" expression and the resulting abstraction from the complementing predicate expressions. One can identify an object through perception only if one discerns the object at the same time as a bearer of specific predicates of perception. For persons this implies that they are identified only in those cases in which they can be perceived by observation as material objects with their physical properties. The knowledge of a person as a perceivable body takes place essentially from the perspective of the onlooker, the third person. Hence, I cannot ascribe predicates of perception to myself from the perspective of the "I" sayer, since from this perspective I do not identify myself, and in particular I do not identify myself through observation.

This may be misunderstood in two respects. First, it obviously does not mean that sentences such as "I have brown eyes" are not justifiable. Rather, their justification rests on the fact that I know that I am someone about whom one can say when one perceives him that "this person has brown eyes." I have previously indicated that different singular terms designate one and the same object from different perspectives, and it is now clear that these perspectives can be relevant for the knowledge of the applicability of predicates. For example, "is a professor at this university" is a predicate whose application to me cannot be established by observing me. Rather, it is established by checking a record in which my name stands; once it is established in this way, one can obviously say "this person [to whom one directly points] is a professor at the University of Hiedelberg," because one knows that this man = E.T. Thus, although one can establish the applicability of a predicate only from the perspective of a specific singular term, one can clearly replace this singular term by any other that refers to the same object. For this reason the expression *I* also obviously can be associated with every predicate that applies to me as a person, even if I cannot establish that it applies to me from the perspective of the "I" sayer.

The other misunderstanding would consist in thinking that this view implies that I myself cannot perceive my physical properties. On the contrary, I can observe myself in much the same way that another can observe me, although it is admittedly the case that I can only observe myself as an entire person on the basis of special arrangements—in the mirror or on film; otherwise, I can observe only specific parts of my body. Nonetheless, it is crucial that the presupposition for identification in every case is the same minimum that applies when another observes me: I refer to the parts of my body by pointing to them and saying "this," and the same thing holds for my mirror image. Hence, I can indeed observe myself, but the predicates that I ascribe to myself on the basis of this observation are assigned, not from the perspective of "I" saying, but from the perspective of "this" saying.

On the other hand, are there also predicates that I ascribe to myself from the perspective of "I" saying? It seems obvious to suppose that these would have to be the "ϕ" predicates. For these were defined in such a way that they designated states of which someone has an immediate knowledge if he has them; and however this immediate knowledge is understood, it is not in any event a type of knowledge that is based upon external observation. Indeed, it was by virtue of this characteristic that the "ϕ" predicates were distinguished from the other predicates that can apply to a person.

Thus, we have now come to a point at which the clarification of the use of the word *I* refers back to the clarification of the use of the "I ϕ" sentences, and this means to epistemic self-consciousness. It appears to be an essential part of the mode of use of the word *I* that the "ϕ" predicates (and only the "ϕ" predicates of the person to whom they apply) are not only in fact ascribed to oneself by "I" saying, but are ascribed from the perspective of "I" saying. This is true in the same sense that it is an essential part of the mode of use of the word *this* that the applicability of a predicate of perception "P" can only be established by means of a sentence "this P."

A specific hypothesis concerning the use of "I ϕ" sentences also directly follows from our analysis of the use of the word *I* that was just elaborated. We saw earlier, at the opening of lecture 3, that two questions had to be answered in order to elucidate these sentences: (1) What constitutes the particular mode of identification of a person by means of the word *I*? and (2) What is the knowledge of epistemic self-consciousness, that is, the knowledge that a "ϕ" predicate applies to me, based upon?

The first question has now been answered. The word *I* designates the ultimate reference point of all identification, though the person referred to by it—the speaker—is not identified; but he is referred to as identifiable from the "he" perspective.

This answer to the first question has implications for the answer to the second question. That is, if there are predicates that I ascribe to myself not only by actually saying "I" but also from the perspective of "I" saying, this means that I do not have knowledge of their application to me by identifying the entity to which I ascribe them; thus, it also follows, as we have seen, that I do not know of their application to me by perceiving or observing this entity. Hence, the immediate knowledge of epistemic self-consciousness not only does not rest upon external observation but also does not rest upon any observation at all. For if the "I ϕ" sentences rested upon an inner observation, one would either have to assume that they were based on an identification of items in the so-called inner sphere by means of *this*, or one would have to construe the reference by means of *I* as analogous to the one by means of *this*. The second possibility is excluded on the basis of the analyses that we just elaborated. The first possibility is similarly excluded, because I am the entity to which the predicate is applied in an "I ϕ" sentence, and not something in me. Thus, at least we already have a negative result with regard to the immediate knowledge of epistemic self-consciousness: It cannot rest upon inner perception, and even the concept of inner perception appears nonsensical.

Our analysis of the use of *I* also has another consequence for a proper understanding of the "I ϕ" sentences. We have seen that the explanation and hence the meaning of the word *I* implies that someone who says "I" knows that the same thing to which he refers as "I" can be referred to by another person as "he" or "this person." In order to avoid a misunderstanding, I should add that this does not exclude a Robinsonade situation as a limiting case. For example, if someone survives after a nuclear war as the only speaker, he obviously can say "I" in its aftermath. When the intersubjective aspect in understanding the word *I* is stressed, it must be noted that this involves a possible intersubjectivity and not an actual one. But this possibility of intersubjectivity is itself necessary, because it follows from the meaning of the word *I*. It is necessary that someone to whom I refer as "I" *can* be referred to by others as "he"—and hence also by name.

Now this has consequences for the "I ϕ" sentences. For if a predicate applies to an entity, it applies to it irrespective of which singular term designates it. This is the so-called Leibnizian law, which is grounded in the meaning of the equal sign: If a = b, then every predicate that applies to a also applies to b. For the "I ϕ" sentences this yields the following result:

The sentence "I ϕ," if uttered by me, is true if and only if the sentence "he ϕ" is true if uttered by someone else who by *he* refers to me.

In reality the connection is even closer than the one that is formulated here as a consequence of the Leibnizian law. For when two corresponding demonstrative expressions such as *here* and *there* or *I* and *he* refer to the same object, they stand in a closer connection than any arbitrary pair of singular terms that refer to one and the same object. In the case of an arbitrary pair of singular terms it is an empirical question as to whether a = b; hence, while it may indeed be correct to say of a predicate that if it applies to a then it also applies to b, someone can believe that it applies to a and at the same time deny that it applies to b if he does not know that a = b. Thus, two different states of affairs are involved in this instance. In the case of indexical expressions, of course, someone also can refer, for example, to a different person by *he*; but *if*, as stipulated in the principle just formulated, he refers to me, then it is necessarily the case that the person to whom he refers by *he* is the same as the one to whom I refer by *I*. Consequently the following stricter principle is valid:

It is necessary that the sentence "I ϕ," if uttered by me, is true if and only if the sentence "he ϕ" is true if uttered by someone else who by *he* refers to me.

For this reason we must also conclude in this case that one and the same state of affairs is involved, which I express by "I ϕ" and he expresses by "he ϕ." For example, if I say "I have a toothache," someone can repeat this statement by saying "He has a toothache." He thereby asserts the same thing that I do, if by *he* he is referring to me. Or he can, for instance, say to me, "You are lying, you don't have a toothache," and in this case we would say that he contradicts me; but this presupposes he is referring to the same state of affairs that I am, that he denies precisely what I have asserted.

Since the one sentence is true necessarily if and only if the other is true, I will refer here to the principle of (necessary) *veridical symmetry*. Now although both speakers refer to the same state of affairs, only the one who ascribes this sort of a predicate to himself has an immediate knowledge of it; from the "he" perspective this same state of affairs is ascertained through the observation of the other person—with reference in part to his behavior, and in part to his statements. Hence, an *epistemic asymmetry* exists. The "ϕ" states are known in a different way by those who have them—and this difference is obviously based on the nature of the states themselves, and not on contingent factors.

This fact that on the one hand veridical symmetry exists between "I ϕ" and "he ϕ," and on the other hand there is epistemic asymmetry, must appear puzzling; for in general a close connection exists among (1) the meaning of a predicate, (2) the truth conditions of the corresponding sentence, and (3) the way that we ascertain that the sentence is true. For example, we explain the meaning of the predicate "red" to someone by presenting different objects to him that are and are not red; we show him under what conditions a sentence "X is red" is true, or how one ascertains whether such a sentence is true. Since in the case of the "ϕ" predicates their applicability is ascertained in two fundamentally different ways, one might think that they must have a different meaning depending upon whether they occur in "I" sentences or in "he" sentences. Nevertheless, the possibility that they have a different meaning is excluded in light of the veridical symmetry of these sentences. Hence, the following line of thought seems to be suggested. As indicated above, in the use of the word *I* it is already implied that the same person to whom I refer with this word can be designated by others as "he," and in the reverse sense "he" refers back to "I"; therefore, it would have to be the case to the same extent that the use of a "ϕ" predicate from the "I" perspective is implied in the use of the predicate from the "he" perspective and vice versa. Thus, the unitary meaning of the "ϕ" predicate would be preserved. In this case, however, the elucidation of the "ϕ" sentences in the first person can only take place in conjunction with the elucidation of their use in the third person. The first philosopher who advanced this conception was Wittgenstein.[8]

Lecture 5

Wittgenstein, I:
The Impossibility of a
Private Language

After his renewal of philosophical work in 1929, Wittgenstein was concerned with the problem of the "ϕ" states. At that time he first had advanced a solipsistic position, as he also had done earlier in the *Tractatus*. I will not go into these phases preliminary to his later position, and for such background I refer you to P. Hacker, *Insight and Illusion*, chapters 4 and 7. The breakthrough to the later position took place in the *Blue Book*, which was composed in the years 1933–1934. The final position was attained in the "Notes for Lectures" (NL), which was first published in 1968 and written in the years 1934–1936; in the *Philosophical Investigations* (PI) it is further developed, above all in sections 243–315, which are devoted to the refutation of a so-called private language.

In NL there are also German notes, which are scattered throughout the English text; they are notes that Wittgenstein had written down for himself and not for his audience. One of these German notes could be used almost as a motto for this and the next lecture: "The atmosphere surrounding this problem is terrible. Dense mists of language are situated around the crucial point. It is almost impossible to get through to it" (306). But Wittgenstein also thinks: "We want to *understand* something that is already in plain view" (PI 89). "The aspects of things that are most important for us are hidden because of their simplicity and familiarity" (PI 129). Thus, Wittgenstein proceeds from the conviction that what we inquire about in philosophy is really quite simple, but that we are not capable of seeing it because our mode of sight is bewitched by misleading linguistic analogies and metaphors. "Philosophy is a battle against the bewitchment of our intelligence by means of language" (PI 109). In this context one can understand the note in NL that it is almost impossible to press through the fog of language to the crucial point. He experiences the atmosphere that surrounds the problem as terrible, and he did not attempt to spare others the path that he traversed in order to present them with results. He wanted rather to indicate the path only as a path, so that his reader himself would have to work his way through the fog; thus, anyone who attempts to understand Wittgenstein and to press forward with him toward clarity must also experience the atmosphere as terrible. You should therefore not expect any results from me either. What one can do in such a lecture is always only to open up the path a bit wider, and at least to bring the problems into view. I will get bogged down, and it is up to you to try to advance further.

What is the problem that Wittgenstein is talking about here? In PI (309) he asks, "What is your aim in philosophy?" And he answers, "To show the fly the way out of the fly bottle." It has only become clear since the publication of NL how this oft-quoted sentence is to be understood.[1] For there we read—again in a German note—"The solipsist flutters and flutters in the fly glass, strikes against the walls, flutters further. How can he be brought to rest?" (300). Hence, the problem is the overcoming of solipsism. Of course, this can be understood genetically, since Wittgenstein himself had earlier advanced a solipsistic position, but one must also understand it systematically. At another point in NL he says, "But here solipsism teaches us a lesson. It is that thought which is *on the way* to destroying this error" (297). What error?

The error involves a conception of the "I ϕ" and "he ϕ" sentences that Wittgenstein refers to in the *Blue Book* as the conception of the common-sense philosopher (48).[2] He emphasizes at the same time, however, that this common-sense philosopher is not the man of common sense. He also calls this conception realism. It can be characterized roughly in the following way: Each person knows only his own inner states (designated by the "ϕ" predicates) on the basis of inner perception. If this is the case, how can I believe that other people also have such states? Indeed, it is clear that I cannot externally observe these states in others. But I can have access to them on the realist view by means of an inference from analogy. Since I observe that certain inner states of mine, such as feelings of pain, are regularly accompanied by a specific type of bodily behavior, I conclude *per analogiam* that when others exhibit a similar behavior they have states of the same type that I perceive in myself in connection with this behavior.

There are familiar skeptical objections to this view, which Wittgenstein also underscores in the *Blue Book*. How do I know when the other perceives objects that I perceive as red that he has the same sensation of color that I have? But once one begins to doubt here, where does one stop? Do I actually know that the other has an inner state at all, or do I merely believe it? And if I merely believe it, then don't I have to leave open the possibility that I am the only one who has inner states? In the *Blue Book* Wittgenstein argues still more strongly in the following way: If one cannot know something in principle, then it also does not make any sense to claim that one merely believes it, since to believe something means to think that something is the case without yet having sufficient justification; but what can it mean to believe something if even a mere partial confirmation is in no way attainable (54)? At another point he takes note of the fact that one cannot even legitimately speak here of a hypothesis that other people have inner states, since absolutely no experience is conceivable that might support or weaken the hypothesis.

The upshot of these skeptical objections is solipsism, according to which only I have inner states. What is characteristic of this position is that it surrenders one side of the realistic conception—that one can also know the inner states of others by means of an inference from analogy—but it adheres to the point of departure of the realistic conception, namely, that one knows one's own inner states through inner perception. Hence, when Wittgenstein states that solipsism is "on the way" toward destroying the error that lies at the basis of the realistic conception, he means only that solipsism represents the true theoretical outcome of the realistic conception. Solipsism is only a more consistent variant of realism: Insofar as solipsism merely denies what realism asserts, the former takes its stand on the same basis as the latter. The common-sense conception still grants the use of third-person "ϕ" sentences; indeed, it seeks to concede the veridical symmetry of the first- and third- person "ϕ" sentences that is characteristic of our actual use of "ϕ" predicates, but its theoretical approach does not really allow for it. The theoretical approach is from the outset a latently skeptical one, and in pursuing this latent skepticism to its conclusion solipsism leads to the point at which the implicit conflict between the common-sense conception and language becomes quite evident. At this point it becomes clear that a solution is possible only if the presuppositions that were unexamined by realism and taken over by solipsism are called into question.

Nevertheless, classical solipsism is still not the final step in the inner dissolution of realism, since it continues to retain the "I" talk. According to Wittgenstein, there is an inconsistency in this. What is designated by *I* has "neighbors" (compare NL 283), since this is implied by the rule of use of the word *I*; it is one of many who can be designated by *he*, and who respectively can say "I" to themselves. For this reason Wittgenstein himself abandoned the "I" talk in his solipsistic phase.[3]

Thus, if the goal for Wittgenstein is to get out of the fly bottle of the solipsist, this does not mean to escape from what is designated by *I*; rather, it means coming out *to* what can be designated by *I* if what can be designated by *I* can only be a being whom others, who designate themselves by *I*, can designate by *he*. In NL Wittgenstein observes, again in a German note, "I am trying to bring the whole problem down to our not understanding the function of the word *I*" (307). The problem Wittgenstein is addressing here is admittedly the special issue of solipsism. I do not want to go into this.[4] In PI there is little discussion of the use of the word *I*, because the aim there is only to critically analyze the fundamental presupposition that is common to solipsism and realism. This involves the assumption that the "ϕ" states are inner events that are given in an inner perception. Against this view Wittgenstein wants to demonstrate that the "ϕ" predicates have a meaning that from the very beginning is a unitary one based on the "I" and the "he" perspective. Thus, on the one hand his project is a destructive one — that is, as a critique of the aforementioned presupposition. On the other hand, it is constructive, since its purpose is to lead to a new understanding of the "ϕ" sentences.

In the present lecture I will consider only the destructive part. It consists in the critique of the conception of a private language. To begin with we have to ask first, what does Wittgenstein mean by a private language, and, second, to what extent can one say that the essential presupposition of realism and solipsism rests on the assumption of a private language?

Wittgenstein indicates in PI (243) how he wants his talk of a private language to be understood. By a "private language" he does not mean a state of affairs in which someone speaks to himself, and it is also not to be understood as an entire language that is spoken only by one man. "We could even imagine human beings who spoke only in monologue." This is not a private language in Wittgenstein's sense, assuming that one could translate the language of such a man "into that of our own." Furthermore, this would still not qualify as a private language if someone in this language would "write down or give vocal expression to his inner experiences—his feelings, moods, and the rest—for his private use." For one can also do this "in our ordinary language." On the other hand, in the language that Wittgenstein calls a private language, "the words . . . are to refer to what can only be known to the person speaking. . . . So another person cannot understand this language." The emphasis here lies on the words *cannot*. The distinguishing feature of a private language is not that it is in fact used only by a single individual, and also not that the words of this language refer to the experiences of the individual; rather, a private language in the relevant sense is involved only if someone else *cannot* understand these words, or, more precisely, if the words of this language refer to something "of which only the speaker can know."

One can now easily see how the common presupposition of realism and solipsism is connected to the conception of a private language that is understood in this way. For insofar as both of these theories address the question of what a language would have to be like to correspond to their conceptions, it is clear that at least the "ϕ" predicates, if not all the expressions of this language, would have a meaning for each individual that would be accessible only to him.

Now the fact that Wittgenstein immediately conceives of the theory he is criticizing as a theory about a corresponding language might be considered a problem. The traditional theories did not understand themselves in this way, and one might raise the following objection to Wittgenstein: "Perhaps a *private language* is not conceivable, but the real privacy of the 'ϕ' states is that they are not accessible through words at all." Wittgenstein examines such an objection at the beginning of NL. He first formulates the objection in German: "Some things can be said about the particular experience and besides this there seems to be something, the most essential part of it, that cannot be described" (275). After an initial critical account, which is still formulated in German, he writes in English: "It is as though, although you can't tell me exactly what happens inside you, you can nevertheless tell me something general about it. By saying e.g. that you are having an impression which can't be described. As it were: There is something further about it, only you *can't say* it; you can only make the general statement. It is this idea which plays hell with us" (276).

Wittgenstein is not very explicit here, and one might reply to him in this way: "Yes, this is just the way it is. We have states that we can generally characterize as sensations, but we cannot describe them; that is, we have no linguistic expressions for them." As an example, think perhaps of a situation in which one has a headache; one does not simply have pains in one's head, but one has a fully distinct sensation. Thus, at this point we may say something like this: I have a fully distinct sensation of pain here in my head, which I nonetheless cannot describe. Or, for example, think of the sensations of taste or smell. Here we are inclined to say that when I taste a pear or try a specific wine, I have a distinct, but indescribable sensation of taste.

Wittgenstein would answer more or less in the following way: "Do you really think that this indescribable sensation is fully distinct? If it is, this obviously means you can distinguish it from other comparable sensations, that you can identify it as qualitatively the same and recognize it again; for example, you can identify and recognize this fully distinctive taste of wine in contrast to that other one. But if this is the case, surely you can give a name to the respective sensation; indeed, you will only have a consciousness that it is a distinct, identifiable sensation if you give it a name. It is not necessary here for the purpose of naming to employ a specific name or a definite predicate; it suffices if you simply say 'this is now once again the same headache that I had the day before yesterday, and not the one that I had yesterday.' Once one is this far along it is quite natural, though not essential, to distinguish the headache from the day before yesterday as type A, for example, in contrast to yesterday's headache, type B. If, on the other hand," so Wittgenstein might continue, "you mean by the indescribability of the sensation that it is not at all distinct or distinguishable from others, then you have described it linguistically in a fully adequate way by saying that it is indescribable and indistinct; and there is once again nothing here that escapes the grasp of language."

Wittgenstein frequently has his interlocutor—the voice within himself that he wants to silence, so to speak—reply by advancing the following kind of objection: But precisely what is essential, precisely what is living, escapes the grasp of language. To which Wittgenstein again answers, What essential thing? What do you mean by this if you want to designate it neither as a distinct sensation nor as an indistinct sensation? "So in the end when one is doing philosophy one gets to the point where one would like just to emit an inarticulate sound" (PI 261), and Wittgenstein adds, "But such a sound is an expression only as it occurs in a particular language-game, which should now be described."

One might want to reproach him for committing a *petitio principii* when he interprets the allusion to the inexpressible merely as something that is again linguistic. But let's reflect: If we talk about the inexpressible, we are still talking, and for this reason we must ask ourselves, for example, how we use this linguistic expression *the inexpressible* if we want to become clear about what is meant by it. You might answer, But what would happen if we did not talk about the inexpressible, but simply experienced it? The difficulty is that precisely when we raise such questions we obviously cannot help raising them linguistically. If we philosophize about the experience of the inexpressible, we are already involved in language, and otherwise we must remain silent. Wittgenstein appears to want to say: Someone who wants to be silent should be silent, but in this case he should also really remain silent; one cannot on the one hand enter into the discussion, and on the other hand resist the fact that one is taken seriously as a speaker. "Isn't what you reproach me of as though you said: 'in your language you're only *speaking*!' " (NL 297).

Hence, Wittgenstein appears to be justified in interpreting the epistemological problem of whether only I can have knowledge of my "ϕ" states as a semantic problem. From this perspective, the problem assumes the form of the question of whether a private language is possible, or whether it is characteristic of all speech that it *can* also be understood by others.

One can divide Wittgenstein's procedure into two steps. In the first step he proceeds from the question of how sensations are referred to in our actual language. He demonstrates that this does not happen in the way that would correspond to the thesis of a private language. This is certainly not surprising, since our actual language as it stands is an intersubjective one, which we have also learned intersubjectively. Wittgenstein's opponent can accept this and still advance the view that the "ϕ" predicates have a double semantic function: On the one hand they have an intersubjective meaning, but on the other hand they also have a private meaning for each person. For this reason Wittgenstein must show in a second, crucial step that such a private component of meaning simply cannot exist; and he does this by demonstrating that a private language contradicts general principles for the meaningful use of linguistic expressions.

How do the words of our actual language refer to "ϕ" states? After he has clarified what he means by the concept of a private language (PI 243), Wittgenstein begins with this question in the following paragraph (244): "How do words *refer* to sensations? There doesn't seem to be any problem here; don't we talk about sensations every day, and give them names? But how is the connection between the name and the thing named set up?" (Now take note of the following step.) "This question is the same as: how does a human being learn the meaning of the names of sensations?—of the word 'pain', for example." (Thus, the question "How does a name refer to the thing it names?" has the following meaning in our ordinary language: How can we explain the use of the expression to someone, or, seen from the other side, how can he learn to use it? And this is now applied by Wittgenstein to sensations.) "Here is one possibility: words are connected with the primitive, the natural expressions of the sensation and used in their place. A child has hurt himself and he cries; and then adults talk to him and teach him exclamations and, later, sentences. They teach the child new pain-behavior." Wittgenstein designates crying as a "natural expression of the sensation." 'Exclamations,' on the other hand—like "ouch"—are already conventional linguistic expressions of pain; they are not natural, because they vary from language to language. And by *sentences* what is meant, of course, are the "ϕ" sentences like "I am in pain." They are closely assimilated to exclamations by Wittgenstein. " 'So you are saying that the word "pain" really means crying?'—On the contrary: the verbal expression of pain replaces crying and does not describe it."

This paragraph already contains the elements of Wittgenstein's own positive conception of the "ϕ" sentences, and it may be useful here to take account of it in the form of theses. If intersubjective understanding is to be possible with regard to states of consciousness, then they must be able to manifest themselves in behavior. Hence, there must be a connection between an observable, external form of behavior and the state of consciousness. This much has also been assumed by the theory of analogy, but what is now crucial is the side from which the reference of the word is apprehended. The analogy theory found it necessary to assign the name to the sensation from within, so to speak; and this implied that the relationship between the expression of the sensation and the sensation was a merely contingent and inductive one, with all the disastrous consequences that followed for the "ϕ" sentences in the third person. If by contrast the assignment of the sensation's name takes place so to speak from the outside—and it does in fact take place just in this way in learning our ordinary language—then an essential connection emerges between the expression of the sensation and the sensation. For the word that we learn is indeed a sensation word; that is, it stands for the sensation and not for the behavior. On the other hand, we only learn the use (i.e., the meaning) of the sensation word in connection with the behavior. Consequently, a connection that is grounded in the meaning of the word, that is, one that is analytic or essential, necessarily exists between the sensation and the corresponding behavior, that is, the natural or conventional 'expression of the sensation' (and the sensation always functions here only as an example for any "ϕ" state). According to Wittgenstein, the occurrence of the expression of the sensation is a so-called criterion from the perspective of the third person, that is, an analytic indication of the existence of the sensation; of course, an indication does not mean a guarantee. On the other hand, the "I ϕ" sentence is not based upon an observation, but takes the place of a natural expression of the "ϕ" state, as Wittgenstein says in the paragraph just cited; thus, the expression of the sentence in the first person is itself to be regarded as an expression of the state. In the next lecture we will have to investigate how all this is to be understood more precisely.

In paragraph 244 Wittgenstein does not yet employ his concept of the criterion, and he does not speak of an essential connection. As long as he only says generally that the sensation words of ordinary language are learned in connection with the expressions of sensations, the common-sense philosopher can still agree with him. In NL Wittgenstein indicates how this philosopher would react to the reference to the intersubjective use of sensation words. He has his opponent say, " 'Toothache' is a word which I use in a game which I play with other people, but it has a private meaning to me" (289). Thus, the common-sense philosopher now travels on a double track: On the one hand the sensation words have an intersubjective meaning, but on the other hand they have a private one. The latter is something inexpressible, and one cannot know (a) whether others have it at all, or (b) whether they have it in a way similar to or different from one's own.

Let's examine this position in light of a slightly different example. In the central part of PI the primary example that guides Wittgenstein's analysis is that of "pain." Aside from this, color sensations are also taken into consideration, beginning with paragraph 272; and in NL this example receives extensive attention alongside the example of the toothache. Of course, here one must make a distinction between, for example, *red* and *seeing red*. Only "seeing red" is analogous to "having pain," a "ϕ" predicate. One can say "I see red," but not "I red," unless one means that one is red in color; in this case "red" is obviously not a "ϕ" predicate. For this reason the treatment in NL, in contrast to that in PI, adheres to the expression *seeing red*. The term *seeing red* is indeed ambiguous. One can understand seeing here in the sense of perception, but one can also understand it in the sense of representation, so that the merely imaginative representation of a red patch can also be designated as seeing red; and the use of the term *seeing red* in NL must be understood in this way. Such an inner seeing of something red, which is not given in the form of perception, poses additional problems in its relation to the perception of something red, and Wittgenstein tackles these in NL and at later points in PI. An attempt to examine these difficulties now would make matters too complicated. I will address this problem only in the simplified form in which it appears in our section in PI, where the issue simply involves the words *red, green*, and so on. The common-sense philosophy speaks here of red sensation and in general of color sensation; these sensations are grasped in a way similar to the pain sensations as something inwardly perceivable, although such a conception is not necessary for the traditional position. It is also characteristic of the traditional position here to insist that, just as in the case of the other "ϕ" predicates, what each person means by the words *red, green*, and so on can be known only by him. A different perspective immediately emerges if one attends to how one actually learns and uses such words.

In NL Wittgenstein first allows the advocate of the traditional position to present his view: "Our teaching connects the word 'red' (or is meant to connect it) with a particular impression of his (a private impression, an impression in him). He then communicates this impression—indirectly of course—through the medium of speech" (279). But how do we in fact teach the word *red*? We do so by demonstrating how it is applied to objects. "We grasp the criterion for this in the fact that he refers to the same things as 'red' that we do, that in general he gives the colors of the objects the same names that we do." In the cases that involve the application of predicates to material objects, behavior is no longer the criterion; rather, it is how the objects are classified.

The opponent also can concede here that we have to explain the intersubjective meaning of color words in this way, but he will again insist that in this case these words have a double meaning: "What am I to say about the word 'red'?—that it means something 'confronting us all' and that everyone should really have another word, besides this one, to mean his *own* sensation of red? Or is it like this: the word 'red' means something known to everyone; and in addition, for each person, it means something known only to him?" (PI 273). "The assumption would thus be possible—though unverifiable—that one section of mankind had one sensation of red and another section another" (272).

This conception of color words, just as the earlier one of sensation words, may perhaps appear to us as very attractive. Could it be correct? But if, in accordance with the very sense of the question, nothing can be adduced that could decide for or against it, then isn't it really a meaningless question?

Thus the conception that the sensation words have an additional private meaning appears empty in the context of our ordinary language. The question of whether two "ϕ" predicates have the same meaning would always be decided on the basis of their use in the common language; and one would now merely add this: In the case of every meaning that is determined through the criteria of use, I nevertheless also still refer to something inexpressible, and I do not know whether this applies similarly for others.

But couldn't the idea of a private language have a sense that is independent of ordinary language? And isn't there actually also a meaningful use of sensation words, which someone can constitute for himself but cannot communicate to others? For instance, wouldn't the previously mentioned example of headache A, which is distinguished from headache B, fall under this type? Aren't there sensations that we can distinguish from others and recognize as distinct, without being able to specify external criteria for them? It is such questions that make it necessary for Wittgenstein, in a second step, to contest even the possibility of a private language. This argument takes place in PI (256–270). A first version can also already be found *in nuce* in NL (290ff.).

If one wants clearly to envision the possibility of a pure private language, it is useful to abstract completely from the realm of behavior. For this reason Wittgenstein begins in paragraph 256 in this way: "But suppose I didn't have any natural expression for the sensation, but only had the sensation?" In paragraph 257 he has the representative of the private language theory say first, "What would it be like if human beings showed no outward signs of pain (did not groan, grimace, etc.)? Then it would be impossible to teach a child the use of the word 'tooth-ache'." The opponent here concedes that in this case there is indeed no intersubjective learning of sensation words. In order to enable him to see what is actually at stake, Wittgenstein makes the following proposal: "Well, let's assume the child is a genius and itself invents a name for the sensation!" Wittgenstein thereby wants to say that the real problem is not that of learning the word but that of learning the word's use. But it still appears as if the difficulty would only be that one could not make oneself understood intersubjectively. Wittgenstein has his interlocutor reply: "But then, of course, he couldn't make himself understood when he used the word." Now the dialogue has advanced to the point at which Wittgenstein can raise the problem to the crucial level: "So he understands the name without being able to explain its meaning to anyone?" In posing this question Wittgenstein anticipates his thesis: It is not only that one cannot explain the meaning to someone else in such a case, but also that one cannot understand the name oneself.

Why not? At first we receive the following answer: "When one says 'He gave a name to his sensation' one forgets that a great deal of stage-setting in the language is presupposed if the mere act of naming is to make sense. And when we speak of someone's having given a name to pain, what is presupposed is the existence of the grammar of the word 'pain': it shows the post where the new word is stationed."

By itself alone, of course, this first answer is still not an argument against a private meaning. Even if Wittgenstein turns out to be right that for the use of such a name "a great deal of stage-setting in the language must be presupposed," he still has not demonstrated that this cannot also take place within a private language.

Only the following paragraph 258 offers the crucial argument. It is the decisive one for the entire series. Wittgenstein begins in this way: "Let us imagine the following case. I want to keep a diary about the recurrence of a certain sensation. To this end I associate it with the sign 'S' and write this sign in a calendar for every day on which I have the sensation." This corresponds roughly to my headache example. Indeed, one can imagine that I write down my two types of headache, A and B, in this way in a calendar. Note also that the way Wittgenstein conceives the problem here not only places a radical theory of private language into question but also challenges a conception that concedes that a "great deal of stage-setting in the language must be presupposed" for the giving of names and that the intersubjective language serves this purpose, but which still claims that within the framework of this language private differentiations of sensations can be made. The question now is this: Is there any possibility that such private-linguistic naming can give a meaning to the sign? If not, then the possibility of a private language is refuted. To give a meaning to a sign means—if one understands this word in a broad sense—*to define* the sign. Thus, the question amounts to the following: Can one define the names of a private language? If not, then they simply do not exist.

Wittgenstein's first step is thus: "I will remark first of all that a definition of the sign cannot be formulated." I do not believe that Wittgenstein means here that a definition cannot be formulated publicly, since in this case we would no longer have a private language. Rather, what he must mean is that a verbal definition, that is, a definition of the sign by means of other words, is excluded, and it is excluded because an elementary predicate is involved. There can be no disagreement between Wittgenstein and his opponent on this point. One ordinarily distinguishes verbal definitions and ostensive, demonstrative definitions. Hence, if no verbal definition of the sign "S" is possible, then an ostensive definition in particular appears to be at issue. And for this reason Wittgenstein has his opponent say in the next sentence: "But still I can give myself a kind of ostensive definition!"

Wittgenstein subjected the conception of ostensive definition to a critique near the beginning of PI (27–35), and A. Kenny maintains in his interpretation of the private language argument that with this critique Wittgenstein already divested the theory of private language of its foundation.[5] We will see that this is fundamentally correct, but we must be very cautious here. For in the first place this critique—and this holds especially for the parallel section at the beginning of the *Blue Book*—can be easily misunderstood. "The ostensive definition explains the use—the meaning—of the word, when the overall role of the word in language is clear. Thus, if I know that someone means to explain a color-word to me, the ostensive definition 'That is called Sepia' will help me to understand the word" (30). Wittgenstein here appears to want to say: If I do not already know that a color-word is meant by the word *sepia*, then I cannot know that someone who points to something and says "This is called sepia" does not mean some other aspect of the object, such as its shape. The assumption that this may be what Wittgenstein means in paragraph 258 is apparently also well supported when viewed in connection with the claim of paragraph 257 that in order to understand an act of naming "a great deal of stage-setting . . . must be presupposed." But in the first place the following objection has correctly been raised against this argument: One becomes aware of whether *sepia* refers to the aspect of color by noticing as more objects are shown that they all have this same color but vary in their other aspects.[6] Hence, one does not have to be told that a color word is involved. If, therefore, this were the purport of Wittgenstein's critique of ostensive definition, it would be completely implausible. But it becomes quite clear from the rest of the text of paragraph 258 that Wittgenstein by no means bases his argument here on a general rejection of ostensive definition. For Wittgenstein replies to the claim of his opponent that he can establish the meaning of the sign "S" through an ostensive definition by saying, "How? Can I point to the sensation? Not in the ordinary sense." This answer presupposes that an ostensive definition is possible in those cases in which we can point to something in the ordinary sense.

If we can point to something in the ordinary sense, we can designate it as "this." Thus, it seems that in this way we can define words such as *red* and *beetle*, that is, by saying "this is red" or "this is a beetle." Here something is identified by *this*, and it is then characterized or classified by the predicate that follows; and by repeating this many times with a predicate, one comes to recognize how objects are classified or characterized by means of this predicate, and thus one understands the meaning of the predicate. On the other hand, we already have seen that in the case of the use of first-person "ϕ" predicates there is no corresponding use of the word *this*, and that here nothing can be identified at all. When I use my headache predicates A and B and say "this is A" or "this is B," *this* does not identify something that one could then ascertain by observation is either A or B, and that could also have not been either A or B; rather, *this* refers directly to the state of being A or being B, and not to *something, which is* A or B.

Thus, Wittgenstein is entirely correct that an ostensive definition "in the ordinary sense" cannot be involved. His opponent also accepts this, and now explains his conception in this way: "But I speak, or write the sign down, and at the same time I concentrate my attention on the sensation—and so, as it were, point to it inwardly." Wittgenstein answers, "But what is this ceremony for?—for that is all it seems to be!" If, as his interlocutor now explains, only the concentration of attention is expressed in the talk of pointing (with or without *this*), then it is in fact an empty ceremony, for the pointing (with or without *this*) has no semantic function in this case.

Wittgenstein continues: "A definition surely serves to establish the meaning of a sign." For clarification one can also take into account two parallel sections from NL: "In our private language game we had, it seemed, given a name to an impression—in order, of course, to use the name for this impression in the future. The definition, that is, should have determined on future occasions for what impression to use the name, and for which not to use it" (291). "In the use of the word 'meaning' it is essential that the same meaning is kept throughout a game" (289). It is admittedly still not clear why, if something cannot be pointed to in the genuine sense—that is, identified— the word cannot have this function of being adhered to in the same meaning. But Wittgenstein points out that it is not clear how the word is to acquire this function by means of a process in which one concentrates on, or becomes absorbed in, what is present. "But what is it like to give a sensation a name? Say it is pronouncing the name while one has the sensation and possibly concentrating on the sensation—but what of it? Does this name thereby get magic powers?" (NL 290).

In PI (258) the representative of the theory of private language answers in the following way: "By the concentration of my attention . . . I impress on myself the connection between the sign and the sensation." To which Wittgenstein replies, "But 'I impress it on myself' can only mean: this process brings it about that I remember the connection *right* in the future. But in the present case I have no criterion of correctness. One would like to say: whatever is going to seem right to me is right. And that only means that here we can't talk about 'right'."

We have arrived at the end of paragraph 258, and the correct understanding of the last quote is, of course, crucial for understanding the thrust of Wittgenstein's argument against the private language theory. In contrast to earlier interpretations, the understanding of this passage has been advanced substantially by Kenny;[7] for he has established that the thesis here is not that we cannot check the correctness (truth) of statements of recollection, but that we cannot check the correctness of the *association of sign and meaning*, which is alleged to rest upon recollection.

Is the private language theory cogently refuted in this way? Certainly only if it is the case that without the possibility of checking there can be no meaning, that is, no meaningful use of a sign. How does the justification of the use of a sign in our language take place? In other words, what does Wittgenstein have in mind in a positive sense? Only if we clarify this will we be able to understand what is actually missing on his account from the private use of a sign. We heard, "But in the present case I have no criterion of correctness." But what does Wittgenstein mean here by a criterion of correctness?

As Kenny presents the case, it would appear as if everything would be in order if we had a perceptible sample instead of a mere memory sample of the sensation. If the difficulty consists only in the fact that in the case of recollection I can no longer check whether the memory sample is still the correct one,[8] then the difficulty would be eliminated in those cases in which one could have a perceptible sample; thus, for example, it would be eliminated for color words. For in order to check the correctness of our use of a word like *red*, we can refer here in a given case to a real color sample—perhaps in a color catalogue—which one can compare directly with the given red; one can perceive both of them at the same time.

But the fact that in the parallel section in NL (291) Wittgenstein uses precisely the word *red* as an example without discussing the issue of memory already speaks against this interpretation. And this interpretation is directly refuted by the fact that at an earlier point in PI Wittgenstein equates the recourse to a perceptible sample in a real table in principle with the recourse to a memory sample. "This table might be said to take over here the role of memory and association in other cases" (53). "But what if no such sample is part of the language, and we *bear in mind* the color (for instance) that a word stands for?" (56). In assessing this case Wittgenstein points to the difficulty we are familiar with from paragraph 258: "But what do we regard as the criterion for remembering it right?" But now he turns the tables. He goes on: "When we work with a sample instead of our memory there are circumstances in which we say that the sample has changed color and we judge this by memory. But can we not sometimes speak of a darkening (for example) of our memory-image? Aren't we as much at the mercy of memory as of a sample?" This last question, of course, implies its reversal: Aren't we as much at the mercy of a sample as of the memory?

In what, however, does the criterion of correctness consist if not in any kind of sample? To this Wittgenstein answers: in the application (146). And *application* here does not mean application to a recurring sensation content, but application to objects. The criterion of correctness in the use, for example, of the predicate *red* is that we can distinguish objects that are red from objects that are not red. A sample can sometimes be useful to us for this (53). But—and this is a decisive link in the argument—there is no sample that already contains in and for itself definite instructions for how it is to be used; it can always be applied in one way or another (73, 85ff., 139ff.). The criterion for someone's correct understanding of the color words is that when he is to sort out a bunch of flowers according to colors, for example, he roughly knows how to separate the red flowers from the blue ones, and whether he uses a color catalogue or a memory sample is irrelevant (cf. 53). The crucial point is that in the case of a classification expression—and the names of sensations and, of course, also all "ϕ" predicates are classification expressions—we can apply the word *correct* only to its use in the classification of objects. Thus, when Wittgenstein says in paragraph 258 that if the use of the name is founded upon a remembered sensation we would have no criterion of correctness, he does not mean that we would have such a criterion if the use were founded upon a perceived sensation, but rather that the criterion is the correct use in classification.

We can also now understand in what sense one can nonetheless speak of "correctness" to a *certain* extent in the case of a perceptible sample. A real color sample is, of course, an object that has such and such a color. We can point to this object—not to the sensation content perceived in it—and say "this is sepia." We thereby display in a paradigmatic case the function of classification—or discrimination— which the predicate *sepia* is to have. We can say, "If you use it the way it was used in this case, then you will use it correctly"; and now the other person must first demonstrate in its use whether he has understood *which* way had been meant.

Only now is it possible to understand what Wittgenstein is actually criticizing in ostensive definition at the beginning of PI. Wittgenstein there invokes an extremely narrow concept of ostensive definition, according to which the meaning of a word is defined ostensively by pointing to *one* given situation. If one sometimes actually can explain the meaning of a word in practice by means of such pointing on a single occasion, this is only because it is assumed that one already knows, for example, that a definition of a color word is involved. But the point that Wittgenstein is driving at is that the meaning is really only understood (even in these special cases) if one knows how to make "use of the word defined" (29). Thus, if one understands by ostensive definition the demonstration of usage, then Wittgenstein has no objection against such a definition; on the contrary, words are defined in such a way, and it also is not necessary to add, for example, that the word *sepia* is a color word. On the other hand, if one under- stands by ostensive definition the alleged association of the word with a content, then such a definition is an absurdity, and it is this primitive conception of semantics that lies at the basis of the idea of the possibility of a private language.

Now we also can understand a sentence that I previously skipped in interpreting paragraph 257: "How has he done this naming of pain? And whatever he did, what was its purpose?" One might ask, What is the point of asking about the purpose here[9] when the issue is only the meaning? Wittgenstein is referring, not to some extra-semantic purpose, but to its semantic function. We already heard, We give the impression a name "in order . . . to use the name for this impression in the future." In the interim it has become clear, however, that the meaning of a predicate lies in its discriminatory function. This is the semantic purpose that the use of a predicate has; and it is precisely this that the private language theory cannot make intelligible.

Now this has been a long theoretical reflection, and you might object: "Haven't you proceeded from extremely specific assumptions about how the meaning of a word is constituted; further, aren't they assumptions that the theoretician of private language is perhaps not compelled to accept? And don't we have to begin with the fact that we can distinguish and distinctly designate sensations without regard to external criteria—for example, sensations of taste or the two head-ache types, A and B? And must we not then proceed to see which semantic theory lies at the basis of this fact?" You are right. Of course, we have to check Wittgenstein's theses against those examples for which the possibility of private use appears particularly well founded.

Let's take as an example the nuances of taste, the taste of pears or of wine. A wine expert is someone who—apart from the added evaluation—has the capacity to distinguish many nuances of wine taste with relative reliability. In so doing he always uses one and the same word for one and the same taste (or for one of its aspects); let's use "W_1" and "W_2" as examples. A good judge of wine is obviously only someone who uses these words with some degree of reliability when he tastes the wine blindly, that is, when he has no independent criteria for the discrimination of the wine. Let's now proceed to the private language situation. In specific cases I use the expression W_1 and in others W_2. How do I know that W_1 stands for a distinct—and always the same—sensation? The defender of private language will reply: "Well, I remember . . . " and now Wittgenstein can ask, as in paragraph 258, "How can you check that?" But we didn't now want to theorize in general, but only to develop that private language argument as far as is suggested by a real context such as that of the wine expert. And, of course, the wine expert does not appeal to the reliability of his memory of taste when asked how he knows that W_1 stands for some-thing distinct, since he would thereby be involved in a circle. Rather, he appeals to the fact that it has been proven that by means of his taste—that is, by means of his use of the predicates W_1 and W_2—he can distinguish different types of wine, which are established as different through criteria that are independent of taste; and it is only through this process that his memory of taste is confirmed as a reliable one.

Thus, we always *in fact* regard the capacity to discriminate objects (in our case, wines), whose diversity is fixed independently, as the criterion for whether a taste word stands for a distinct taste. Once this capacity is demonstrated, we can then use the word without attending to the external criteria—and it is in this possibility, of course, that the relevance of this capacity lies. But the meaning of the word is determined through the correlation with these external criteria, and can be determined through no other criteria. Naturally it does not follow from the correlation of W_n with an external criterion C_m that W_n is to be considered synonymous with C_m; in this case W_n would no longer be a sensation word. But W_n is a word that we use when we discriminate wines by *tasting* them; and if we ask ourselves what the distinct taste is with which the use of W_n is associated, then we must say it is the one by means of whose tasting precisely those wines are recognized that are made from such and such grapes in such and such a way (C_m).

Thus we arrive at the conclusion that even when one might think that there is a strictly private use of sensation words, one not communicable to others, this use is in reality connected with observable criteria, at least insofar as it makes a claim to determinacy (and otherwise one cannot speak of a meaning). This means that if one looks more closely at how one establishes the meaning of such words for themselves, one finds that it takes place precisely in the way that one might explain the meaning to someone else: Such and such a taste is the taste of such and such grapes. And it is not even *conceivable* how one could otherwise fix the meaning.

All predicates "F" that are involved here can only be explained on the basis of sentences of the form "x is F" through a correlation with observable properties C of x; this is precisely because they are predicates, and this means that they are classification expressions. Now these predicates include either predicates of perception, such as those just mentioned involving taste (as well as those of color), or the "ϕ" predicates, which do not stand for perceptible properties of material objects but for sensations or other states of consciousness of persons. In PI (270) Wittgenstein develops a line of reflection with regard to bodily sensations such as my two headache types, A and B, which is entirely analogous to what I just elaborated for the sensations of taste. Here it also proves meaningful to use a sensation word irrespective of observable criteria, but here too the meaning of this use is not an association with a sensation content but a characterization—in this case of the person himself. And the criterion for whether a distinct sensation is involved here also lies in the existence of a correlation with observable criteria—in this case in the physical state or behavior of the person.

All names for sensations—and beyond this all "ϕ" predicates—are classification expressions; by their means something is characterized, discriminated, or recognized. The mistake of the theorist of private language was that he either (a) grasped these expressions as simple names, and thereby also assumed an untenable conception of name giving, which made it impossible to understand their further use, or (b) acknowledged their discriminatory function, but was compelled to assume that what is classified, characterized, or recognized are *the sensations*. He thus failed to see that what we characterize are *the objects* through *sensing* them—and associating sensation words with them—whether the objects are those that we perceive through the senses or the experiencing person himself. Hence, the fundamental mistake of the theory of private language was that it hypostatized the "ϕ" states into peculiar, inwardly observable objects. This mistake is not primarily a semantic one, but a false ontologico-epistemological assumption that, certainly as soon as it expressed itself semantically, only allowed for a theory of private language. To the reproach "And yet you again and again reach the conclusion that the sensation is itself a nothing," Wittgenstein replies, "Not at all. It is not a *something*, but not a nothing either" (PI 304).

Lecture 6

Wittgenstein, II: The Way Out of the Fly Bottle

The knowledge that is expressed in first-person "ϕ" sentences appeared unproblematic to the traditional theory—it is based upon inner perception—and for this reason, the knowledge that is expressed in third-person "ϕ" sentences had to appear correspondingly problematic. On the other hand, if one proceeds, as Wittgenstein does, from the actual use of "ϕ" sentences, the question concerning the basis of the knowledge that is expressed in these sentences appears in the opposite direction from the outset. For we learn "ϕ" predicates in connection with their use in third-person sentences, or in connection with first-person sentences that are uttered by other persons. Therefore, in attempting to understand Wittgenstein's own conception of "ϕ" sentences, it is advisable to begin with the "he ϕ" sentences.

I have already alluded to the fact that Wittgenstein's concept of the *criterion* is fundamental for his understanding of the "he ϕ" sentences. "An 'inner process' stands in need of outward criteria" (PI 580). What does Wittgenstein mean by *criterion*?[1] The word has a meaning for him that is not limited to its use in "ϕ" expressions. The only place at which he fully explains what he means by it is to be found in the *Blue Book* (pp. 24–25): "Let us introduce two antithetical terms in order to avoid certain elementary confusions. To the question 'How do you know that so and so is the case?', we sometimes answer by giving *criteria* and sometimes by giving *symptoms*." The concept of the criterion is therefore to be understood as antithetical to that of the symptom. Where does the difference lie? Wittgenstein provides an example: "If medical science calls angina an inflammation caused by a particular bacillus, and we ask in a particular case 'why do you say that this man has got angina?', then the answer 'I have found the bacillus so and so in his blood' gives us the criterion, or what we may call the defining criterion of angina. If on the other hand the answer was 'His throat is inflamed', this might give us a symptom of angina. I call 'symptom' a phenomenon of which *experience* has taught us that it coincided, in some way or other, with the phenomenon which is our defining criterion."

Wittgenstein further explains that in practice the two concepts *symptom* and *criterion* are not sharply separated. It is often the case in science, for example, that something which is first taken as the defining criterion for the application of a predicate is later taken as a mere symptom when something more suitable is found to serve as the defining criterion. But Wittgenstein emphasizes that this vacillation over whether this or that is to be taken as the symptom does not affect the conceptual distinction between *criterion* and *symptom*.

What is the higher concept to which these two concepts belong? In both cases the issue involves an empirically given state of affairs p that warrants the assertion that another state of affairs q exists. In English the word *evidence* is used for such a connection, and since a corresponding word in German is lacking, the expression *Evidenz*, which was earlier used in a different way in German, has also come into use in this context. *Evidence* in this sense is defined in the following way: p is evidence for q if p is an empirically given state of affairs that warrants the assertion that q exists. With the help of this concept of evidence we can now define Wittgenstein's terms *symptom* and *criterion*: p is a symptom for q if p is inductively acquired evidence for q, that is, evidence that rests upon experience; on the other hand, p is a criterion for q if p is evidence for q that is not inductive but is grounded in the meaning of q.

From the way in which Wittgenstein explains the concept of *criterion* in the angina example of the *Blue Book*, it appears as if a criterion would also always be a necessary and sufficient condition of the thing for which it serves as the criterion. But Wittgenstein uses the concept of criterion in other contexts in such a way that this does not have to be the case. Thus, at another point in the *Blue Book* he says (p. 51): "The grammar of propositions which we call propositions about physical objects admits of a variety of evidences for every such proposition. It characterises the grammar of the proposition 'my finger moves, etc.' that I regard the propositions 'I see it move', 'I feel it move', 'He sees it move', 'He tells me that it moves', etc. as evidences for it." When Wittgenstein says that something lies in the grammar of an expression, he always thereby implies that it belongs to its meaning. The statement that these different types of evidence belong to the grammar of such a sentence therefore indicates that different criteria are involved. A connection exists between these types of evidence and the sentence for which they are evidence that is not merely inductive but definitional; that is, it is grounded in the meaning of the sentence.

This example of the "propositions about physical objects" is different from the angina example in several respects. First, a criterial connection does not exist here between two sentences, but between two sentence types; second (and this is connected to the first point), this example does not simply involve a criterion for the application of a specific predicate to an object, but criteria for how sentences of a definite sentence type are generally to be justified. On the one hand we have a sentence about an objective, perceptible state of affairs ("my finger moves"), and on the other hand we have a large number of 'subjective' sentences, in which a person and his cognitive relation to this state of affairs are specified. And now Wittgenstein claims that it is part of the essence — or the meaning — of the objective sentence (hence of this sentence form) that if someone asks for its justification, one or more of the subjective sentences must be specified. The following connections exist between the objective sentence and the subjective sentences. (1) The objective sentence can only be justified by sentences of the subjective type. (2) The subjective sentences that are related to one and the same objective sentence can reciprocally confirm or refute one another. For example, I can justify the sentence "my finger moves" by the fact that I feel it moving, but this criterion can fall into contradiction with others, for example, I do not see it moving; but then other subjects can say to me, for example, "Of course it is moving; we all see it, you must be a victim of an optical illusion." Hence, many subjective sentences are contraposed to the one objective sentence, so that no single one of the criteria is a necessary or sufficient condition for the truth of the objective sentence. It follows from these two points that (3) what has been justified by subjective sentences can be refuted only by sentences of the same type. The objective state of affairs is not conceivable as something independent of its subjective modes of appearance. Nonetheless, it is not a subjective mode of appearance or a sum of such modes of appearance; this is a function of the fact that the 'grammar' of the two sentence types is different, although they are anchored in one another in the ways just indicated.

There is a far-reaching analogy to this situation in the case of the third-person "ϕ" sentences. "An 'inner process' stands in need of outward criteria" (PI 580). If this connection is to be criterial, it must be essential—that is, grounded in the meaning of the "ϕ" sentences— to the same extent as the connection just elucidated between the objective sentences about perceptible states of affairs and the subjective sentences about their modes of appearance. Here we also have on the one hand *one* sentence about a sensation or some other "ϕ" state of a person, and on the other hand a *large number* of sentences about the behavior of this person; each sentence out of this plurality is a noninductive evidence for whether the "he ϕ" sentence is true. Here it is also the case that (1) the "he ϕ" sentence can only be justified by sentences about the behavior of the person. Though in the first case the *modes of appearance* of the objective state of affairs were involved, here we speak of the behavior by which the "ϕ" state characteristically is *expressed* or *manifested*; and the use of the corresponding "I ϕ" sentence certainly has a special place among the different possibilities of how a "ϕ" state can attain expression. Thus, an essential connection exists between the "ϕ" state and its expression, since the "ϕ" predicate can be defined only in connection with the behavior by which the state is expressed. On the other hand, it is also the case here that (2) a single manifestation cannot be a necessary or sufficient condition for assuming that the person is in the "ϕ" state, because here also a great number of sentences about modes of behavior are contraposed to the single "ϕ" sentence; and these sentences can reciprocally confirm or refute one another. For this reason it is also true here (3) that the "he ϕ" sentence can be refuted only by sentences of the same kind, namely, by sentences about behavior.

The problem of dissimulation is especially pressing in this connection, particularly in the case in which the behavior is the utterance of an "I ϕ" sentence, that is, in the case of lying. Dissimulation (and the special case of lying as well) consists in intentionally behaving in such a way that one expresses a "ϕ" state that one does not have. Obviously Wittgenstein can and will not deny that there is characteristic behavior without the "ϕ" state. To the objection "But surely you will admit that there is a difference between pain behavior accompanied by pain and pain behavior without any pain?" he replies, "Admit it? What greater difference could there be?" (PI 304). But there are "criteria in behavior" for dissimulation (*Zettel* 571). Otherwise we would not have been able to acquire the concept of dissimulation (ibid.). "A child has much to learn before it can pretend. (A dog cannot be a hypocrite, but neither can he be sincere.)" (PI, p. 229)

Thus, the possibility of dissimulation still does not indicate an "inner" sphere that is independent of behavior; rather it is founded on a higher-level form of behavior: "The language games with expressions of feelings are based on games with expressions of which we don't say that they may lie" (NL 293). "The word 'lying' was taught us in a particular way in which it was fastened to a certain behavior, to the use of certain expressions under certain circumstances. Then we use it, saying that we have been lying, when our behavior was not like the one which first constituted the meaning" (NL 295).

The analogy between the criterial grounding of the justification of "he ϕ" sentences and the criterial grounding of the justification of sentences about perceptible objects has its limits. First, we must confront the following problem: If we look more closely it turns out that those sentences that function as criteria for the truth of sentences about perceptible objects are a type of "ϕ" sentences; for they are 'subjective' sentences in which a person is said to see something, feel something, and so on. Thus, the curious situation arises in which "ϕ" sentences function as criteria for sentences about perceptible objects, and in precisely the reverse sense sentences about perceptible objects function as criteria for "ϕ" sentences. For this reason it might be thought that a circle must arise here.

It nonetheless follows from an important reflection that Wittgenstein developed in *Zettel* (Z 410ff.) that this is not the case. Wittgenstein shows there that in the case of sentences about perceptible objects the understanding of the straightforward sentence necessarily precedes the understanding of the sujectively modified sentence. "Why doesn't one teach the child the language game 'It looks red to me' from the first?" (422). Answer: Because the understanding of this sentence presupposes that one already knows what is meant by *red*, and this can only be explained by means of a sentence "it is red" (cf. 420). "Imagine that a child was quite specially clever, so clever that he could at once be taught the doubtfulness of the existence of all things. So he learns from the beginning: 'That is probably a chair'. And now how does he learn the question: 'Is it also really a chair?' " (411). If we wanted first to teach a child the sentence "That is probably F," then the word *probably* would be an empty addition, and "That is probably F" would have the same meaning for the child as the sentence "That is F" has for us. "That is probably F" only can be learnt together with "That is really F," and more specifically it is connected to the experience of having one's expectations disappointed (415); this experience pre-supposes that the corresponding unmodalized sentence has already been understood. "The red visual impression is a new *concept*" (423), that is, a concept that only can be acquired if one already has the concept of redness. "The language game that we teach him then is: 'It looks to me . . .', 'it looks to you . . .'. In the first language game a person does not occur as perceiving subject" (424). "You give the language game a new joint" (425).

This reflection implies a radical reversal of the entire modern tradition of epistemology. Since this tradition neglected the semantic problematic, it conceived of the knowledge of objects by assuming that the process of knowing originated entirely from sense perceptions or, linguistically speaking, from sentences such as "it appears to me. . . ." In fact, it is only when the language game has received the "new joint" of the subjective sentences that the originally unmodalized sentences acquire a specifically "objective" sense; this is indicated by the fact that each straightforward sentence p about perceptible objects is equivalent to "really p." In this way the contrast to "it looks (to me) that p" is incorporated into the meaning of p; and its criterial connection with these subjective sentences or its justification through them, which pertains to the 'grammar' of sentences about perceptible objects, only emerges at this level.

It is at this point that the analogy between the criterial justification of "he φ" sentences and the criterial justification of sentences about perceptible objects breaks down. We cannot directly explain the mean-ing of "φ" predicates in the way we can and must directly explain the meaning of *red* before we can understand the sentences that function as criteria for the justification of "this is red." We can only explain the predicate "has pain," for example, by means of external criteria. Therefore, what is primary here from an epistemic standpoint is also semantically primary. And for this reason the previously suspected circle between sentences concerning the 'outer' and 'inner,' between sentences about observable objects and those about "ϕ" states, does not exist. The semantic point of departure, which lies at the foundation of the criterial language game about perceptible objects as well as the criterial language game about "ϕ" states, is straightforward sentences about perceptible objects.

In this connection, we are directly faced with perhaps the most questionable aspect of the account of "ϕ" predicates that has been given so far. If "ϕ" predicates are explained by indicating under what behavioral conditions they can be ascribed to a person, then doesn't one have to conclude that Wittgenstein reduces the "ϕ" predicates to complicated behavioral predicates? Of course, I have already said that according to Wittgenstein the sensation words on the one hand designate precisely the sensations, while on the other hand they are explained by means of external criteria; in this way an analytic connection between the statements about sensations and the statements about modes of behavior is established that stands in contrast to the analogy theory. But this contention still appears open to question, since one can raise the following objection: In what sense do the sensation words designate sensations if they are explained only by way of behavior? Aren't the sensations thereby reduced to mere dispositions to express the sensations?

In PI, paragraph 307, Wittgenstein protests against the charge of behaviorism. The justification he gives, however, consists only in the claim that when he denies that "mental processes" are inwardly perceivable (as they are according to the private language theory),[2] the "mental processes" as such are not thereby "denied." This justification remains a negative one. What is there in Wittgenstein's positive conception of "ϕ" predicates that entitles him to repudiate the charge of behaviorism?

It is his account of first-person "ϕ" sentences. If we consider what is missing from the preceding explanation of "ϕ" predicates by means of external criteria, this can be expressed roughly in the following way: Someone who has only learned to speak about pain, for example, in the third person, can indeed know when someone has pain, but he lacks the feeling of what it means to have pain. But this can also be expressed more simply: He has not yet felt pain. But this merely means that he has not yet had pain, for to feel pain means to have pain. And what it means to have pain would have to become clear when one explains how the sentences "I have pain" and "I know that

I have pain" are used. Perhaps you might contradict me here and say no, the right way to understand what it means to have pain cannot be to inquire into the modes of use of these sentences; rather, it would have to consist in describing the having of pain, and for this purpose one must observe it. Of course, if we formulated our task in such a way, we would again be committing ourselves to the private language theory. But why, so you might ask in reply, don't we at least formulate the task in the way that I characterized it myself at one time: as a question of what our knowledge is based upon when we say "I know that I have pain"?

The reason is that as early as the beginning of his critical examination of the private language theory Wittgenstein claims, "It can't be said of me at all (except perhaps as a joke) that I *know* that I am in pain. What is it supposed to mean—except perhaps that I *am* in pain?" (PI 246). This argument sounds admittedly curious. We have already seen in the first lecture that it is characteristic of "ϕ" states that someone who has them also always immediately knows that he has them. Hence, when I am in a "ϕ" state, I can also always say "I ϕ," and this statement is an expression, not of a mere opinion, but of knowledge; in fact it is always the case that if I can say "I ϕ," then I also can say "I know that I ϕ." But now why should it follow from the equivalence of these two sentences that one cannot speak of knowledge here, as Wittgenstein claims? At another point Wittgenstein justifies his conception by noting that "I ϕ" sentences are not susceptible to doubt, and by claiming that when doubt is logically excluded one also cannot speak of knowledge (PI, p. 221).

This argument is also not immediately plausible. But we cannot do justice to Wittgenstein's reflections on this question until we have become acquainted with his conception of "I ϕ" sentences; and the task now can only be to formulate the problem in such a way that it is not prejudiced toward any particular side. And this only seems to be attainable by adhering to the formulation that I just proposed: Namely, how are "I ϕ" sentences used? For the question posed in this way leaves it open as to whether or not they are used in such a way that they express knowledge—and whether or not for this reason they can always be expanded into the form "I know that I ϕ." When posed in this way the question even admits the private language conception as a possible answer; according to this conception, "I ϕ" sentences are *used* in such a way that they express, or are justified by, an act of inner perception.

For Wittgenstein, of course, the elucidation of the use of "I ϕ" sentences must proceed in a different direction; for if a sentence "I have pain" were to be justified through an act of inner perception, the word *pain* would have a different meaning when used in first-person sentences from that when used in third-person sentences. Furthermore, it would—in terms of my formulation at the end of the fourth lecture—transgress the principle of the veridical symmetry of first- and third- person "ϕ" sentences. Even the moderate supporter of a private language theory, who persists in assuming an additional subjective meaning, had to admit that the "ϕ" predicate in the first place has an intersubjective meaning, even when it is used in first-person sentences.

Thus Wittgenstein faces the following problem: On the one hand, the "ϕ" predicate in first-person sentences must be explained in a way that makes intelligible how its use in first- and third- person sentences can be learned unitarily; on the other hand, one must take account of the fact that an epistemic asymmetry—as I called it—exists between these sentences. Wittgenstein solves this problem by also seeing the "I ϕ" sentence in the context of the behavioral *expressions* of the "ϕ" state; but he does this in such a way that the expression does not—as in the case of third-person "ϕ" sentences—supply the criterion by which the sentence is justified, but rather the first-person sentence is itself to be understood as an expression of the "ϕ" state. We already saw this in the last lecture: The sentence "I am in pain" takes the place of the natural expression of pain, it "replaces" the cry or groan (PI 244).

The sentence "I am in pain" is therefore interpreted by Wittgenstein in such a way that in its use the pain is expressed or comes to expression, and not in such a way that in it knowledge, that is, a cognitive act, is expressed. The "I ϕ" sentences are expressive and not cognitive sentences. By a cognitive sentence, a sentence of the form "a is F" is to be understood. By means of "a" an object is *identified*, of which it then can be *ascertained* that the predicate "F" applies to it on the basis of the *criteria* that pertain to the predicate; in this way we come to know (*erkennen*) that a is F. The simplest example of a cognitive sentence is a sentence of the form "this is F," when "F" is a predicate of perception. The predicative sentence "a is F" does not itself express

knowledge that something is the case, but only belief; but when such
a sentence is expressed, it is assumed that it can be *known* (ascertained)
that a is F. To be sure, if an "I ϕ" sentence were cognitive *at all*, then
knowledge—and not merely possible knowledge—would always be
expressed in its use; for I cannot merely believe that I ϕ, but *if* I ϕ
then I always also already know it. "It has sense to say 'it rained and
I knew it', but not 'I had toothache and knew that I had'. 'I know
that I have toothache' means nothing, or the same as 'I have toothache' " (NL 309). Of course, this is simply a consequence of the fact
that it is is characteristic of "ϕ" states that someone who has them
has an immediate knowledge that he has them.

Thus if the "I ϕ" sentence has a cognitive sense at all, knowledge
would always be expressed in its use (even in those cases in which it
was only simulated). The knowledge that would be expressed would
have to consist in the fact that when I identify myself by means of
the singular term *I*, I can ascertain that the predicate "ϕ" applies to
the object identified by this term on the basis of the criteria that hold
for the predicate. But we already have seen—and it is just this that
is also emphasized by Wittgenstein in the present context (PI 404)—
that I indeed refer to a person by *I* (namely, myself), but I do not
identify him. In contrast to *this*, by means of *I* one does not pick out
a distinct object in the perceptual field, of which it then may be
observed, perceived, or ascertained that it fulfills the criteria of "ϕ";
and it is also equally the case from the other side—from the side of
the predicate—that the correct use of the "I ϕ" sentence is not justified
by ascertaining that the criteria that hold for "ϕ" are present (PI 290).
"One wishes to say: In order to be able to say that I have toothache
I don't observe my behavior, say, in the mirror. *And this is correct*, but
it doesn't follow that you describe an observation of any other kind"
(NL 319). One might think thus: If a predicative sentence is used
correctly then it must be grounded upon a type of verification, and
if the verification is not external it must be an internal one. But the
"I ϕ" sentence is not based upon verification at all (Z 472). The transfer
of concepts such as perception, observation, and verification to the
so-called inner sphere does not make any sense.

We will, of course, have to ask how correctness in the use of the
"I ϕ" sentences is to be understood positively, if they are expressive
and not cognitive. But we can now already make clear to ourselves
what Wittgenstein achieves by means of the thesis of the expressive

sense of "I ϕ" sentences. He thereby succeeds in distancing himself equally from the introspective *and* the behavioristic conceptions, which both grasp "I ϕ" sentences as observation sentences. With the expressive conception of these sentences Wittgenstein delineates how a predicate like "having pain" is learned in a unitary way for first- and third- person sentences in the context of behavior, without assimilating the two types of sentences to one another epistemically. A "ϕ" predicate can be learned in its unitary meaning with reference to one and the same mode of behavior in such a way that this mode of behavior represents the criterion for the use of the predicate in the third person from the perspective of the observer, while the use of the "I ϕ" sentence is itself a modification of the mode of behavior from the perspective of the agent. "They teach the child new pain-behavior" (PI 244).

But does Wittgenstein overcome behavioristic reductionism in this way? One might object that if the "I ϕ" sentence is understood as an expression of the "ϕ" state, we are once more dealing merely with a mode of behavior. But a fundamental difference exists between sentences about sensations that are based upon the expressions of sensations and sentences that are themselves expressions of sensations. You still might object that we have only the expression of sensation here and not the sensation. Now what sort of conception do you have of what it means to have the sensation itself? Of course, a distinction is to be made between the sensation and the expression of the sensation. But how can the sensation be expressed linguistically? Let us assume the impossible is possible and we can inwardly perceive sensations; will we be closer to the sensation with a sentence in which the *perception* of the sensation is expressed than with the expression of the sensation? (Furthermore, a regress would arise here, since the perception of the sensation would also be a "ϕ" state, which for its part would also have to be perceived and so on.) "For how can I go so far as to try to use language to get between pain and its expression?" (PI 245). In order to be convinced of the correctness of Wittgenstein's conception, it is useful to imagine any given sensation or feeling; when we imagine ourselves in a state of pain, for example, we picture how we would behave.

So far, so good (perhaps). The question now arises as to how these expressive sentences are to be understood semantically, and in what semantic connection they stand to the cognitive "he ϕ" sentences. As

I indicated, the "I ϕ" sentence is not to be understood in its structure as an ordinary predicative sentence of the form "a is F." The word *I* is not to have the function that a singular term otherwise has; but then how is its predicative structure to be understood? Or shall we say that in reality it does not have a predicative structure at all, and that as an expressive sentence it is to be understood analogously to an undivided expressive utterance such as "ouch"? In this case, however, the "I ϕ" sentence could no longer be understood as a statement, and from this it would also follow that it would not be permissible to call such sentences true or false. And finally one would not be able to speak of knowledge in relation to these sentences, and consequently it would not be possible to claim for them a type of certainty that one ordinarily associates with "I ϕ" sentences; this would follow either from the fact that these sentences cannot be true or false or that they are not 'cognitive.' Under such circumstances, the definition of "ϕ" states with which I began—that is, that they are those states of which one has an immediate knowledge if one has them—would be untenable. And, of course, the talk of a veridical symmetry and epistemic asymmetry of first- and third- person "ϕ" sentences would also be untenable if it were not permissible to speak of either truth or knowledge in relation to the first-person sentences.

These consequences seem to have little intuitive plausibility, and thus the question arises as to whether such consequences really follow from the noncognitive character of these sentences. Wittgenstein did not systematically pursue this problem. The thesis that the "I ϕ" sentences cannot be called true or false is advanced by some of his interpreters,[3] but not by Wittgenstein himself. What one does find are passages in which he denies that these sentences have the character of statements (Z 401, 549), but in other passages he expresses himself more cautiously (PI p. 224). On the other hand, in NL he extensively discusses the problem of lying with respect to the "I ϕ" sentences; and in contrast to other expressions of "ϕ" states, in the case of lying not only dissimulation but also (intentional) untruth is involved.

Wittgenstein's conception appears more unequivocal in his insistence that one cannot speak of knowledge in relation to the "I ϕ" sentences. His crucial argument appears to be that one cannot speak of knowledge in those cases in which doubt is logically excluded. When Hacker objects to this by saying that one can certainly speak of knowledge in the case of the equation "2 + 2 = 4" although doubt is senseless, he probably has not understood Wittgenstein's point.[4] Doubt is logically possible for every statement, though it may immediately prove to be unjustified. When Wittgenstein maintains that doubt is logically excluded in the case of "I have pain," he means that its exclusion is based upon the expressive character of the sentence. In the case of an inarticulate exclamation like "ouch" doubt is in fact logically excluded; it could not grammatically "take hold" here. And we thereby confront the essential point of the entire problem: It is Wittgenstein's fundamental thesis that "I ϕ" sentences are not essentially different from inarticulate exclamations; but the qualification "not essentially" still leaves open the prospect that they are different, and it is here that we will have to take up the argument.

Wittgenstein distinguished in PI, paragraph 244, between (a) the "primitive, . . . natural expressions of the sensation" (cries, groans), (b) "exclamations" like "ouch," and (c) "sentences" like "I am in pain." It is implied by his thesis of the expressive character of "I ϕ" sentences that (b) and (c) belong closely together, but Wittgenstein elaborated nothing more specific regarding the connection and the difference among these forms. Alston has made a significant contribution to this question in his essay "Expressing." Alston first points out that the structural difference between (a) on one hand and (b) and (c) on the other hand does not consist in the fact that (b) and (c) must be learned; rather, it rests upon the fact that (a) is a so-called natural sign, a symptom, while (b) and (c) are cases of rule-governed behavior. Like all use of linguistic expressions, they are based upon the learning of a conventional rule, a norm, in relation to which one can speak of a 'correct' or an 'incorrect' use of the expression ("Expressing," pp. 21ff.). Hence, Alston correctly subsumes those nonlinguistic expressions of "ϕ" states that are rule governed—as, for example, the shrug of one's shoulders—under exclamations ("Expressing," 27); they also can be designated as 'linguistic' in a broad sense of the word.

One understands the meaning of a linguistic expression when one knows its rule of use. We thereby have a simple means with whose aid we can go beyond the overall assimilation of "I ϕ" sentences to exclamations, and attain a clarification of their precise connection. Which rules of use are constitutive for "I ϕ" sentences, and which are constitutive for exclamations? By exclamations here we mean all conventionally rule-governed expressions of "ϕ" states that are not predicatively structured. Alston answers these questions in roughly the following way: An exclamation "A_1" is correctly used by someone only if he is in state "ϕ_1." Thus, for example, the rule for the exclamation "ouch" is the following: If S says "ouch" and S has no pain, then S is using the exclamation incorrectly. If he admits that he doesn't have pain, then we would say that he has not understood the meaning of the word *ouch*.

With respect to the "I ϕ" sentences, Alston does not proceed by presupposing the expressive character of these sentences; rather, he treats them as a special form of an assertoric sentence. According to Alston, the following rule holds for the use of any given assertoric sentence: a sentence z is only correctly used if p; if someone says "it is raining" when it is not raining, then he is using the sentence incorrectly. If he admits that it is not raining, then we would say that he has not understood the meaning of the expression "it is raining." Thus, by means of the rule about z ("it is raining"), which was just specified, the meaning of z is fixed in a way completely analogous to the previous fixing of the meaning of "A_1." If we now apply this to the special case of the "I ϕ" sentences, we get the following result: If someone uses the sentence "I ϕ_1" and is not in the state "ϕ_1," then he is using the expression incorrectly. The rule that thus follows for the sentence "I ϕ_1" is identical to the rule that had been established for the exclamation "A_1." Thus, Wittgenstein's thesis appears to be confirmed in a startling way: The exclamation "ouch" and the sentence "I have pain" appear to have exactly the same rule of use.

This account of the situation certainly is in need of modification. For it would follow from it that the corresponding "he ϕ" sentence also has the same rule of use as the exclamation; in particular, the "he ϕ" sentence and the "I ϕ" sentence would have the same rule of use. What Alston has specified as the rule for assertoric sentences is in reality merely their truth condition, and the fact that these are identical for first- and third- person "ϕ" sentences merely corresponds to the principle of veridical symmetry. One can in fact say that the exclamation "ouch" is used *correctly* by S precisely in those cases in which he has pain, and it is precisely in these cases that the sentence "I have pain" is also used *correctly* by S; further, it is in these cases that the latter sentence is *true*, and it is precisely in these cases that the sentence in the third person, "S has pain," also is *true*. Alston did not pay attention to the fact that in the case of an exclamation one can speak only of correctness and not of truth, while in the case of an assertoric sentence there are two levels of correctness; one uses an assertoric sentence correctly if one uses it in accordance with the meaning that it has, but this still does not mean that it is correct in the further sense that it is true. The rule of use of an assertoric sentence, for example, "S has pain," does not consist in the condition that the sentence is only correctly used in those cases in which S has pain; rather, knowing the meaning, that is, the rule of use, of an assertoric sentence means knowing how to ascertain that it is true— thus, in this case it means to know how to ascertain that S has pain. Hence, Alston is indeed right that an assertoric sentence p is also linked to the state of affairs that p through a rule, but the rule involves several levels and refers to the *knowledge* through which the sentence is *justified*. This constitutes the cognitive character of this sentence, which was described earlier.

The situation is entirely different in the case of an exclamation. It is not cognitive, it does not refer to a possible ascertaining of its truth, and truth and error cannot be used to characterize it. Here the following simple rule applies: S correctly uses the exclamation "ouch" precisely in those cases in which he has pain. For the exclamation there is only one form of incorrectness, that is, the use of the expression that violates the rule (in instances of dissimulation we have an intentional violation of the rule of use); in the case of the cognitive sentence there is also a possibility of error that stands beyond the possibility of violating the rule of use. Thus, the state of affairs for the two extreme cases— exclamations and the corresponding "he ϕ" sentences—is clear. To which side do we have to assign the expressions that really interest us, the "I ϕ" sentences? We cannot hesitate here, since the following also applies for "I have pain": This expression is used correctly by S precisely in those cases in which he has pain. Thus, as far as we can see up to now, the "I ϕ" sentence has the same rule of use as the corresponding exclamation. In this case as well there is only the possibility of violating the rule of use, and not the possibility of error. I therefore agree with Alston in his conclusion. But this conclusion cannot be properly derived if, like Alston, one proceeds from the assumption that the "I ϕ" sentence is a particular type of assertoric sentence; rather, it is only to be reached if it is already presupposed that the "I ϕ" sentence is not used cognitively.

According to the preceding account, there is no difference at all between the mode of use of an "I ϕ" sentence and that of the corresponding exclamation. But such an analysis does not deal with the fact that the "I ϕ" expression is structured, and that besides the predicate, which might be considered equivalent in meaning to the expression used in the exclamation, it contains the word *I*, which has its own meaning as elucidated earlier.

For the complete understanding of the meaning, that is, the rule of use, of an independently used expression such as a sentence or an exclamation, it is not sufficient to consider its mode of use in isolation; rather, one must also take into account how the expression can be answered. Alston correctly points out that in this respect the "I ϕ" sentence is to be distinguished from the exclamation. In supplementing the word corresponding to the exclamation with the word *I*, the expressive expression acquires a similarity to the cognitive-assertoric sentence in the third person, so that we now have two predicative sentences "I ϕ" and "he ϕ" in which "I" and "he" stand for the same entity and the complete expressions stand for the same state of affairs. Thus, a relation of veridical symmetry arises between these two sentences, and from this it follows that "I have pain" is to be distinguished from the exclamation "ouch" by virtue of the fact that one can reply to the first expression (in contrast to the second) by saying yes or no, "that is true" or "that is false." And this has the further consequence that in the case of the "I ϕ" sentence, as distinct from the exclamation, one can speak not only of dissimulation but also of lying.

This modification turns out to be possible as a result of the fact that, as we have just seen, the expressive expression is used *correctly* precisely in those cases in which the "he ϕ" sentence is true. Thus if there is a possibility of recasting the expressive expression in such a way that it formally acquires the structure of an assertoric sentence, that is, of an expression that can be true or false, then the following results: If it is used *correctly* (in conformity to the rule), then it (or what is asserted by it) is *true*. And this possibility arises precisely through—and only through—the addition of *I*, because by means of this unique singular term the speaker refers to himself in such a way that he does not identify himself, but knows that the same thing to which he refers in a nonidentificatory way is identifiable by other singular terms ("this person here," "Mr. X"). If the predicative expression were supplemented by any other singular term by which this same person is designated, then the person would be identified, and the whole sentence would be cognitive, that is, it would lose its purely expressive sense;

and we would no longer be able to say that if it is only used correctly (in conformity to the rule, whereby the rule to be followed is the same as that of the exclamation), then it is true.

Let us now examine the question from the side of the predicate. In our language, of course, we do not have an exclamation to correspond to every "ϕ" predicate, but we can easily imagine a language in which an exclamation A corresponds to every "he ϕ" sentence in such a way that the "he ϕ" sentence is true under the same conditions in which the exclamation A is used correctly. The fact that most "ϕ" predicates are supplemented by a propositional subordinate clause ("he is glad that you are coming") does not present an additional problem, because exclamations also can be supplemented propositionally (for example, "how fantastic that you are coming"). Let us further assume that this language contains no "I ϕ" sentences. Then everything that we express by "I ϕ" sentences would be expressed in it by exclamations that are employed in accordance with the same rule. If there is a one-to-one correspondence between "ϕ" predicates in third-person sentences and exclamations of type A, then we would obviously have a superfluous reduplication of expressions; it would therefore seem preferable for the sake of simplicity to use the same word for the predicate in the third-person sentences and for the corresponding exclamation, for example, the word *pain* instead of the word *ouch*. Hence, on the one hand we would have, for example, the sentences "he ϕ_1" and "he ϕ_2" and on the other hand the exclamations "ϕ_1" and "ϕ_2." And now, of course, we only have to add the word *I*—and we have just seen to what extent this is unproblematic—and we have our "I ϕ" sentences.

If we ask what distinguishes our actual language with its "I ϕ" sentences from the one just imagined with the "ϕ" exclamations, or if we ask what the function of the word *I* is in these sentences, it obviously amounts only to this: By means of this word an expression is produced that, though used according to the same rule as the exclamation, is true in those cases in which it is used correctly. We thus have the unique case of assertoric sentences that can be true or false and nevertheless are not cognitive. Thus, the supposition already formulated in the fourth lecture—namely, that it is essentially characteristic of "ϕ" predicates that one can ascribe them to oneself only from the perspective of "I" saying—is now confirmed and rendered more precise. This follows, not because by means of *I* the speaker is identified in a special way, but because with this word he designates himself merely as the one who is speaking (exclaiming) without identifying himself; and only in this way can an expressive, noncognitively used predicate be supplemented by a singular term.

Wittgenstein's assimilation of the "I ϕ" sentences to exclamations is therefore essentially correct, although two qualifications are in order. (1) One must not go so far as to say that because nothing is identified by *I*, a person is thereby not designated at all; Wittgenstein sometimes appears to do this (cf. PI 410), and it has been argued more recently by G. E. M. Anscombe in her otherwise instructive essay "The First Person" (p. 60). (2) The peculiar status of this singular term is closely connected to the existence of this special case of assertoric sentences that are nonetheless not cognitive. Wittgenstein tended to deny the assertoric character of these expressions because he thought that it was only in this way that he could establish their expressive character. But they do not exclude each other, and it would contradict our actual use of language if one wanted to deny that one can use the word *true* and *false* in connection with the "I ϕ" sentences. In particular, such a conception would disavow an important communicative aspect of our language, which is expressed in the veridical symmetry of the first- and third- person "ϕ" sentences.

How does the situation stand with regard to the question of whether one can meaningfully speak of knowledge in the case of the "I ϕ" sentences? The argument that one cannot speak of knowledge because in the case of an exclamation doubt simply cannot "take hold" in a grammatical sense has now lost its force; since the "I ϕ" sentence is assertoric, doubt is 'logically' possible here in contrast to the exclamation. On the other hand, we have seen that for "I ϕ" sentences, just as for exclamations, the possibility of error that is characteristic of cognitive sentences does not exist. Now if the possibility of error is excluded for an assertoric sentence, this means precisely that one knows what is asserted by it, since one cannot doubt it. If Wittgenstein were to mean by the logical exclusion of doubt *this* impossibility of doubting, then he would be dogmatically stipulating the meaning of the word *to know* in a way that once again would contradict our actual linguistic usage. It is probable that Wittgenstein (and at any rate this holds for the discussion that followed him) made the noncognitive character of these sentences determinative in refusing to grant them the character of knowledge. But to know (*wissen*) and to ascertain (*erkennen*) are not the same thing, and not all knowledge has to rest upon an act of cognition (*Erkenntnisakt*).

Let us make clear to ourselves why the possibility of error is excluded. It is characteristic of expressive expressions that one learns their meaning in such a way that they are used when one is in the state that corresponds to them. I learn to say "ouch" or "I have pain" only in those cases in which I have pain. It is important to stress that such a direct correlation between the linguistic expression and the facts does not obtain for a cognitive sentence. In every case that involves getting to know in the sense of *ascertaining* whether p, one cannot learn simply to say "p" if p. Even in the case of the most elementary perceptual judgment, such as "it is raining," what one learns at best is to say "p" only if one *perceives* that p. And it is in the necessity to ascertain whether "p" is true that the room for error arises. If I say "ouch" when I do not have pain, then I have unintentionally or—for the purpose of deception—intentionally used the expression incorrectly. The same thing is also true for "I ϕ." We have already seen that if the "I ϕ" sentence merely is used in conformity with its rule, it is also true. But it further follows from this that I can be certain that the "I ϕ" sentence is true if I merely have used it in conformity with its rule. Thus, we have here a type of knowledge that does not rest upon an act of ascertaining—upon a cognitive process. In contrast to all other types of knowledge, therefore, here we also cannot pose the question *How* do we know that P? The fact that we can no longer pose this question does not contradict the meaning of *knowledge*. Rather, every form of empirical knowledge refers to a subjective state with regard to the question how do we know it? For example, how do I know that P? Because I perceive it. And it would be absurd to repeat this question with regard to the subjective state.

My earlier introductory talk of a form of immediate knowledge, which was still quite indefinite, has now acquired a precise meaning. At that point I distinguished immediate knowledge only from indirect, inductively justified knowledge, because I was not yet in a position to prejudge the issue of whether or not this knowledge rests upon an inner perception. On the other hand, it now has become clear that immediate knowledge is different in a specific sense from direct knowledge. Empirical knowledge is direct if in response to the question "How do you know it?" one does not appeal to factual evidence from which one has *inferred* what is known; I know it, not because I know something else, but because I observe or have observed it directly. "And how do you know that you are observing it?" This question is no longer meaningful.

Direct knowledge is still a form of mediated knowledge, since it is based upon something. This conclusion is already implicitly contained in the account of the "φ" predicates that I provided at the outset—that is, that they represent those states of which someone who has them immediately knows that he has them. For it follows from this account that if I find myself in this state, I cannot help knowing it, and I do not first have to do something—such as observe it—in order to know it.

Now you might ask, Isn't the regress to which the Heidelberg school called attention simply circumvented arbitrarily here? Isn't this solution of the problem just as dogmatic and unilluminating as the one proposed by those philosophers who—like Brentano—simply claim that in each "φ" state a perception of this state is also immediately contained? The force of Wittgenstein's solution, however, does not consist in evading the regress, but in correcting a phenomenologically false approach that was common to the entire traditional theory of immediate knowledge; the theory assimilated this knowledge to the model of external observation, and hence grounded it in an act of perception. Thus, the fact that the regress falls away is only a consequence, and not the goal of this correction. Wittgenstein succeeds in putting the problem on a new basis by resolving the ostensibly epistemological or cognitive problem ("how do I know it?") into a semantic one ("how is the expression used?").

To be sure, a special semantic case is involved. In the case of assertoric sentences that are not "I φ" sentences the rule of use of the expression *refers* to an act of ascertaining. But this is precisely not true in general for the rule of use of an expression. It does not hold for expressive utterances. Here, for example, a rule such as the following applies: If someone cries in a certain way, he can just as well say "ouch" instead. It is absurd to amplify this rule so that it reads: If someone is *aware* that he is crying in a certain way, then he can. . . . The question "How do I know that I am crying?" is just as absurd as the question "How do I know that I am in pain?"

You still might find it paradoxical that someone can learn the use of an expression according to the rule that he is to use "A" or "p" if p. You might ask the following question: Don't we actually have to assume that the speaker is somehow aware that p? But this would be a pure construction. It does not belong to the rule of use. The speaker uses the expression incorrectly if not-p (that is, if he is not in this state); this is all we can say. And to the contrary we have to ask: Why are we actually inclined to find this semantic state of affairs paradoxical? Obviously it is simply because we are so strongly oriented by the model of perception that we assume that there cannot be any non-inductive empirical knowledge that is not based upon perception or something analogous. In opposition to this, it should be evident that in those cases in which the use of language is so closely linked to us that we are no longer talking about other entities but are expressing ourselves in it, it is absurd once again to postulate precisely that mediating relation between the use of the expression and one's own state or one's own action which is indeed necessary for the knowledge of other entities. And whether it is evident or not, it is in the first place simply a fact—as was shown very clearly by Shoemaker—that we can learn to use certain expressions under specific conditions *without* having to *ascertain* that these conditions hold; and second, one can show that our capacity to learn to use certain expressions when we have ascertained that specific conditions obtain presupposes that there are also expressions that we learn to use under specific conditions *without* having to ascertain that such conditions obtain. As Shoemaker remarks, this fact is no more paradoxical than the fact that "a child who was burned in the past now will avoid fire without first establishing that he was burned in the past."[5]

I would now like to conclude the interpretation of Wittgenstein's theory of immediate epistemic self-consciousness. Let us make clear to ourselves what we have attained, and what is still missing from our account. We have acquired a general theory of the "ϕ" predicates, which was exemplified concretely only in the particular case of sensations, especially those of pain. We have thereby developed only a general framework for understanding the rules of use of the remaining "ϕ" predicates. We cannot directly carry over what has emerged from the analysis of pain to other "ϕ" states such as intentions, beliefs, and actions. Unlike a sensation, an intention does not have a 'natural expression' on which the rule of use of the "ϕ" predicate could immediately fasten. Of course, it is also true of intentions, and in general of all "ϕ" predicates, that the states for which they stand are exhibited in behavior. It has become clear on grounds of principle that all "ϕ"

predicates have a unitary meaning in first- and third- person sentences. They are learned from both perspectives in relation to modes of behavior; from the perspective of the observer the modes of behavior function as criteria for the ascription of the predicate, and from the perspective of the "I" sayer the use of the "I ϕ" sentence is itself a modification of these modes of behavior. But how this works out concretely for the different classes of "ϕ" predicates is a task that has still scarcely been undertaken up to the present day.

Lecture 7

Transition to the Problem of Self-Determination: Freud, Hegel, Kierkegaard

In the discussion following the last lecture it became evident how far removed my interpretation of Wittgenstein is from providing a sufficient understanding of the "ϕ" predicates. I pointed out at the end of the lecture that actions are also "ϕ" states, and thereupon I was asked how that can be reconciled with the fact that one obviously can be conscious of doing something although one is not doing it; for example, without being insincere someone can say "I am lifting my left leg," and then in a given case find out that the leg is not raised.

This difficulty involves not only actions but also movements. Movements of a person are also "ϕ" states, if the criterion of a "ϕ" state is that someone who is in this state has an immediate knowledge, which is not based upon observation, that he is in it; and, of course, one can also be mistaken with regard to one's own bodily movements. I can have the sensation that my left leg is rising (that it is being lifted up), and then find out in a given case that it is not being raised. But this same difficulty also concerns feelings insofar as they are localized in one's body. I can have pain in my left leg and then find out that I no longer have a left leg, and the same situation also obviously applies for Wittgenstein's example of a toothache. And for a still wider class of "ϕ" states we can discover the same difficulty—that is, for memories and perceptions. For example, "I see Mr. Theunissen standing at the door of the auditorium"; "I remember having seen Mr. Theunissen at the door of the auditorium yesterday." In the case of the first sentence it can turn out that I am hallucinating, and thus am not seeing at all; and in the case of the second sentence it can turn out that I have merely dreamed it, and thus do not remember it at all.

Should we now conclude that all these predicates are not "ϕ" predicates? For the definition of "ϕ" predicates that was originally given—that they stand for states of which the person who has them has an immediate knowledge—cannot hold true of these predicates, since it cannot involve a type of knowledge in which error is possible. On the other hand, the epistemic asymmetry of first- and third- person sentences that is characteristic of the "ϕ" predicates applies for these predicates, and the immediacy of this consciousness, which was described at the end of the last lecture, also applies to it; I now say *consciousness*, since I must leave open the question of whether it is still permissible to call this knowledge.

Let us consider on what basis these "ϕ" predicates whose use in the first person may involve error and the possibility of correction can be distinguished from the remaining incorrigible "ϕ" predicates. It is best to begin with the predicates of perception, since here we can immediately link up with Wittgenstein's reflections, which were presented at the beginning of the last lecture. We saw that a sentence such as "I see that the finger moves" is a criterion for the sentence "the finger moves." I have a 'direct,' but not 'immediate,' knowledge of the fact that the finger moves; and this knowledge is based upon the immediate knowledge that I see this. The knowledge that the finger moves can prove to be mere belief, that is, an illusion, through further criterial evidence, for example, when I touch the finger. It is important for our problem that in this case I must retract not only the sentence "the finger moves," which refers to the objective state of affairs, but also the psychological sentence "I see that the finger moves"; and this is because the sentence about a "ϕ" state is formulated in such a way that it not only contains a reference to an objective state of affairs but also implies the truth of the sentence about this state of affairs. For this reason, as soon as the objective sentence proves to be untrue, the psychological sentence must also be retracted *insofar* as it implies the objective sentence. Thus the psychological sentence is recast, for example, into "I have the sensation of seeing the finger move." The "ϕ" sentence that is reformulated in this way is incorrigible; it no longer implies an objective state of affairs, but remains merely a sentence about one's own conscious state. It is to be noted that such a sensation is not an immediately given datum like a sensation of pain. Rather, the sentence "I have the sensation of seeing . . ." is semantically secondary to the sentence "I see . . ."; its meaning consists exclusively in the remainder of the sentence "I see . . .", which always continues to be warranted after the withdrawal of its objective implication. Hence, "I have the sensation of seeing . . ." means the same thing as "I have the impression, I believe I see, it appears to me that I see." Such sentences are not epistemological points of departure, but terminal points; they are based upon the contradiction between the objective implication of the original "ϕ" sentence and those other "ϕ" sentences that refer to the same objective state of affairs.

The sentences about memories, bodily feelings, and one's own movements and actions are corrigible for the same reason as the sentences of perception: They are all psychological sentences that imply sentences about facts concerning the physical world or the body. If one removes this implication one must modify the corresponding sentence, and one thereby acquires an incorrigible sentence that is now merely a sentence about one's own conscious state, for example, "I had the feeling that my left arm was raised." (The tendency to formulate such a sentence in the past is a function of the fact that it does not express an original datum, but is the result of a correction.) The sentence about a toothache is ambiguous. One can continue to assert it in a given case if it turns out that one no longer has any teeth. In this case it does not mean "I have a pain that is localized in my tooth," but "I have a pain of the type that is localized in a tooth." Thus, for the corrigible "ϕ" predicates we always have two predicates: the original predicate, which implies a physical state of affairs, and the modified predicate, which merely stands for the conscious state; and in special cases such as that of a toothache, one and the same expression is used for both predicates.

We also have to understand the unmodified predicates as "ϕ" predicates because these predicates are also used expressively in the first person: Their use entails neither an identification of the person to whom the predicate pertains nor a verification of the predicate's application. This expressive use allows no room for error in itself, and for this reason what is stated by such a sentence contains a component that is incorrigible; hence, a correction is not itself possible within this mode of use, but can take place only by way of a different mode of access to the implied physical state of affairs. Nevertheless, we must now retract the unqualified proposition that in the case of the "I ϕ" sentences error is excluded: and similarly we must revise the definition of "ϕ" states as states of which someone has an immediate knowledge if he is in them, unless we understand the concept of knowledge in such a broad sense that it involves the feature of corrigibility.

Let us now consider still another class of "ϕ" predicates that also involve the possibility of error, although this does not concern an implied physical state of affairs. I mean states such as intentions, emotions, wishes, and beliefs. The forms of error that are typical of such states concern the character of the psychical state itself, and not an implied physical state of affairs. Here we encounter that phenomenon of self-deception for which Freud used the concept of the unconscious.

It would be inadequate to try to resolve the problem that is raised here by confining oneself to the statement that I made in the first lecture, namely, that intentional states such as intentions and wishes and conscious states ("ϕ" states) comprise two overlapping classes. If one restricts oneself to this correct statement, then a static conception would be possible on the basis of which there would be on the one hand conscious intentions, wishes, and so on, and on the other hand unconscious intentions, wishes, and so on; this would not take into account the fact that the unconscious intentions, wishes, and so on are potentially conscious states, that is, that we can bring them to consciousness and vice versa. In the case of such a static conception there would be no reason to speak of deception, since one would not deceive oneself about the conscious states, and simply would not know the unconscious ones at all.

Nonetheless, the claim that two overlapping classes are involved contains an essentially correct kernel from which we can gain an insight into the peculiar character of deception that is at issue in the case of these "ϕ" predicates. In contrast to the previously discussed "ϕ" sentences that imply statements about physical states of affairs and for this reason themselves contain the possibility of error and correction, the first-person "ϕ" sentences now at issue do not contain the possibility of deception and correction within their own domain. This becomes evident in view of the fact that there is no possibility of a subjective modification for these sentences; sentences like "I have the impression (or the sensation) of having the intention to avoid Petra" make just as little sense as the sentence "I have the impression of feeling a pain." And if someone says "I *believe* that I have the intention to avoid her," this sentence does not thereby express a correction, but it expresses a different "φ" state, that of undecidedness. If I have the clear consciousness of having an intention, and I express this in an "I φ" sentence, then I really have this intention. This situation corresponds to the statement about the overlapping of the two classes. Those intentions of which I am conscious I also really have, but I also have intentions of which I am not conscious. In what sense, then, can one speak of self-deception?

We first have to clarify the meaning of unconscious intentions, wishes, and so on in order to see how they are connected to our conscious intentions, wishes, and so on. Intentions and wishes, for instance, can also be identified from the perspective of the third person, like all "φ" states, through the observation of behavior. The fact that a person has a specific intention means that he is directed in his action either dispositionally or actually toward the corresponding end. It can be established from the perspective of the third person that he is directed in this way through behaviorally relevant criteria. And the fact that the intention is unconscious does not mean, as is suggested by Freud's hypostatizing, 'topographical' manner of speaking, that the intention exists as a represented entity in a sphere of 'the' unconscious; rather, it means that no expressive utterance in the first person corresponds to what has been determined through observation.[1] Since an utterance in the first person would have to correspond to the third-person sentence on the basis of veridical symmetry, we can speak of self-deception: The person is directed toward an end in his action without knowing it. This makes it possible to extend the concept of untruthfulness in such a way that one can speak not only of untruthfulness in relation to others but also of an inner untruthfulness. I am untruthful only in relation to the outer world if there is a difference between what I express and what I think (or say to myself); I am untruthful in an inner sense if there is a difference "between what I am disposed to say about myself and what I am disposed to do."[2]

This account of the concept of unconscious intentions already implies their connection to conscious intentions. It is one and the same action and will, and one and the same affective state of the person that is determined both by conscious and unconscious intentions. If asked what I intend in relation to Petra, I can truthfully answer "I want to avoid her," and this does not exclude the possibility that my relationship to the same person is also unconsciously determined by different intentions, even the opposite intention. If I am asked how I feel, I can truthfully answer "irritated," without being conscious in a given case of what I am irritated about; and even when I know an answer, this does not exclude the possibility that it contains only part of the truth. The unconscious intentions, wishes, emotions, and so on are, therefore, not unknown entities, but hidden aspects of precisely those "ϕ" states of which I am conscious. This is the reason why we can say that the corresponding "I ϕ" sentences are untruthful, that is, that they represent a form of self-deception; for although these sentences are correct as far as they go, they contain only a part of the truth as answers to the overall question of what I am doing, what I intend, and how I feel. In this respect, they are untrue in the same sense that the report about any historical occurrence (such as an automobile accident) is untrue if it consists of obviously true sentences but covers up the facts as a whole by omitting essential or even the most important aspects.

Thus, in addition to those "ϕ" predicates that imply physical states of affairs, we have a second class of "ϕ" predicates whose use in the first person equally allows for error and correction; but this is not because they imply facts in another ontological category, but because the psychological states they designate stand in more comprehensive connections within the same category. Therefore, in this second class the error involves a form of self-deception, and here *self* stands for one's own "ϕ" states. The understanding of the aspect of illusion for the first class does not create any problems, since (a) it does not involve the "ϕ" state itself, and (b) the linguistic system of rules that governs the possibility of both error and correction can be recognized easily. On the other hand, although the fact that there are unconscious intentions and so on becomes more intelligible when one realizes that what is involved is merely further aspects of something that is conscious and incorrigible, it nevertheless remains something that is still unclarified up to the present day. To be sure, the recourse to a special psychoanalytical knowledge is not necessary after Freud has called attention to this phenomenon. It is an everyday fact of experience that we are conscious of our psychical states only in a restricted way, and that the boundaries of consciousness can become wider and narrower; but this phenomenon is structurally unclarified. For if "ϕ" states are defined through the fact that we have an immediate knowledge of them, it remains puzzling that there are states that are like "ϕ" states and yet are unconscious.

Freud's dynamic conception of the unconscious also can at best alleviate this problem, but cannot resolve it. The dynamic conception claims that precisely because "ϕ" states in themselves would have to be conscious, one can only make their unconsciousness intelligible by assuming that the person involved does not *want* to be conscious of them because they are painful or even unbearable; thus, they become unconscious because the person cannot help quasi closing his eyes to them, or 'repressing' them. This dynamic conception is plausible and empirically well founded. But a state that in itself is unclarified cannot be elucidated by appealing to an activity that brings it about.

Before leaving this confusing topic, I would like at least to draw attention to the fact that recollection and forgetting may occupy a key position in the elucidation of the unconscious "ϕ" states. On the one hand, recollection belongs to the class of "ϕ" states that are corrigible in relation to an objective state of affairs that they imply; on the other hand, the objective state of affairs in this case consists precisely in one's own past "ϕ" state.[3] The fact that one is mistaken about one's own past "ϕ" state is in principle no more puzzling than being mistaken about something that is currently perceived. The forgetting can also be understood in a certain sense as analogous to not perceiving something that is currently perceivable. Now if it could be shown, as Freud suggests, that the unconscious component of any present "ϕ" state is based upon the lack of consciousness of past "ϕ" states, that is, that all self-deception is founded in deception about the past, it is conceivable that the structure of self-deception could be elucidated in this way.

The fact that there are unconscious aspects of one's own "ϕ" states implies that immediate epistemic self-consciousness also stands in a tension between self-deception and self-knowledge, which I earlier noted is characteristic of that form of mediate epistemic self-con-sciousness to which the demand *gnothi seauton* pertains. This demand was related to one's own dispositions to action, volition, and emotion, that is, to what is called character. Character properties are different from unconscious "ϕ" states by virtue of the fact that they—since dispositions are involved—can in principle only be known mediately, that is, from the perspective of the third person, while the unconscious aspects of "ϕ" states *can* be known immediately (and that means expressively). But from the perspective of the demand *gnothi seauton*, no sharp boundary exists between unknown character properties and unconscious "ϕ" states: Both are factors determinative for my willing, acting, and feeling and are unknown to me. And with respect to their content, they also merge into one another: Unconscious aspects of my intentions lead to unknown volitional dispositions in me.

By virtue of its unconscious aspects immediate epistemic self-consciousness itself refers us to the practical relation of oneself to oneself. Both (a) the fact that in principle the "ϕ" states have unconscious aspects and (b) the question of where the border between the conscious and unconscious can be found at any given time seem to be grounded in the practical relation of oneself to oneself. The unconscious does not simply exist; on the contrary, if we may follow Freud, the fact that "ϕ" states are unconscious rests upon our interest in not being aware of them. In the interpretation of Freud developed in his Heidelberg dissertation, Martin Bartels seems to me to have correctly pointed out that since for Freud the phenomenon of not-knowing here in question is a "not wanting to know,"[4] "self-consciousness" is understood as an "accomplishment," "in which the individual himself delimits the range of what he wants to accept as his own being."[5] For this reason Bartels calls this accomplishment an "action that delimits consciousness." On the other hand, there is also the possibility of an interest that is opposed to the interest that sets up these limits, as was shown most convincingly by Stuart Hampshire in connection with Freud;[6] it is oriented toward widening the limits of consciousness, and making conscious as many unconscious factors as possible that determine one's own actions. As Hampshire shows, this interest in self-transparency is or is not present to the same extent as an interest in freedom. Freedom is a gradual phenomenon, just like self-consciousness; the more extensively we recognize the factors that determine our being and acting, our willing and feeling, the freer we are. For only if we are aware of them can we control them in a given situation; thus, we can relate to them selectively, deliberatively, and autonomously, that is, we can adopt such or such a position toward them.

These opposed interests are not directed toward any specific practical intentions, but are interests in which the individual is concerned with himself. The "ϕ" states are repressed by the individual, or as Freud says, by the 'ego,' because *it itself* feels threatened by them. And the interest in freedom implies that the individual is interested in determining his course of action *himself.* We thus arrive at the problem of practical self-consciousness to which I already alluded at the beginning of the semester. This concerns the question of how a relation of oneself to oneself is to be conceived structurally; for it is already presupposed by the interest in repression that one is related in one's volition and action not only to particular intentions but also somehow to 'oneself.' Furthermore, it concerns the question of how we can understand that phenomenon of practical self-consciousness which appears to have the character of a relation of oneself to oneself in an eminent sense: namely, relating oneself to oneself in the mode of self-determination.

In now moving to this second and more relevant part of the problem of self-consciousness, it might appear as if we will find much stronger motives here for assuming a relation of an ego or self to itself than in the case of theoretical self-consciousness. Such a relationship, which is postulated by the tradition deriving from Fichte, proved in the case of theoretical self-consciousness, first, to be phenomenologically undiscoverable and, second, to be absurd; finally, we were able to identify the misguided assumptions that led to this false way of posing the problem. But as soon as we are confronted with the problem of the practical relation of oneself to oneself, you might find that this conception of a self-relation in which the subject makes himself an object immediately comes to mind. Indeed, it seems to be implied when one speaks of a relation of oneself to oneself. On the other hand, we have already learned to be cautious in the face of superficial impressions that are suggested by linguistic expressions. The talk of self-consciousness also seemed to imply a self-relation—and precisely the type that Fichte assumed: a self's knowledge of itself. Thus, we should not mistake such superficial impressions for what is phenomenologically given. An alleged structure either is or is not absurd. If the alleged self-relation of A to A, in which the latter posits itself as identical with itself, turned out to be absurd for theoretical self-consciousness, it will hardly be able to prove meaningful in the context of practical self-consciousness. I have already pointed out that Heidegger, in particular, attempted to disengage the understanding of the relation of oneself to oneself from the reliance upon traditional models; I also noted that G. H. Mead called attention to previously neglected structures in the elucidation of the relation of oneself to oneself, and that the structures brought to light by Heidegger and Mead mutually complement one another. But before I examine these new approaches, we must more clearly outline the traditional conception, which is still quite common today.

This conception especially comes to mind for the understanding of a free, autonomous self-relation, that is, for the understanding of what one can call self-determination. Earlier I introduced this phenomenon myself by pointing out that we apparently have the possibility of taking a step back from our desires, the roles in which we find ourselves and the norms by which we are guided, and asking, What am I in all of this, and what is it that I myself want? As far as it goes this description might actually correspond to a phenomenological fact; but it is tempting to interpret the fact in such a way that there is a self or an ego, a kind of nucleus of the personality, that somehow can bend back or 'reflect' into itself from its concrete desires and roles and thus has a standard in itself according to which it can choose, reject, and integrate the outer and inner claims.

Conceptions of this kind appear to have a certain immediate plausibility, and they are presupposed in those empirical investigations that today are called ego psychology. In the investigations concerning 'the development of the ego,'[7] the issue is not the development of psychical structures in general, but the development of precisely that personality nucleus which is designated in some way as autonomous and integrative. It is thereby presupposed as self-evident that it is justified to speak of something called the ego, although as far as I know this presupposition has not been substantiated anywhere. It is only most recently that one can detect tendencies within ego pyschology to dispense with this hypostatizing mode of speaking, and to understand what is designated by the term *ego* as a mode of being of the person.[8] But ego psychology up to this point has not developed the conceptual means necessary for the realization of these tendencies.

The ease with which one today speaks of the ego in these connections goes back to a large extent to Freud, who relies in this mode of speaking upon the German psychological terminology of that time, which goes back to Herbart and Fichte. I do not need here to examine the development of Freud's concept of the ego from his "Project for a Scientific Psychology"[9] in 1895 to his later conception, which is developed in particular in *The Ego and the Id*.[10] Besides, the 'organization' that Freud designates as the ego comprehends essentially more 'functions' than are relevant for us here.[11] I can also refrain from discussing the additional difficulty (admittedly significant in our context) that

Freud uses the expression *the ego* quite ambiguously. On the one hand, it stands for that particular organization or power within the personality; on the other hand it also stands for the particular person as a whole—especially in his reflections concerning the problem of narcissism.[12] This is an ambiguity that Heinz Hartmann has tried to eliminate by introducing the expression *the self* for the second meaning.[13]

Freud designated as the ego that authority which decides which contents are repressed from consciousness. This function is connected to the fact that the ego is an 'organization,' which is "distinguished by an extremely remarkable striving toward unification, toward synthesis."[14] In contrast to the dispersed desires, it represents a 'unitary will,' which is time related and for which the principle of noncontradiction is valid.[15] It has a mediating function that operates first between the desires (the 'drives,' the 'id') and the reality that opposes them, and then further between the desires and the internalized norms that oppose them (the 'superego'). Thus it is a "poor thing, which stands under three different types of servitude, and accordingly suffers under the threats from three different sorts of danger—from the external world, from the id's libidinal impulses, and from the severity of the superego."[16] On the one hand, the ego is defined through this mediating function, but on the other hand a necessity for this mediating function only exists because the ego—and here we might simply say the person—has a "unitary will," which is distinguished by the "extremely remarkable striving toward unification." Freud locates the decisive factor of psychical maturation in the "strengthening of the ego."[17] What he means by this is that the ego grows out of its ancillary role in relation to its "three strict superiors"—id, reality, and superego.[18] It is thereby directed toward a form of autonomy in which it is subjected neither to the claims of the impulses nor to those of the norms, but instead learns to master them in turn. To the extent that its strength (its capacity to integrate) grows, the compulsion to resolve the conflicts through repression and mere compromise lessens. And this apparently implies that the "synthesis," which always must be carried out in one way or another, generally loses its coercive character.

In this account an aspect of freedom is ascribed to the ego that does not directly follow from the conceptual framework that Freud employs for it. If we compare Freud's conception of the ego as something standing opposed to the claims of the drives, reality, and the superego with the preliminary description that I just outlined, it is striking that Freud not only does not refer to the ordinary way of talking about the "I" but also does not even speak of a relation of oneself to oneself. The 'ego' is an objective power within the psychical reality, just like the 'id' and the 'superego'; the only difference is that in contrast to the latter it is an 'organization' and has a synthetic function. Freud hypostatizes not only the side of freedom but also the side of coercion; for he opposes the latter to the 'ego' in a quasi-personifying manner as the 'id' and the 'superego.' In so doing he stands in an old tradition. Plato already presented 'reason' and the 'passions' as powers within the soul struggling against one another. Thus, Freud himself also says: "If we adhere to the popular modes of speaking, we might say that the ego represents reason and circumspection in psychic life, while the id represents the untamed passions."[19] The following simile also brings Plato to mind: "One might compare the relation of the ego to the id with that of the rider to his horse."[20] But Plato arrived at these metaphorical modes of speaking from a phenomenological basis, namely, that of talking to oneself practically (especially in the form of self-admonition).[21] In Freud we also find a similar conception in the case of the superego. But Plato and the entire tradition of practical philosophy before Fichte were still not oriented toward a concept of the "I." This fact can be described in Freudian terminology by saying that the older tradition still had no need to distinguish between the superego and the ego, or in other words, between heteronomous and autonomous conscience. It is only since Fichte and Kierkegaard that it has seemed to us necessary to relate the question concerning the right mode of conduct not only to normative contents but also to the way and means in which I appropriate them for myself as an individual, that is, to the way in which I relate myself to myself in their appropriation. Since Freud grasps not only (like Plato) sensuality and normative consciousness but also what he calls the ego as an objective power, the ego is reduced to an anonymous organization with an integrative function. In so doing he discards precisely that aspect which was the basis for the orientation toward the expression *I:** the relation of oneself to oneself. Since Freud simply left this aspect out of consideration, he avoided the structural absurdities that result if one is intent upon understanding the relation of oneself

---

*In German no distinction is made between *I* and *ego*: The word *Ich* is used in both contexts (Trans.).

to oneself in accordance with the traditional model of the subject-object relation. Hence, Freud's own theory of the ego has the advantage of not containing absurdities, and it has only the disadvantage that it is in no sense a theory of the relation of oneself to oneself. But such a theory would have to follow from his own assumptions as soon as one attempted to translate the substantives *id*, *ego*, and *superego* into terms that are behaviorally relevant, that is, as soon as one specifies the modes of being of the person for which the substantives stand. In the case of the term *ego* this would mean examining the relation of the person to himself, and without a concept of the relationship of oneself to oneself it does not appear possible to understand something like self-determination. Moreover, it is no accident that although we find a concept of an autonomous conscience in some of Freud's followers, we do not yet find this concept in Freud's own work.

Which possibilities do the traditional ontological models offer for a structural comprehension of the relation of oneself to oneself? In raising this question I adhere to the notion, in contrast to Freud, that it seems to be a phenomenological fact that one relates oneself to oneself in one's volitions and actions. We must examine how the tradition following Fichte attempted to grasp this phenomenon. For this purpose I would like to examine the first theoretical steps that Hegel and Kierkegaard made toward comprehending this phenomenon. Since I will refer only to the first step in each writer's theory, I will not do justice to their positions. In Hegel's case I will later attempt to redress this to some extent. If you find it disturbing that important philosophers are criticized in such a cavalier manner, I suggest that you replace their names with arbitrary pseudonyms. For I am not interested in a critique of these philosophers, but in the question of which means the traditional conceptual models offer for understanding the practical relation of oneself to oneself.

Hegel deals with the practical relation of oneself to oneself in the introduction to his *Philosophy of Right* under the concept of freedom of the will. In order to understand the terminology, one must realize that it was an established part of the philosophical tradition since Aristotle to distinguish between 'sensuous,' 'immediate' volition and volition that is determined by understanding, reason, and deliberation. The two modes of volition are distinguished in that for immediate volition the scale pleasant-unpleasant is the standard, while for volition based upon deliberation the scale good-bad is employed. There are two possible answers to the question of why one does something, that is, why one wants to do something: One can say either "because I like to do it, because I find it pleasant" (the present subjective state is then the ultimate reference point), or "because I find it good"; and in the latter case this means that I have objective grounds to act in such a way. Here we encounter another established element of the entire tradition; it consists in the assumption that this second justification either (a) concerns only the relation of means to ends, with the ultimate reference point resting in pleasure—certainly not the pleasure of the present moment but of life as a whole—or (b) is a 'moral' one, and is related to a conception of the right form of life. In order to understand Hegel's terminology it is also necessary to keep in mind that in the German conceptual framework bearing a Kantian stamp the expression *will* is reserved for the 'higher faculty of desire,' namely, that form of volition which is determined or determinable by reason; on the other hand, the words *inclination* and *desire* are used for immediate volition. Thus in this terminology one cannot speak of a will in the case of animals; the word *will* always stands for a so-called free will. Kant makes a further distinction between *Wille* and *Willkür*. *Wille* in the narrow sense designates the type of volition that is *determined* by reason; *Willkür*, in contrast, designates the type of volition that is *determinable* by reason. Two concepts of freedom correspond to this distinction: For Kant the so-called positive concept of freedom stands in the foreground; according to it, the will is only free when it is determined by reason. But, of course, Kant also needs the other concept of freedom, according to which the will as *Willkür* is free insofar as one can act *either* immediately *or* deliberatively; in Kantian terms this means insofar as one can allow oneself to be determined either by inclination or by reason.[22]

Hegel supplements these traditional distinctions (as Fichte had already done) by viewing the rational will in connection with self-consciousness or the relation of oneself to oneself. With this addition, the problem to which I alluded at the beginning of the first lecture begins to exert itself: namely, the question of the connection between a form of life grounded upon reason and an autonomous self-relation. A first step in this direction can already be found in Kant, since he conceives of the rational determination of action as autonomy or self-determination. But Kant does not yet mean by autonomy a self-determination of the person as a person or of the I as an I, but a self-determination of reason.[23] It is first Fichte who attempts to understand the rationality of the person on the basis of the I's relation of itself to itself.

It is here that Hegel takes up the argument. He begins the exposition of the concept of the free will with these sentences:

The will contains (a) the element of pure indeterminacy or the pure reflection of the ego into itself, which involves the dissipation of every restriction and every content either immediately presented by nature, by needs, desires and impulses or given and determined by any means whatever. This is the unrestricted infinity of absolute abstraction or universality, the pure thought of oneself (*Philosophy of Right*, paragraph 5).

I want to limit myself now to this first step in Hegel's exposition, but we should at least take a look at the further exposition so that we are familiar with the context. The second element of the structure of the will is "(b) . . . the transition from undifferentiated indeterminacy to the differentiation, determination and positing of a determinacy" (6). Finally, "(c) The will is the unity of both these moments. . . . It is the self-determination of the ego, which means that at one and the same time the ego posits itself as its own negative, i.e. as restricted and determinate, and yet remains by itself, i.e. in its self-identity and universality. It determines itself and yet at the same time binds itself together with itself. . . . This is the freedom of the will" (7).

Thus on the one hand this reflection into oneself as against one's individual intentions, inclinations—the 'contents'—is considered one element of the freedom of the will, whereas on the other hand we have the process of allowing oneself to be determined by these contents, and finally the unification of these two moments; this unity consists in the fact that the ego identifies itself with determinate contents and nonetheless preserves the form of universality. This synthesis of the first two moments is intentionally left undefined by Hegel, because in the following paragraphs he distinguishes two forms of this synthesis on the basis of whether the contents remain external to the ego or whether the ego recognizes itself in the contents confronting it. In the first case the will is only formally free, for it can abstract from every given content but has no standard in itself (17); and since it thus remains subject to the given content in choosing, it is dependent upon the latter and therefore it is not truly free. "At this stage the freedom of the will is *Willkür*" (15). One must distinguish this will, which is free merely "in itself" or "in concept," from the free will "for itself," which has "universality, or itself qua infinite form for its content" (21). The subject is only truly free when it knows itself as one with the objectivity to which it relates itself in acting, because it is no longer dependent upon something foreign to it; and since the agreement of subjective and objective spheres constitutes the meaning of truth for Hegel, it is also only when the will is free "for itself" that it is "true, or rather the truth itself" (23).

I will examine Hegel's conception of a true and free relation of oneself to oneself later. Today I would like to limit my attention to the conceptual means that Hegel uses in addressing the problem of the relation of oneself to oneself in the first step of his exposition. The purpose of our present recourse to Hegel is only to assist in answering the question of which possibilities the traditional ontological models offer for structurally comprehending the relation of oneself to oneself. Let me once more recall the fact with which I began—it was something that I claimed could be considered a phenomenological fact. It is the fact that in all one's action and volition one is always somehow related to oneself, and that this relation of oneself to oneself is realized in a special way when one reflectively asks, Am I really myself in what I am doing? What is it that I myself want? Obviously it is precisely this fact that Hegel attempts to grasp in his exposition of the freedom of the will. He also provides an answer to the demand for a model of an autonomous relation of oneself to oneself with this concept of the true, free will that is for itself, but I will defer consideration of this aspect, since it constitutes a higher level. At the outset the question is merely this: How is the relation of oneself to oneself grasped structurally?

Two of the traditional models that we were earlier able to identify for the problem of epistemic self-consciousness are united in Hegel's approach to the problem—the model of the substance with its accidents (determinations) and the subject-object model. The different inclinations and so on of the person are understood as the determinations of the ego. And it is then said that the "reflection of the ego into itself" is characteristic of the ego (5). This reflection 'into itself' is the practical counterpart to the reflection 'upon oneself' that we encountered in the traditional conception of epistemic self-consciousness. The subject can now practically 'abstract' from his objects, as he earlier did theoretically, and turn himself back upon himself: In the relation of oneself to oneself the subject himself becomes the object.

By uniting these two models—that of the substance with its determinations and the subject-object model—the relations contained in both of them are made dynamic: As we already saw in the case of Fichte's conception of theoretical self-consciousness, the ego not only is identical with itself but also 'posits' itself as such, and it has its determinations not simply in itself, but it is a "transition . . . to differentiation, determination and positing of a determinacy as a content and object" (6); and the union of the two moments is similarly a "positing" (7). Of course, one can say (and in fact it is customary to say) that German Idealism 'overcame' the substance model precisely through this process of dynamization. But in the first place it is questionable whether it is necessary at all to overcome the substance model rather than merely to supplement it; second—and this is obviously the main consideration—the conceptual terms by which this dynamization is effected are obscure; and third, it seems that because it is merely 'dynamized,' the substance model is retained. We already saw earlier that the concept of positing, which Hegel uses as if it were self-evident, is unclear. This lack of clarity increases even more when one combines the concepts of identity and difference with that of positing by speaking of a positing of identity and self-identity and a positing of difference and self-differentiation. If these expressions have a trace of intelligibility, it is only because in the sphere of the will actions must be involved. Since Fichte understood the structure of "I = I" as the most fundamental action (as the action of self-positing), the concept of action, which rightly attained a central position in German Idealism, was improperly linked with the ontological concepts of being, identity, and difference, so that these were turned into pseudoconcepts. It thereby became possible to incorporate actions within the dynamic substance model, and thus to leave the actual concept of action unelucidated. In our text of Hegel this had the consequence that the entire thematic of "freedom of the will" is developed on the foundation of an abstract ontological framework in which one speaks only of an ego, its 'contents' and 'determinations'; the phenomenological basis for concepts such as the will, inclination, and decision is not worked out at all, but these concepts are merely grafted onto the dynamic ('dialectical') conceptual framework of ontology.

The main difficulty for our problem of the relation of oneself to oneself, however, lies not in the dynamized substance model but in the subject-object model. The reflection of an ego "into itself," which is understood in a practical sense, is afflicted with the same structural absurdities as the reflection of an ego "upon itself," which is understood in a theoretical sense. If one understands the word *reflection* literally as a bending back toward oneself, we can associate a distinctly vivid image with this, but how does such an image contribute to the understanding of the relation of oneself to oneself? Let us therefore refrain from entertaining such figurative conceptions, and instead attempt to focus upon what is termed reflexive in logic; this consists of a relation that an object has to itself and only to itself, so that the following applies for some x and y: x R y, only if x = y. This relation would not be described simply by characterizing it as reflection, but the question of what constitutes the reflexive relation that is assumed in this formula would now first have to be raised.

Is seems to me the best one can do with the talk of a "reflection into oneself" is to formulate the question in this way. We thereby would have freed the question at least in small measure from the subject-object model. For it now no longer would be presumed that this relation of the subject to itself is a representing of itself or otherwise analogous to a relation that the subject supposedly has to objects. But is seems to me that as soon as we have reduced the talk of a reflection upon or into oneself to its formal structure, it becomes evident how useless it is for elucidating the relation of oneself to oneself, and this is clear precisely in light of this formal structure. In the case of theoretical self-consciousness as well, the difficulty was based, not on some peculiar characteristic of the so-called subject-object relation, but on the fact that both intentional consciousness in general and self-consciousness in particular were supposed to be a relation of something to *something*; in both cases the fact that intentional consciousness is propositional was overlooked. Since knowledge is involved in the case of theoretical self-consciousness, it was indeed easy to show from the outset that it consists formally in an intentional relation to a proposition; the "self" of which I have knowledge is a specific proposition that I ϕ. You might, however, raise the following question: Isn't the practical relation of oneself to oneself to be distinguished from epistemic self-consciousness precisely by virtue of the fact that the 'self' to which a person relates himself is not propositional, but is simply he himself or his ego? I have not yet advanced far enough at the present stage of our reflections to be able to show that this is not the case, and thus at first I intend only to oppose one view to the other: I do not believe that there is a nonpropositional relation of oneself to oneself, and in any case I cannot conceive of anything that conforms to this concept. If my intuition is correct, we would also have to expect for the practical relation of oneself to oneself (although it is not as evident here) that the second 'self' in this expression must be capable of expansion into propositional form in the same way as the 'self' of epistemic self-consciousness. The question would only be: How?

A first indication that not only my own subjective intuition is involved can be seen in the fact that at any rate all practical (volitional-emotional) relating of oneself to other persons is propositional. The grammar of the relevant expressions discloses this almost immediately for the volitional relation of oneself to others: An "I want" that is related to another person always requires an entire subordinate clause as its grammatical object. This is not as obvious for emotional expressions such as *to fear* or *to love*. In the case of *fear* the grammatical object of the verb is sometimes an expression that stands for a person, whereas in the case of *love* this is always true. I indicated earlier that these intentional relations are also at least implicitly propositional because they imply a belief about existence. But one can and must go further here. "I fear N" is obviously a shortened version of "I fear that N can do something harmful to me." "I love N" is a shortened version of "I am glad that he exists, I want things to go well for him, I want to be together with him," and so on. A corresponding relation is evident for all of the other verbs that stand for a relation of oneself to a person.

You will point out that very little has been gained by this, because the relation of oneself to oneself is simply different from the relation of oneself to others. Certainly! The propositional structure of the relation of oneself to others is intended only as a hint. Nevertheless, this hint acquires more force when one considers that there is, as far as I can see, only a single intentional or mental relation that is only implicitly propositional—on account of the presupposed existence implication— and not itself propositionally expandable; this is the relation of *reference* in the sense in which one says, for example, that "by *him* I am referring to Mr. X." If this is correct, it would mean that the only intentional relation to a simple object is one that consists in the use of a singular term; indeed, this is in fact the only intentional relation that clearly cannot be propositional, because it is precisely the function of a singular term to serve as that independent part of a propositional expression which specifies which object the remaining part of the propositional expression is to characterize. Thus it would be, to say the least, very curious if in addition to the relation of 'reference' there were *another* nonpropositional intentional relation, the relation of oneself to oneself; or in other words, if in addition to the possibility of referring to oneself there were another way of relating oneself to oneself. It is no wonder that in view of such a peculiar state of affairs it is tempting to say that the one who refers to himself by means of the word *I* is the person; the one who relates himself to himself is the 'ego,' a nucleus within the person. But one hopes no argument is necessary to show that such a doctrine of two persons would be absurd. It is one and the same being who says "I" and who relates himself to himself.

Can we give the talk of reflection another sense than that of a reflexive relation? It is obviously possible and it also seems well founded to understand the talk of reflection, not in the sense of a relation of the person to himself, but in the sense of a relation of the person to his own further behavior. In this sense one can also designate epistemic self-consciousness as reflection: From a formal point of view it is a relation of knowledge to one's own states, although we saw that the conception of this knowledge as a relation is misleading. But it only now becomes clear why there is so much resistance to understanding the practical relation of oneself to oneself propositionally. It is obvious that this resistance is not merely based upon the reliance upon the subject-object model, as is the case for epistemic self-consciousness; rather, the conception of the relation of oneself to oneself as a relation to one's own behavior appears to contradict the fact that a relation to *oneself* should be at issue here, and not a relation to this or that behavior. But this formulation of our problem seems to suggest a possible perspective on its solution: The task would consist in identifying a distinctive bearing of the person that does not represent a specific behavior but constitutes the basis of all specific behavior; we would be able to say of this phenomenon that insofar as the person relates himself to this bearing, he relates himself to himself. Thus the task would involve the identification of a distinctive propositional state of affairs that fulfills this condition.

Kierkegaard came close to apprehending this phenomenon, though he remained enmeshed in the inadequate traditional terminology that he adopted from German Idealism. At the present stage of our reflections it is worth taking a brief look at his approach. His fundamental structural characterization of the relation of oneself to oneself is to be found in the opening sentences of *Sickness unto Death*:

Man is spirit. But what is spirit? Spirit is the self. But what is the self? The self is a relation which relates itself to its own self, or it is that in the relation by virtue of which the relation relates itself to its own self.

Kierkegaard attempts to break away from the substance model decisively by no longer speaking of a subject that relates itself to itself; he speaks instead of a 'relation.' Indeed, Hegel also meant the same thing. But it is a mistake to think that one evades the real structural difficulty by treating the thing that relates itself to itself as the 'relation' of the subject instead of as the subject itself. The difficulty lies in the concept of a reflexive relation of a to a, regardless of whether by "a" one means the subject or its relation in whatever way one understands it; for in the latter case the relation itself would have a subject-object relation to itself.

Nevertheless, Kierkegaard makes a distinction between a first relation that is a relation of the subject and a second relation that is that of reflection. This provides a justification for modifying Kierkegaard's description of the structure, so that one gets rid of the unintelligible idea of a reflexive relation; and this can be done by restoring a restricted domain of validity to the substance model and insisting that it is the person who relates himself to his relation.

Whether this formulation makes sufficient sense depends upon the question that I left open just before—namely, what the character of the relation is to which the person relates himself. Now Kierkegaard understands the word *relation* here, not in the sense of a mode of behavior, but in the sense of "an objective relation"; and indeed in this case a "relation between two elements" or a "synthesis" is supposed to be involved. Kierkegaard understands human existence as a precarious synthesis of antithetical factors, as a "synthesis of the finite and the infinite, the temporal and the eternal, freedom and necessity." As long as that to which the person relates himself is described merely as a relation between two antithetical factors, it remains unintelligible, of course, in what sense the person relates himself to himself in relating himself to this relation. This difficulty could remain unnoticed by Kierkegaard himself because he mistakenly identified the relation of oneself to oneself with a reflexive relation that the relation has to itself. If, as I just proposed, one does not adhere to this, then one will have to determine what lies at the basis of this synthesis; this is something that is not explicitly disclosed by Kierkegaard. If one were to take Kierkegaard literally, it would appear as if the basis of the structure of the 'self' were composed of the two elements of possibility and necessity, between which there existed a relation that related itself to itself. But this can only mean, of course, that possibility and necessity—and whatever else is to be brought into the synthesis—are not subsistent elements, as Kierkegaard's traditional substantival mode of speaking suggests, but that they are determinations of something; and the question now is, Determinations of what? It certainly conforms to his further analysis if we say that possibility and necessity are antithetical determinations or features of human existence or human life.

If we look at it this way, *possibility* and *necessity* are not expressions that stand for something substantial; but also they are not predicates that are directly to be applied to the person; rather they are second-order predicates that characterize the existence or life of the person. When Kierkegaard's conception is spelled out completely, it contains three different 'relations': (1) the person's behavior in the sense of his existence, which is not especially brought to light by Kierkegaard, (2) the relation in the sense of a relation between the fundamental determinations of existence, and (3) the person's relation of himself to his existence. Since one's existence is determined by the second relation—the 'synthesis'—the person's relation of himself to his existence is a relation of himself to this synthesis. And, of course, the converse of this sentence also holds: The person's relation of himself to the synthesis is a relation of the person himself to his existence, and *this means* it is a relation of himself to himself. With this implicit reference to the existence of the person Kierkegaard hit upon the special propositional state of affairs that we were seeking; it thus becomes possible to speak of a relation of oneself to oneself that does not have the structure of a reflexive relation. That to which the person relates himself in relating himself to himself is neither he himself as an entity nor his various modes of behavior, determinations, or actions, but the relation of himself underlying these determinations, which one can call the existence or life of the person.

The question of whether this is a correct interpretation of Kierkegaard is, of course, secondary for us. If one claims that an author obscures what he really means by relying on traditional concepts, and that he only implicitly refers to a structure, then it is no longer crucial whether one is still entitled to identify the result with the author. I certainly believe that it is only on the basis of this interpretation that Kierkegaard's conception becomes free of absurdities. But the interpretation of Kierkegaard is not an end in itself for us. Its outcome has yielded an important consequence for our argument: We have found a possible answer to the question of the structure of a relation of oneself to oneself in which the relation does not take a reflexive form but has a propositional structure; it consists in my relating to the fact that I exist.

This result also fully harmonizes with what was disclosed in the case of the relation of oneself to other persons. We saw that the so-called intentional relations to others are modes of relating oneself to their modes of behavior; and to the extent that the relation of oneself to the other person is not a relation of oneself to this or that mode of his behavior, but a relation of oneself to this person *himself*—for example, when we respect or despise, love or hate him—it is a relation of oneself to his existence, a saying of yes or no to his existence. The relation of oneself to oneself appears in the same way to stand in a tension between self-love and self-hate, and a saying of yes or no to one's own existence seems to rest upon this. In the same way that we want things to go well for someone we like, we always want things to go well for ourselves (and we will have to investigate what this means). This structural correspondence between the relation of oneself to oneself and the relation of oneself to others is, to be sure, limited. What Kierkegaard means by the establishment of synthesis in the relation of oneself to oneself—the freedom to determine oneself or to fail to be oneself—has no corresponding feature in the relation of oneself to others.

What we have gained up to now is only a starting point: the possibility of understanding the relation of oneself to oneself propositionally, as a self-relation, not of the person to the person, but of the person to his life, his existence. The absurdities of the traditional model are thereby eliminated, but it is still uncertain whether the perspective that now has been gained can provide what is required. It is at first unclear what *existence* means here; further, it is unclear how we must grasp the relation of oneself to this propositional fact of one's existence if it is to be understood, not as a form of epistemic self-consciousness, but as a practical relation of oneself to one's own actions. Finally, in what sense can the relation of oneself to one's own existence provide the basis for understanding something like self-determination?

These are precisely the questions that define Heidegger's point of departure. Whereas Kierkegaard understood existence in terms that were structurally traditional, Heidegger attempted to sever the understanding of the existence of human beings from the traditional concept of existence, and to show that a relation of oneself to oneself can be found precisely in the relation of oneself to one's own existence. Moreover, he argued that this relation corresponds to the phenomenological facts, and is free from the paradoxes of the earlier theories of self-consciousness that resulted from the reliance on the subject-object model. We will have to see how far he advances on this basis, since his method is intuitive and phenomenological and lacks the discipline that is demanded by the analysis of language.

Lecture 8

Heidegger on the Relation of Oneself to Oneself, I: The Approach

The interpretation of Heidegger's theory of the relation of oneself to oneself as developed in *Being and Time* has a special significance for this course of lectures as a whole, in both a substantive and a methodological sense. Its significance is substantive because Heidegger succeeded in displaying the fundamental structure of the relation of oneself to oneself, although this has hardly been understood up to now; and all of the theories that are perhaps more comprehensive, such as Mead's or the one based on the notion of an 'ego identity,' must be integrated within it if they are to attain structural coherence. It has special methodological importance because here the language-analytical interpretation of pre-analytic philosophy must demonstrate its strength in a constructive sense. The language-analytical interpretation had to exhibit its destructive side more strongly in those cases in which we were dealing with a phenomenologically unverifiable approach to a problem resting on opaque traditional models, for example, in the case of the Heidelberg school or the conceptual constructions of German Idealism. In Heidegger's case we are confronting a completely different methodological situation. For he himself was concerned with radically placing the traditional concepts and structures into question, and he attempted this by means of a descriptive method and by recourse to the 'phenomena'; and in this he went much farther than analytic philosophy. But since his descriptive method lacked a criterion of verifiability, his ideas remained intuitive and unproven theses, as we shall soon see; for this reason they require language-analytical examination.

The application of a language-analytical interpretation is not only justified here in the sense in which it is justified for every type of philosophy, that is, insofar as every reflection upon concepts is raised to the level of an inquiry that can be checked and verified only by assuming the form of linguistic analysis—rather, Heidegger's philosophy is receptive to linguistic analysis from the outset, since for Heidegger the subject of philosophy is understanding, that is, language, and he understands his "phenomenological description" as "interpretation," and his method accordingly as "hermeneutic" (BT, pp. 61–62).* But Heidegger did not try to work out any criteria for such a hermeneutic method; and his procedure in fact remained closely oriented toward Husserl's conception of intuitive generalization or an intuition of essences, although the object of analysis is no longer, as in Husserl's case, contents of consciousness or 'experiences' but understanding. In this way Heidegger surrendered even that—albeit questionable—degree of verifiability which Husserl still had at his disposal. The only thing that remained was language, and this in itself was correct. But in the first place Heidegger committed one of his gravest mistakes when, in radicalizing Husserl's idea of pre-predicative experience, he also regarded the orientation toward the *logos*, the statement and the sentence in general as a traditional prejudice (section 7B, section 33); the orientation toward the individual word became the standard for him—granted, not yet explicitly in *Being and Time*, though it was implicit in his methodological procedure. Second, the orientation toward words remained methodologically unchecked, since Heidegger does not attempt to specify their modes of use; this is true both in those cases in which he attends to existing words—as in the case of the word *being*—and in those cases in which he coins new words for the designation of a structure he finds intuitively evident. This has the consequence that the communicative character of his procedure remains evocative: Those essential connections that the author intuits are to be evoked in the reader by means of words. This is where the starting point for the language-analytical interpretation is to be found. It will be necessary again and again to ask to what extent the insights that Heidegger only evokes can be translated into controllable statements. In part, I will only be able to elaborate the difficulties and to indicate the direction in which I think further interpretive work would have to go.

*All pages citations from *Being and Time* refer to the Macquarrie and Robinson translation (New York, 1962) (Trans.).

I will proceed with the interpretation of the conception of the relation of oneself to oneself as developed in *Being and Time* in three steps. In the first step I want to explain in its general significance Heidegger's thesis that the relation of oneself to oneself is a relation, not to oneself as an entity, but to one's being, to one's existence. In the second step, which I will only reach in the next lecture, I will interpret Heidegger's elaboration of this structure through his explication of consciousness of one's own being as temperament (*Befindlichkeit*) and understanding. The third step will be devoted to the question of how on this basis Heidegger can explicate the phenomenon of that exemplary relation of oneself to oneself which is referred to as self-determination.

First, we must clarify the context within which Heidegger analyzes the relation of oneself to oneself. The object of inquiry in *Being and Time* is the question of the "meaning of being." Heidegger regards this question as the most comprehensive philosophical question, and through it he believes that he can evade all the mistakes and confusions of modern as well as ancient philosophy (cf. BT, section 6). He thinks the errors of ancient philosophy can be evaded in this way because it raised the question of being, but not the question of the meaning of being; rather, it presupposed as self-evident that being has the meaning of being-present-at-hand (*Vorhandenheit*). In contrast to ancient thought, which was oriented toward being and substance, modern philosophy asked the question, Why precisely being as the universal horizon of inquiry? Why not rather the subject, knowledge, life, history, society? And Heidegger's thesis is that in these modern concepts the ancient sense of being is actually implicitly retained. The subject, history, and so one also *are* in some way or other. But then the point is not to grasp them as concepts that are opposed to being in general, but rather only as concepts opposed to a specific sense of being; and one must now ask in what sense they themselves possess being. And thus the real task in relation to modern as well as ancient philosophy is to raise the question of the *meaning* of being. The fact that by means of this question Heidegger has a perspective in mind that advances beyond the modern concepts can be seen in his thesis—which admittedly always remained only a thesis—that in opposing (or in deepening) the ancient orientation toward being-present-at-hand the meaning of being is to be understood in the context of *time* (section 5); hence the title of the book. In contrast, the subject-object model fundamental for modern philosophy is, according to Heidegger, the result of the unreflected adoption of the Greek orientation toward a representation of the present-at-hand.

But perhaps you may find that this entire way of posing the question is difficult to comprehend or quite nebulous. Whenever we used overly grandiose expressions in his seminars, Heidegger time and again demanded, "Let's have the small change." This is a demand that we also continually will have to apply to him himself in the course of the interpretation. "Being," the "meaning of being"—what does this mean? How do we attain an understanding of what is meant? Being—this is not any arbitrary thing, an object; an object would rather be something, that is, a being, and we have to distinguish the individual thing from its being, as Heidegger tells us.

It seems that we only find the being of entities, their "is," in language. Thus, the question of the meaning of being appears to be the question of the sense of the word *is* in its different meanings. Did Heidegger intend it in this way? By insisting upon the question of the *meaning* of being did he want to return to the question of what we mean by the expressions *being* and *is* in opposition to the established terminological use of *being* in traditional ontology? It might seem this way, since Heidegger begins his book with the following quote from Plato: "For manifestly you have long been aware of what you mean when you use the expression 'being'. We, however, who used to think we understood it, have now become perplexed." Heidegger continues: "Do we in our time have an answer to the question of what we really mean by the word 'being'? Not at all. So it is fitting that we should raise anew *the question of the meaning of being*." I have written the last two sentences on the blackboard so that you can immediately recognize the ambiguity: In the first sentence the talk is explicitly of the word *being*, and for that reason *being* stands in quotation marks; but in the second sentence it remains open as to whether the word is still meant, and that it is not the word that is meant is indicated by the fact that *being* no longer stands in quotation marks.[1]

Thus, from the very outset we encounter a fatal lack of clarity stemming from Heidegger's ambivalence toward language. On the one hand, he intends the question of the meaning of being as a question concerning the meaning of the word *being*; but on the other hand he does not intend it in this way. He too remained subject to the traditional prejudice that as long as one appeals only to language one does not get at the thing itself. The question of the meaning of being is not at all to be understood merely as a question of the meaning of this word, but as a question of the meaning of being itself. But if the question is not understood as a question of the meaning of the word *being*, it remains obscure as to what the question about the meaning of being is supposed to signify, and what *being* is to signify. And indeed it remains necessarily obscure; if someone says *being* and thereby thinks that he has evoked something that is not merely what we understand when we understand the word, this does not allow for elucidation as a matter of principle. For the sole possibility of an elucidation would consist in recourse to the word.

In this respect an ambiguity in the word *meaning* is also involved. We speak not only of the meaning of linguistic expressions but also of the meaning of actions; and correspondingly we employ the word *understanding* not merely in the sense of understanding linguistic expressions and other signs but also in the sense of understanding an action, or something produced by an action (a work), or finally a person (in his actions). The question of meaning here always implies something like this: What does the or an agent intend by this, what is he aiming at? Ultimately the talk of the meaning of a linguistic expression is also a special case of this talk of the meaning of an action. For the question of what sense—what meaning—a linguistic sign has means something like, What does one intend to say with it, what function does the expression have? In those cases in which we have linguistic expressions that on the basis of their meaning stand for something that itself has or can have meaning—in particular an action—the possibility of a progressive series of questions arises. For example, what sense does *mountain climbing* have, that is, what meaning does this expression have? What is the sense of mountain climbing, that is, what does one attain in doing this? In these cases it is clear that (a) two sharply distinguished questions are at issue, and (b) the second question presupposes that the first has been answered. Now there is a meaning of the word *being* for which the question of meaning can be posed in precisely this serialized fashion, namely, of being in the sense of human existence or life. The life of a person is the entire connection of his actions. For this reason we also ask about a meaning in relation to the life of a person, in particular, in relation to one's own life—and here with a special concern: Is something aimed at by it, or what is it that I myself intend with it? In the case of this being—but also only in this case—what the question of the meaning of being signifies is thus intelligible, but it is derivative with regard to the question of the meaning of the word *being*; this is all the more clear in this case, because it is possible only with regard to *one* of the meanings of the word *being*. It can be surmised from section 32 of BT (pp. 193ff.) that Heidegger actually had this further question of the meaning of one's own being in view in connection with the question of the meaning of *being*. But he did not distinguish between these two questions, and this has further contributed to the lack of clarity of his question concerning the meaning of being.

If Heidegger's question as to the meaning of being were not meant ambiguously, that is, if he had intended it unequivocally as a question of the meaning of the word, then the unavoidable first step would have been to ask whether this word has a unitary meaning at all. And if—as is obviously the case—it has different meanings, one must ask whether a unitary connection exists between them. For it is only when this has been clarified that there is an evident sense to raising the question of *the* meaning of *being*. Heidegger mentions in passing several meanings of *being* (p. 26), but he assumes as self-evident that they stand under a unitary meaning. In truth this is by no means self-evident; it is not clear that being in the sense of existence, being in the sense of the copula, being in the sense of identity, and being in the sense of truth (as when we say "it is as you say") are to be brought under a uniform meaning. But this implies that what Heidegger is talking about in raising the question of the meaning of being remains unclear not only when he passes over the meaning of the word but also when he considers it.

Nevertheless, Heidegger furnishes us with two indications on whose basis we can extrapolate his intention in raising the question of the meaning of *being*. The first indication is that according to Heidegger we can only clarify *being* by recourse to the understanding of *being*, the '*Seinsverständnis*' (section 2). This is the specifically 'transcendental' turn by means of which Heidegger distinguishes himself from traditional, objectivistic ontology. But beyond this Heidegger talks in such a way as if *all* human understanding is based upon an understanding of *being*. For this reason one might also conceive of Heidegger's undertaking—the question of the meaning of *being*—as a question about the essence of human understanding. The thesis then appears to be that the understanding of a certain word—the word *being*—somehow underlies all other understanding. This would imply, of course, that in relation to understanding only the understanding of sentences is at issue, since the word *being* only occurs in sentences. But it does not occur in all sentences. A second indication helps us further here. In the lecture *What Is Metaphysics?*, which appeared two years after *Being and Time*, Heidegger advanced the thesis (which was already implicit in *Being and Time*) that there is only an understanding of being in conjunction with an understanding of nothing; and if we dispense with the tendency to speak only in substantives (which Heidegger shares with the tradition) and replace the talk of the 'nothing' with the word *not*, it follows that Heidegger wants to grasp the extension of the word *is* in strict correlation with the use of the word *not*. Thus, according to his conception it is the connection between affirmation and negation—the yes/no—that underlies the understanding of sentences; and if understanding extends even further, it underlies this as well. This is the interpretation that I attempted to provide in my essay "The Language-Analytical Critique of Ontology." It certainly does not correspond exactly to Heidegger's self-understanding, but it is the best I could make of Heidegger's question of being; and as far as I know, it is the only attempt that has been made up to now to understand what Heidegger means by *being* in a way that can be intersubjectively checked.

How does Heidegger get from the question of the meaning of *being* to the question of man's relation of himself to himself? We have just seen that Heidegger conceives of the question of the meaning of being as a question of man's understanding of being. Heidegger explains that human beings have an understanding of being by appealing to the fact that they have an understanding of their own being, that they relate to their own being in the mode of understanding (p. 32). Note that if we are talking about an understanding of one's own being, it is clear on the basis of the reflections just advanced that we can speak not only of an understanding of *being* but also of an understanding of being; this is a complication to which Heidegger himself never pays attention. Now if one accepts the interpretation of what Heidegger means by *being* that I just offered, the thesis that all understanding of being is based upon the understanding of one's own being means that the yes/no structure in general is founded upon the particular yes/no relation that we have to our own being. This connection does not appear justified in the form in which it is presented in the introduction of BT. The justification is prepared only in the third chapter of the first division, and it was to be carried out in the third division of the work, which Heidegger did not write. In the third chapter of the first division Heidegger develops the thesis that all understanding and knowledge of entities is based upon an understanding of the world, whereby *world* is understood, not as the "totality of entities," but as "relative to human Dasein."[2] One might interpret it to mean the totality of situations of action. I would like to leave open the question of whether we can elaborate a proof from this starting point that would establish that the relation of understanding to one's own being as being-in-the-world underlies the understanding of being in general. The fact that the third division of BT was not written shows in any case that Heidegger himself encountered difficulties in attempting to elaborate this proof. For our purposes the correctness of the thesis plays no role. Nonetheless, the thesis itself can only be welcome to us, for it had the consequence that the undertaking that was originally conceived as the question of the meaning of *being* actually turned into the question of the self-understanding of human beings in the sense of their relation to their own being.

The way in which Heidegger grasps a human being's relation to his own being as understanding is formulated on page 32, and this approach is further elucidated beginning on page 67. To begin with, a preliminary terminological remark is necessary, so that the quotations do not remain unintelligible. Heidegger does not speak of human beings or persons, but employs the term *Dasein*. On page 32 he says, "This entity (man) we denote by the term Dasein." He justifies this later by saying that man is "his there"; and the word *there* is explained by the claim that it stands for the "disclosedness" of this entity (pp. 171ff.). The word *disclosure* (*Erschlossenheit*) is again a fundamental term of BT, which Heidegger obviously chose in place of the word *consciousness*; this is because he wanted to get away from Husserl's concept of an intentional consciousness directed toward objects, and he needed a wider concept for which even the word *understanding* was not sufficient. Understanding is a mode of disclosure for him, but moods are also modes of disclosure. In light of Heidegger's evocative use of words it is no wonder that he did not explain the word *disclosure*; this task is no doubt further complicated by the fact that it involved a technical term coined by Heidegger himself. If he had written in English, perhaps he might have chosen the word *awareness*; there is no equivalent for this in German, and its meaning seems to me to come closest to what Heidegger means by *disclosure*. If you recall the difficulties that arose in trying to define the word *consciousness*, you will not want to take Heidegger too severely to task on this point. The situation is substantially worse in the case of the expression *Dasein*. The problem with this term is not so much that the expression *da* (Eng. "there") is unclear, but that the word *Dasein*, just like the word *consciousness*, is a *singulare tantum*: In contrast to the substantive predicates "human being" or "person" it has no plural, and therefore it seems absurd when Heidegger says that he wants to designate this entity, man, as Dasein. One cannot adopt a different expression for a word when it has a different grammar. In so doing Heidegger remains entrapped in precisely the tradition he wants to overcome; for *the* consciousness was analyzed in just the same way that he analyzes *the* Dasein. Although Heidegger subsequently also analyzes the relation of oneself to others (as the theory of consciousness ultimately did as well), a peculiar and misguided egocentrism nonetheless survives as a result of this reliance on a *singulare tantum*. I cannot see how the introduction of the term *Dasein* has had any positive sense. It is only a stylistic device that has unfortunate consequences, and we can better appropriate Heidegger's contribution to our complex of problems if we refrain as far as possible from the use of this term.

Heidegger presents his most crucial statements about the relation of oneself to one's own being abruptly and dogmatically. They also stand in the context of the conflation of the question of being with the question of the being of man, which we just discussed. Thus it is not clear that they are to be understood as an answer to the question of how a human being relates himself to himself, an answer that stands antithetically opposed to the conception that he relates himself to himself reflexively in such a way that the subject himself turns into his own object. It becomes amply clear from the later arguments (§25) that this antithesis is not simply my own interpretive addition, but that it is intended by Heidegger as the foil to his own formulation. The crucial sentence that Heidegger begins with reads: "Dasein is an entity. . . [for which] in its very being that being is an *issue* for it" (p. 32). He then further elucidates: "The essence" of Dasein lies in the fact "that in each case it has its being to be, and has it as its own." He concludes by drawing the following consequence: "But in that case it pertains to this constitution of the being of Dasein that in its being it has a relation of being to this being. . . . It is peculiar to this entity that with and through its being this being is disclosed to it itself." And this means that it has an "understanding of being," an understanding of this being that it "has to be."

The first question that arises is what is meant here by *being (Sein)*. Though what Heidegger means by the universal question of being is unclear, it is nonetheless relatively clear what he means in the present concrete connection by *being*, by "the being" of a particular human being. What is meant is obviously his existence. Heidegger appears to confirm this, since in the same connection he says, "The being . . . to which Dasein . . . always relates itself in some way we call existence." But at the point at which Heidegger resumes his exposition on page 67, he emphasizes that he does not intend the word *existence* to be understood in the sense of the traditional concept of existence: "But here our ontological task is to show that when we choose to designate the being of this entity as 'existence,' this term does not and cannot have the ontological meaning of the traditional term 'existentia'; ontologically existentia is tantamount to being-present-at-hand, a mode of being which is essentially inappropriate to entities of Dasein's character. To avoid confusion we shall always use the interpretive expression 'presence-at-hand' for the term 'existentia', while the term 'existence' as a determination of being will be allotted solely to Dasein."

If one is content with such a sheer opposition of existence in the traditional sense and existence in Heidegger's sense, however, there is nothing at all to be understood here. Heidegger would have made himself much more intelligible if he had acknowledged a general generic concept for existence, and then had distinguished between existence in the sense of being-present-at-hand and existence in the sense of to-be. The fact that he did not do this is not simply an oversight, of course, for the admisssion of a unitary genus would have contradicted Heidegger's tendency toward the total opposition of his conception to the traditional one. We will repeatedly encounter this tendency toward a total opposition in the further course of our interpretation; it is a self-stultifying intention that has repeatedly hindered clarification. In the concrete case it is a requirement of the language-analytical interpretation that first the grammatical position of that being which Heidegger has in mind must be fixed before it can be more precisely elucidated; and it is this grammatical position which constitutes the generic unity linking this being and the general concept of existence. The grammatical position of this "is" is, as one usually says, that it is used 'absolutely', i.e., as an independent predicate with a noun or pronoun; for example, "I am" or "he is no longer."

The justification of this concept of existence has been called into question in analytic philosophy. For it can be shown that normal existence sentences like "unicorns exist" are only syntactically, not semantically, predicative sentences; for example, in the sentence "unicorns exist" existence is not predicated of unicorns, but the sentence means that among all real objects there are some that are unicorns. Thus, such sentences are in reality general sentences, and existence has the meaning that is expressed in modern logic by the existential quantifier. It also can be shown that singular existence sentences like "the devil exists" actually have this structure as well. The sentence means that "among all real objects there is one and only one to which the attribute of being-Satan belongs." I am only summarizing the conclusions here, and I must refer you to the literature for the arguments.[3] I can only pursue the ontological problems here as far as is necessary for our present context.

This also holds for the next step.[4] We must now note that not all singular existence sentences can be understood as general sentences in the suggested way. It would follow from the thesis that all existence sentences are general that it is meaningless to predicate existence of an individual object. But in the case of material objects, which come into being and pass away and have a continuous existence in time, it is essential to be able to speak of their existence as individuals, for otherwise we would not be able to say that they begin to be, that they cease to be, and that they exist from such and such a time to such and such a time. Now these formulations also show that in such sentences we do not predicate existence pure and simple of an object, but we always predicate it in connection with a temporal reference, and if necessary with a spatial reference ("he existed at such and such a time in such and such a place"). If the material object at issue is a living being, one can also speak of life instead of being or existence. "He existed at such and such a time in such and such a place" means the same thing as "he lived at such and such a time in such and such a place," and "he is no longer" means the same thing as "he no longer lives." This shows that existence in the present sense really is a predicate; however, it is not a predicate that can be used absolutely, since the temporal reference pertains to it explicitly or implicitly. But it would also be false to maintain that existing in this sense simply means living, and to think that we could evade the ambiguity of the concept of existence in this way. For there are, of course, also material objects that do not live and in relation to which we nonetheless have to be able to speak of a beginning and an end and a continuation of their existence. Thus, living is that special case of existing which is characterized by the fact that a process is necessary within the living being in order for it to maintain itself in existence, that is, a process of self-preservation; and since such a being exists precisely as long as this process lasts, one can equate this process—living—with its existence.

Why is it that in the case of spatiotemporal objects general existence sentences fail to suffice? Why are singular existence sentences also necessary here, and how is their meaning to be understood? I can only intimate an answer here.[5] All predicative speech only has meaning with reference to something, that is, an object, and this must be identifiable. In the case of spatiotemporal predication space and time constitute the unified dimension of identifiability. Therefore, the presupposition of predicating something of a spatiotemporal object is that this object is identifiable relative to space and time, and it is this relation that receives expression in the singular existence sentence. In Heidegger's terminology one might say this: The fact that a material object is or exists means that it is present (anwesend) during a specific period of time somewhere in space (and this holds correspondingly for the other kind of spatiotemporal objects, i.e., events).[6] Existence in the sense of singular existence sentences signifies presence, and this is to be understood as a relational predicate that refers to spatial and temporal positions. I can leave the question open here as to whether it is still possible to reduce existence in this sense to the existential quantifier (as I once maintained),[7] or whether a genuine—though unique—two-place predicate is involved in this sense of existence.

These abstract ontological distinctions and differentiations seem to have led us far away from Heidegger. In reality they make it possible to classify his concept of existence correctly. We have seen that there are two concepts of existence with two different grammars; one is expressed by the phrase there are or by the existential quantifier, whereas the other is the singular (predicative) concept of existence, which implies a temporal and if necessary a spatial reference. The concept of life is a special case of the latter concept, and we can now see that the particular concept of existence Heidegger has in mind is a special case of this special case. It is that form of existing in the sense of living in which the being that thereby exists or lives understandingly relates itself "in its being" (as Heidegger says) to this being, existence, or life.

How is this relation to oneself to be understood and how can one grasp the specificity of this existence in language? At the beginning of these lectures we saw that Heidegger attempted in his earlier approaches (for example, in his review of Jaspers) to grasp the difference linguistically in the distinction between the sentence "I am" and the sentence "it is." But he rightly abandoned this attempt in *Being and Time*. "I am" has a descriptive, observational mode of use just as does an "is" sentence, and the point is to identify a reference that is other than descriptive in the relation of oneself to one's own existence if "being" here is not to have the meaning of being present-at-hand. Heidegger expresses the fact that the relation of oneself to one's own being has a practical-voluntative sense, first, by stressing that "for this being . . . its being is at *issue*." But this teleological, deliberative aspect does not quite do justice to the phenomenological facts. Hence, we find the further formulation that this being relates itself to its being as something that it "has to be" (p. 32), whether it wants to or not. Heideggger regards this aspect of a certain kind of "facticity" as so fundamental that at the point at which he resumes this crucial topic he characterizes existence immediately as the "to-be." "The 'essence' of this entity lies in its to-be" (p. 67).

It is only *prima facie* that this talk of the to-be appears artificial and contrived. Actually at this point Heidegger adhered exactly to the formulation that is used in ordinary modes of speech when we are confronted in a concrete and existential fashion with our being in that general way which Heidegger analyzes abstractly. I already alluded earlier to Hamlet's question "to be or not to be." What does this question refer to, and what kind of interrogative character does it have? It is obviously not a theoretical question whose answer would consist in a statement; rather, it is a practical question in the precise sense that its answer can consist only in a sentence that expresses an intention or a decision. The practical sense of the question is disclosed in what follows it: "whether 'tis nobler. . . ." The being to which it refers is not the existence that has already transpired, but my existence as it impends at the time. I can only describe the existence that has already transpired as it also can be described by someone else. In contrast, the existence that impends at any given time is of such a kind that I have it to be, that is, I have to carry it out in one way or another, or I must decide no longer to go on with it. The relation that I have to my existence as it impends is different from the relation that someone else can have to it. Someone else can only relate to it theoretically, prognostically, and I can do this as well, but I cannot thereby avoid practically relating to my existence as it impends at any given time. I have to carry it out, I have to decide *to be* in one way or another, and since I am in this respect irreplaceable (i.e., no one can assign his carrying out of being to someone else), the to-be has the "character of being in each case mine" (p. 68). Thus, Heidegger's thesis is this: As long as we exist we relate ourselves to this existence, and we relate to it as our respective future; in this context, the future means the being that is to be carried out at the present moment, and beyond this our entire prospective being. This being is given to us as something that we have *to be*, and that is *at issue* for us; in this respect, the relation of oneself to the being that is so experienced can only be a practical one, that is, a voluntative and affective relation.

We will be better able to grasp what is special about Heidegger's conception if we compare it to the corresponding traditional conception. Indeed, the doctrine that man's being is at issue for him is by no means novel, but originates with Aristotle and has characterized a substantial segment of the tradition. Aristotle extended it to animals as well, and at one point he claims it for all living creatures, even plants: They strive to preserve their being.[8] In a similar way we find the conception in Aristotle that the being (existence) of living creatures consists in their life.[9] In the case of plants one cannot speak of a striving in the strict sense. But it is still permissible to speak of an objective teleology, and thus one can roughly say here that the function of life processes is the maintenance of these life processes; and this is precisely what Aristotle meant: The *télos* of life activities is being, and in those instances in which one can speak of desiring and striving, for example, for animals, all striving is directed toward that which is useful for the preservation of being or the species, that is, toward what is 'good' for this end.[10] Since the nonrational animals do not have conscious states that they can express in sentences, however, they are not consciously related to their being and to what is good for it. What they strive toward, therefore, is not exactly being but pleasure; this is the representative in consciousness of the good, and through it the striving is objectively mediated with the preservation of being.[11] Only a human being is consciously related to this being and what is good for him, because (as Aristotle expressly says) he speaks in sentences (*logoi*).[12] As a consequence his striving is not only determined by feelings but also can be directed toward facts (ultimately toward the fact of being), and can be affected by means-ends deliberations. This striving is designated as the will.[13] Sometimes Aristotle reserves the word *praxis*—"action" or "activity"—for this deliberative, no-longer-automatic life process, though he also uses it in a more general sense.[14] Being is now not only life but also activity, and at this level in which striving is founded upon deliberation, the issue is not only the preservation of being. Rather, for the deliberative person the question arises as to *how* he wants to be—that is, in accordance with a conception of life—and this means that the question arises not only as to what is good for the preservation of life but also as to the good life itself.[15]

Thus Aristotle already had a concept of a nontheoretical, practical relation to one's own being, and this relation is also the ultimate reference point of all willing for Aristotle. What distinguishes Heidegger's conception, then, from this traditional conception? I would like to focus on three aspects.

First, Aristotle one-sidedly developed the active aspect of one's relation to one's own being—namely, that man's being is *at issue* for him. Heidegger supplements this through the passive aspect, so to speak—namely, that man has his being *to be*, whether he wants to or not. Heidegger designates this "that he is and has to be" as the "facticity of being delivered over" and as "thrownness" (BT, p. 174). While the first, voluntative aspect has the character of a practical *possibility*, since one chooses what one is concerned about within a range of possibilities, the second aspect represents the moment of unavoidability, of practical *necessity*. In the practical sphere possibility and necessity belong essentially together; every situation of choice is determined by both of these moments. The fact that one finds oneself in a specific situation of action is the moment of unavoidable facticity, but there is no situation of action that does not contain a range of practical possibilities, for otherwise it would not be a situation of action. And what holds for the single situation of action holds for one's relation to the fundamental situation underlying all situations of action: the facticity of the to-be. I face a range of decisions as to which way I want to carry out my being, but the fact that I have to carry it out is given to me. Of course, I can also decide by means of suicide not to carry it out, but the fact that I must choose between life and death is also given to me as unavoidable—an unavoidability that is expressed in the word *must*. This conception that the two complementary aspects of practical possibility and practical necessity pertain to human existence was probably suggested to Heidegger by Kierkegaard.[16] We saw in the last lecture that Kierkegaard, who was conceptually still completely under the influence of German Idealism, speaks merely of a synthesis of these two moments. It is Heidegger who first succeeds in descriptively grasping these two aspects in an unobjectionable way, for he understands them (I anticipated this in my interpretation of Kierkegaard) as aspects of that being to which I relate myself practically; thus he relocates them within the context of Aristotle's practical concept of existence, which had fallen out of consideration in German Idealism. In contrast to Aristotle, however, the acknowledgment of the passive aspect of the relation to one's own being implies that the voluntative relation can just as well assume the form of a rejection. For this reason words such as *striving* or *willing* are not employed by Heidegger, and instead of these he chooses the expression *care*. The voluntative relation of oneself to one's own being is care for this being that I have to be, and both possibilities, wanting to live and wanting to die, are contained in this relation.

The second aspect in which Heidegger differs from the Aristotelian conception does not concern the descriptive aspect of the phenomenon, but relates to the fact that Heidegger attempts for the first time to extract ontological capital from this phenomenon; he does this by advancing the thesis that the meaning of *being* is fundamentally different when it is given as something to be carried out as opposed to something to be stated. This aspect was, of course, the most important one for Heidegger, and I must deal with it somewhat more fully. Aristotle and the tradition following him did not draw any conclusion for the concept of being from the possibility of the practical reference to being. Heidegger's interpretive thesis that *being* in the tradition means something like "presence-at-hand"—an existence that is to be stated—appears to me to be correct. And Heidegger's explanation that this conception followed from the exclusive orientation of ontology to the assertoric sentence also seems to me correct (sections 13, 33). But the question is, What is the alternative to this orientation to the assertoric sentence? A stronger and a weaker thesis can be distinguished here. In *Being and Time* Heidegger advances the stronger thesis, but as far as I can see he originally proceeded from the weaker thesis; only this weaker thesis follows directly from our present context, and in my view only the weaker thesis can be corroborated from a language-analytical standpoint. In the analytic approach to philosophical texts it seems to me important to learn not to view them as monolithically as they themselves are presented. The hermeneutic method, which merely wants to understand an author and to consider his work as a unified whole, leads to the consequence that either one does not take a position with regard to the truth of what is said at all, or one can only completely accept or reject it. But the truth claim of a philosopher can only be taken seriously if one distinguishes the different steps and the different aspects of a train of thought, and then weighs them individually.

In the present connection I mean by the weaker thesis the contention that the meaning of being differs in accordance with whether it is taken theoretically, as something that is asserted, or practically in the previously specified sense, as something to be carried out. The stronger thesis is that *being* in the sense of presence-at-hand is not only not the only sense of *being*, but also a sense of *being* that is derivative in contrast to that of the to-be.

Let us first consider the weaker thesis. When we refer to two meanings of *being* here, we must again raise the question of which of the grammatically distinguishable meanings of *being* are involved. On the basis of the preceding reflections it might seem plausible to assume that two meanings of *being* are involved in the sense of the previously elaborated concept of singular (predicative) existence. But the fact that Heidegger (as we just noted) relates being in the sense of presence-at-hand to the assertoric sentence indicates that a grammatical meaning of being must be involved here that would be expressed in all assertoric sentences, and not only in the singular existence sentences. Everything that is capable of being stated, and not just predicative existence, is to have the sense of presence-at-hand. Thus, if the distinction to which Heidegger alludes can be understood as a distinction of two modes of "being," it involves a type of being that would have to belong to every assertoric sentence. This type of being can be identified as 'veridical being.'[17] This is the meaning of the word *is* when we say "it is as he said," "it is the case that p," where instead of "it is the case that . . ." we can also say "it is true that. . . ." This word *is* appears to express nothing other than the assertive aspect of the assertoric sentence, for the expression "that p" says the same thing as "p" except for the fact that the assertive moment or the assertoric mood is missing from it. If one supplements ". . . that p" by "it is the case that . . ." a sentence results that is equivalent to the original sentence ("p"); thus, in "it is the case that . . ." the assertive moment, which is normally not explicit, stands out by itself in the same way that it does when we answer an assertoric sentence by yes or no. In this case the content of what is affirmed or denied is presupposed — it is expressed in the sentence that one answers by yes or no; *yes* means the same thing as "it is the case," and *no* means the same thing as "it is not the case." I already intimated my thesis earlier that what Heidegger means by *being* extends as far as the use of yes and no.

If that yes/no by which we answer assertoric sentences has a descriptive meaning and expresses being in the sense of presence-at-hand, and if there is still to be another sense of *being*, then there has to be another mode of use of yes/no for which the content of what is affirmed or denied is not that of an assertoric sentence. And this other mode of use does indeed exist. It is related to imperatives and sentences of intention. Sentences of intention are indicative sentences in the first-person future that are not used as assertoric sentences; they are employed in those cases that involve one's own actions or activities, for example, when I say "I shall go home after the lecture." Whether or not the fact that is formulated in such a sentence will exist is not a question that is independent of the speaker, as is the case for an assertoric sentence. On the contrary, it depends upon the speaker himself (more precisely, upon whether he intends this). If I do not do what I have said, my sentence does not prove to be false, and I have not made a mistake; rather, I have not acted in conformity with my expressed intention. Hence, such future-oriented sentences are not prognoses, and in fact they are not assertoric sentences at all, since they are not true or false. These sentences are the sentences in the first person that correspond to imperatives in the second person. If someone tells me to "go home after the lecture," I can answer either by yes or by the corresponding sentence of intention. They are equivalent. Thus, a sentence of intention is the affirmative answer to an imperative. But instead of answering the imperative by yes or by executing the action, one can answer by saying no. Correspondingly, one can regard every sentence of intention as an answer to a practical question ("is it best—or better—*to* go home?"); this is a question to which one would also have been able to say no.

Thus, the yes/no of sentences of intention has the meaning of choosing to act (to be) in such and such a way, and generally we only speak of actions in those cases in which this latitude of freedom obtains. If a sentence in the first-person indicative future involves a fact whose occurrence does not depend upon me—for example, "I will be thirty-five years old tomorrow," or "I will arrive in London tomorrow according to my kidnapper's plan"—then it is an assertoric sentence, and the relevant event is not my action. The imperative is also related to this yes/no of choice. One can only address imperatives to beings that have the freedom to do or not to do what is demanded by the imperative. Indeed, we also use expressions, in relating to animals, that seem like imperatives but in reality function as signals, because the animal cannot answer by yes or no; it cannot assume a position toward the sentence. Thus there are two fundamentally different ways to assume a position toward sentences, the assertoric yes/no and the practical yes/no; in the first case something is stated or asserted, whereas in the second case (if it takes place in the first and not in the second person) the decision is expressed to carry out or not to carry out something, to act in such or such a way. These two different modes of assuming a position are explicit or implicit answers to different types of questions, the theoretical and the practical question. The two corresponding sentence forms can be understood as two distinct modes of veridical being (in a broadened sense): (a) "(it) is (the case that . . .)" and (b) "Let (it) be (the case that . . .)."

Does this distinction imply that a different *meaning* of *being* is involved? I think it does. For we say that the meaning of a word is different in two different contexts if (1) the rule of use of the word differs in the two contexts, and (2) if one case cannot be subsumed under the other as a special instance. In this respect the to-be differs more fundamentally from the general concept of life than the latter does from the (even more general) concept of the singular existence of a material object. In this regard I must modify the account I gave earlier that the to-be is a special case of a special case of predicative existence. The general concept of life simply can be subsumed under the concept of predicative existence. It is for this reason that the word *exists* has the same meaning when we say that something living exists as when we say that a lifeless material object exists. In the case of a person, a being that relates itself practically to its existence, the word *exists* can stand in a sentence that by virtue of its changed sentence form effects a change in the meaning of veridical being and in this way also lends a modified 'coloring' to all its constituent expressions.

Of course, this is still not a fully convincing argument. For you will object that although two different meanings of veridical being are involved, the existence expression *as such* retains the same meaning, especially since we can also apply it in assertoric contexts to persons. But as I have just indicated it must be noted that the possibility of this practical modification of veridical being is not independent of the propositional content of the sentence. The possibility of practical sentences (imperatives, sentences of intention, practical questions) is grounded in a specific class of predicates; namely, those whose application to the subject depends upon the subject itself, that is, predicates that stand for activities. When these predicates occur in practical sentences, they are not just any constituent expressions in these sentences; rather they are those expressions that make the practical modification of veridical being possible; and for this reason when they occur in assertoric sentences, they also have a different semantic from that of other predicates.

How are these predicates connected to existence? The freedom a person has in relation to his to-be is expressed not only in the form "to be or not to be" but also always in the question, How do I want to be, how do I want to live? For a person can never carry out his being abstractly, but can only be in one way or another. Thus, the person relates himself to his being in such a way that he always chooses specific *possibilities* of being (as Heidegger expresses it), and this means specific activities. If all being-in-a-certain-way (*So-Sein*) of human existence (life) consists in activities and actions, then it also seems plausible conversely to understand all activities (and all actions are rooted in activities) as modes of being. This is the way I interpret Heidegger's statement: "Accordingly those characteristics which can be exhibited in this entity are not 'properties' present-at-hand of some entity which 'looks' so and so and is itself present-at-hand; they are in each case possible ways for it to be, and no more than that. All being-in-a-certain-way of this entity is primarily being" (p. 67).

Heidegger cannot possibly have meant by this statement that a person does not have properties that are present-at-hand, and that all the things that can be said of him are ways for him to be. Perhaps he would have argued that the properties that are present-at-hand belong to the person, and not to Dasein. But then one would have to speak of two subjects and explain how they are connected. Such peculiarities are a function of Heidegger's tendency to see an unbridgeable chasm between his new conceptions and those of the tradition. Thus, he believed that his conception of the being of human beings as something to be carried out contradicted the conception that this entity is a substance with properties or a subject of predicates. Apparently he believed that an entity can only be either one or the other, that it can only be grasped either as present-at-hand or as an entity in the mode of being of existence as to-be. If we want to seize the chance to appropriate Heidegger's new insights productively, we have to free them from these self-contradictory eccentricities. If a person were not something present-at-hand, something whose existence could be stated, he would not exist at all. And one can state, in the third person, that he exists in such a way that he relates himself, in the first person, to his existence as to-be. Furthermore, we can state that on the one hand predicates pertain to him that can be characterized only as present-at-hand. These are in part the type of predicates that even the person himself can only ascribe to himself from the perspective of the observer; and in part they are ϕ predicates that also stand for states of the person and thus for properties by virtue of their veridical symmetry. On the one hand, there is a special class of "ϕ" predicates that are distinguished from the other predicates by virtue of the fact that their application to the person depends upon the person himself; that is, they are "ϕ" predicates that stand for activities and actions. Now these predicates stand for "ways to be" — this is the essential point of Heidegger's account — and this means that they are to be grasped, not as predicates of the first level, but as adverbial determinations of existence. Of course, these predicates can also be employed descriptively in assertoric sentences in the same way as the existence predicate that underlies them. But at the same time it is clear on the basis of the meaning of these expressions that when they are used in first-person interrogative or future indicative sentences, or in second-person imperatives, the modification of the theoretical yes/no into the practical yes/no results. Thus, a modification in the meaning of veridical being is involved that rests upon the special character of a class of predicates; and since these predicates stand for ways to be, their character is most intimately bound up with the special character of human existence as to-be.

In my view, Heidegger's thesis that a different meaning of being is given with the existence of "Dasein" can be explicated and justified along language-analytical lines in roughly the way just presented. This is the thesis that I called the weaker one. For Heidegger it is bound up with the stronger thesis that being in the sense of to-be is more primordial, and that being in the sense of presence-at-hand is derivative. I cannot simply ignore this stronger thesis, since it overlies the weaker thesis for Heidegger and was crucial for the speculative turn in the construction of *Being and Time*. But an extensive explanation and criticism of these connections would lead us too far astray. They do not contribute anything to the topic of self-relation, which is our main focus of interest. I will therefore confine myself to a few remarks.

We have just seen that Heidegger (incorrectly) thought that if Dasein relates itself to its own being as to-be, its being cannot be understood simultaneously as presence-at-hand. For this reason the being as presence-at-hand that he considers is only that which is not in the mode of Dasein. Heidegger advances the ostensibly plausible thesis that we do not relate to entities in isolation, but in their "involvement" (*Bewandtnis*) within an interest-determined situation of action; he designates this situation as the "world" (BT, sections 13, 15, 18). For Dasein the fundamental issue is always its own being. Its being is its ultimate "for-the-sake-of-which" (*Worumwillen*, BT, p. 116). Thus, the "involvement" in which the entities "within-the-world" (*innerweltliche*) are encountered in a situation of action ultimately rests upon their usefulness or harmfulness for the being of Dasein. Correspondingly, the entities within-the-world are not originally encountered theoretically, that is, in the detachment of knowledge, but in one's "dealings" (*Umgang*): as "ready-to-hand" (*Zuhandenes*), not as "present-at-hand" (section 15). Heidegger claims that the disclosure of entities within the world as ready-to-hand can be interpreted as a pre-predicative mode of encounter (section 32). An entity can always only be disclosed in its orientation toward something and hence as something. The "as" structure that manifests itself in predication is based upon this. The primordial orientation (*Woraufhin*) of the disclosure, however, lies in the totality of involvements. Thus, it is accessible pre-predicatively as ready-to-hand. In this respect assertion is a "derivative mode," since it no longer allows the entity to be encountered within a totality of involvements, but considers it in isolation. The basis upon which the entity is disclosed in the "as" is now no longer the totality of involvements, but the properties that are to be found in the entity itself.

Thus, Heidegger establishes the derivative character of the present-at-hand as opposed to the to-be by introducing a third meaning of being—namely, the ready-to-hand. On the one hand, he claims that this ready-to-hand is related—by way of the phenomenon of the 'world'—to the being of Dasein, and on the other hand he asserts that the present-at-hand is founded upon it. The weakest link in this chain of reasoning seems to me to be the last: that is, the thesis that in the modification of the "as" structure, the property-structure and thereby the structure of predication takes the place of the totality of involvements. Heidegger attempted here as well to draw novel ontological conclusions from a phenomenon that was quite familiar to the Aristotelian tradition—the teleological constitution of things of use. But the argument is not effective in establishing that those features that a thing has as a result of its relation to a totality of involvements and a for-the-sake-of-which are not expressible through predicates. In any case, it is evident here what makes this stronger thesis of Heidegger so much more problematic than the weaker one. While the thesis that the to-be represents a different meaning of being than the present-at-hand is confirmable because one can demonstrate the nonassertoric sentence forms in which it is expressed (though Heidegger himself does not do this), the thesis that the ready-to-hand is a distinct meaning of being points beyond the domain of language. Although the idea that "disclosure" only takes place in connection with an interest and care (*Sorge*) and that all care ultimately refers back to the care for one's own being and the being of others is plausible, it does not thereby follow that the descriptive disclosure articulated in assertoric sentences is the derivative mode of a primordial disclosure. The thesis that asserts such derivativeness is speculative in the sense that one cannot specify which criteria are to be relevant in evaluating its correctness. The same thing holds for the thesis that there is a meaning of being—the ready-to-hand—that cannot be grasped in language, and hence is not a meaning of *being*.

I thus conclude my discussion of the second aspect that distinguishes Heidegger's conception of the practical relation to one's own being from the Aristotelian conception. This aspect, which concerns the ontological consequences that Heidegger draws from this phenomenon, was the most crucial one for Heidegger himself. The thesis that is contained in the title *Being and Time* must also be understood in the context of this aspect. The being that is to be carried out is essentially a futural one, though this future is in a certain sense an instantaneous future; it concerns the being that is to be carried out now and not later moments that can be foreseen descriptively. Heidegger advanced the thesis, following Bergson, that the future and hence temporality in general can only be understood from the situation of freedom and the to-be. Thus, his ontological objective was to rethink the meaning of time from the standpoint of the to-be, and to rethink the meaning of being in general from the standpoint of time understood in this way.

I can finally proceed to the third aspect that distinguishes Heidegger's conception of the practical relation of oneself to one's own being from the Aristotelian conception. It is the most crucial aspect for our context of inquiry. Just as Heidegger attempts in contrast to the ancient tradition to understand the meaning of being in a new way on the basis of the phenomenon of the to-be, he also attempts in contrast to the modern tradition to conceive of the structure of the relation of oneself to oneself in a new way on the basis of this phenomenon; and it seems to me that his success is undoubtedly greater in the latter case than in the reorientation of the ontological problematic. In this regard the fact that man relates himself to his to-be with care (*sorgend*), that is, in a voluntative-affective mode, acquires its special significance through the thesis that this is not only a phenomenological fact, but that man relates himself to himself by relating himself to his *being*; thus, this does not take place in a reflexive relation conceived in accordance with the subject-object model.

You might object that one should not designate the relationship of the person to his being as a relationship of the person to himself; this would be ungrammatical, since the expression *to oneself* can only be understood reflexively, so that a relationship of the person to himself can consist only in the relationship of the person to the person and not in a relationship to his being. On the other hand, it seems obvious that in relating oneself to one's further life, to one's to-be, one relates oneself to oneself. You might reproach me with the charge that I am using a double standard; for I immediately declare other theories invalid when they involve ungrammatical structures, but on the other hand I want to portray them as harmless in those cases in which a violation of grammar suits my purposes. Let me address this objection by making the following proposal. Instead of saying that the relation of the person to himself proves to be a relation of oneself to one's being, we can say this: What one regarded as a relation of oneself to oneself proves not to be a relation to oneself, but a relation to one's being. Nevertheless, I will still follow the looser mode of speaking from time to time.

Thus, the assumption that was developed at the end of the last lecture in connection with Kierkegaard has now been confirmed. This concerned the claim that even in those cases in which the person relates himself not merely to his own states but to himself, this self-relation must be understood as a relation to a proposition, which then must have a special status; and it was further assumed that this proposition consists in the existence of the person. The question that still remained open there—in what sense can the relation of oneself to this propositional content be understood as a practical one—is now answered. My capacity to relate myself in a voluntative-affective mode to my existence rests upon the fact that the proposition to which I thereby relate myself is not the *fact* that I exist, but my existence as it impends; and *this means* the (practical) *necessity* that I have to be, and together with this the (practical) *possibility* to be or not to be, or to be or not to be in such and such a way.

But our problem consisted not only in the fact that an analytically possible and phenomenologically correct structure had to be found for a practical relation of oneself to oneself. Rather, the phenomenological state of affairs from which I proceeded in thematizing the practical relation of oneself to oneself was the following: first, that *in all doing* and *wanting* one always also somehow relates *to oneself*, and second, that one does this in a particular way when one thinks one can speak of self-determination. Thus we must anticipate that an adequate elucidation of the structure of the relation of oneself to oneself will also include an adequate understanding of the connection between the relation of oneself to oneself and what Hegel called the 'determinations' (*Bestimmtheiten*); this understanding is no longer to lead to the aporias that result when this connection is conceived in accordance with the substance model and the 'self' as "I" nucleus. Now we have just seen that in Heidegger's conception of the relation of oneself to one's own being one finds a natural and structurally un-problematic connection to that which is done and wanted: The activities of the person are nothing other than his ways to be. The person understands himself as that which he does or wants to do, and *himself* here means his life. According to Heidegger, of course, this voluntative relation to one's own being involves only one side of the matter—the side of the active self-relating to one's own being that is experienced as practical *possibility* (to be in such and such a way). For Heidegger this side of the disclosure of one's own being stands under the title "understanding" (one understands oneself as the so-and-so, i.e., the one who is active in such and such a way). And Heidegger now advances the further thesis that the side of practical *necessity*—which he terms "thrownness"—also has its own mode of disclosure: In accordance with this passive side one's own being is disclosed in one's emotions and moods. Thus, Heidegger succeeds in incorporating the voluntative as well as the affective states into the relation of oneself to oneself. The person encounters himself, his being, both in what he wants and in what he feels.

In this account, we still have not reached that particular mode of the person's relation to *himself in* his doing and wanting that can be characterized as self-determination. For if this characterization is to have meaning, it does not suffice that the person relates himself to himself insofar as he does or wants to do this or that; rather, the relation of oneself to oneself somehow would have to be itself deter-minative for what one does and wants. Heidegger claims that this possibility of self-determination also can be understood on the basis of the structure of the relation of oneself to oneself as presented by him. At the beginning of *Being and Time* Heidegger already refers to the possibility of being-oneself (*Selbstsein*) at the same point at which the concepts of existence and to-be are first introduced (p. 33): "Dasein always understands itself in terms of its existence—in terms of a possibility of itself: to be itself or not itself." The formulation that someone is also capable of not being himself seems paradoxical. The sentence just quoted is elaborated by Heidegger in the statement that follows: "Dasein has either chosen these possibilities itself, or got itself into them. . . ." This concept of choosing oneself appears at first glance equally paradoxical. It yields the impression that the person has a substantial criterion for the choice of his purposes and activities in what he 'himself' is, or in his to-be as such. We will have to see whether Heidegger's conception of the relation of oneself to oneself is capable of providing a structurally clear meaning to the idea of self-determination.

Lecture 9

Heidegger on the Relation of Oneself to Oneself, II: The Elaboration

I have the impression that I have only partially succeeded in making Heidegger's position intelligible to you—that is, the idea that persons are beings who have to be their being, and for whom their being is at issue. Perhaps the best access to this position can be found in the question that is often designated as the fundamental question of ethics; this is the question: What should one do? What is the best thing to do? Or again: How should I or how do I want to live and be? What is the best possible way to live? We saw last time that since every sentence expressing intention stands in a yes/no framework of choice, every intention must be understood as an answer to a practical question that does not have to be posed but always can be posed. It is characteristic of human freedom that we do not have to devote ourselves immediately to a purpose but can, so to speak, step back from it by asking or considering whether or not it is better to want (or to do) what is expressed in a sentence of intention. It pertains analytically to practical questions and to the meaning of deliberation that such questions can be formulated in this way: What is good, better, the best?

You will ask, The best for what? This can obviously vary. The practical question—the question about what is good, better, best— can have a very narrow significance, but it also can have a quite comprehensive and fundamental significance. It is narrow if our purposes are not put into question, but only the means and method. But even if we put our purposes into question, the practical question can still remain relatively circumscribed in certain instances; this is the case if we merely put immediate purposes into question in light of long-range purposes, or if we put our purposes and our way of life into question in light of social norms, which themselves are not subject to question.

When does the question have a fundamental significance? Surely in those cases in which we do not put individual actions into question in view of something else, but instead place our actions and thereby our life as a whole into question. But this last formulation is misleading. It might suggest that the practical question is only raised fundamentally if it is directed toward one's life plan, and that it would not be raised fundamentally if one asked, What is the best thing to do at this moment, for example, in which I find myself presented with an unexpected situation? Or that it would not be raised fundamentally if I asked, What is the best way to behave in view of such and such circumstances, which I recognize apply to me? The practical question is indeed not fundamentally posed if circumstances that I can change are presupposed as given. On the other hand, to disregard given circumstances and the concrete situation would imply that the practical question was not seriously posed. And even the question directed toward one's life plan can be oriented to purposes or social norms that are not themselves questioned; furthermore, the practical question stands in danger of being regarded as something that is to be resolved once and for all. Thus, the criterion for whether the question is fundamentally posed is the one that was just cited: namely, whether I put my life as a whole into question; but this "as a whole" does not exclude (but includes) the fact that the question is situationally related and is to be raised anew in each respective case. Nonetheless, this question comprehends my life as a whole because it has the following sense: Who do I want to be, that is, what do I find is the best way to understand myself as someone who is living and acting? And when the question is posed in this way, it always also stands in the horizon of the limiting question: Is it generally better to be or not to be?

I trust that you are familiar with such questions in one way or another. Let us consider what is presupposed by them. First, a practical question always concerns one's own or a common acting, doing, living, or being in the first-person singular or plural. Second, it always concerns one's own or a common future that is more or less immediate or distant. Third, the question (whether narrow or comprehensive) would not be raised if I were not concerned or did not care about my activity (or in some cases my life), that is, if this were not an *issue* for me (and this is also true when the caring involves others). Fourth, the practical question (whether posed narrowly or comprehensively) implies that I have a certain latitude for free decision, since otherwise there would be nothing about which to raise a question. Fifth, the practical question also implies that there are boundaries to the freedom; in those cases in which nothing is given, there is nothing that requires deliberation. It is given to me that I find myself in precisely such and such a situation, that I have such and such a character, and finally that I exist at all. Sixth, we not only find ourselves in a specific framework of free choice *when* we raise the practical question, but we also have the freedom to raise or not to raise the practical question. Seventh, the practical question always signifies, What is better?

Thus, I have once again presented the very moments that are contained in Heidegger's position by proceeding from the practical question, which is accessible to everyone; although I presented them the last time in connection with Heidegger's own statements at the beginning of BT, I have now refrained as far as possible from relying upon his terminology. Only the aspect that was indicated last—the reference to the good—appears to be missing in Heidegger, and we will have to inquire about what is implied by this, and why this is missing in Heidegger. The aspect that I indicated in the next-to-last point—that part of our freedom consists in either raising or not raising the practical question—explains why the framework of possibility and the interrogative character of our existence do not have to be evident. It is not only that whether we pose the practical question at all is open and depends upon our interests; in particular, it is open as to how fundamentally we pose it. It is thus understandable why we can scarcely avoid practical questions that only concern the means to predetermined ends, whereas we can overlook those that also arise in relation to the ends themselves, that is, in relation to our being. The fact that they arise even if we are not conscious of them—thus the fact that unquestioned existence also is to be understood as an answer to a question that is merely not explicitly posed—is a consequence of the fact that (as Heidegger formulates it) the understanding of "not" is part of the understanding of being (BT, p. 331); or, as one can also formulate it, every sentence that expresses intention can be negated. According to Heidegger, the fact that the fundamental practical question is generally not conscious can further be explained by the fact that it puts us in a state of insecurity in which we can no longer hold on to our previously established opinions; hence, as a result of our need for security we have a motive for evading or concealing it (§40). Heidegger designates the two possibilities of openness and evasion in the face of the practical question as those of authentic and inauthentic existence, whereby by *authentic existence* he means an existence that has "made itself its own" (*sich zueigen*, pp. 68ff.).

In this respect it once again becomes clear that if the practical question is posed fundamentally, it involves me in a confrontation with myself. For this reason evasion in the face of freedom is a fleeing from oneself (§ 40). Thus, according to Heidegger self-consciousness— the relation of oneself to oneself—has "at first and for the most part" (pp. 69ff.) the mode of a fleeing from oneself. The choice at which the practical question is aimed has the character of a "choosing oneself" (*Sich-selbst-wählens*, p. 232), and this has a double sense. In the first place the act of questioning and choosing must be carried out by me myself—it cannot be delegated to somebody else; and second, what I thereby choose is what I myself am: In this act I determine who (how) I shall be.

Thus, the concept of self-determination and self-choice has now lost the paradoxicality that consistently afflicted it when it was conceived in light of the traditional model, according to which the 'self' could only be understood as an "I" nucleus. At the end of the last lecture, however, it seemed that this paradoxicality might still persist even if one speaks (like Heidegger) of a relation of oneself to one's own being. We saw on a first level that Heidegger could solve the problem of how man relates himself to himself *in* doing or wanting to do this or that by claiming that the activities of the person are nothing other than ways to be. But in order to be able to speak of self-determination, it appears essential that in relating himself to himself the person does not already *eo ipso* want this or that. The possibility of a self-relation to one's own to-be is now envisioned, which offers the prospect of detaching the to-be as such from its concrete determinacy. The reason that a difficulty does not arise here corresponding to the one endemic to the traditional conception of an "I" nucleus is that this distinction of the self from its determinations now simply can be understood as the practical question, whereas before it had to assume the structure of a 'reflection into oneself.' It admittedly cannot be understood as any arbitrary practical question, but must be specified as the one that no longer has as its point of reference any pregiven purposes or norms; and *this means* precisely that it is no longer any given determination of my being that constitutes the point of reference, but only my being as such. The latter is not encountered in the practical question as something isolated, but in such a way that it is directly related to *possible* determinations; and this takes place insofar as I ask who or how I want to be. Thus, the reference to my own being as such actually contains no substantial criteria for the choice of concrete possibilities. Rather, it consists precisely in leaving all pregiven substantial criteria for the determination of my being aside, and in focusing the choice upon my being as such; and this means nothing other than, Who do I want to be? To the extent that we adhere to substantial criteria, we have shifted the burden of choice from ourselves onto the criteria. The reference to my being as such is the formal condition of the fact that *I* choose *myself*; and I do not do this merely in a general sense and without direction, but in knowing what is at issue, namely, *myself*, my own life.

I can easily imagine that you are not satisfied with these accounts, and I will of course return to the problem of being-oneself. What has just been said, however, suffices for the purpose of concluding the first step of my interpretation of Heidegger—the elucidation of the general structure of the relation of oneself to oneself. The next two steps are devoted to the question of how Heidegger elaborates this conception. We have seen that for Heidegger the problem of the relation of oneself to oneself arises on two levels that correspond to the two levels on which I had already presented the problem of practical self-consciousness at the beginning of the semester. At the first level the general structure of all relations of oneself to oneself is involved: how the person relates himself to his to-be in his purposes and emotions—or, as Heidegger says, in understanding and temperament (*Befindlichkeit*). The second level concerns this structure in the mode of its 'authenticity,' that is, the relation of oneself to oneself in the special sense of self-determination.

According to Heidegger, the general structure of the disclosure of one's own being is constituted in 'temperament' (having a mood) and in 'understanding'; in understanding existence as the for-the-sake-of-which (possibility) is disclosed, and in mood existence as to-be (facticity) is disclosed. Before we examine these modes of disclosure in detail, we still have to take into account a characteristic of the being of Dasein that is fundamental for Heidegger and crucial for both modes of disclosure. This is the characteristic of 'being-in-the-world' (*In-der-Welt-Seins*). I have already mentioned the concept of world in passing, and in that context I explained it as a situation of action. This is not completely correct. Rather, one would have to say that in the same way that the individual activity or action is always embedded in the more comprehensive context of life, the situation of action is embedded in the comprehensive phenomenon of the world. What the individual situation of action is for the individual action, the world is for one's life activity as a whole.

Aside from the concept of the to-be, the concept of being-in-the-world is the second model by means of which Heidegger broke through the subject-object schema. This concept is directed against the idea that the primary correlate of 'disclosure' is always an individual object, so that consciousness would have to jump, so to speak, from object to object. The language-analytical conception is also subject to this criticism insofar as it assumes that the respective correlate of 'disclosure' is what is understood in an individual sentence. For under this conception understanding would also splinter, so to speak, into clearly discrete units. Against this conception Heidegger advances the thesis that the primary correlate of disclosure is a totality of entities in which one finds oneself; every reference to an individual entity always takes place within the disclosure of this totality. This can be illustrated to some extent by the reference to spatial objects: We can only refer to an individual spatial object within a previously disclosed totality of spatial objects. The analogy to space also makes it clear that by the word *totality* one does not mean a closed totality, but an open dimension to which everything that ever may be encountered belongs. Finally, I am mentioning the spatial analogy also because one can see by it that the totality Heidegger designates by the word *world* does not necessarily fall beyond the reach of language-analytical analysis. For the reference totality of spatial positions can be elucidated through the semantic connections of reference between expressions of localization.[1] For Heidegger spatiality is only one aspect of the world (BT sections 22–24); for a language-analytical reconstruction of the concept of world, however, the spatiotemporal dimension would seem to be fundamental, since it provides the basis for the experience of an open totality of entities. In any case, for Heidegger "world" is not the objective totality of the present-at-hand, but it is that totality of entities within which man finds himself as an agent. The totality within which things are encountered is not (or at least not primarily) their spatial connection of reference, but the significance or nonsignificance they have for our 'care' (section 18); Heidegger designates this aspect of world as 'environment' (BT, p. 94). But the world is always at the same time 'with-world' (*Mitwelt*, p. 155); as being-in-the-world, Dasein not only stands in an open dimension of entities about which it can 'care' or not 'care,' but also in this dimension it exists at the same time 'with' or 'against' others of its own kind. The others are similarly defined by care for their own being, and this aspect of the world is itself defined by care; for the others are encountered as those for whose being I can care or not care in different ways, and who can care or not care for my being (BT §26).

By means of the concept of being-in-the-world Heidegger does not merely indicate (first) that the relation of the person to other entities—things or persons—always already stands within a disclosure of 'entities as a whole'; nor does he restrict the significance of being-in-the-world (second) to the insight that this disclosure is grounded in care, that the perspective in which the "as a whole" is constituted rests upon my and other's care about my being and that of the others. Rather, a third point is involved here and this is the most crucial one for our purposes—namely, that conversely one also experiences one's own being as being-in-the-world. The person experiences *himself* as in a world—as in an encompassing situation of action—and the being that is at issue is always already a being-in-the-world, that is, a being *with* others who care *in the midst of* entities about which one can care. Thus, the person does not relate himself on the one hand to himself and on the other hand to other entities. The fact that the relation of oneself to oneself can be conceived in this intimate structural connection to the "as a whole" and to the plurality of entities that are encountered on its basis is a consequence of Heidegger's understanding of the relation of oneself to oneself as a relation of oneself to one's own existence. We saw last time that in accordance with its general concept this existence has an (even in the case of inanimate objects) essential spatiotemporal qualification. Hence the existing being stands in a relation to all other spatiotemporal objects, and this relation must become a conscious one as soon as the being relates itself to its existence; of course, this relation is also modified by the care character of this self-relating. It should be obvious that this last remark is my own explanatory addition, which would not be accepted by Heidegger, since such a grounding of the to-be in the present-at-hand contradicts his thesis of the primacy of the to-be.

I shall now consider the two modes of disclosure of one's own being as being-in-the-world, which Heidegger deals with under the concepts of temperament (*Befindlichkeit*) and understanding.

Heidegger means by the term *temperament* the phenomenon of mood, and beyond this he means affectivity in general (§29). His thesis is this: Having a mood is not simply having a conscious state characterized by feeling; rather it is a mode of disclosure, and it brings "Dasein . . . before itself" as being-in-the-world in such a way that it discloses the "facticity" of the "that it is and has to be"; Heidegger also designates this facticity of existence as "thrownness" (*Geworfenheit*, pp. 173ff.).

Heidegger complicated the evaluation of this thesis as well by proceeding (as he did everywhere) in a nonargumentative and evocative fashion, and by not following an analytic method. The first chapters of Kenny's book *Action, Emotion, and Will* provide a model of how one would have to proceed here. Following Wittgenstein, Kenny focuses upon the question of how we use expressions that stand for individual emotions, and it is clear that one cannot have a rational discussion about these (as well as other) concepts in any other way. In Kenny's analysis it becomes evident that in contrast to physical feelings (such as pain or hunger), it is constitutive for the concept of an emotion that not only (a) a specific expressive behavior and (b) specific actions that are motivated by the feeling pertain to it but also (c) an intentional object is involved (pp. 14, 60, 67).

Thus, analytic philosophy rediscovered in its own way the characterization of emotion that Aristotle already provided in the second book of his *Rhetoric*. Anger, fear, envy, and so on are related to propositional objects; according to Aristotle, every emotion is defined by being related to a state of affairs of a specific type (Kenny's [c]) and by motivating a specific way of acting (Kenny's [b]). For example, Aristotle defines *anger* as a "painful impulse for visible revenge (b) on the grounds of a putative and unjustified slight of the person himself or someone related to him (c)" (1378a 31f). Thus, an emotion always implies a *belief* that is characteristic for it; for example, in the case of anger the belief is implied that the person to whom the anger is directed has unjustifiably behaved in a contemptuous way toward me.

The fact that this cognitive moment characteristic of judgment pertains to the concept of an emotion is universally accepted today in analytic philosophy. Heidegger himself closely adhered to the Aristotelian description in section 30, where he treats fear as a "distinct mode" of temperament; but he thereby restricts himself to the propositional aspect since he generally overlooked the motivational-volitional component. To be sure, he did not claim to provide a comprehensive characterization of emotions, but wanted to concentrate upon their disclosive character; and we will presume that the latter is most likely to be found in the propositional, cognitive component. In any case, we can attempt to approach Heidegger's thesis on this basis.

In this context, the indeterminacy of the concept of disclosure makes things more difficult. By insisting that knowledge is only one (and indeed a derivative) mode of disclosure (section 13), Heidegger leaves us without a clear criterion for deciding whether a state of consciousness is a mode of disclosure. I see no other alternative than to recur to the concepts of knowledge, experience, and belief, which certainly can be grasped in a wider sense than the concept of pure theoretical knowledge that is presupposed by Heidegger. Thus, I proceed from the assumption that we may only assign a disclosive character to an emotion or to a mood if by means of this state we experience something in some way as something.

Is it correct to say of an emotion that it involves the experience of something as something on the basis of its cognitive component, and in this respect discloses something? This does not appear sufficiently justified if the emotion merely implies a cognitive component by virtue of being based upon it. Thus, for example, Aristotle defines *fear* as "aversion or confusion resulting from the imagination of some harmful or painful evil in the future" (1382a 21ff). The belief that an evil threatens me is obviously not based upon the fear, but the fear is grounded in the belief. Of course, Heidegger would like to deny this: "In fearing as such, what we have thus characterized as threatening is freed and allowed to matter to us. We do not first ascertain a future evil and then fear it" (p. 180). In ascribing the idea of succession ("first . . . and then") to the opposing conception, Heidegger unfairly makes it implausible. And obviously Heidegger's own conception that we can only experience something as threatening in fear is untenable. To be sure, we can only *feel* something as threatening insofar as we fear it—indeed, fear consists precisely in this—but it is possible without doubt to regard something as threatening, and at the same time to feel absolutely no fear of it.

From this distinction one can recognize in a preliminary sense what would have to be shown in order to establish the disclosive character of emotions. It should first be clear that the essence of emotions is underdetermined if it is merely noted that they are related to states of affairs; rather, they are always concerned with states of affairs in which something appears as good or bad for me or for someone else. In the case of fear a future evil is involved, in the case of anger the fact that someone has slighted me, in the case of gratitude the fact that someone has done something good for me, in the case of envy the fact that something good happens to someone else instead of me, and so on. In every case we have first a descriptive state of affairs—for example, something is expected or something is said or has been done—that appears in the second place as good or bad for me or others. And we can now ask whether or not the experience that a state of affairs is, in this respect, good or bad only takes place in and through the emotion.

In the case of fear this certainly is not true. I do not know that an anticipated state of affairs is bad through fear, but because I know inductively that a state of affairs of this kind has such and such consequences for me. But you might ask, Is it not my affectivity that makes that future state of affairs appear as bad for me? Even this is not necessary in the least. Aristotle specified the two relevant possibilities precisely and stringently: The expected evil can be harmful (destructive) or painful. No feeling is required as a criterion for the first instance. It is only in the second case that a feeling is, of course, the criterion, but if it involves a physical pain, this is not an emotion; thus, in either case it is not the *fear* that functions as the criterion of the evil.

Nevertheless, in this explanation one case has now become apparent in which affectivity is constitutive of the fact that we experience something as good for us, that we reckon something as contributing to our well-being. Let us consider pleasure in an activity. This admittedly has a different structure from the phenomena that Aristotle ranks among the emotions. But it can certainly be placed in the domain of the emotions to the same extent as moods. For Spinoza, joy and sadness were the fundamental emotions. The question of which activities—modes of being—we consider as contributing to our well-being, that is, which activities make our life worth living, is ultimately a question of which activities we consider to be part of a good life; and this is decided and can only be decided on the basis of which activities we take pleasure in.

Aristotle also ranks love or friendship among the emotions, and these are obviously closely connected to pleasure. Whom we like is decided on the basis of whether we enjoy being with them. Thus, we can also say it is our affectivity that 'recognizes' the other as someone whom we like.

The situation is different with emotions such as envy, compassion, gratitude, and admiration, which also involve a relation to others. I choose the case of compassion here because it is analogous to fear in the following respect: In compassion we are concerned with someone else's evil, whereas in fear we are concerned with our own impending evil. Just as in the case of fear, it is once again not the emotion that discloses the evil that concerns someone else. Compassion is distinguished from the affect-free recognition of the suffering of someone else by virtue of the fact that I am concerned in my own being about the other's suffering. Thus, in compassion—and only in it—my being is disclosed to me as one that is affected by the evil afflicting the other. In compassion—and only in it—I experience that evil as one that affects myself. Hence, in compassion the evil is constituted as something affecting myself in a way quite analogous to the way in which an activity is only constituted as belonging to my well-being through the pleasure taken in it. The corresponding phenomenon holds *mutatis mutandis* for all emotions that are related to others. As long as I only describe the slight to which someone else subjects me, I am not affected by it in my being. It is only on the basis of my disposition to anger that I experience myself—my being—to be affected by the slight.

We can now see that fear represents an especially unfavorable example for Heidegger's thesis. Since fear is related to one's own future evil, one cannot say that such evil is constituted as an evil for me only through fear; one cannot even say that it is only through fear that the future evil becomes an evil that can be experienced now, because this is also quite possible on the basis of an affect-free expectation. Fear is different from such an expectation only by virtue of the fact that in it the future evil is felt as a present one, and this is obviously trivial. Nevertheless, in this triviality the point that is truly crucial for Heidegger is hidden, because the fact that the future evil is felt as a present one means that I am affected by it in my present being, my being that is now to be carried out—exactly as in the case of the other emotions. Thus, in the case of fear (and of course the same holds for hope) the disclosive character is more difficult to recognize, because unlike the case of the other emotions it does not concern the state of affairs (as one that is good or bad for me), but only myself (as affected in my well-being through the state of affairs). But this was the point on which Heidegger wanted to insist: The emotions are modes of relating oneself to oneself, and in them I encounter myself; or, to be more precise, in them I am confronted with my to-be (in relation to a state of affairs affecting its well-being) as something to be, and this means as something to be endured. Pleasure is endured to the same extent as suffering. "To endure" here stands for the passivity that is expressed both in the traditional terms for the emotions (Greek *pathos*, Latin *affectus*, German *Leidenschaft*) and in Heidegger's talk of the disclosure of the thrownness or facticity of the to-be, as well as in my explanation of this facticity as practical necessity. Once again it is only Heidegger's conception of the relation of oneself to oneself as a relation of oneself to one's own to-be that appears to make it possible to do justice to the phenomenological fact that it is the person himself who feels affected in the emotion by the state of affairs that has an effect upon his well-being.

In the case of emotions in the narrower sense the person is primarily related to the respective state of affairs, and he only experiences himself along with this insofar as he is affected by the state of affairs that has an impact upon his well-being. On the other hand, the confrontation with oneself comes to the fore in those affective states that can be designated (following Heidegger) as moods (*Stimmungen*): states such as depression, cheerfulness, happiness, boredom, ill humor, and anxiety. It is apparent that Heidegger had these phenomena in mind in section 29, where he deals with temperament (*Befindlichkeit*); and the fact that in section 30 Heidegger treats fear as a mode of temperament and never explicitly specifies a criterion for distinguishing moods from emotions can only give rise to a certain lack of clarity. Heidegger's designation of fear as an "inauthentic temperament" (p. 391) and his contraposition of anxiety to it as the "fundamental temperament" (pp. 228, 393) can also lead to confusion; he interprets *anxiety* as that mood in which Dasein confronts itself with its freedom, and which in this respect belongs to the context of 'authentic' existence.

For Heidegger this is a special characteristic of anxiety, and in no way holds for all moods (cf. pp. 395–396). Since Heidegger was primarily interested in the distinction between "authentic" and "inauthentic," he left the general structural distinction between moods and emotions unspecified. But it is evident enough. Wittgenstein designated it by distinguishing "among the emotions" "the directed from the undirected" (*Zettel* paragraph 488).

Moods are distinguished from emotions by virtue of not having an intentional object, and one would also have to say that they do not imply a well-defined motive for action. Since the defining character of emotions thereby no longer appears to obtain, Kenny has objected to the recognition of such "objectless emotions" in general (*Action, Emotion, and Will*, pp. 60ff.). Since the emotions are defined by an objective reference, the possibility of objectless emotions must indeed be rejected; but a mood is precisely not an emotion, although it is an affective state.[2] One would rather have to conceive of the behavioral criteria through which the different moods are to be characterized in such a way that they define the affective disposition—"affectivity" (*Angänglichkeit*), as Heidegger says—on the basis of which the person reacts in this or that way to contingent events that arise in the situation of action, and potentially affect his well-being. This merely programmatic characterization, which is no doubt insufficient, demonstrates in any case that mood is a state of the person and concerns his affective openness or closedness with reference to the "as a whole." Moreover, it is characterized by Heidegger in just this way: "The mood-character of the state of feeling existentially constitutes Dasein's openness to the world. . . . In every case the mood has already disclosed being-in-the-world as a whole, and first makes it possible to direct oneself toward something" (p. 176).

Thus, the deeper reason for Kenny's denial of moods can be discerned in the fact that he lacks a concept of world or situation of action. For if such a concept is lacking, the only alternatives appear to be object-related feelings on the one hand and bare sensations on the other.[3] An objective reference can also be found in the world reference of moods, but in contrast to the well-defined objective reference of emotions it is a more open and undetermined one.

It seems to me that a rough criterion for deciding whether an expression of feeling stands for a mood is whether it can be used as a possible answer to the question, How are you, how are you feeling, how is it going? This question can be answered at every moment in which we are conscious, and in this respect one must grant Heidegger that we are always in one mood or another. Of course, there are many expressions for affects that can be used both for moods and in an object-related sense. For example, "I am sad about such and such," or simply "I am sad." If the word is used in the second sense, as an answer to the question how are you?, then the next appropriate question appears to be not so much "what about?" as "why?" Only in this way is it implied that the sadness was meant as a mood, and not as a directed state. Nevertheless, there are any number of borderline cases. In response to the question "How are you?" one can even answer with a simple expression of emotion, for example, "I am angry at you." But this then implies that this emotion is so dominant that it determines my affective temperament as a whole. The borderline cases demonstrate that every emotional involvement with a specific state of affairs exerts an impact upon my affective temperament as a whole. Nevertheless, my temperament does not consist of the sum of my emotional attitudes to diverse states of affairs. The above-mentioned questions such as "How is it going?" presuppose a uniform overall temperament, and the form of the question (How are *you*?) appears to confirm that this involves, not simply any state of the person, but the type of state in which the person is confronted with himself; but this can only mean that the person is confronted with his life, or his to-be.

Now Heidegger's thesis is this: In a mood the to-be is experienced *as* what one has *to be*, that is, in the "facticity of being-delivered-over"; in it Dasein's "that it is and has to be" is disclosed to it. This thesis may have an intuitive plausibility for some of you, while to others it may appear odd. Can it be brought into a context of confirmable explanation? I would like to make an attempt.

Heidegger describes a mood as if it somehow brings Dasein before the—as he says—'naked' 'that it is' (p. 134). On the other hand, he distinguishes between the "brooding" and the "elevated" moods. Evidently the 'that it is' appears in a different 'coloring' depending upon which mood is involved. What lies behind this metaphor? If we focus upon the question "How are you?", there are obviously two standard answers that are the simplest: "good" and "bad." These extremely rough and indefinite answers indicate a scale that extends from "I

am happy" to "I am in despair," and these answers appear to have
something to do with whether life appears 'meaningful' or 'meaningless'
to one. Thus, mood in no way appears to bring us before the 'naked'
to-be; rather, in it we always experience the to-be in a specific way,
as good or bad, meaningful or meaningless. We have also seen in the
case of the emotions that the states of affairs to which they refer
always concern us by affecting our well-being, so that we experience
them in the emotion as good or bad for us. How is this connection
of affectivity with what is good or bad for us to be understood, and
why did Heidegger overlook it?

We call good or better something that we prefer, wish, or in certain
cases intend on the basis of deliberation. In Heidegger the concept of
the good does not appear, but that of the for-the-sake-of-which nonetheless plays a role. One's own being is ultimately the for-the-sake-
of-which of Dasein, the object of its care or—to put it traditionally—
of its will. But this is not true simply in the sense of survival. Rather,
we have seen that already for Aristotle in the case of a living being
that is consciously and deliberately directed toward its being, the
question arises not only of what is good for the preservation of its life
but also of what constitutes the good life itself. Or, to express it in
modern terms with a concept that is subsequently used by Heidegger
(p. 193), the question arises as to the meaning of life. Where the striving
is not determined (as in the case of animals) merely by what is pleasant
or unpleasant, that is, where it is directed toward life in the mode of
a *will*, it must be directed toward a specific way of life, a purpose or
a meaning if the will is not to operate in a vacuum. Now this has the
following consequence: Human life moves on a scale between fulfilled-
meaningful and empty-meaningless.

We have already seen in the case of the emotions that they cannot
be defined at all without the motivational-volitional aspect, and the
same holds for moods. Indeed, Heidegger emphasizes that all understanding (and under this title he treats the for-the-sake-of-which) is
affective and vice versa (p. 182). But in actuality he left the connection
out of consideration. This connection consists in the fact—which is
obvious enough—that it is precisely *the* being that is *at issue* that is
experienced *as such* in mood as what one has *to be*. In mood we endure
the effect of the success or failure of our intentions and wishes. And
in this respect 'it goes' 'well' or 'badly' for us. If finally our intentions
and wishes no longer find points of contact, if nothing has meaning

anymore, a mood of depression or despair results. And just as in the case of the emotions, mood is itself obviously also the motivational point of departure of a type of volition, although here it is not a volition directed toward a specific goal; rather, it is the volition characterized succinctly in colloquial speech as the will to live. Thus, every mood consists in an overall volitional disposition.

Now we can return to Heidegger's thesis. In the first place, the view that is merely asserted by Heidegger—namely, that mood is actually related to one's being (of course as being-in-the-world)—seems to me to be substantiated by the reference to the to-be in the sense of what is at issue. At the same time, it has now become clear that mood always discloses one's being in a specific way, in a way for the will and hence as good, bad, and so on. The fact not only that mood discloses life in this way for the will but also that one must understand the peculiar passivity of this experience—the 'pathic' dimension of mood—as the experience of this being in its 'that' and 'to-be' appears initially obvious for the negative moods. In these moods, as Heidegger says, the "burdensome character of Dasein" (p. 173) is experienced: In ill humor, or even more clearly in boredom, and most acutely in depression we experience ourselves confronting the unavoidability of having to exist. In depression the being-in-the-world as such, the 'naked' 'that it is and has to be,' is disclosed to us, since we can no longer become absorbed in a specific activity. Of course, we can now see that this 'nakedness' does not belong to mood in general, but to that extreme mode in which life is experienced as meaningless. This is consequently also the constellation from which the question arises as to whether not to be is better than to be. If the question is not merely theoretical, it derives its meaning from the fact that I have hit upon the 'that I am and have to be.' In the "I refuse" or "I am no longer willing" one experiences the 'I must.' Thus, Heidegger's thesis seems to me to be confirmed for the negative moods. But it also holds true for the positive ones as well. I find the objection, which is frequently raised against Heidegger, that he has a partiality for the negative moods to be unjustified. The primary orientation on the negative moods is justified methodologically because the structure can be more easily recognized in these instances, as is usual in most negative cases.[4] The same thing that is affirmed in happiness is denied in unhappiness, that is, being-in-the-world, and the yes takes place—like every yes—within the background of a possible no, and vice versa.

The possibility of meaninglessness is the foil of happiness. But you might ask, Can the mood, the feeling, be understood as a "yes" or "no" saying? Certainly not. Rather, in the "yes" and "no" saying that is at issue here the will, the 'will to live,' expresses itself; but the will to live is only what it is on the basis of being affected in such and such a way by the 'that I am and have to be,' and this is experienced in mood.

Thus I conclude that Heidegger's thesis that moods are modes of self-consciousness—of the relation of oneself to oneself—withstands analytic scrutiny, and is to be regarded as a genuine discovery. It was, of course, only to be achieved on the strength of the presupposition that the relation of oneself to oneself is a relation of oneself to one's being. It thereby becomes clear that this presupposition not only makes possible a concept of the abstract structure of the relation of oneself to oneself, but also discloses perspectives that indicate that the relation of oneself to oneself involves a much richer phenomenon than one might suppose by relying on the concept of reflection.

Furthermore, it has also become clear that a being that relates itself to itself depends upon being able to give meaning to its being. We just saw that this second aspect of the relation of oneself to one's own being, that is, Dasein's concern with meaning, is actually more closely connected with the aspect of affectivity than it appears to be in Heidegger's account. I think that Heidegger's exposition of this side of the relation of oneself to oneself is less productive than the treatment of temperament. With regard to the for-the-sake-of-which, one would have expected Heidegger to try to interpret the familiar anthropological phenomena on the basis of the relation of oneself to oneself, just as in regard to temperament he had presented emotions and moods as modes of disclosure of one's own being. As we have just seen, these relevant phenomena are those of volition and of actions and activities. But Heidegger's need to disengage himself from the tradition was so strong here that instead of casting these familiar phenomena in a new light, he chose to elucidate the subject matter by means of a series of terms that were idiosyncratically adopted and insufficiently explained. This procedure of explication through the accumulation of words is frequent in *Being and Time*, and it is connected to what I have called the evocative method. The most important terms by which Heidegger describes this aspect of the relation of oneself to oneself can be presented in their interconnection as follows.

Dasein is related to its being as its for-the-sake-of-which. This being is always possible being or potentiality-for-being. This disclosure of potentiality-for-being takes place in understanding. Understanding has the structure of projection, and projection is always related to meaning.

Therefore, the most important terms are these: *for-the-sake-of-which, possible being, understanding, projection,* and *meaning.* In explaining Heidegger's accounts of these terms, I will attempt at the same time to comply in outline with the desideratum just suggested, which was not fulfilled by Heidegger; I can thereby at least indicate how in my view one would have to proceed here.

The concept of the for-the-sake-of-which is the only one that is traditional and whose understanding causes no special difficulties. "For-the-sake-of-which" is the translation of the Aristotelian expression *hu heneka*: It signifies that which is the object of interest, which Aristotle also simply designates as *télos*—end or purpose. Both for Aristotle and for Heidegger the ultimate for-the-sake-of-which of man's actions and activities is his own being. We have already seen that it is not the mere preservation of being that is thereby involved, but the way of being. And this implies the following: One should not understand the talk of the for-the-sake-of-which as if we had on the one hand an activity and on the other hand the for-the-sake-of-which as something that is to be effected through the activity. Rather, life or being consists in nothing other than activities. I already alluded to this in the last lecture, and at that point I referred to activities *and* actions, but I have not yet defined these concepts. We speak properly of doing in all those cases in which we demarcate intentional and deliberate events from mere occurrences. It thereby follows that where something is done or enacted we are dealing with a process whose continuation into the next respective phase depends upon whether the agent wants it. Within this comprehensive concept of action one can speak—corresponding to a distinction that goes back to Aristotle—on the one hand of actions in the narrower sense and on the other hand of activities.[5] Actions in the narrower sense are defined by an end that is to be attained through them, whereas activities are deliberate processes in which each phase is like every other. In this sense, for example, it is an action to swim to the other shore, but an activity merely to swim. A criterion of this difference consists in the fact that one can speak only of speed but not of duration for actions, whereas conversely for activities one can speak only of duration and not of speed.

In the present context the distinction is important because we apparently can engage only in activities as ends-in-themselves; consequently, only activities would be candidates for modes of being, for the partial concrete units within which we carry out our own being. Since actions are defined by the ends that are to be attained through them, one can apparently only will an action as a means for the end that is to be attained through it. Here, of course, the objection arises that one can do something for an end and at the same time as an end in itself. Nevertheless, it must be noted that a reciprocal relation of grounding exists between actions and activities. First, every action is grounded in one or more activities: I can only swim to the other shore by swimming for a while, I can only repair a machine by working on it in a specific way for a while. Second, the reverse also holds: I can only swim by covering a specific route, and even more fundamentally and universally, by performing specific goal-directed bodily movements. Since being (life) itself can only be designated structurally as an activity, it seems plausible to say I carry out my life in various activities, although on the one hand the latter are grounded in actions and on the other hand they ground actions. Now should one also say this: If one does something both for an end and as an end in itself this involves an action grounded in an activity, and one wants both the end of the action (e.g., to reach the other shore) and the activity itself (e.g., to swim)? It seems to me that this account does not do justice to the possibility that we can want to engage in an activity as an end in itself precisely by virtue of its characteristic of being directed to a specific end. This difficulty indicates that the connection between activities and actions would have to be conceived as being even more intimate than I just suggested.

Now if one's own being is the for-the-sake-of-which of human beings, then it follows that however a human being may determine his active being, he must in any case be interested in being able to do what he does for its own sake as well. I believe that this old-fashioned Aristotelian conceptual framework provides a much better basis for grasping what Marx meant by alienated labor than the Hegelian framework, which is oriented to the subject-object model and to an obscure concept of identity; I maintain this although Marx himself tried to grasp this phenomenon within the Hegelian framework. An activity is alienated to the extent that one does not or cannot do it for its own sake as well.

Heidegger himself does not speak of actions and activities, but designates the modes of being in which man carries out his being concretely as *possibilities* (of being). We thus come to the second term. Why did Heidegger select this title? I think that there are two reasons.

The first reason, which I have to go into in more detail, consists in the fact that Heidegger wanted to emphasize that aspect of one's relation to oneself which follows from the yes/no polarity of the understanding of being and, in particular, of sentences of intention. What is now involved is not the passive or responsive answer of yes/no that we encountered in temperament as the affirmation and denial of the necessity to exist, but the active yes/no of choice, which is part of wishing and willing themselves and therefore also part of our doing. We find ourselves both in relation to our being in general and in relation to our particular doings within an open range (*Freiheitsspielraum*) of possibilities. This range is expressed in sentences of the form "I can . . ." ("I can do such and such, I can also refrain from it"). Hence, as Heidegger says, all being in the sense of existing is a potentiality-for-being such and such (p. 183). Every sentence of intention—and consequently also all doing—is always an explicit or implicit (obviously normally implicit) decision within the range that is disclosed to us in the sentence "I can . . . and I can also not. . . ." Instead of the term *disclosure*, we can here also use the clearer expression *know*. In those cases in which the consciousness of a range of possibilities exists, we can say "I know that I can either do it or not." Hence we are here dealing with *practical knowledge* about *oneself*, which in contrast to epistemic self-consciousness is not knowledge that I am in such and such states or that I have such and such characteristics; rather, it involves knowledge that I have the possibility to act in such or such a way, and at the same time this means that a specific situation of action is given. Thus, the question arises as to the distinctive meaning of these "can"-sentences and correlatively one must ask what possibility means here.

Heidegger emphatically stressed that the meaning of *possibility* or *potentiality-for-being* in the case of possibilities of existence or action (and I am now using the word *action* in the broad sense of "doing," which also includes activities) differs from other meanings of *possibility* or *potentiality-for-being*; but as is so often the case, the intensity of this emphasis is the reverse side of the deficiency in analytic elucidation. He writes: "Dasein is not something present-at-hand which possesses its capability for something as an addition; it is primarily possible-being. . . . The possible-being, which Dasein is existentially in every case, is to be sharply distinguished from both the empty logical possibility and the contingency of something present-at-hand insofar as such and such can 'happen' to the latter. As a modal category of presence-at-hand possibility signifies what is not yet actual and what is not at any time necessary. It characterizes the *merely* possible. . . . On the other hand, possibility as an *existentiale* is the most primordial and ultimate ontological determination of Dasein" (p. 183).

This quotation contains two statements: (1) the declaration that possibility as an existential term is "the . . . ultimate positive ontological determination of Dasein," and that Dasein is "primarily possible-being"; these claims can only be rendered intelligible by assuming that here actual-being is to be understood itself as possible-being. (2) This possible-being is to be distinguished both from logical possibility and from the 'contingent.' But Heidegger does not explain *how* it is to be distinguished from these meanings of possibility. But if the first statement—that in the existential sphere actuality and possibility somehow coincide, or that possibility takes the place of actuality—is to have a meaning at all, this can only be inferred from the justification of the second statement, i.e., from the special meaning which the word "can" has here; and this justification is lacking.

Let us attempt to reconstruct it.[6] Compare the sentence "I can (could) now break off the lecture" with the sentence "the ceiling of the auditorium can (could) now give way." In the second sentence both logical possibility and the "contingency of something present-at-hand insofar as such and such can 'happen' to the latter" can be exemplified. In the first case we would say that on logical grounds it is not certain beforehand that the opposite is true; in the second case we would say that on empirical grounds it is not certain beforehand that the opposite is true. In both cases we can place the expression of possibility in front of the whole sentence and say "it is possible that the ceiling of the auditorium will now give way." The aforementioned grounds pertain to the truth of the sentence that follows the "that" expression. Let us try the same thing with the first sentence. Can it also be reformulated as "it is possible that I will now break off the lecture"? If we reformulate it in this way, it has the meaning corresponding to the other sentence: It expresses a prognosis; thus, it involves an indefinite reference to empirical grounds that speak for the occurrence of this event but do not exclude its opposite. If one reformulated the sentence in this way, for example, if you were to express this sentence in the third person, it would suggest the following: "(As far as we know him and in the state that he is in now) it is possible (there is evidence for it) that he now will break off the lecture." In this sense, however, the sentence does not have the meaning that it has when I use it to express the fact that I am considering acting in this way. In the latter case I mean whether the lecture is broken off or not depends on me. But now we have to find a formulation in which this meaning is expressed unequivocally.

Thus, our first result consists in the fact that the word *can* has a meaning here that precludes the reformulation "it can be that. . . . " The *can* is not to be understood propositionally, as a mode of "veridical being," but predicatively: It expresses a qualification of the subject— in this case a qualification of me. The fact that there are such modes of use of the word *can* that cannot be understood propositionally may at first appear surprising, but it has recently been demonstrated in analytic philosophy. I refer here to the work of R. M. Ayers, A. Kenny, and U. Wolf.[7] This also holds, as was shown by these authors, for a use of *can* that is less controversial than the one that concerns us here. That is, it also holds when we use the word *can* to express the fact that something has an ability—for example, "this glass can break." This sentence cannot be translated as "it can be that this glass will break." Rather, it signifies that when specific conditions occur, the glass breaks (not: it is possible that then the glass will break). Thus, the sentence refers back to regularities, but not to sentences expressing possibilities. Of course, this is not a proof, but I can refer you to the literature for the details.

Now there is a special kind of ability for which an additional complication arises. Kenny designates abilities of this sort as "volitional powers."[8] What is meant here are abilities whose actualization depends not only upon relevant conditions but also upon whether the being that has this ability wants the actualization. For example, someone can play the violin, that is, he has the ability to do so, but this does not mean that when the relevant conditions for the exercise of this ability are present (the availability of a violin, and so on) he will play; rather, we always have to add: "and if he wants to." I now have the ability and the opportunity to break off the lecture, but do I want to? Just as the actualization of the ability depends not only on the opportunity but also on the desire, it is obvious that the opposite is also the case: I can only want to do something if I have the ability and the opportunity to do it. The presupposition of my being able to consider doing something is that I have both the ability and the opportunity. This seems to be precisely the meaning of the sentence "I can now break off the lecture" if it is meant as a sentence that expresses a possibility of action; it says that I have both the ability and the opportunity, and it thereby implies that the performance of the action only depends upon whether or not I want to do it.

From this viewpoint, the curious expression "I can if (only) I will," which has been the object of a great deal of controversy, becomes intelligible.[9] It appears that we can regard this directly as a criterion for whether a "can" sentence is used in such a way that it expresses a possibility of action; in all instances in which this is the case, it can be reformulated as, for example, "I can now break off the lecture if only I will." What is meant is more precisely: I can break off the lecture (ability and opportunity), and whether I will break it off depends only upon whether I want to do so.

For the purposes of greater elucidation we can also clarify this question with reference to the past. If I say after the lecture "I could have broken it off in the middle," I can add "if only I had wished to"; and by this I mean that I would have broken it off if I had wished to. The opportunity to do so was present; the fact that I did not do it depended only on me. "Only on me," of course, does not mean upon a mysterious I within me, which thus once again suggests itself from an unexpected perspective: the problematic of freedom. Rather, it means that it depends upon my will, and this substantival mode of speech also obviously does not refer to something within me that decides the issue; on the contrary, it is obvious that when we say "it depended only on my will," we mean "it depended only on whether I wanted to do it."

Now, of course, you will ask, And what does this depend upon? If one's reply to this question is that this depends upon my psychological state, my character, and so on, many people see such an answer as a denial of the possibility of free action. In such a case I have not decided at all, but my supposed decision was only the (in principle predictable) result of an inner play of forces. The argument can also be applied at an earlier stage in our chain of reasoning: Is it correct that the so-called volitional abilities are different from the others by virtue of the fact that their actualization depends not only on conditions but also on willing? One could claim that it is indeed correct that they depend upon the opportunity and the desire, but that these jointly constitute the conditions of actualization; the desire to do so is only a further condition.

Kenny has raised the objection against this argument that one cannot identify "to want x" independently of "to do x."[10] If someone has the ability and opportunity to do x, it does not follow that an identifiable occurrence of wanting must precede the doing of x; rather, the fact that he does x voluntarily means that he wants to do it. I decide the question of whether or not I now want to break off the lecture by doing one thing or the other. But if the wanting is not an occurrence that is identifiable apart from the doing, then it cannot be designated as an additional condition upon which the action would be causally dependent. And U. Wolf points out that the same thing also holds for the case in which we form the corresponding intention *prior* to the action, because such an intention is also analytically connected with the action, that is, it is not an independent empirical condition.[11]

The outcome of these considerations is that the sharp distinction between opportunity and willing that was made in the aforementioned analysis is in any case correct and necessary. But the problem of determinism is thereby only deferred by one step. If the respective wanting is not an independent causal factor, the problem nonetheless remains that the wanting itself is conditioned by one's psychological disposition. But why should this really bother us? The conception that a decision is not a decision because it is itself psychologically conditioned seems to me unjustified, and the problem of what constitutes free action is only obscured by associating it with the metaphysical problem of determinism-indeterminism. For the problem of free action is purely descriptive, and it concerns the empirical conditions that function as criteria for calling a mode of behavior free; and this holds independently of whether or not the behavior is predictable either individually or statistically—a question that is entirely unsettled. And it is far more relevant to criticize Kenny's analysis, not for its indeterministic implications (which it has in his view), but because it fails to provide an appropriate account of the descriptive structure of free action.

Indeed, the question arises as to whether one can properly call an action free if what one does depends upon what one wants to do. This thesis has the implication—expressly accepted by Kenny[12]—that we also have to call the action of animals free. Now it is open to Kenny to define a concept as broadly as he wishes. But then the question can be raised as to (a) whether the given definition corresponds to the way we normally use the words *free* and *responsible*; one can further ask (b) whether this account actually describes that meaning of *can* which is contained in sentences that express possibilities of action, and this is the question that is crucial for our purposes. Among other considerations we have to deal with the fact that we can speak of being "free" in a gradual sense; for example, we speak of diminished responsibility in the case of someone who is drunk. The inebriated person does what he wants to do, but would we say "it depended upon him"? If this is not the case, then obviously the thesis that "it depended upon me" means that "it only depended upon whether I wanted to do it" must be revised.

It is the capacity for deliberation that is missing in the case of animals and is assumed to be present to a diminished degree in the case of someone who is drunk. Now those "can" sentences that were to be elucidated also appear to belong to the context of deliberation, and it is this feature that is not taken into account by Kenny. We saw that "I could now break off the lecture" is the typical sentence form used when we are considering a possibility of action. And now an entirely different justification from the one provided by Kenny and Wolf for why we should not class the "if I want to" among the conditions of action suggests itself: The "if I want to" occupies a special position because it is essential for the *agent who deliberates* to distinguish what is given in the situation of action, which makes the action possible *for him*, from what depends *upon him*. The latter concerns the question of whether he wants to do it, and this means what position he takes toward it. At the same time it is clear that what is at issue is not any arbitrary situation of deliberation, or just any practical question; it does not involve deliberation about the best means for presupposed ends. Rather, we are deliberating about what we want to do, and this contains the question of who we want to be. In the case of animals what they do depends upon what they want, but they cannot ask themselves what they want; and this means that they cannot become aware of possibilities of action, that is, there is no correlate for them to the "can" sentences of the type "I can now break off the lecture."

What does it mean to ask oneself what one wants? Since this is a practical question, the issue is not to ascertain what I in fact want, what my inclinations are, but to determine what position to take toward my inclinations. Thus it is necessary here to return to the old distinction between immediate desiring, that is, inclinations, and reflective desiring, that is, willing in the strict sense; this is the distinction that Freud also had in view with his concepts of the "id" and the "ego" (although he thereby hypostatized the problem). The immediate desiring that Kenny has in view (he speaks of "wants") is to so little an extent what the deliberative agent is referring to when he says "I can if I want to" that we rather have to regard the inclinations among the conditions that are presupposed by the willing.[13] If I say "I could now break off the lecture," I thereby imply that I have not only the ability and opportunity for this but also an inclination to do it; and under certain circumstances I am also implying that I have inclinations opposed to this inclination, which come perhaps from shame or a feeling of duty; but now as I deliberate the question arises: What do *I want* to do? We have already seen that this question does not presuppose an "I" nucleus; it does not signify "what does 'the I' want?," but "who (or how) do I want to be?" The "it depends upon me" now certainly has a deeper meaning, so to speak, than it did in accordance with the previous version in which it merely signified "whether I want to do it" in the sense of immediate desiring; but it does not have this deeper meaning because it involves a different I. Rather, it is always the same person who is involved, and the "it depends upon me" again only means "whether I want to do it"; it is merely implied that the wanting now stands in the domain of deliberation. If the inclinations themselves belong to the conditions that are presupposed by the willing, this implies that the choice that is considered in deliberation is (in being a choice between possibilities of action) also a choice between inclinations; and if one wants to concede to Kenny that choosing is also part of immediate desiring, a second-order choice is at issue in the case of willing that involves taking a position.[14]

If this is the correct interpretation of the "can" sentences in question, it might seem as though an asymmetry would have to arise between first- and third-person "can" sentences. For I had claimed that the meaning of the "can" sentence can only be understood if one views it from the perspective of the deliberating agent. But if one speaks in the third person one can certainly assume that the person of whom one is speaking stands within the context of deliberation; and we also actually speak of someone precisely in this way if we take him to be accountable. And it is only in this case that we use a "can" sentence in the third person in such a way that it expresses a possibility of action and not a prognosis. I already noted that if you say "he could now break off the lecture" it suggests that you actually mean "it is possible that . . ." or "his psychological disposition does not appear to make it unlikely that . . .", but you can also use the sentence in the same sense in which I use it; and the criterion for whether you are using it in this way is (now as before) whether you would complete it in the following way: "he can if he wants to." You are talking about me in such a way that you put yourself in my position, and I talk about myself in an entirely equivalent way when I say with reference to a past situation that "I could have done otherwise if I had wanted to." In order to be able to talk in this way one does not have to presuppose that the person involved actually has deliberated, but only that he had the capability to deliberate, that he stood within a framework of deliberation even if he was not aware of it. By contrast, in the case of someone who was drunk we do not say without hesitation that "he could have done otherwise," because his ability to adhere to his long-range intentions, particularly to the intention not to act thoughtlessly, was reduced or nonexistent at this point just as was his capacity for deliberation itself. What the drunken person does depends merely upon his psychological disposition; *merely* here means without the intervening link of the framework of deliberation. But this does not mean that the willingness to deliberate and the extent to which the framework of deliberation is perceived are not themselves also psychologically conditioned in the other case. As Hampshire has shown, it is also meaningful from this point of view to speak of more or less freedom.

Thus Heidegger's thesis concerning the difference between 'existential' possibilities or possibilities of action and possibility in the sense of contingency would have to be elucidated in roughly this way. How can we make his second thesis intelligible (which is obviously crucial for him) that "possibility . . . is the ultimate positive ontological determination of Dasein"? Here a statement Heidegger makes two pages later helps: Dasein "is continually 'more' than it is factually, supposing that one wanted to make an inventory of it as something present-at-hand and list the contents of its being, and supposing that one could do so. But Dasein is never more than it factually is, because its potentiality-for-being belongs essentially to its facticity. But as possible-being Dasein is also never anything less; that is, it *is* existentially that which it is *not yet* in its potentiality-for-being" (BT, pp. 185–186). It is clear in this quote that Heidegger would like to express here something for which he lacks the appropriate words. He apparently can only describe the state of affairs by assuming something he himself considers false—namely, that one may "list the contents of Dasein's being as something present-at-hand." This idea is again taken up in a later and more central passage—where the structural totality of Dasein is characterized as care (section 41): "Dasein is in each case already *ahead* of itself in its being. Dasein is always 'beyond itself,' not as a mode of relating to other entities which it is not, but as being toward the potentiality-for-being which it is itself" (p. 236).

The last quote is without doubt the most intelligible. Indeed, we already saw in the preliminary analysis of the relation of oneself to one's own being that it only can be understood as a relation of oneself to one's own future being. Heidegger himself still did not mention the future at all in that context, and it is only at a later point in *Being and Time*—the systematically central point of the entire work, in which the move to temporality as the being of Dasein takes place—that he identifies as futurality (*Zukünftigkeit*) what he designates here as being-ahead-of-itself (section 65). Now I have characterized this relation of oneself to one's impending further life merely as a fact. Nevertheless, this fact that I can only relate myself to myself in my present existence by relating myself to my future being (which is not a subsequent being but the being that immediately impends) is puzzling enough; in this respect I forge a quasi-unextended, punctual bridge between the now and the moment that immediately follows, which, according to Heidegger, first makes possible all further relation to the future as futural. And it is this fact that Heidegger would like to make intelligible by means of the concept of existential possibility.

Thus his thesis is that through the relation of oneself to possibilities of action this being-ahead-of-oneself is made possible. In Heidegger's more abstract terminology, only because I relate myself to my being as possible-being can I relate myself to it at all, and this at the same time implies that I relate myself to it futurally. If the explanation that was just elaborated of how the "I can" of action possibility is to be understood is correct, this means a being is not 'ahead-of-itself' simply by virtue of being volitionally active, but this futural reference emerges first in the deliberative "I can," that is, in the open range of action that becomes explicit in deliberation.

Perhaps this thesis can be made clearer by attending to another aspect of deliberative action. We have already seen that deliberation is directed toward a decision, and conversely that all action that is articulated in sentences of intention can be put into question at any time; thus, the open range of possibilities remains constitutive for it. Now Hampshire has pointed out that one can illuminate the phenomenon that Heidegger has in mind in the expression *being-ahead-of-oneself*, that is, the peculiar unity of the present and the succeeding moment in acting, by noting that whenever someone is interrupted in doing something he can always say what he would have done next.[15] In a certain sense the purpose continually runs ahead of the doing. This does not happen explicitly, but it can be made explicit in the experiment envisioned by Hampshire. In this way Heidegger's thesis that Dasein "is continually 'more' than it is factually" can acquire a clear meaning. The "more" is the purpose that is constitutive for the intentional activity and runs ahead of it. The next step in the action, however, is a possibility of action, and this can again be confirmed through an experiment in which the agent stops himself and raises the practical question. Now I need only cite Heidegger's statement again, which had previously appeared obscure: Dasein "is never more than it factually is, because its potentiality-for-being belongs essentially to its facticity" (p. 185). And for this reason "possibility as an *existentiale* is the most primordial and ultimate positive ontological determination of Dasein" (p. 183).

Lecture 10

Heidegger on the Relation of Oneself to Oneself, III: Choosing Oneself

I will continue immediately from the point at the end of the last lecture where I had to interrupt the interpretation of the second aspect of the relation of oneself to oneself, namely, the relation to one's own being as the for-the-sake-of-which and possibility. I wanted to explain the terms that are fundamental for Heidegger's account of this side of the relation of oneself to one's own being in the following sequence: *for-the-sake-of-which, possibility, understanding, projection,* and *meaning.* We are still concerned with the second of these terms. I claimed that there are two reasons why Heidegger designates the activities in which man concretely carries out his being as possibilities. First, he wanted to underline the range of freedom that pertains to our activity on the basis of the yes/no polarity of our understanding. We then saw that this is connected to the further thesis that we can only relate ourselves to our being as something impending because we relate ourselves to our actions as possibilities of action and to our being as potentiality-for-being; and it is only on this basis that a consciousness of the future emerges.

The second reason for Heidegger's choice of the term *possibility* is still to be identified. I have already pointed out that Heidegger neglected to elucidate the traditional concepts for the volitional self-relation by means of his elaboration of the relation of oneself to oneself because he wanted to separate himself as sharply as possible from the tradition. The choice of the term *possibility* for the concrete units in which Dasein carries out its being seems to me to be an expression of this neglect.

On the one hand, the choice of this term undoubtedly has the positive significance of emphasizing that the person relates himself to himself in his activities, since these are designated as possibilities of being. In this way the connection of the basic units in which one's own being is concretized with the global unit of existence is secured, but the characterization of the basic units as possibilities leaves their descriptive character completely indeterminate. The question of how these possibilities are to be understood concretely—for instance, as actions, connections of actions, activities, and roles—is left open, and the choice of the term *possibility* somewhat obscures this fact.

The three remaining terms—*understanding*, *projection*, and *meaning*—can be explained in connection with one another. *Understanding* stands for the specific disclosure of one's own being as possible-being. The best possible mode of access to what Heidegger means by *understanding* seems to me to be the connection between understanding and meaning, although Heidegger himself does not introduce the concept of understanding in this way. I pointed out earlier that we use the expressions *understanding* and *meaning* correlatively and that one must distinguish between the understanding and meaning of linguistic expressions and the understanding of the meaning of an action. Meaning in this second sense (really the primary sense as indicated earlier) signifies the same thing as purpose and end. Understanding an action means understanding its meaning, and this means understanding its purpose. We understand a thing that was deliberately produced when we understand its function—its purpose—and this involves knowing what end it serves, and how one has to use it in order to attain this. We understand a person when we correctly grasp the intentions of his action, the interconnection of his motives for acting.

We have already seen that Heidegger does not clearly distinguish this understanding of meaning from the understanding of linguistic meaning. This is connected to the fact that he makes excessive claims for the concepts of understanding and meaning. Thus he advances the thesis that "all sight is grounded primarily in understanding" (p. 187), and that meaning is the focal point "in terms of which anything becomes intelligible as something" (193). This also led Heidegger to neglect the specifically practical, volitional aspect of *meaning*. We will have to disregard these excessive claims and this illicit shift in the concept of meaning.

The understanding of intentions as I have just described it is a mode of knowledge. I understand an action, a person, a thing, when I know the purpose that the action has or the end that the thing serves. The volitional aspect here belongs, not to the act of understanding, but to the object of understanding.

But Heidegger wants the word *understanding* to be grasped in such a way that it stands for the disclosure of one's own possible-being. Just as a specific disclosure of one's own being in emotions and moods was elaborated under the title "temperament," so the specific mode of disclosure that pertains to willing itself is now to be presented under the title "understanding." Thus, a kind of understanding is at issue for which it is constitutive that it is understanding in the first person. Heidegger describes three aspects of such an understanding that pertain to potentiality-for-being, although he does not himself distinguish between these aspects.

As to the first aspect, when I myself do something, we would not normally say that I understand the intention. This is connected with the epistemic asymmetry of "ϕ" predicates. I do not first have to interpret a form of behavior in order to know what intention *I* am pursuing. In acting I pursue the intention, and I do not first have to apprehend it. But we have now seen that the intention or purpose guides the action, so to speak; the action would lack orientation in its absence. And this can be regarded as a first form of the disclosure that pertains to the action itself.

Heidegger takes recourse here to another mode of use of the word *understanding*: "We sometimes use . . . the expression 'understand something' in the sense of 'being able to manage something', 'being a match for it', 'being able to do something' " (183). Heidegger even uses this phrase to introduce the concept of understanding. He thinks that through this connection of the use of "understanding how to do something" and "being able to do something" he can make understanding plausible as the mode of disclosure that is constitutive for possibilities of action. But here his deficient analysis of the concepts of possibility had unfavorable consequences. The "can" that is used when we say "someone can do something" obviously stands for the "can" of ability and not for the "can" of the possibility of action. Nonetheless, Heidegger seems to me to have seen something correct here. I just pointed out that we understand a thing that has a function when we know how it is used. But one can only demonstrate this knowledge and (if necessary) convey it to others by actually dealing with the thing correctly. And this way of dealing with things requires a specific disclosure. Heidegger designates it as circumspection. In English and the Romance languages one can use the word *know* in place of the word *can* when it has this sense, for example, "I know how to drive" in place of "I can drive." The specific disclosure that directs the activity itself, which Heidegger called circumspection, was later identified and analyzed by G. Ryle as "knowing how." It is not limited to the correct way of dealing with a thing. Rather, we also speak of a circumspect mode of behavior in a situation of action— and Heidegger tries to take this into account (cf. BT, p. 373). To be sure, Heidegger did not analyze this phenomenon more closely, and it is doubtful whether he even would have been able to elucidate the understanding of a thing more precisely without the concept of a rule.

I turn now to the second aspect. In the preceding account the disclosure that guides the action was considered only in the context of determinate and particular ends of action. Now we have already seen in connection with the interpretation of moods that a being that volitionally relates itself to its own being depends upon finding a meaning for its life if its will is not to fall into a void. Thus it is now not only the meaning of an individual action that is involved but also the meaning of life; here *meaning* implies something like a conception of life on whose basis one can understand oneself in one's willing and doing. Heidegger considers this aspect right at the beginning of his exposition; after he has alluded to the use of the expression *understand something* in the sense of "being able to do something," he continues: "In understanding as an *existentiale*, that of which we are able is not a what, but being as existing" (p. 183). The unfortunate mixture of the two meanings of *can* is retained in this sentence; in addition, it seems unclear how one is supposed to be able to apply the idea of "knowing how" to existing as such. The characterization of understanding as "projection" that subsequently follows is more illuminating (185). For Heidegger, *projecting* means understanding oneself in terms of a conception of life. The thing that is projected is meaning (193). The concept of projection suggests the view that man creates his conception of life himself, but what is meant is only that this conception must be posited in one way or another; we have no volitional ends that are predetermined by nature, because we relate ourselves to our being. Since as Heidegger says the projection is also always thrown

(BT, p. 315) or pregiven, we actually find ourselves in the context of socially pregiven conceptions of life to an extent that obviously varies according to the historical situation. With this statement I am touching upon a social problematic that Heidegger completely neglects. Of course, he does analyze being-with others, and he also analyzes the dependence of one's self-understanding upon what most people consider correct under the title of the "they" (das Man). But his analysis lacks a proper appreciation of social and institutional interconnections, and the roles that are determined on this basis; and it is doubtful whether understanding oneself in terms of a conception of life is even conceivable outside these social interconnections. This is one of the points in Heidegger that refer us to the interpretation of Mead.

Heidegger assigns still another meaning of the word *understanding* to this projective aspect of understanding by virtue of which I understand myself in terms of a meaning (although he does not do so explicitly). He says that in understanding Dasein "knows" "how things stand with itself, i.e. with its potentiality-for-being" (184). He thereby alludes to a meaning of *understanding* in terms of which one can say "I understand myself as the so-and-so." We have already encountered this aspect, since it has been repeatedly shown that the question of how I decide about my potentiality-for-being is decisive for the issue of who I am. At a first level *who* can simply mean the social role that I have, for example, I understand myself as an auto mechanic, as a father of a family, and so on; but on a broader level *who* can also mean the kind of person I am.

Let me recapitulate. When the word *understanding* is intended in the sense of understanding actions, persons, and things, we normally use it in such a way that it does not refer to ourselves; and here understanding is a completely normal (if nonetheless distinctive) kind of knowledge. Heidegger wants to use the word *understanding* in a partly unconventional sense to designate the disclosure that belongs to willing and to deliberative activity itself. We have now become familiar with two aspects of this disclosure. In the first case the word *understanding* cannot be used in such a way that it is related to meaning; rather, it refers to understanding how to do something. Furthermore, a disclosure of *oneself* is still not at issue here, but only the circumspect execution of an action. An understanding of oneself is clearly involved in the case of the second aspect, and here we can use the word in its normal sense; but this understanding is not a kind of knowledge: one understands *oneself*—one's being—in terms of a meaning.

The form of disclosure in volitional self-understanding that emerged in the discussion of the existential concept of possibility comes to the fore only in the third aspect. When we explicitly consider our potentiality-for-being—although not theoretically—this takes place by raising the practical question, by deliberating. In the section in which Heidegger deals with understanding, the possibility of the explicit practical disclosure is only touched upon in passing. This may be connected to the fact that deliberation is not well suited to be designated as understanding. The word *deliberation* does not occur at all in *Being and Time*; we will later have to ask ourselves why this is the case. The point at issue is expressed, nevertheless, in the following statement by Heidegger: "The projection is the existential constitution of the being of the *open range (Spielraum)* of the actual potentiality-for-being" (185, my emphasis).

Deliberation in the form in which it has been encountered in the discussion of possibilities of action is still not *eo ipso* existence in the mode of self-determination; for deliberation concerning who I want to be can still be oriented toward accepted and conventional points of view. But deliberation *can* assume the form of the practical question that is understood in a fundamental sense. Existence in the mode of "authenticity" is an exemplary mode of understanding one's own being in an 'open range of possibilities'; and this is why the analysis of understanding leads directly to the third stage that I proposed for the interpretation of Heidegger's conception of the relation of oneself to oneself—that is, to the question of Heidegger's conception of the relation of oneself to oneself in the strict sense of being-oneself and self-determination.

Heidegger introduces this problem by raising the question of the "who" of Dasein (section 25). The way that he deals with this question again reveals a curious mixture of insight and confusion; and the confusion seems to me to result once more from a lack of language-analytical reflection.

In addressing the question of the who it seems plausible, he says, to proceed from the assumption that "Dasein" is the "being" "that I myself always am." From this one might infer the following: "The who is defined in terms of the I itself, that is, the 'subject' or the 'self.' The who is the thing that maintains its identity through the change

of behavior and experiences, and is thereby related to this multiplicity."
Heidegger thus suggests that the concept of the I in the tradition
deriving from Fichte arose from such an interpretation of the who
question and that for this reason the independence and constancy of
the I are understood as substantiality. In contrast, he insists that the
question of the who, the self, the I, and the independence and constancy
of the I must be understood from the standpoint of existentiality
(p. 152, cf. also pp. 369ff.).

How does the question appear from this standpoint? Heidegger
writes: "It could be that the who of everyday Dasein is precisely *not*
the I that I myself always am" (p. 150). This sounds curiously paradoxical. We will reply, Who am I supposed to be if not I myself?
Heidegger answers in response: Initially and for the most part I am
not I myself, but the "they-self" (*man-selbst*) (27). "The *they* . . . answers
the question of the *who* of everyday Dasein" (pp. 165–166). Heidegger
thereby wants to say, I allow what I respectively do and intend and
how I understand myself to be determined by what *one* (the they)
regards as good, and I do not determine it myself. "With Dasein's
lostness in the they, that actual potentiality-for-being that is closest
to it—the tasks, rules and standards, the urgency and extent of con-
cernful and solicitous being-in-the-world—has already been decided
upon. The they has always kept Dasein from taking hold of these
possibilities of being. The they even hides the manner in which it has
tacitly relieved Dasein of the burden of explicitly *choosing* these possibilities" (312).

This also indicates the conditions under which I am 'I myself': "the
existentiell modification of the they-self into *authentic* being-one's-self
must be carried out as the recovery of a choice. But the recovery of
choice means choosing this choice, i.e., deciding for a potentiality-of-
being on the basis of one's own self" (313).

Thus the state of affairs that Heidegger has in mind is now clear.
In the terminology that I used it concerns the practical question insofar
as it is posed fundamentally. Since we stand existentially in an open
range of possibilities of being, we have the possibility either to consider
this range or to conceal it from ourselves, to question ourselves and
to choose who we want to be or to evade this question. The account
of the they now indicates how this question can be evaded, namely,
by doing those things and living in that manner which 'one' generally
regards as correct. This implies that one cannot simply exist within

a possibility; all human existence apparently must be grounded in one way or another in something that is regarded as correct. This may be what is generally regarded as correct, or what I myself believe to recognize as correct. If someone does not make the choice himself, he must be relieved of it.

Thus, when Heidegger distinguishes the "I myself" from the "they-self," he is referring to a distinction that he also designates as one between 'authentic' and 'inauthentic' existence. Existing authentically means existing in the mode of self-determination, and Heidegger also employs the term *resoluteness* (*Entschlossenheit*) in this context (343). When Heidegger first presented his ideas in lectures at Marburg, the students remarked jokingly, "We are resolute, but we do not know to what purpose." The word one-sidedly emphasizes the aspect of the outcome of a choice. We can make Heidegger's point more accessible if we take into account that a decision (resolution) is the end toward which deliberation proceeds; thus, one might say, the term *resoluteness* represents the entirety of the question, deliberation, choice, and decision, although we will later see that this does not exactly fit Heidegger's conception.

It remains to be noted that Heidegger speaks not only of a choice but also of "choosing this choice." This description addressses the fact that we can either pose the practical question or not pose it: We have the *possibility* to make ourselves open to the range of possibilities. Thus we have the possibility of choosing among possibilities or, as this has also been expressed, we are free either to be free or not. For this reason choice always implies a choosing of choosing, and since in choosing we exist in the mode of being-oneself, Heidegger also speaks of a "choosing oneself" (*Sich-selbst-wählens*) (232, 334).

The last formulation leads us back to the formulations that Heidegger used in connection with the question of the who. The meaning of Heidegger's paradoxical claim that I can be either I myself or not I myself has now been elucidated. As Heidegger himself notes, these expressions refer to "certain ways to be" (163)—that is, to a person's existence that is either in the mode of self-determination or not. The discussion of self-determination finally loses the last appearance of paradox when it becomes clear that it merely addresses the question of whether or not someone himself chooses what he does or wants; in other words, the issue is whether the person himself decides who he is. In the latter formulation—whether he has chosen it himself—

the emphasis upon *himself* is suitable, but it can also just as well be omitted. Perhaps you will protest and insist that not every choice is a self-choosing. But in this case you simply mean that not every choice is a choice in which the person decides about his being, about who (how) he wants to be.

Hence if the word *himself* is even dispensable in the formulation "whether he chooses himself," it is plainly misused when it is employed outside this context in order to express the mode of being of choosing. On this basis the contradictory formulation "I am not I myself" emerges, from which Heidegger had proceeded. Heidegger's talk of being-oneself and choosing oneself are also to be rejected for the same reason. The latter expression certainly would be meaningful if its function were only to express in shortened form that someone chooses who (how) he wants to be. It is misleading, however, if (as is obviously the case with Heidegger) it means that I choose myself or to be myself. We have already seen that the descriptive meaning of this way of speaking is that I choose to choose.

Thus the talk of the self and of being-oneself is based upon a misuse of the word *self* that proceeds in two phases; first, it is torn out of its natural context and, second, it is converted into a substantive. This conversion into a substantive always harbors the danger of hypostatizing a second subject within the person. In Heidegger's case this does not occur, but an analogous paradox arises: He puts *Dasein*, which can either be itself or not itself, in the *place* of the person. We are told that Dasein is not something present-at-hand, that is, a substance, subject, or person; *rather*, it is existence. This is only the more radical position in appearance. In truth existence can only substitute for substance through a failure to grasp it as what it is—namely, the being of a person. And this happens in Heidegger through his conversion of the modes of being themselves into substances: he speaks of "the they," the "being-oneself," and so on. Fortunately, he also provides descriptive formulations that permit an adequate conceptual account of the phenomena and are free of paradox. He has shown that the meaning of the talk of the relation of oneself to oneself is the relation to one's own being; and he shows that the meaning of the talk of self-determination lies in the mode of being of choosing. The difficulty arises through his failure to adhere to these verbal formulations as the only ones that are legitimate for these states of affairs. If one does this, the substantival mode of speaking remains available for the designation of the person. To be sure, Heidegger would not have consented to this because (as we have already seen) he wanted to have a rift between existence and the being of the present-at-hand.

It is now also clear that the orientation toward the question of the who of Dasein is fundamentally misguided. We know from our earlier discussions that the force of the question who is a request for an identification of the relevant person. Thus Heidegger immediately makes a mistake in his basic approach when he assumes that the question "who am I?" can be answered by "I" or "I myself." We have seen that I cannot identify myself by the use of the word *I*. Now you might point out that I have myself repeatedly used expressions such as "the question at issue is who I want to be." Nonetheless, for the purpose of avoiding misunderstanding I have frequently added "who signifies how, or what kind of a person, I want to be." The word *who* here is not used for individual identification, but for so-called qualitative identification. For example, if a beetle collector wants to identify an exemplar, his goal is not to identify this exemplar as an individual, but to determine the type to which it belongs. And in the present context when we ask "who is that?" with reference to persons, we can obviously mean "what sort of person is he?"

Just as Heidegger presented the misleading talk of being-oneself as an alternative to the conception of the person as subject and substance, he also placed two additional determinations (both illuminating in themselves) in an analogous contrast. These are the determinations of the independence (*Selbständigkeit*) and constancy (*Ständigkeit*) of authentic existence, on whose basis he characterized the difference between authentic and inauthentic existence (351, 369, 381, 426ff.).

The talk of independence or self-sufficiency is easily understood in this context: We call someone independent if he does not act in conformity with what is commonly believed, but deliberates and decides himself. But if the independence that is understood in this way is treated as a competitor to the Aristotelian concept of self-sufficiency (by means of which Aristotle distinguished substance from the determinations that are ontologically dependent upon it), this merely leads to unnecessary paradoxes.

By means of the concept of the constancy of the self Heidegger wants to address the problem of "the 'connectedness of life', i.e., the stretching-along, movement and persistence that are specific for Dasein" (427ff.). I already alluded to this problem when I noted that if the practical question is posed fundamentally it refers to life as a whole. Heidegger works out this reference to the totality of one's own being through the concept of being-towards-death. The possibility of death is the possibility of no-longer-being. I have so far only referred to this possibility in Hamlet's question of whether it is better to be or not to be. But now we must recognize the more general state of affairs that is contained in this question—namely, the fact that one only perceives the possibility of life (like every possibility) in unity with its negation. But this implies the following: The confrontation with myself (i.e., with my life as such) that is required for choice only takes place in the simultaneous confrontation with the ever-present possibility of the end of my life. Heidegger's talk of being-toward-death has been the object of ridicule, but this has been completely unjustified. From Heidegger's point of view, the confrontation with the "unsurpassable" possibility of death concerns "Dasein's being-in-the-world as such" (294). And I regard as incontestable his thesis that this confrontation (a) sets one free "from one's lostness in those possibilities which may accidentally thrust themselves upon one" (308), and (b) in this respect is a necessary condition for the authenticity of choice (section 62). His thesis is well grounded analytically and can be confirmed through a thought experiment. Furthermore, the principal importance of the confrontation with one's death for the entire problem of self-consciousness must be acknowledged. A subject or an expression standing for a subject cannot be negated, but only a propositional content. Therefore, for the traditional theory of self-consciousness there *could* not be a correlative relation to one's own nonbeing; in 'reflection' the subject relates itself simply to itself. And consequently as soon as one understands the relation of oneself to oneself as a relation of oneself to one's own life, one must also see it as a simultaneous relation of oneself to the possibility of death.

The reference of authentic choice to death (and this means to life as a whole) leads to a way of relating oneself to oneself that Heidegger terms the "stretchedness" (*Erstrecktheit*) of authentic existence; and the type of continuity that he characterized by means of his concept of constancy is also part of this. He does not mean that life proceeds according to a preconceived plan, or that one is not open for a change in one's life conception (cf. pp. 308, 355ff.). But if the change is chosen at the time for a purpose, there is a reason for it; and in this way the continuity in the discontinuity is also restored. This process stands in contrast to allowing oneself to live from day to day, which is not continuously related in an existential sense—in one's way of acting— even if it always remains the same.

Heidegger not only provided the concept of self-determination with a structurally sound meaning, but he also clarified the sense in which there are two levels of the practical relation of oneself to oneself, as I indicated at the beginning of these lectures. The understanding of the fact that we relate ourselves to ourselves *in* our wanting and doing (and in our emotions and moods as well) has become clear through Heidegger's conception of the relation of oneself to oneself as the relation of oneself to one's own to-be, and through his elaboration of this conception in light of the facticity and possibility character of this to-be. The dual possibility within such a relation of oneself to oneself of self-determination and of evasion in the face of such self-deter- mination is a result of (1) the yes/no polarity that pertains to the understanding of being (or more precisely to the understanding of possible-being) *and* (2) the fact that there is a motive for concealing from oneself the possibility of placing one's own being into question.[1]

But now we must also examine the limits of Heidegger's conception of self-determination. When I introduced the concept of self-deter- mination at the beginning of these lectures, I presented it in immediate connection with what I termed a reflective self-relation. I characterized the latter as that relation of oneself to oneself which places the beliefs implied in one's actions and purposes into question; these involve beliefs about facts as well as normative beliefs. Thus this self-relation stands for the question of truth insofar as it pertains to the presup- positions of one's own action. The appropriateness of the term *reflective* for this mode of the relation of oneself to oneself is not based upon the meaning of the word *reflection* in the traditional theory of self- consciousness; rather, it is grounded in the use of this word in the sense of "deliberation." Thus the reflective self-relation signifies a self- relation that is deliberative. As we have already seen, deliberating means posing a practical question, and a deliberative relation to *oneself* is one in which the practical question becomes fundamental, that is, in which it concerns one's own being. We have also already seen that when we deliberate or pose the practical question, we always ask, What is good?, or more precisely (since one always deliberates about alternatives), What is better or the best? At that point we saw that *good* or *better* is a word that expresses the fact that we prefer something;

but this is not the only thing at issue, since in contrast to *pleasant* the word *good* expresses an objective preference. In the sentence "I prefer it because it gives me more pleasure," the present subjective state is the basis of the decision; in contrast, if we say "because it is better," this implies that there are reasons to prefer it. Sentences with the word *pleasant* are therefore sentences about myself, that is, about a "ϕ" state of mine; sentences with the word *good* predicate a character of preferability of a state of affairs, and they are objective statements that raise a claim to be justified. And it is for this reason that deliberation is directed toward the issue of the better and the best, since we surely do not have to trouble ourselves about what is more pleasant. Deliberation aims at an objectively justified choice. Therefore advice or counsel is also possible in those cases involving deliberation. When we advise someone we are deliberating about what is preferable for him to do for objective reasons.

We have encountered the issue of the good in the interpretation of Heidegger on several levels, and there actually seems to be a hierarchy of modes of use of the word *good* that is not readily transparent.[2] On the lowest level it obviously does not yet have its objective connotation, for example, when we say "it tastes better to me." If we consider specific activities as part of our 'well-being' because we like doing them, what is good in this sense of goodness is so not because it is to be justified as such through deliberation, but because it serves as a basis for the deliberation about what constitutes the good life for me. We have a particularly difficult situation in the case of the emotions. The emotions and moods are modes of an *immediate* state of being-concerned by something that is good or bad for my being or that affects me through my conception of what the good life is for me. It is for this reason that one can argue with someone (or also with oneself of course) about the justifiability of his emotion or mood. ("You say that things aren't going well, that you are in despair, but actually you have every reason to be satisfied when you consider that your conditions of life are such and such.") We obviously have a more unequivocal situation in those cases in which we deliberate about which possibility of action we should choose, since here we have to deal with a practical question. Nonetheless, it must give us pause to realize that precisely in those cases in which the practical question is posed fundamentally a formulation with the word *good* does not recommend itself; rather, the question who or how do I want to be seems more appropriate.

Still, one can always also pose the question in this way: What is the best thing for me to do? But in this context, when we ask someone for advice about a concrete life decision, he will first adduce reasons, but in the end he will say, "It is your life, only you can decide what the best thing is for you, who you want to be." Thus, there is an ultimate point in deliberation at which we simply can no longer justify the decision objectively; rather, what is best for me at this point is itself only constituted in my wanting it. What is involved here is that second-order wanting in which we adopt position such and such toward our immediate wishes and inclinations. If this were not the case, if wanting in the final instance could still rest upon reasons, the will would lose its significance or force, so to speak; and this means it would no longer be *my* adoption of a position. (You should no longer fear that 'the I' is again returning here. I am challenged in fact, but this means I have to take a position.)

If we now return to Heidegger's concept of self-determination after this excursus on the concept of the reflective self-relation, we must note that the aspect of reflection is missing in Heidegger's conception of self-determination. In any case, no explicit reference is made to the aspect of deliberation at all, and this is related to the absence of the concept of the good from the analysis in *Being and Time*. It is present only in the form of the concept of the for-the-sake-of-which. But this merely stands for the ultimate reference point of wanting. The point of view of objective justification to which the practical question is related is missing entirely. This is connected to the fact that although regard for the well-being of others is incorporated into the preliminary discussion of being-with in a purely descriptive way (section 26), it is missing entirely (or almost entirely) from the subsequent account of self-determination. If we understand by morality those norms that specify what is good or bad for me to do in light of a consideration of the interests of others, such an understanding of morality is not to be found in *Being and Time*. But it would seem clear that either positively or negatively this aspect pertains essentially to the question of who or how I want to be. And the claim of objective justification seems especially apparent for this component of practical deliberation. Of course, it is also the case here that the question of the extent to which I take the moral point of view into account is ultimately a matter to be decided by my choice of what kind of a person I want to be.

The fact that the concept of the good—and correlatively both the concept of deliberation and that of the justification of evaluative and normative statements—cannot be found in Heidegger is a consequence of his concept of truth. I would like to examine this problem only very briefly here, since I have dealt with it extensively in my book *Der Wahrheitsbegriff bei Husserl und Heidegger*. The concept of the good also falls under the concept of truth, since all statements contain a truth claim (and this means a claim to justification); and sentences that say that something is good or better are statements. Now Heidegger did not (as might have been expected) also jettison the concept of truth along with the concept of the good. The issue here is more complex. Heidegger began with the assumption that a statement 'discloses' something, and he formalized the concept of truth in such a way that he ultimately grasped it as coextensive with the concept of disclosure (section 44). But the specific meaning of *true*—namely, the claim to justification and proof—thereby drops out of the account. Yet since the word *truth* is retained, it simultaneously appears as if the concept of truth is preserved and even deepened; and on this basis a peculiarly illusive situation arises. For example, Heidegger designates resoluteness, that is, existence in the mode of authenticity, as "the truth of Dasein which is most primordial because it is authentic" (p. 343); and this is completely consistent, of course, since resoluteness is the disclosure in the mode of authenticity. If one adheres to the genuine concept of truth, however, one cannot designate authentic existence directly as truth; rather, one must characterize it as a state of being-directed toward truth in the sense of the practical question regarding the true good. This question includes (1) *gnothi seauton*, the "self-knowledge" that is also touched upon at one point by Heidegger (BT, p. 186), or the process of "becoming transparent to oneself" in the motives underlying one's intentions. And it also involves (2) the question of whether the following set of assumptions has been properly justified: (a) the factual assumptions implied by my intentions, (b) the normative assumptions regarding my obligation toward others that are also implied in my intentions, and finally (c) the evaluative assumptions regarding my own well-being. These objective deliberations constitute the basis for the decision (although it is not deducible from them) concerning who (or how) I want to be. Since Heidegger designates resoluteness directly as the essential truth, this objective basis of deliberation that precedes the decision is not merely overlooked; rather, the form of resoluteness that is understood in this way is unequivocally separated from the question of truth precisely because it already is the truth itself.

If we understand the word *reason* in its traditional meaning, as the capacity for justification, Heidegger's step here must be characterized as an attempt to banish reason from human existence and particularly from the relation of oneself to oneself. At the beginning of these lectures we noted that the problem of self-consciousness in modern philosophy up to Fichte and Hegel was regarded as philosophically so central only because self-consciousness appeared constitutive for a form of life related to reason. It is therefore all the more surprising that precisely the philosopher who first developed an adequate structural conception of the relation of oneself to oneself abandons the concept of reason.

It might now seem plausible to suspect that Heidegger's concept of the relation of oneself to oneself does not allow for a concept of reason at all. I consider this suspicion unjustified. We have seen that the concept of self-determination as Heidegger developed it can be conceived without violence in conjunction with the concept of deliberation, and therefore it can be understood as a reflective self-relation. Of course, you can object that my interpretation was forced to a certain extent. But this was done intentionally. My intention was not to provide a faithful account of Heidegger, but to extract what we need from Heidegger for our actual formulation of the problem. In my view Heidegger's approach is the only one that permits a structurally irreproachable elucidation of the relation of oneself to oneself in general, and of self-determination in particular.

I would like to go another step further and argue that Heidegger's concept of self-determination not only admits of extension through a relation to reason but also demands this extension on its own grounds. In my view, the concept of self-determination without reason as presented by Heidegger is untenable, and even his own conception is imperceptibly sustained by a relation to reason. Thus, my thesis is that there simply cannot be a form of self-determination that is not understood as a reflective self-relation.

The proof of this rests upon the analytic connection that was established in the last lecture between the strict concept of freedom in the sense of responsible freedom and the concept of deliberation. We saw just now that self-determination means that the involved person himself chooses who (how) he wants to be. But we also saw that a decision is fundamentally to be understood as the outcome of a deliberation. This does not mean that an actual process of deliberation must precede a decision, but it does mean that a decision implies a deliberation. A choice that cannot even be justified after the fact is not a decision. A choice that is not deliberated, that is not made in light of reasons, is a choice in which I leave how I choose to accident; and in this respect we have to say it was not I who chose. Does our old phantom 'the I' return here for one last time? Of course not, since we have already seen that the meaning of talking about whether it was I who chose consist in establishing whether I have chosen in a certain way.

According to Heidegger, authentic choice is supposed to bring Dasein back from its lostness in the arbitrariness and contingency of the possibilities in which it actually finds itself. If this is to be the meaning of the choice, it requires a criterion or standard. It became clear early in our discussion that Dasein does not possess a material criterion in something like its 'self,' which it would merely have to apply to its possibilities; indeed, a material criterion is out of the question here. The only thing a standard can mean here is a way of confronting one's possibilities in authentic choice, namely, a manner of raising questions about them. The only criterion that Heidegger furnishes is the confrontation with death, and this is certainly a necessary condition. But is it sufficient?

Heidegger himself writes: "One's anticipatory projection on that possibility of existence which is not to be outstripped—on death—guarantees only the totality and authenticity of one's resoluteness. But those possibilities of existence which have actually been disclosed are not to be gathered from death" (p. 434). But then where are they to be found? Heidegger's answer is from one's own thrownness, and this means from one's historicity (435–437). Although it is correct to say that it is part of authentic existence to accept oneself as what one is and has become, it is still trivial to say that the possibilities that are to be chosen are those that are in fact given; such a strategy provides exactly no criterion for the choice between possibilities. Heidegger moves in circles here: On the one hand, the choice is supposed to free one from the contingency of possibilities in which one actually finds oneself; on the other hand, he refers the choice itself to historicity, to the possibilities in which one actually finds oneself. Since Heidegger envisages no justification for why one of several historically given possibilities is chosen instead of another, it is an irrational choice in the strict sense of the word.

In the case of an irrational choice we tend to adopt the following description: Something has chosen rather than I have chosen. Why? We saw earlier that if the will could still rely upon reasons in the final instance, my adoption of a position would lose its force, and would not be my adoption of a position. But the following is equally true: If the will were not obliged to rely upon reasons in the penultimate instance, my adoption of a position would be without force, and would not be my adoption of a position. Thus, the upshot of this is that the distinguishing feature of that choice which can be characterized as self-determination is that the choice is carried out in the mode of *rational volition*. The choice cannot be understood as self-determination either (a) if one denies its irreducible volitional character, that is, if one claims to be able to reduce it to rationality, or (b) if (like Heidegger) one denies that it must be able to rest upon justification, that is, that it is grounded in the question of truth even though it cannot be fully resolved in this question.

The fact that Heidegger still retained the concept of truth (though in the illusive mode suggested) can be regarded as evidence that even his derationalized conception continues to be imperceptibly sustained by a relation to reason. The consequences of this derationalized conception of choice and the derationalized concept of truth, however, can be seen in a speech that Heidegger gave in November 1933. The speech was given in support of Hitler prior to the national referendum on Germany's withdrawal from the League of Nations. It begins in this way: "The German people are called upon to choose by their leader [*Führer*]. But the leader does not demand anything of the people; rather, he offers the people the immediate possibility of the supreme free decision: whether the people as a whole will claim their own Dasein, or whether they will fail to claim it. Tomorrow the people choose nothing less than their future." And it then continues: "What kind of an occasion is this? The people recover the truth of their will as Dasein, for truth is the disclosure of what makes a people certain, clear and strong in their acting and knowing."[3] These quotes indicate that Heidegger's Nazism was no accidental affair, but that a direct path led from his philosophy—from its derationalized concept of truth and the concept of self-determination defined by this—to Nazism.

Nonetheless, we would be relinquishing philosophical insight if we did not want to learn what we can from Heidegger for this reason. The point is to recognize precisely the position that led to irrationalism, and not to throw the baby out with the bath water.

Lecture 11

Mead, I: Symbolic Interaction

Aside from Heidegger, George Herbert Mead is the only philosopher I know of who has attempted to free the relation of oneself to oneself from the conception of a reflexive relation. He thereby sought to extricate it from the traditional subject-object model, and to reconceptualize it in a structurally new way. Perhaps Gilbert Ryle should also be mentioned in addition to Mead; I will return to his work later in this lecture. According to Mead, the relation of oneself to oneself must be understood as talking to oneself, and this in turn is to be understood as the internalization of communicative talking to others. Therefore, the relation of oneself to oneself is essentially both linguistically and socially conditioned. But for Mead the reverse of this conditional relation is equally operative: Only beings that can relate themselves to themselves by virtue of their capacity to talk to themselves can speak the specifically human form of language and can have the specifically human (i.e., normative) form of sociality. The thesis of the connection of language and normative sociality is old—going back to Aristotle[1]—but the addition of the relation of oneself to oneself to this complex of conditions is new.

Thus we are confronted with two conceptions: (a) the Heideggerean account, which insists that the relation of oneself to oneself is to be understood as a relation to one's own to-be, and (b) Mead's conception, which claims that it is to be understood as a form of talking to oneself. If Mead's conception should prove (when properly interpreted) to be as valid as Heidegger's, we will have to assume that the two conceptions do not represent alternatives, but supplement one another; for there is surely only one truth regarding these matters.

We have already been able to locate weak points in Heidegger's conception that demand supplementation. It became clear at the end of the last lecture that Heidegger cannot grasp that eminent form of the relation of oneself to oneself which is termed self-determination as a reflective self-relation because he abandons the standpoint of reason. Deliberation and justification, however, are precisely modes of talking to oneself, and they represent a form of talking to oneself in which the deliberating agent counsels himself from an objective perspective, that is, from the perspective of any given partner. Moreover, in the clarification of relation of oneself to one's own being that preceded the discussion of self-determination, we encountered the question of whether the projection of one's own being in terms of a meaning is not essentially dependent upon the social dimension. And this question can easily lead to the assumption that there cannot even be something like a relation to one's own being outside an intersubjective context.

On the other hand, Mead's structural approach contains a clear possibility of connection with Heidegger's structural approach, especially if the latter is understood in light of my interpretation (which deviates a little from Heidegger's own). We saw that Heidegger himself emphasizes the linguisticality of the understanding of being, although he shrinks back from the necessary conclusion that the understanding of being, and particularly the relation of oneself to one's own to-be, is expressed in sentences. Now the yes/no polarity proved to be a fundamental aspect of the understanding of being—and, on my interpretation, of the understanding of sentences. This yes/no-polarity contains a reference of all speech to a possible reply. And conversely we will see that Mead's unelaborated conception of the semantics of human language as essentially anticipating the reaction of a partner only attains a clear meaning through recourse to the yes/no-structure. Furthermore, you are now already in a position to anticipate that Mead is mistaken when he claims that a relation of oneself to oneself is contained in talking to oneself as such. This relation to oneself is given only if the act of talking to oneself concerns one's own to-be; thus, Mead's conception is itself tenable only when it is linked with Heidegger's framework.

These preliminary remarks are intended both to provide an orientation and to justify myself, since such an attempt to connect Heidegger and Mead may appear somewhat peculiar from an external point of view.

Mead did not systematically present his conception of the "self" in a published work but elaborated it in a continually revised course on social psychology that he gave at the University of Chicago during the first third of this century. The relevant source for us is the book *Mind, Self and Society*, which was edited by Charles Morris on the basis of two sets of lecture notes from the years 1927 and 1930. The German translation that appeared in 1968 is entitled *Geist, Identität und Gesellschaft*. Thus, the translator rendered "self" as "identity"—not only in the title, but throughout the text—although in German there is a word "*Selbst*" that corresponds precisely to the English term "self." The term "identity" in the sense that is relevant here came into use in the school of social psychology that originated with Mead, but it was not used by Mead himself; and I must say that this was fortunate because the term is quite unclear. Since it plays such an important role in the contemporary discussion, I will return to it after the interpretation of Mead. Such an overly interpretive translation would be unacceptable even if there were substantive grounds for it, because it denies the reader the chance to be able to evaluate the term for himself. Still, I would like to show you an example of the grotesque consequences to which it leads in the case under consideration. In his concluding reflections on the concept of the self Mead explains: "It is the characteristic of the self as an object to itself that I want to bring out. This characteristic is represented in the word 'self', which is a reflexive, and indicates that which can be both subject and object" (pp. 136ff.). I was curious to see what the translator would make of this, since here Mead explicitly uses the word *self*. He translates the second sentence in the following way: "In the case of identity a subject as well as an object can be involved" (p. 178). This sentence not only fails to render what Mead says but is also unintelligible. The example may suffice to indicate that the translation not only contains a faulty choice of terminology but also is so unreliable that it should not be used. For this reason I will always refer only to the page numbers of the English edition in what follows.

The book is divided into four sections. The first is entitled "The Standpoint of Social Behaviorism," and it serves as a general characterization of Mead's position in contrast to other contemporary schools of psychology. The second section is entitled "Mind," and in contrast to *self* this term is really quite difficult to translate; in the context of Mead's usage it signifies the form of intelligence that is specifically human. In this section Mead develops his conception of human speech as a special kind of interaction, and he characterizes human intelligence as a capacity essentially characterized by the ability to speak. The third section is entitled "Self," and the fourth is entitled "Society." In our context, of course, the third section is the most important. I will begin with a consideration of it, and will subsequently have to return to the second section.

The substantival expression *the self* might lead us to expect the worst. We have already encountered this term in Kierkegaard. Isn't a nucleus within the person again postulated here just as it was in talking about 'the I'? In fact Mead will later discuss "the I" as a particular aspect of the self that is distinguished from another aspect that he calls "the me." But we already know that it is not the substantival mode of speaking in itself that is bad, since nothing rests upon the expression as such; rather, the question is how the expression is explained. The issue is whether one allows oneself to be misled by the expression into claiming that it involves a something, or whether the explanation discloses that the expression only indicates a mode of behavior of the person. Since Mead understands himself as a kind of behaviorist, he considers only the latter possibility. In contrast to vulgar behaviorism, which disregards the so-called inner sphere, Mead's program (as sketched in the first part of the book) is precisely to show how an inner sphere is constituted on the basis of a specific form of external behavior, namely, communicative behavior. This means that a very specific type of inner sphere is envisioned. It is not the inner sphere that the tradition concerned with the problem of epistemic self-consciousness had in view, but an inner sphere in the sense of the relation of oneself to oneself; and the word *relation* is now meant in the sense of "behavior." Mead is also familiar with the topic of the epistemic self-consciousness of "ϕ" states to which (as he says) only the person himself has access (166). But in contrast to Wittgenstein he did not make it his task to elucidate this sphere of the (in his words) "subjective" in behavioral terms. For him it is a sphere of mere consciousness, and not self-consciousness. He says that this subjective sphere is not "reflexive" (ibid.), and we can acknowledge that he was correct in this regard in view of what we have seen from Wittgenstein. On the other hand, the term *self* is supposed to signify a reflexive mode of relation, and we therefore will have to see how he explains these concepts of self and reflection in behavioral terms.

At the outset Mead introduces the term in an entirely traditional way. I have already cited the following remark: "It is characteristic of the self that it is an object for itself." Thus Mead begins with the traditional subject-object model. The self is basically characterized as that which is "both subject and object"; and Mead also subsequently uses the term *self-consciousness* synonymously (138). At first glance this seems just like the conception that we found in the Fichtean tradition. But Mead only uses this conception as a formal indication of the phenomenon that he is seeking. In the tradition this relation of reflection was conceived as an immediate inner relation. But in Mead's view the point is to find criteria for it in behavior.

The following reflection represents a first step for Mead. From a behavioral standpoint, it seems relatively intelligible that a person relates to other people as objects. The question then arises: "How can an individual get outside himself (experientially) in such a way as to become an object to himself?" The answer reads: "The individual experiences himself as such, not directly, but only indirectly . . . he becomes an object to himself only by taking the attitudes of other individuals toward himself" (138).

Now, this thesis is so general that it is not tied to the specific subject-object model. It can also be formulated with the aid of the expression *relation of oneself to oneself*, which does not prejudge the structural question. It then reads: Something like a relation of oneself to oneself cannot be conceived as something immediate; a person can only relate himself to himself by relating himself to others and adopting the relation of others to himself. In this formulation the thesis also acquires relevance against Heidegger. But admittedly it is still only a thesis. It is not only not yet justified but also completely unclear with regard to the structure that it postulates. It is unclear how the relation of others to me is to be understood, and which 'attitudes' are involved; and in particular it is unclear what my capacity to take on the attitude of the other toward me is supposed to mean. And above all we must not forget that according to Mead's own methodological claim this entire complex structure is supposed to be explicable in behavioral terms. But from a behavioral standpoint we are not allowed to talk about 'attitudes' at the outset, and we are also not permitted to speak of a relationship to another person as object or of relating oneself to him; rather, we are to speak only of the responses of two or more organisms to mutual stimuli. Hence Mead must confront the task of specifying those stimuli and responses on whose basis something like an attitude toward the behavior of another is constituted; for this is in turn supposed to be the condition for the possibility of constituting a relation to oneself.

Such modes of behavior or action of an organism whose function is to serve as stimuli for actions of members of the same species have a communicative function. If an action Z of organism A functions as a stimulus for an action of organism B, then it serves B as a signal that a state of affairs S that is relevant for B is present. This state of affairs can involve either the organism A itself (e.g., one dog indicates to the other by his aggressive bearing that he is about to attack him) or another state of affairs in the environment that is relevant for B (e.g., the existence of food or the proximity of an enemy). The signaling character of Z can also be understood quasi-prescriptively instead of quasi-indicatively, so that Z has the function of evoking a response from B that is appropriate in the social context of cooperation among organisms. In the normal case of animal communication as exhibitied in any of the ways indicated, B obviously does not grasp the stimulus originating from A *as a signal*; indeed, B does not 'relate' to Z at all, but simply responds to it.

If the 'attitudes' the two organisms that we can call persons are to have to one another must be constituted in a specific interplay of stimuli and responses, this implies that the relation of persons to one another under consideration must consist in a special form of communication. And Mead's thesis is that the constitution of the specifically human form of communication is identical with the constitution of the relevant relation of persons to one another and to themselves. Thus the thesis is not merely that the relation of persons to one another, which itself is supposed to make the relation of oneself to oneself possible, is made possible by the structure of human communication. Rather, it is equally true in a reverse sense that communication only attains the structure that is characteristic of human language when the sending and receiving of signals proceeds in such a way that the sender not only has an effect upon the receiver but also anticipates his reaction, and the receiver does the same thing.

Mead calls the signs of the human language "significant symbols" (46) in contradistinction to the signs of the animal languages that function as signals; the former have a "meaning." What does this mean? Mead provides the following definition: "Meaning is that which can be indicated to others while it is by the same process indicated to the indicating individual" (89). Thus, the characteristic feature of human language is supposed to be that its signs mean *the same thing* for everyone, for those who employ them and for those who apprehend them, and this is the case in spite of the fact that they are responded to in a great diversity of ways (54, 56). This implies two things: The meaning is not simply contained in the response, but is detached from the latter; and in this way it becomes possible that something like an *identical meaning* for sender and receiver is constituted. The communication does not take place in a one-way direction as it does in the simple stimulus-response schema; rather, the sender also indicates the same thing to himself that he indicates to the receiver. It thereby becomes possible for sign giving to be experienced *as* sign giving— and from both sides. This stands in contrast to a situation in which the sign is merely produced or responded to. Here the thesis again reads: The two partners can only relate themselves to an identical meaning of the sign, and hence to the sign as sign, insofar as they relate themselves reciprocally to one another. But the reverse is also true: They can only relate themselves reciprocally to one another insofar as they employ significant signs, and this requires that they use signs in such a way that they have an identical meaning.

This is still merely a thesis, but we now know more precisely what is being sought. The task that emerges for Mead is to discover an interplay of stimuli and responses that fulfills the specified conditions. A preliminary presupposition appears to be that there must be a reciprocal interplay of stimuli and responses that involves more than the mere procession of stimuli from A to B and B to A; rather, it is further required that B responds to the stimulus originating from A with a stimulus that reacts back upon A, and that A itself again responds to this reactive stimulus from B, and so on. Mead locates a phenomenon of this structure in the ritual through which members of the same species adjust to one another in preparing for a social action like fighting, sexual intercourse, or feeding their young. An example is the fighting ritual between dogs (42ff.). The attacking dog does not immediately attack, but makes a gesture that gives notice of the impending attack; the dog under attack responds to this gesture by adjusting in one way or another to the indicated attack, namely, by assuming a specific position; and this position functions once again as a stimulus for the first dog to change his position, and so on. Thus a "conversation of gestures" (43) emerges. As Mead emphasizes, however, these gestures are "not gestures in the sense that they are significant" (43). Mead also wants to avoid as far as possible the connotation of the word *gesture*, which implies that gestures are signs of inner states. *Gestures* are to signify merely "that part of the act" which "is responsible for its influence upon other organisms. The gesture in some sense stands for the act as far as it affects the other organism" (53). Thus the word hardly implies more than the word *stimulus* in this context.

It is clear that the 'dialogue of gestures' described above still does not fulfill the condition that was stipulated by the concept of meaning, since nothing is constituted as identical here and a "separation of the stimulus and the response" (121) also does not yet take place. The two dogs merely respond alternately to the behavior of the other, and they do so in respectively different ways; one still cannot speak of an adoption of the attitude of the other. But it might be argued that this would be attained as soon as each of the two not only responded to the stimulus of the other but also responded to his own stimulus in the same way that his partner does. For under these circumstances it might seem as if each one takes on the attitude of the other, and each also indicates to himself what he indicates to the other. At the beginning of his exposition Mead in fact asserts: "The vocal gesture becomes a significant symbol . . . when it has the same effect on the individual making it that it has on the individual to whom it is addressed" (46).

It is possible that a mistake in the lecture notes is involved here, because in the first place it is easy to see that such a simultaneous self-stimulation by itself in no way fulfills the specified condition. If each member responds in the *same* way as the other, this still does not mean that he takes on the attitude *of* the other; and nothing is constituted as identical for both of them as long as they only behave in the same way. Second, Mead himself subsequently points out that there is a form of behavior that possesses this characteristic of simultaneous self-stimulation, but is precisely not symbolic — namely, the vocal behavior of birds and small children, which (as he says) is mistakenly designated as imitation.[2] In the case of birds he states that if the gestures that serve for the reciprocal accommodation to a social action are (a) largely the same for both partners and (b) perceived by the creature itself that expresses them (as is the case for vocal gestures), then the reciprocal stimulation functions at the same time as self-stimulation (361ff.). In addition, a sound that originates from A can be imitated by B in order to stimulate himself to respond appropriately. Mead interprets the behavior of the small child in this way when it alternates between crying and imitating the calming voice of the parent (364). At this point Mead adds: "This childish type of conduct runs out later into the countless forms of play in which the child assumes the roles of the adults about him." This connection appears quite dubious. An understanding of norms is a necessary part of role playing in the strict sense, and hence role playing is linguistically founded; it certainly cannot be linked up so immediately with the vocal interplay of the small child described above. To be sure, Mead also does not want to claim that this interplay already represents a symbolic form of behavior. According to Mead, gestures that are perceived by the being itself that performs them (such as the vocal type) are a necessary presupposition for symbolic behavior. In order for a sign to have the same meaning for communication partners, they both must be able to perceive the same sign; sameness here is to be understood on a phonetic level, although the medium can be a different one. But this sameness, of course, still does not provide the constitution of identity on the crucial semantic level.

What is still missing? Let's grant that one could characterize the child's behavior described above by noting that the child alternates between the adoption of its own attitude and that of the mother; in contrast, the characteristic feature of symbolic communication would be that the speaker anticipates the response of the hearer while performing his speech act. In an essay written in 1922, Mead formulates this point with idealistic exaggeration in the following way: "It is through the ability to be the other *at the same time* that he is himself that the symbol becomes significant."[3] Mead indicates what this is supposed to mean concretely on page 47: "When, in any given social act or situation, one individual indicates by a gesture to another individual what this other individual is to do, the first individual is conscious of the meaning of his own gesture—or the meaning of his gesture appears in his experience—insofar as he takes the attitude of the second individual toward that gesture, and tends to respond to it implicitly in the same way that the second individual responds to it explicitly. Gestures become significant symbols when they implicitly arouse in an individual making them the same response which they explicitly arouse, or are supposed to arouse, in other individuals, the individuals to whom they are addressed."

This is the most extensive account that Mead provides, and we must rely upon the wider context for a more precise understanding. Two questions immediately arise. First, it might be argued that Mead strays from the behavioristic model of explanation through his recourse to implicit responses. But this is not the case if an implicit response is understood as a disposition to the corresponding explicit response; and this is obviously how Mead meant it. Thus the second question becomes all the more pressing: How do we have to conceive of the implicit response of the speaker? That is, what is the explicit response to which it is the disposition? In the passage cited and in other, similar passages Mead has an imperative expression in mind (the gesture indicates to another individual "what he is to do"). This seems to indicate that the disposition of the speaker is the readiness to perform the action himself that is required of the other person, and Mead occasionally provides this interpretation (67) without systematically developing it.

This conception is untenable, and it also cannot be reconciled with other things that Mead says. In the first place it is obvious that if the speaker merely produced the disposition in himself to do the same thing that the hearer is supposed to do, he still would not thereby relate himself to the hearer or to the action that is demanded of him; we still would not have gone beyond the structure of a simultaneous self-stimulation. It does not follow from the fact that one of them has a disposition to do the same thing to which the other is stimulated that there is something identical to which they both relate. Furthermore, the difficulty arises as to how such a conception is to be applied to nonimperative expressions, in particular, to assertoric expressions; and in many contexts it is clear that Mead has the latter in mind as well. What could the hearer's response be here, which is implicitly produced by the speaker in himself? Perhaps the belief that something is the case? A belief, however, is not a response; it is itself a disposition. Indeed, it is correct that the speaker indicates to himself the same thing that he indicates to the hearer; if he is not lying he has the same belief. But how this takes place is what must be explained by means of the behavioristic model, and we cannot simply smuggle in the concept of belief in this context.

The solution to the problem emerges if we take note of two aspects of Mead's conception: First, the response of the hearer is supposed to be able to react back upon the action of the speaker; an *interaction* is supposed to be involved. This was already taken into account on an elementary level in the "conversation of gestures," but it has fallen out of consideration in the present interpretation of imperative expressions. The second aspect is closely connected to this: The symbolic interaction is supposed to be "internalizable," and this internalization of the relevant relation to the behavior of the other provides the basis upon which the 'self,' the relation of itself to itself, is to be constituted. Now, whenever Mead deals with this internalization, he makes it clear that it involves a form of talking to oneself: The person "talks and replies to himself as truly as the other person replies to him." For "thinking . . . is simply an internalized or implicit conversation of the individual with himself" (47).

Now this also means that communication, talking to others, has the character of a dialogue. The consequence for our question regarding the explicit response of the hearer and the corresponding implicit (dispositional) response of the speaker is that it must always involve a symbolic response. The response must itself be verbal. This may not appear very plausible for the example of the imperative that is favored by Mead. But the reflections that Mead himself develops in paragraphs 14–16 confirm this hypothesis. Here the understanding of the imperative is dealt with from the perspective of the hearer. "The dog cannot give to himself that stimulus which somebody else gives to him. . . . In significant speech the person himself understands what he is asked to do, and *consents* to carry out something. . . . The hearer is not simply moving at an order, but is giving to himself the same directions that the other person gives to him" (108–109, my emphasis). Thus the verbal stimulus of the speaker is not directly related to the requested action of the hearer, but is mediated through the verbal answer of the hearer. Mead speaks merely of consent, but consent only has significance against the background of the possibility of refusal. The response of the hearer, which is implicitly anticipated by the speaker, is thus his answer of yes or no. Mead does not formulate it explicitly in this way, but the fact that he speaks of a "separation between stimulus and response" in this connection, and of a "delayed response" (98, 117), can only be understood on this basis. This hiatus between stimulus and response differentiates not only imperative communication but also all action that is motivated by symbolic thinking from "reflex" and "habitual behavior"; and this hiatus is characterized by "reflection" (98). Reflection is connected to choice for Mead as well, and is always related to "alternative possibilities of response" (98, 117). Someone who reflects or deliberates speaks to himself in adopting yes/no positions in the same way he would speak to others with whom he was consulting about what to do. As we have already seen, this same yes/no structure is constitutive for the sentences of intention that are considered in deliberation, and also provides the foundation for the range of free possibilities that serve as the presupposition for understanding and employing an imperative as an imperative and not as a signal. Mead clearly recognizes the connection when he says that the addressee of an imperative does not immediately carry it out, but must first give himself the directions that the other gives to him.

Mead's ideas concerning symbolic communication remained in outline form, and he did not develop them into an actual theory of meaning. Thus he explicitly examined neither the special character of the yes-or-no response nor the difference between imperative and assertoric expressions. It would have been plausible within his framework to have expanded upon the characterization of symbolic language in terms of the indicated "separation between stimulus and response" by noting that symbolic language is particularly distinguished from signal language by virtue of its clear separation of practical and assertoric expressions. While the presymbolic organism responds immediately to a given fact in the environment, the symbolically thinking organism apprehends a state of affairs in assertoric sentences and then deliberates in practical sentences about how to respond. A presymbolic communication can be described in both the assertoric and the imperative mood, depending on whether one considers the outlook of the speaker or the addressee; for example, a warning cry can be viewed as information that an enemy is in the area, or as an order to run away. It is neither one thing nor the other, because it does not yet have a unitary meaning for the speaker and addressee. The question of whether the addressee understands the expression assertorically or practically is only decided when the addressee can assume such or such a position toward it; and according to Mead, this adoption of a position is anticipated by the speaker. To be sure, understanding is not exhaustively explained by the adoption of a yes/no position; but the adoption of a yes/no position of speaker *and* hearer refers to rules of action, which in one case govern the justification of what is affirmed and in the other case govern its practical execution. The concrete elaboration of the theory of meaning would consist in the systematic formulation of these rules in behavioral terms.

Of course, the adoption of a yes-or-no position is not the only possible verbal response to a practical or assertoric sentence, and Mead did not even explicitly characterize it in this way. Thus I must emphasize that this is an interpretive addition that seems to me to be indispensable; for it is solely on this basis that Mead's claim regarding the essential feature of symbolic communication—namely, that the response is anticipated by the person who expresses a sentence—can be sustained. It is part of the meaning of both assertoric and imperative sentences that the person who expresses them anticipates in uttering them a possible no from the addressee, and thereby enters into a yes/no dialogue. This yes/no dialogue is readily internalizable, and all further assumptions of a position to what is said (or in any case those that are internalizable) presuppose the adoption of a yes-or-no position. It is also on this basis that it becomes comprehensible that the speaker and hearer relate to something identical, for this is precisely what is affirmed or negated. To be sure, it cannot be argued that the identity of what is said is constituted in the adoption of a yes/no position; it is presupposed in adopting a position. Mead did not demonstrate how this identity is constituted, and this can only be demonstrated in my view by attending to those rules of action to which the yes/no structure itself refers. Mead also did not take another characteristic feature of symbolic speech into account: namely, the fact that its elementary expressions—sentences—contain component expressions that signal languages do not contain; these are the singular terms. In my view, it is in the rules of use of these sentence components that an identity is constituted that makes it possible to speak also of an identity of what is expressed by the sentence as a whole.[4]

Thus Mead did not succeed in establishing those modes of behavior that make a symbolic language possible in his sense. He merely specified criteria that a behavioristic theory of symbolic language would have to fulfill; and in this respect he still seems to me to be a reliable guide for a contemporary theory of meaning. These criteria include an identical meaning for hearer and speaker, and a separation between stimulus and response. This separation is to be understood behavioristically in the following way: A special type of response intercedes between stimulus and response, that is, a verbal response, and it arises in such a way that a dialogue results, which is itself internalizable.

The incomplete character of Mead's theory of meaning is not a problem in our context, since for us the issue is only the extent to which a relation of oneself to oneself is constituted in symbolic interaction as characterized by Mead. Mead's thesis is this: As soon as someone "talks and replies to himself as truly as the other person replies to him, we have behavior in which the individuals have become objects to themselves" (139). One can only relate oneself to oneself in talking to oneself: "I know of no other form of behavior than the linguistic in which the individual is an object to himself, and, so far as I can see, the individual is not a self in the reflexive sense unless he is an object to himself. It is this fact that gives a critical importance to communication, since this is a type of behavior in which the individual does so respond to himself" (142).

This thesis can be evaluated from various positions of proximity and distance. As long as one considers it from the remote perspective of the intuitive reader, it seems entirely plausible that we can only become objects to ourselves by somehow getting outside ourselves, and that this can happen precisely by putting ourselves in the perspective of others who make us their objects.

On the other hand, if we examine Mead's thesis through the language-analytical magnifying glass, we must conclude that the genuine insight it may contain is presented in a structurally absurd way. First, he proceeds from the untenable traditional conception of a reflexive relation in which the subject is itself turned into an object for itself; second, he makes something bad even worse by thinking that he can provide a behavioral foundation for the subject-object model through the stimulus-response model. A way of responding to objects, however complex, still remains a response; a reference to objects only arises through a special type of symbol and its rules of use, that is, the singular terms; and it is in this context that the use of the word *I* is constituted, which makes a reference of the speaker to himself possible. This reference is reflexive in the logical sense, but it does not presuppose a reflexive act.

Let us now make a third attempt by retreating one step. We shall disregard both the traditional and behavioral conceptions through which Mead presents his thesis, and focus only on the aspect of symbolic interaction. The thesis then reads in this way: A relation of oneself to oneself is contained in talking to oneself; and we can add that it is a different type of relation of oneself to oneself from the one that is involved in the mere reference to oneself by means of *I*. In examining the validity of Mead's thesis we must set aside the practical inner dialogue, since in this case one might argue that one's own being is always at issue and therefore that a relation of oneself to oneself is implied. The question is whether Mead is correct in claiming that a distinct relation of oneself to oneself is already contained in the structure of the inner dialogue as such. If the thesis is correct, it must also apply to the theoretical inner dialogue, and Mead obviously has this in mind. Let us therefore imagine that we have to solve some theoretical problem. Such a dialogue might have the following structure: "p because q, and q because r; or is it false that p, since s and t obtain; furthermore, it is surely true that u, but u and p are contradictory. Then wouldn't r have to be false? Or perhaps p doesn't follow from r after all." A relation of oneself to oneself is not contained anywhere in such an argumentation, not even in the adoption of a negative or questioning position toward a preceding simple assumption of a position. In such a train of thought I do not think of myself. Thus, the word *I* also does not even normally occur, and this would be the most minimal condition for being able to talk about a relation of oneself to oneself. And if it does occur, such as when we say "I believe that p," it does not have a meaning that extends beyond epistemic self-consciousness.

Such a meaning is present, however, as soon as the inner dialogue is a practical one, that is, a deliberation. When I deliberate about what I want to do, I relate myself reflectively *to my doing*. Now is this a relating to *oneself?* It certainly is if we grant the Heideggerean conception that in all one's relating to one's own possibilities of action one also implicitly relates oneself to one's own being. But one can also reply affirmatively to this question without recourse to Heidegger's thesis. For it can be argued that in adopting a position toward one's activity one always thereby relates oneself to oneself in just the same way that in adopting a position toward another person's activity one thereby always relates oneself to this person.

Here we encounter a structure that is also discussed by Gilbert Ryle in the *Concept of Mind* in connection with the problem of self-consciousness. Ryle does not limit himself either to the adoption of positions or to linguistic actions in general; rather, he proceeds from a general concept of higher-order actions that are defined by virtue of being related to another action in such a way that the "performance of the former involves the thought of the latter" (191). Some of the many examples cited by Ryle are replying, retaliating, scoffing, buying, bribing, extorting, resisting, rewarding, criticizing, and approving. This concept of higher-order actions is somewhat larger than the sociological concept of interaction, because it does not presuppose that the actions are those of two individuals who are reciprocally related to one another (e.g., one can scoff at someone behind his back). To be sure, this is connected with an obscurity in Ryle's concept. He did not realize that the relatedness of one action to another cannot be generally understood by assigning the first action to a higher level than the second; for it is characteristic of some of the actions that he himself specifies that the actions to which they are related are related to them in just the same sense, such as the action of buying. The crucial point for Ryle was to make clear that there are such complex actions not only with reference to the actions of other persons; on the contrary, one also learns as a child to perform such actions with reference to one's own actions (193). Ryle certainly speaks as if such a self-reference is conceivable for all actions of this type, although it is quite evident that one cannot, for example, blackmail oneself or sell oneself something. Perhaps Ryle's primary interest in actions that are related to one's own actions also explains why he could overlook reciprocal actions. As far as I can see, actions that are related to one's own actions are always of a higher level: One cannot cooperate with oneself, make a contract with oneself, and so on. And if we say that someone talks to himself or plays with himself, this only means that he talks or plays without someone else, but not that his talking or playing is related to another instance of talking or playing. But it seems to me that still another qualification is necessary. Ryle emphasizes that it is an intellectual prejudice always to conceive of higher-order actions as linguistic (192). As far as I can see, however, all higher-order actions that are related to one's own actions are linguistic.

If this is correct, one would have to concede to Mead that a relation of oneself to oneself is involved in talking to oneself practically, but this is not (as he contended) because it is a form of talking to oneself in which one talks to oneself as one would talk to someone else. Rather, it is a function of the fact that in deliberation one relates oneself to future possibilities of action with a view toward adopting a position (and also evaluatively toward one's past actions). Mead's broader thesis that the relation of oneself to oneself has "essentially a social structure" is not particularly convincing in light of what he has argued so far about the self. It is certainly correct that talking to oneself—both theoretically and practically—is genetically a derivative of communicative speaking, and it is also correct that all talking to oneself can be extended into conversation with others at any time. But it is not clear what is supposed to be *structurally* communicative about speaking to oneself. Indeed, one is obliged to say that from a structural standpoint speaking to oneself is precisely not communicative. Although we sometimes address ourselves by *you* in talking to ourselves, there are here not two quasi-persons who communicate with one another. In a monologue nothing is communicated, and no process of understanding someone takes place; and for this reason there is also no possibility of a misunderstanding, but only one of a lack of clarity.

It is essential to realize that (a) speaking to oneself as such does not constitute a relation of oneself to oneself, and (b) even the form of speaking to oneself that can be understood in a certain sense as a relation of oneself to oneself—namely, the practical form—is still not essentially interactive. This is crucially important for recognizing the special character of the structure that Mead elaborates in the following sections, where he speaks, first, of the "genesis of the self" (sections 19–20) and then distinguishes between "the me" and "the I," which describe the two structural aspects of the self (sections 22, 25). In my view Mead succeeds here, in his theory of roles, in showing that a relation to oneself is only constituted in conjunction with a relation to another. But this relation to oneself is not just any form of talking to oneself, but an adoption of a yes/no position toward one's own being; and it is not just any adoption of a position on the part of others that is involved, but a set of normative expectations. Mead obscured both his theory of language and his theory of roles by not separating them clearly—something that many interpreters regard as his special merit. Thus in his general remarks on language, he speaks as if the anticipation of the other's assumption of a position already involves taking on his role as well. The indefinite talk of "taking the attitude of the other" had unfortunate consequences. An adoption of a position is not yet a role.

Mead, II: The Self

In section 19 in which he discusses the "genesis of the self," Mead introduces the problem in such a way that it appears as if the same self is involved that is supposedly constituted in the talking-to-oneself-and-others. But in my view it is clear, first, that a more specific structure is involved, although Mead can correctly claim that this structure is only conceivable symbolically. But the reverse is precisely not true: Talking to oneself and to others does not in itself have this structure. Second, I believe that Mead can correctly claim only that this relation of oneself to oneself is structurally and not merely genetically interactive. Finally, it is my view that a relation to oneself is implied here that can only be understood with the aid of Heidegger's concept of the relation to one's own to-be. Thus if Mead is correct, this relation would have to be understood as something that is constituted through interaction.

In the "genesis of the self" Mead distinguishes "two general stages" (158). The distinction is described differently by him in two places. In the first passage the distinction is not directly elaborated, but is specified in connection with the kinds of children's play that are typical for the respective stages (150ff.). It is characteristic for the first stage that the children play at being something, such as a mother, a teacher, or a policeman. In doing this "they take on different roles" (150). The children only learn that form of play which Mead calls games at the second stage (he mentions baseball as an example). He describes them as "organised games"; and they are essentially games for several people in which each individual performs a specific role in such a way that he must be ready to take the role of everyone else. This description is somewhat misleading. It is not essential that one must actually be ready to take the role of someone else; rather, the point is that each role can only be understood in the context of its interplay with the other roles. The characteristic feature of such games is that they are constituted through rules (152); and the rules determine the reciprocal rights and duties of the players. A child can only play such a game if he has understood what it means to join with others in a common activity that is determined by rules and to act in accordance with such rules. (One reason why Mead's successors also did not make a sharp distinction between his theory of language and his theory of roles is that speaking is also performed according to rules. But linguistic rules do not define rights and duties; linguistic rules are not norms in the narrow sense, but technical rules: Failure to comply with them does not lead to a sanction, but to a lapse in understanding.)

In the second passage in the text Mead describes the two stages directly instead of circuitously indicating the kinds of play that are characteristic for them: "At the first of these stages, the individual's self is constituted simply by an organisation of the particular attitudes of other individuals toward himself and toward one another. . . . But at the second stage in the full development of the individual's self that self is constituted not only by an organisation of these particular individual attitudes, but also by an organisation of the social attitudes of the generalised other or the social group as a whole to which he belongs" (158).

These descriptions give rise to many questions, and some of them can be answered on the basis of Mead's further explanations. I find it particularly difficult to bring together the accounts of the first stage that Mead provides in the two places; and it is correspondingly difficult to form a clear picture of his conception of the first stage. The first characterization suggests that at the first stage roles can only be played and not exercised, because an understanding of the rights and duties that are constitutive for roles does not yet exist. Other places suggest that Mead is also concerned with the difference (that has been extensively analyzed in subsequent role theory) between the capacity to exercise an individual role and the capacity to exercise different roles in different social contexts without (as is often said) losing one's identity. Mead sees this identity ensured in the development of what is called

"character" (162ff.), and he thinks that this "organisation of the personality" arises as an "individual reflection" out of the organization
of the group to which the individual relates at the second stage (158ff.).
This thesis is not particularly convincing, and it would seem more
plausible to regard the transition from role identity to character identity
as an additional gradation within the second stage. I will return to
this later.

The question of precisely how Mead wanted his first stage to be
understood is not that important here, because we are mainly concerned, not with genetic, but with structural questions. And these
pertain above all to the second stage; only at the second stage is "self-
consciousness in the full sense of the term" supposed to be attained
(152). And it is not difficult to see how the descriptions that Mead
provides in both places for the second stage harmonize with one
another: The structures of the games described in the first characterization correspond to the structures of real social life described in
the second characterization. In both places Mead's principal term is
the *generalised other*. This term signifies the "organised community or
social group" (154). An organized community is a totality of individuals
who stand in a relation of "cooperation" (155). Aristotle had already
defined the term *koinonia* in this way, and it was subsequently translated
into Latin as *societas*.[1] A *koinonia* is a free association of individuals for
the reciprocal promotion of their well-being. And Aristotle calls a
koinonia politike a community that is indispensable for the existence of
its members; thus it is a community that is entered into, not for the
sake of a particular end, but for the sake of existence itself. This is
to be distinguished from a merely contractual community, of which
the game group is also an example. The qualification "free" is employed
neither by Aristotle nor by Mead, but it seems to me to be necessary
in order to distinguish a human community from an animal one. And
this qualification is also implied both for Aristotle and for Mead by
virtue of the fact that such a community is mediated by the form of
language that is specifically human. If someone is a member of an
"organised community," he is free to resign his membership despite
the fact that this may mean his death (as is certain in the case of the
slave). Even in the fundamental community of the *koinonia politike*
cooperation is based upon a yes that is at least implicit.

Upon this the special character of the regularities that govern cooperation in the context of a human community is founded: They are
norms. Mead does not employ this concept, but it is implied by him.

Indeed, he uses the even more general concept of rule (152) without explaining it more precisely. The meaning of rules of action, and specifically of norms,[2] can be elucidated by contrasting them from two sides; a form of rule-governed behavior is on the one hand different from a form of behavior that is merely *regular* as a result of causal factors, and on the other hand it is to be distinguished from behavior that is governed by imperatives. An "imperative" is an *individual* order to action; someone who follows a rule acts in accordance with a *general* standard for action under specified conditions. In this respect rule-governed behavior is similar to behavior that exhibits regularity, but it is different from the latter by virtue of the fact that the rule 'demands' an action just as an imperative does. This is expressed linguistically in a prescriptive sentence, and is manifested in behavior through the agent's capacity to respond by yes or no just as he does to an imperative. This implies that the agent is free to follow the rule or not; and the fact that the agent does or does not follow the rule *for reasons* (just as he does or does not follow an imperative *for reasons*) indicates that freedom is involved here in the strong sense that pertains to the sphere of the practical question and deliberation. Someone who follows a rule may merely have good reasons to adhere to it—for example, in order to avoid a greater evil (such as punishment). But he also can adhere to it of his own accord, and in this case he not only has good reasons to follow it but also considers the rule itself to be well justified. Rule-governed behavior is most often distinguished from cases of behavioral regularity by looking at the way that exceptions are handled. In the case of a behavioral regularity, an exception necessitates the admission that the assumed regularity only takes place with a certain frequency; in the case of rule-governed behavior, it is presumed that the rule is 'broken,' and the behavior can be criticized in this respect. But a critical attitude involving words of praise or blame is also possible in relation to the behavior of an animal or a small child, which is only more or less regular. The crucial aspect of rule-governed behavior is that the agent himself can criticize his behavior. This presupposes that he *recognizes* the rule, whether he acknowledges its validity as such or relative to his other ends. Thus the criterion of criticism is founded upon the criterion according to which the rule represents a reason for action.

Norms are a type of rule. Many authors even employ the term coextensively with that of *rule*. But it seems more plausible only to designate social rules as norms. These involve rules that are followed out of regard for others, and for this reason are also ordinarily socially sanctioned in one way or another in contrast, for example, to technical rules or private maxims of action. We can now understand more fully what Mead means in talking about the "attitudes" of the social group. He is referring to the normative expectations that members of the group reciprocally have regarding their behavior. (I should note here in parentheses that it was customary for a while in sociology to define norms simply as "expectations of expectations." But this expression can only mean that the agent expects (and this means he *knows*) that the others expect (and this means they *require*) a specific action from him. Thus the expression *expectations* has a different meaning at the first point in this formula from the one it has at the second point. Since at the second point it stands for expectations that are themselves already normative, this formula does not fulfill its claim to define the concept of norm; on the contrary, it presupposes it.)

Within the domain of norms, those norms that govern cooperative practices form an essential nucleus; their eminent status derives from the fact that it is only on their basis that a community is constituted. Furthermore, it is only in the case of norms governing cooperative practices that it seems self-evident that for every obligation of one individual there are corresponding rights of other individuals. The concept of cooperation should not mislead one into thinking that co-operation must be coordinative, so that all members have equal rights; rather, it can just as well be a largely subordinative relation, the extreme case being that of the slave who has no rights and only duties. Now Mead calls the nodal points of organized social cooperation roles. Someone who occupies a specific role—for instance, a mother, teacher, or policeman (to return to the examples cited by Mead for children's role-playing)—has specific cooperative duties and rights; in other words, the role consists in a collection of cooperative rights and duties.

We can now understand what Mead means by the "generalised other" and his "attitudes." Mead speaks of the "generalised other" not just because attitudes of the "social group" are at issue but also because these attitudes are normative expectations; and this implies that they are generalized demands. These expectations do not simply arise from all the individuals of the group, but they are grounded in the organization of cooperation within the society. They are directed toward the individual, not as an individual, but as the bearer of specific roles; they are directed "toward the various phases or aspects of the common social activity" (155). In this respect the "reaction of the community" has "what we call an institutional form" (167).

The structure developed by Mead has now been sufficiently clarified so that the following question can be raised: To what extent can he claim that an individual attains what he calls self-consciousness (or what we may term self-relation "in the full sense of the word") merely on the basis of this structure (152), that is, merely by taking on roles and thus situating himself in one way or another within the totality of cooperative activities of a society? A relation of oneself to oneself is obviously implied here that does not merely consist in an assumption of a position toward one's own possibilities of action, as is the case in any practical form of talking to oneself. In the relation of oneself to oneself that is currently under consideration, the individual no longer relates himself merely to individual actions; or more precisely, since he always relates himself to individual possibilities of action, he relates himself to these in light of the extent to which they correspond to how (or as what) he wants to understand *himself*. In adopting a role I understand *myself* as a so-and-so; and since I develop a definite character in the multiplicity of roles, the issue in a more significant sense becomes who (what kind of a person) I want to be, that is, how I understand *myself*. What is contained in this "myself" or "oneself"? Mead did not pose this question, because he thought he had already explained the meaning of this reflexivity by means of the structure of speaking to oneself. The mistaken character of this belief can also be seen from the fact that when Mead designates the second stage in the genesis of the self as the "fully developed self" and as "self-consciousness in the full sense of the term" (152), he does not want to contrast this designation with that "self" which is supposedly contained in the formal structure of talking to oneself; rather, he contrasts it with the first stage of role behavior (whose precise structure admittedly has remained unclear). But this means that the talk of a "self" and of a relation to oneself has a specific meaning in the context of role behavior, and in *this* sense a "self" and a relation to oneself still cannot be found in talking to oneself as such, even if the latter is practical.

We have already encountered this structure of understanding oneself as a so-and-so in Heidegger, and it seemed clear at that point that this structure can only be understood in connection with the to-be. The fact that I understand myself as a so-and-so means that my to-be, my life, has this meaning for me. Must we return to this structure of the to-be for the purpose of understanding Mead's thesis that a relation to oneself is constituted in role behavior? You might say that understanding oneself as a so-and-so simply means ascertaining that such and such role predicates apply to oneself, such as being a mother or a teacher. But there are other predicates that apply to me for which it is obviously not appropriate to say "I understand myself as . . . "— for example, "I understand myself as having black hair or as now giving a lecture." And even role predicates can apply to someone without one being prepared to say "I understand myself as a so-and-so." For example, it is conceivable that someone could say "Indeed I am a teacher (or a mother), but I don't understand myself as a teacher (or a mother)." The implication here is that one occupies the role, but does not 'identify' oneself with it. What does this mean? It obviously means that the cooperative activities that exist through this role do not 'fulfill' me, that is, my will to live; in other words, they do not constitute or help to constitute the meaning of my life.

The following consequences can be drawn from these considerations: First, a relation to oneself (i.e., to one's to-be) is contained in the assumption of roles, because roles as cooperative activities are con- stitutive of meaning. Second, the role is only an offer of meaning, and whether I make it my own or not depends on me. Thus, we also encounter the phenomenon of the adoption of a yes/no position here, and we will later see that this aspect of role behavior is crucial for Mead himself. The tension between identification and distance has relevance for the aspect of the self that he designates as "I." But taking a position toward roles is a relation to oneself, not because it involves taking a position toward something, but because it is taking a position toward possibilities of understanding *myself*; and here *myself* means my life. Even if one experiences a role that one occupies as not meaningful for oneself—for one's life—one relates oneself precisely in this way to oneself, to one's life and its potential meaning.

Thus we can only understand Mead's thesis that a self-relation is contained in the performance of cooperative activities that are main- tained through roles if we align it with Heidegger's concept of the relation of oneself to oneself. But Mead claims not only that a relation to oneself is contained in role behavior but also that a relation to oneself is constituted only in role behavior: "One has to be a member of a community to be a self" (162). Or if we want to formulate this point in terms of the perspective that was just outlined, he is claiming that the cooperative possibilities of action marked out by roles are not only offers of meaning but also the only possible offers of meaning. This thesis cannot simply be refuted by pointing out that to a great extent we are unable to identify ourselves with our roles, and that so many of the socially given cooperative activities can be experienced only as 'alienated labor.' Rather, the fact that given forms of cooperative activity are experienced as meaningless can equally be regarded as an indication that cooperative activities always involve the claim to provide a basis of meaning; hence, it is only for this reason that they can be experienced as meaningless. Thus a critique of socially given cooperative activities from the standpoint of their meaning would always be conceivable only on the basis of a model of a better society — or in any case this is Mead's conception. Such a critique cannot be developed from the perspective of an activity that is not socially related; the latter is not a possible source of meaning at all.

Mead merely advanced this position as a thesis, and perhaps this was a consequence of his mistaken belief that the essentially social character of the relation of oneself to oneself already is established through the supposedly communicative structure of talking to oneself. Mead seems to me to have come closest to a proper justification of his thesis in his reflections on the connection between recognition and self-respect (26). We will again find in Hegel this conception that self-consciousness is only constituted in the process of being recognized by others. Here we finally encounter the colloquial meaning of *self-consciousness*,* which implies something like the feeling of self-worth. This self-consciousness has nothing to do with theoretical self-consciousness, but is a mode of the relation of oneself to one's own to-be: It is the consciousness that one's life has value and is not worthless. And this seems to be the condition of the capacity to affirm one's life in the sense of being willing to continue to live. We must apparently experience ourselves as worthy of affirmation in order to be able to affirm ourselves. And we only experience ourselves as worthy of affirmation, at least genetically speaking, if others have affirmed us — that is, have loved and recognized us; and structurally speaking, this occurs only if we believe that others can affirm us.

---

*That is, the colloquial meaning of the German *Selbstbewusstsein* (Trans.).

Here I must again introduce a wider perspective. We have already seen in the interpretation of Heidegger where I referred to Aristotle that the characteristic feature of human volition is that it is not only indirectly related to the preservation of its own life through the feelings of pleasure and pain (as is animal volition); thus, a human being not only is directed toward the satisfaction of his needs but also, as a user of language, has a consciousness of his life. Consequently, he no longer blindly does what is good for the preservation of his life by being guided by his sensations; rather, he can himself reflect upon what is good or bad for him. And since a human being has a directly volitional relationship to his life—that is, relates himself to himself—he is dependent upon being able to affirm his life; hence he must give his life a 'meaning' and seek to live a good life.

The last-named expressions—"affirming one's life," "giving it meaning," "wanting to live a good life"—are not equivalent. It is no accident that Aristotle only focuses upon the last of these three expressions, and that in Heidegger precisely this expression or one equivalent to it is missing.

In order to see the interconnections correctly, we first have to clear up an ambiguity that can have confusing consequences for the first of these expressions. We obviously are only dealing here with practical affirmations. But these can themselves have different meanings. The yes to one's own life in the sense of a willingness to continue to live has the meaning of a sentence of intention: It expresses a volition. On the other hand, when we say that one person affirms another, *affirm* always means something like "esteem"; and *esteem* means to find something good: It involves a value judgment. And if it is correct that we can affirm our life in the sense of wanting to continue to live only if we think that our life has 'value' (i.e., that it is worthy of affirmation, which means worthy of esteem), then self-affirmation in the first sense of "affirmation" presupposes or requires self-affirmation in the second, evaluative sense. And this second sense is essentially an intersubjective one.

The requirement that life have a 'meaning' stands, so to speak, between these two meanings of affirmation. This requirement is more formal than the second meaning and merely implies that there is something in terms of which one can understand oneself in one's will to live. Now if Mead had talked to Heidegger, he would have advanced the following thesis: (a) we only find meaning in a form of life that we can regard as worthy of esteem along with others; and in connection with this, (b) the relevant activities are those that we engage in not only for ourselves but at the same time for and with others: that is, cooperative activities.

There are views in Heidegger that approach the second half of this thesis, since it is also true for him that human existence is essentially being-with (*Mitsein*), a being with and for (or against) others (BT §26). But this aspect remained peculiarly faint and undeveloped in his work. On the other hand, there is nothing in Heidegger that corresponds to the first part of the thesis—namely, to the idea that the will can only fulfill itself in something that is 'good' in the sense that it requires intersubjective recognition. He merely touches upon this idea in discussing that inauthentic albeit widespread form which he designates as "distantiality" (BT, p. 164) and which also belongs to inauthentic existence for him. This form is characterized by "concern about one's difference from others" in which the issue is merely one's "priority over others," and one is only intent upon either "catching up" to the others or "holding them down." In contrast, Mead points out that the productive possibility of a "sense of superiority" (208) should not be overlooked simply because of this "disagreeable type of assertive character" (205); in particular, one must not overlook the fact that a structure is involved that "seems to belong essentially to self-consciousness" irrespective of all moral evaluation. I can also reformulate what Mead means here by saying that self-consciousness in the ordinary [German] sense of the word seems to belong essentially to the relation of oneself to oneself.

Heidegger's neglect of this structure in its constitutive meaning for the relation of oneself to oneself results from his lack of consideration of the concept of the good; and this in turn is connected to the fact that Heidegger eliminated the aspect of reason—of objective justification—from the relation of oneself to oneself. Something is called good—or, more precisely, better—if it is preferable on objective grounds, and accordingly I was able to interject some aspects of the good into the context of the practical question that is constitutive for authentic existence. Nonetheless, the ultimate reference point of deliberation remained one's own well-being. On the other hand, we now come across a use of the word *good* that could not even be acknowledged in a supplementary way in the interpretation of Heidegger because its reference point is not one's own well-being, although as soon as it does come into play it becomes relevant for the question of what is best for me.

It is generally characteristic of human abilities that they can be developed in ways that are better or worse; they stand on a scale of preferability. Whatever one 'can' do, one can do better or worse, and this also means better or worse than others, for example, singing, swimming, cooking, or repairing cars. Depending upon how important a particular ability is to us or how much we like to exercise it, we will be intent upon exercising it as well as possible. Aristotle tended to understand *good* in this sense as aptness for the production of the work to which the activity is related.[3] But this account cannot be sustained universally,[4] first, because there are activities such as swimming and singing that are not directed (like repairing a car) toward the production of something, and, second, because there are activities such as cooking that are directed toward the production of something, but the produced work does not provide a simple criterion for their good (as it does in the case of a repaired car). On the other hand, it is obvious that my formal definition of *good* also works here. X can sing, swim, cook, repair cars, better than y if those who properly understand the activity in question prefer the performance of x to the performance of y. A subjective element thus enters in here, although the preference is not simply subjective and arbitrary but is objectively justified. The criterion for this claim to objective justification, however, is merely that those who properly understand the matter make the decision on what is to be preferred. I see the look of doubt in some of your faces, but I must let this stand as a thesis. For this reason I also only want to give an equally programmatic answer to the next question that arises here—namely, the question of how it is to be decided which people understand the matter properly if there are no objective criteria. The answer runs as follows: It is those individuals who are most experienced in the affair at issue; and a person x is more experienced in something than a person y if there is a course of experience from y to x that results in y sharing the value judgments of x, but no course of experience from x to y. Thus, good or better in this sense is what would be acknowledged as such by everyone once they have had the necessary experiences: The consensus (qualified in the way just indicated) is not a consequence of objective criteria, but is itself the sole criterion. Heidegger's complete neglect of this meaning of *good* does not seem to be based merely upon the fact that like every other use of *good* this use appeals to objective justification. Rather, this form of justification contains an indissolubly social, intersubjective aspect; thus if *good* in this sense were also to be relevant for the relation of oneself to oneself in the mode of authenticity, a form of self-determination would no longer be conceivable in which one could simply choose for oneself without referring to the agreement (even if only potential) of others.

But you might raise the following question: Why must the striving for excellence in some abilities be relevant for the relation of oneself to oneself, especially if the latter is considered in the mode of authenticity? In my view we can distinguish three levels in both a structural and genetic sense, even if there are no sharp boundaries. Of course, that affirmation which we experience at the beginning of our lives and which constitutes the basis of our feeling of self-worth cannot yet be related to roles. But at a very early stage it does contain moments of esteem that refer to various kinds of ability, to the development of abilities that have a social significance in at least a broad sense.

Now Mead's thesis is that it is only when abilities are expanded into roles that a dimension is opened in which the individual relates himself to himself. This involves two aspects. First, roles are also contexts within which abilities are exercised; and this implies that the exercise of a role stands on a continuum ranging from "better" to "worse," and here these words have the same meaning that they have in relation to abilities generally. Second, it is not sufficient for the individual merely to perform particular socially recognized actions more or less well; rather, he can only develop a relation to *himself* and a feeling of self-worth in the strict sense when he attains a specific social place for himself (and this means for his life) with a long-term cooperative function.

The third level, which is only intimated by Mead through his reference to the development of a character, arises as a consequence of the fact that the exercise of roles is constitutive but not sufficient for the development of a relation of oneself to oneself. We say, for example, that "as a teacher he is excellent, but as a person I cannot approve of him"; and obviously the question "Who do I want to be?" with reference to myself is not exhausted by answers such as "a good teacher," "a good mother," but always has the more comprehensive sense of the question "What kind of a person do I want to be?" I do not have a theory of how this question is to be understood more precisely. I will therefore restrict myself to critical remarks concerning the way in which both Heidegger and Mead deal with it; and in both cases I will return to Aristotle.

As criticism of Heidegger: Aristotle bases his ethics on the idea that the same mode of use of *good* and *bad* that applies in general to human abilities and activities also applies to the activity of human life as such; thus since every person is concerned about his being, he must be concerned to carry it out in the best possible way.[5] And in this context the question of which life is a good one is again decided by those individuals who properly understand this matter, that is, those who have the greatest practical wisdom.[6] I do not think this is a theoretical trick on Aristotle's part, but rather corresponds to our ordinary understanding. This understanding is not to be found in our use of the expression *good person* (here the word *good* has assumed a more specific connotation in modern usage), but it appears in many other expressions; it is evident, for example, when we say "I admire or think highly of him as a person," "he is a wonderful or exemplary person," or "I find such a way of life right." By virtue of their form such value judgments raise the claim to be objectively justifiable statements, which present two possibilities: Either they prove to be mistaken or one-sided, or we must be able to convince others of their validity. This implies neither that there is only *one* ideal possibility of human existence nor that someone could simply adopt some ideal conception as his own; furthermore, the irretrievably individualizing and volitional components in choosing oneself that we established in the interpretation of Heidegger do not have to be denied. It is certainly true that every path of self-discovery and self-determination must be an individual one; nevertheless, this does not preclude but rather accommodates the insight that a criterion of the correctness of this path is that it would have to meet with the approval of those who 'understand something of this matter.' We saw earlier that one cannot speak of self-determination if either the volitional or the rational aspects are omitted. And we can now see that the rational aspects are omitted to the extent that one either dispenses with learning from others in relation to one's own decisions, or gives up being able to convince others of their merit. Heidegger made a mistake in thinking that the 'self' in the talk of "I myself" is only to be understood on the basis of the contrast with others. In reality this manner of speaking is to be understood in terms of the decision that I myself make, and in this respect it stands in contrast to a decision that is not made by me but by something in me; and this is precisely the case when the rational aspects (which involve intersubjective aspects, as we have just seen) cease to assert their role.

As criticism of Mead: It seems that the only perspective that Mead has in mind with regard to the question of transcending individual roles is that of integrating various roles. But one can readily ask whether the 'question of identity' should be so exclusively oriented toward the concept of roles, especially when the meaning of this question is what kind of a person I want to be. It might be argued that the question of what kind of a person I want to be always means the following: What kind of a person do I want to be in relationship to my fellow men? But precisely at this point one must ask whether it is warranted to understand the relationships between people exclusively as normative relationships (as has become customary in sociology). Although the normative relationships are the ones that count from the perspective of the institutional organization of society, this does not apply from the perspective of the individual. Here affective relationships have at least as much fundamental significance, and it is worthwhile in this context to recall that for Aristotle the question of what it means to be an excellent person focused entirely on this aspect. Since in affective relationships I relate myself *to myself in* my relationships *to others*, the task in these affective relationships is to strike an optimum, that is, a proper mean;[7] and one must grant Aristotle that what is called character is the affective behavioral disposition of a person. Thus the question concerning the right way of being of a person cannot center upon the integration of various roles, because in the first place this question can be crucial in deciding which roles I select for myself to the extent that this falls within my freedom. More important, however, this question can also already be relevant within the context of exercising a *single* role; thus, for example, a postal clerk can impress us in the way he does his work, not because of the way he functions in his role (e.g., as a good postal clerk), but because of the human qualities by which he exercises it. And if he has found such a standard in himself, in his affective character, it naturally follows that he also will remain 'the same' in another role.

Does this problem concerning the question of what kind of a person one wants to be represent the same stage in Mead's work that Heidegger addresses in his account of 'authenticity'? No, this is still not the case. For even if one explicitly raises this question, it does not have to be raised from an independent standpoint; it can be exclusively oriented toward what 'one' regards as appropriate. And it is noteworthy that in his distinction between *me* and *I* (§§22, 25) Mead envisages a contrast that is similar to the one made by Heidegger by means of his concepts of 'the they' and authentic existence.

Mead defines the "me" as "the organised set of attitudes of others which one himself assumes. . . . The taking of all of those organised sets of attitudes gives him his 'me' " (175). Thus, the me constitutes the picture of the normative expectations that others have of me. It is the projection of expectations emanating from the society onto me. Mead obviously selected this expression because he thereby wanted to refer to what I am as an object of social expectations; or, more simply, he wanted to refer to how I ought to be in my roles and in my other behavior from the standpoint of society. Mead comes very close to Heidegger's description of 'the they' when he says, "The 'me' is a conventional, habitual individual. It is always there. It has to have those habits, those responses which everybody has" (197).

In contrast, the "I" is "the answer which the individual makes to the attitude which others take toward him . . . the 'I' gives the sense of freedom" (177). This concept is more extensive than that of self-determination. It represents in a general sense the response of the individual to the expectations directed at him—the yes or no (accepting or declining, 194). Thus, Mead fixes the conceptual boundary at a different place from that of Heidegger, but this difference is relatively unimportant; it can be done in one way or the other. For Heidegger, the 'they' is a mode of being-oneself; hence, he speaks of the 'they-self'—that is, the self that accommodates itself to what is regarded as correct. In Mead's conceptual framework this is *one* possible response of the 'I' to the 'me.' For Mead, the entire spectrum of possible responses to social expectations pertains to the "I." The person acts in his own peculiar way no matter how he responds, no matter how he performs the role expected of him. Thus an aspect of innovation always pertains to the 'I' (177, 203). But the crucial alternative is the one between yes and no, between "devotion" and "self-assertion" (192), and this means between "adjusting one's self or fighting it out" (193).[8]

It is important to understand this concept of self-assertion correctly. First, there is no connection between this concept and that of the sense of superiority. Rather, the need to distinguish oneself from others functions within the context of what is universally acknowledged. In contrast, by means of the concept of self-assertion Mead considers the possibility of giving a negative reply to what is universally acknowledged. Second, it must be noted that for Mead such a negative reply cannot consist in a simple refusal in which the individual goes his own way; rather, it can only consist in a new universal conception that is directed toward gaining recognition against the others. For this reason, this "self-assertion" is a "fighting it out." "If one puts up his side of the case, asserts himself over against the others," this implies that he "insists that they take a different attitude toward himself." Mead continues: "Then there is something important occurring that is not previously present in experience" (196). Innovations in the real sense rest upon such acts of self-assertion, which in some instances are collective; this promotes the development of society and prevents its ossification.

We have now reached the point at which the real contrast to Heidegger's conception becomes evident, since Mead's concept of self-assertion represents his concept of self-determination. Although Mead scarcely elaborates his conception, it contains the essential characteristics of self-determination in germ: that is, that the individual himself chooses who (how) he wants to be, and does not therby orient himself toward any accepted or conventional points of view. Mead does not describe this as self-determination but rather as self-assertion, because the individual relates himself to himself in such a way that he thereby relates himself to others who relate themselves to him; and for this reason he cannot understand himself in a new way without at the same time understanding social relations differently. Thus the individual is directed toward asserting and implementing his new view of the being of persons—of social being—against the others. If it seems in Heidegger as if authentic existence is a turning away from the 'they,' one has to ask: Where can it turn to? To be sure, a turning away from the 'they' is required, but only in the sense that the existing normative conceptions are no longer accepted simply because *one* accepts them. But this only happens to the extent that one grapples with precisely these normative conceptions; if one tries to turn one's back on them, one remains bound up with them in reality. While the 'they' in Heidegger has no positive significance aside from constituting the actual structure of our everyday existence, the 'me' for Mead has the positive connotation that normative conceptions must first be existent in conventional form in order for a society as well as a relation of oneself to oneself to be constituted. Furthermore, conventionally preexistent norms provide the only material on whose basis an autonomous self-relation can be worked out; and the result of this work can only be improved conventional conceptions.

How is the self-assertion that Mead has in mind to be understood concretely? "The demand is freedom from conventions, from given laws. Of course, such a situation is only possible where the individual appeals, so to speak, from a narrow and restricted community to a larger one, that is, larger in the logical sense of having rights that are not so restricted" (199). "A man has to keep his self-respect, and it may be that he has to fly in the face of the whole community in preserving his self-respect. But he does it from the point of view of what he considers a higher and better society than that which exists" (389). Mead conceives of such a higher society as one in which more "democracy" in the sense of more "brotherhood" is realized, that is, in which "every individual stands on the same level with every other" (286); thus the subordinating structures of social cooperation are dismantled.

"The only way in which we can react against the disapproval of the entire community is by setting up a higher sort of community which in a certain sense out-votes the one we find. A person may reach a point of going against the whole world about him. . . . But to do that he has to speak with the voice of reason to himself. He has to comprehend the voices of the past and of the future. That is the only way in which the self can get a voice which is more than the voice of the community," and it is the only way in which it "can change the attitude of the community" (167ff.).

Mead's conception remained a sketch. Although the irreducibly individual and volitional aspects of self-determination that we were able to extract (and want to retain) from Heidegger's conception are lacking, we now see that Mead's view corrects Heidegger's conception not only with regard to its social deficiency but also with regard to its rational deficiency. Both aspects essentially belong together for Mead. The appeal to reason in practical matters is the appeal to a consensus that would have to result if there were "universal discourse," that is, a discourse of all rational beings (157ff., 195). This appeal is necessary if an individual arrives at a conception of the good life different from that held by others. We saw earlier that "good" is something that is preferable on objective grounds, and we have no material criteria for this; rather, it is the most experienced who decide on this matter. When I advanced this position you may have suspected that the decision regarding the good is thereby surrendered to what is merely conventional. But there is a difference between those who are most experienced and those who are regarded as such. For this reason an individual can assert the correctness of a divergent view in opposition to the prevailing one, but he cannot simply appeal to his intuition or his authenticity in so doing; rather, he has to be aware that the criterion for the correctness of his view is the possibility of ultimately convincing the others.

This is a troublesome affair in any concrete case. Let us therefore find consolation in the fact that at least it sounds noble in the abstract. We now have a concept of a reflective self-relation in which a position is deliberatively taken toward the existing individual and social beliefs that are implied in one's own actions, in social actions and in institutions; and deliberating here means raising questions regarding what is actual, possible, and better. This deliberative adoption of a position pertains in particular to the beliefs implied in one's own conceptions and social conceptions of the right form of life or, more precisely, the right form of communal life. And this form of talking to oneself at the same time is implicitly a discourse with all rational beings.

Appendix: The Concept of Identity in Social Psychology

I had promised after concluding the interpretation of Mead to examine the term *identity*, which is widely used in contemporary social psychology. The use of this term essentially originates with E. H. Erikson, who writes in his essay "The Problem of Ego-Identity": "I can attempt to make the subject-matter of identity more explicit only by approaching it from a variety of angles. . . . At one time, then, it will appear to refer to a conscious sense of individual identity; at another to an unconscious striving for a continuity of character; at a third, as a criterion for the silent doings of ego synthesis; and, finally, as a maintenance of an inner solidarity with a group's ideals and identity. . . . After an attempt at clarifying this relation, the term itself still retains some ambiguity."[9] I have cited this passage first because it indicates that at least Erikson himself is aware of the indefiniteness with which he uses the word *identity*. Second, it lends expression to the complexity of the problem encompassed by this term. In particular, it refers to genetic aspects of the relation of oneself to oneself that pertain to developmental psychology; these aspects go beyond what has been discussed in these lectures, and would require their own extensive conceptual elaboration. Since I cannot accomplish this here, I must restrict myself to an external critique, and I will refer only to one author. I have selected J. Habermas's theory of identity because it has distinct conceptual contours and because Habermas stands in close connection to Mead (in his own self-understanding as well).

Habermas's theory of identity is also developmental in character. He distinguishes three stages. Let me quote at length to characterize them: "In learning to differentiate his body from . . . his surroundings, the child acquires a 'natural' identity, so to speak; this is a function of the durable character of an organism that preserves its integrity over time. Indeed, plants and animals are already systems in an environment, so that they not only have, like moving bodies, an identity 'for us' (the identifying observers) but in a certain sense possess an identity 'for themselves.' But the child only constitutes himself as a person to the extent that he learns to localize himself in his social life-world. When the child internalizes the general symbolic patterns characteristic of the few fundamental roles of his familial setting and later the actions of larger groups, the child's *natural identity*, which is centered upon the organism, is superseded by a symbolically constituted *identity of roles*. The character of role identity in sustaining continuity rests upon the stability of behavioral expectations, which also are established in the person himself through the ego ideals. . . . This conventional identity generally disintegrates during the phase of adolescence. During this period the young person learns the important difference between norms on the one hand and fundamental principles on the other. . . . Such principles can serve as a standard for criticizing and justifying preexisting norms. . . . [The ego] must reckon with the possibility that the traditional, customary forms of life prove to be merely particular and irrational. Hence, it must take back its identity, so to speak, behind the lines of all *particular* roles and norms, and must stabilize it merely through the abstract capacity to represent itself in given situations as that agency which can still fulfill the demands for consistency . . . even in the face of incompatible role expectations. The *ego identity* of the adult confirms itself in the ability to develop new identities and at the same time to integrate them with those that have been overcome, thus placing itself and its interactions in the context of a unique life history. Such an ego identity makes that capacity for autonomy and for individuation possible which is already potentially contained in the structure of the ego at the stage of role identity."[10]

Before examining this three-stage conception of identity, I would like to remind you that the question "Who do I want to be?" does not refer to a numerical identification, but to a qualitative identification. This should not be a matter of controversy, since my numerical identity is fixed and is not something that is left to the discretion of my will. I can want to become different from what I am, but I cannot want to become a different person from who I am; and this is true entirely on logical grounds. And it is in any case clear that in the formulation "I understand myself as a so-and-so" a qualitative identification is involved. This was obviously also confirmed in the context of the interpretation of Mead: When one understands oneself as a mother, a policeman, and so on, it is clear that these are role *predicates*, that is, general characterizations; and in the interpretation of Mead this gave me the opportunity to use the terminology of identity several times as a matter of course. Finally, it is equally clear that the question of what kind of a person I want to be, or what kind of a character I want to have, is a predicative question, although it is obviously not to be answered by only one predicate.

If we now consider Habermas's three-stage schema from this background, a puzzling impression emerges. It is obvious at the second stage of "role identity" that a qualitative identity is involved. On the other hand, Habermas's characterization of the first and third stages indicates that they involve individuality, that is, numerical identity. But then it is unclear *what* it is whose development is actually being analyzed. We are told that the development of *the identity* of the person is under consideration; but *identity* is only a word, and we have just seen that it is a thoroughly ambiguous word. You might reply in the following way: Identity simply has two aspects, the numerical and the qualitative; and why shouldn't the first be developed at the outset, then the second, and then at a higher stage the first again? I have difficulties following such an argument; for if you claim that identity has two aspects, I do not understand what this third thing is that is alleged to have two aspects. Someone who thinks that it is meaningful to talk about a unitary concept that encompasses predicative and numerical identity would first have to explain what is supposed to be meant by this. Until such time we have no choice but to insist that a word that has two meanings is involved.

Nonetheless, Habermas's theory offers the advantage of permitting the relatively easy identification of the two meanings—and this is because Habermas explicitly stresses one aspect, that of numerical identity. As far as I know, both meanings are found together throughout the relevant literature without being distinguished, and they are mixed together in an extremely confusing way for the logically oriented reader. I refer to the passage from Erikson just cited only as a further example: On the one hand he speaks of the "sense of individual identity," and on the other hand of the "maintenance of an inner solidarity with a group's ideals and identity." Levita's book *Der Begriff der Identität* is devoted exclusively to this issue, and seeks to shed light on the problem through a long historical-philosophical introduction. Instead of relying on Frege, however, it is guided by a book concerning "the doctrine of identity in the discipline of German logic after Lotze," and this makes the confusion complete. More recently Henrich has correctly observed: "Any number of individuals can be autonomous in precisely the same form and manner. If this is the case, they cannot be distinguished as individuals through their 'identity.' If this is not taken into account, discussions under the topic of 'identity' will suffer from a confusion that is really irremediable."[11]

What is to be done in light of such a situation? It may be that both meanings are important for the problem that is at issue; but if one wants to speak, like Habermas, of a development *of* identity, one must try to distinguish one of the two meanings as irrelevant or secondary for the problem. Henrich's view is that the ambiguity has to be resolved in favor of qualitative identity; and the reflections to which I alluded in connection with the question "Who do I want to be?" obviously also point in the same direction. Since the word *identity* in ordinary usage primarily means numerical identity—in contrast to "identification" and "identifying-oneself-with" (which also has been disregarded)—it can be assumed that once the word was introduced it led to a misguided search for a numerical identity behind it, even if in reality a numerical identity was not at issue; the opposite development would be more difficult to envisage.

To be sure, Habermas has attempted to resolve the ambiguity in the other direction, that is, in favor of numerical identity. Although the texts that I have cited give the impression that Habermas shifts from one meaning to the other, he attempts in an earlier text to establish that the identity of the second stage is also numerical; in this case my formal critique would have been premature. It was obviously Habermas's belief that *identity* cannot mean anything but numerical identity, and this is a view that Henrich also seems to hold. But Henrich concludes from this that the use of this word in social psychology is not a strict one, whereas Habermas considers it a reason to treat identity as numerical at all stages. He attempts to accomplish this for the second stage by designating the "primary roles of sex and age" as "identifying characteristics" in his "Notizen zum Begriff der Rollenkompetenz" (Notes on the Concept of Role Competence);[12] and it is clear from the context that *identifying* is meant there in the sense of "numerically identifying." But this seems contrived in several respects. First, if it is correct that sex and generation are the primary roles that the child learns in the Oedipal phase, generation is nonetheless not the same thing as age. Age is not a role. A child is not numerically identified relative to his family through sex and generation. Second, if this conception were valid at all, it would only be true for the primary roles. Finally, there is a third difficulty: At each stage of development of identity, the identity in question is supposed to represent a problem to be resolved; does Habermas seriously want to claim that the child's numerical identification of himself within the family represents a problem for him at this stage?

Let us now examine Habermas's descriptions of those stages of the development of identity that he regards as self-evidently involving numerical identity. At the outset he claims for the first stage that "already plants and animals" have not only an identity "for us" but also an identity "for themselves." This might be construed as a gesture of homage to Hegel, since Habermas delivered this lecture on the occasion of his reception of a Hegel prize; but this same formulation also appears in other writings. The state of affairs that Habermas has in mind is that when processes in an organism (which can be characterized as life processes) cease to function, the organism dies; and when a creature dies, its identity obviously also vanishes. It may be permissible to describe this phenomenon teleologically (and in this respect anthropomorphically) by saying that the organism is carrying out these processes in order to preserve its life. But it does not follow from this that either its existence (life) or its identity is 'for it.' Organisms do not have an identity 'for themselves' at all, and I cannot imagine what the criteria of an identity 'for itself' could possibly be in the case of beings that cannot identify anything linguistically. In contrast, children obviously have an identity for themselves in the sense that they can identify themselves numerically in the same way they identify other persons and objects; and this capacity is acquired precisely at the point at which they learn to apply singular terms to themselves and to others.

Why does Habermas overlook this linguistic identification? It is the only one by virtue of which it is undoubtedly certain that one acquires a numerical identity 'for oneself.' Presumably this form of theoretical identification of oneself is not sufficient for his purposes. It is also not sufficient from my point of view. But the question is whether or not this linguistic reference to oneself as an individual is the necessary condition for what is still missing. And what is it that is still missing? In my view it is the volitional-emotional relation to oneself. According to Heidegger, this turns out to be a relation to my to-be; and since it is *my* to-be that is at issue, the linguistically constituted numerical identity is presupposed. What is added to this is the interest of the individual that things go in such and such a way for him, for example, that he is active instead of passive and thus attains independence, or that he can have confidence that he is loved and recognized. But this implies that numerical identity does not constitute an additional emotional-volitional problem. The volitional-emotional problem is how the individual (whose individuality is established) acquires specific qualifications for himself or for his being (that things go in such and such a way for him, that he behaves in such and such a way). I am a relative novice in matters of developmental psychology, and hence I cannot speculate on what the preliminary stages of the relation of oneself to oneself are that possibly even precede the linguistic phase. But in Habermas's case the preoccupation with a nonlinguistic identity motivated his recourse to a supposed organismic self-identification; thus he not only disregards the actual self-identification in language but also fails even to raise the question concerning the preliminary stages of the volitional-emotional relation of oneself to oneself. On the other hand, when we find in Erikson titles for the early phases such as "primordial trust," "autonomy," and "initiative," it is clear that these stand for such preliminary stages even if the conceptual connection is more tentative and unclear than it is in Habermas's case.

Habermas describes his third stage of identity by means of three characterizations: (1) the capacity to remain consistent with oneself in different and even contradictory systems of roles, (2) the readiness to question preexisting norms (development of "autonomy"), and (3) the capacity "to place oneself in the context of a unique life history," and thus to represent oneself in one's difference from everyone else, that is, in terms of one's identity ("individuation").[13] Habermas assumes in his description of the third stage that an analytic connection exists between these three characterizations; and his understanding of the concept of identity requires that the third characterization be considered the most crucial one.[14] The first characterization corresponds to what I analyzed in connection with Mead under the title "character identity"; and the second characterization corresponds to what I analyzed in connection with both Heidegger and Mead under the titles "self-determination" and "reflective self-relation." On the other hand, we have not found anything in our preceding analysis that would correspond to the third characterization. If my arguments in this regard were correct, the connection between the first two characterizations should not be conceived as intimately as Habermas suggests; a character identity or consistency in contradictory systems of roles can also be attained within the limits of the conventional. Two stages of increasing autonomy are involved, and Habermas is correct that the problem of consistency raised by contradictory systems of roles can be resolved more adequately at the level of the reflective self-relation.

But now in what sense is a special problem of individuation (or a special capacity to solve this problem) supposed to pertain to the truly autonomous, reflective self-relation? The numerical identity of the individual is fixed, and it ultimately rests upon spatiotemporal determinations. Thus if a 'problem' is still presumed to exist regarding the individual's numerical identity,[15] it can only lie in the individual's attempt to obtain this spatiotemporal identity, so to speak, in terms of the particularity of qualitative determinations in which he understands and presents himself so that he appears in this sense as 'unmistakable,' and this means as *unique*. This would imply that when the question "Who am I and who do I want to be?" is raised from an autonomous standpoint, it is characterized by a concern about one's own uniqueness, and is to be understood as a question about how one can "maintain one's identity *in contrast with* others."[16] I find this conception implausible, and in my view the only thing that recommends it is the misleading numerical conception of identity. Someone who autonomously raises the qualitative identity question "What kind of a person do I want to be?" will *in fact* arrive at results that allow him to appear unique; but if he turns his uniqueness into a problem and makes it his *aim*, an inappropriate factor is thereby introduced into the practical question of truth. Instead of simply directing the question to how matters actually stand and what the best possibility would be for my existence and that of others, the issue now would be how I can distinguish myself from others; that is, there would be a concern about one's "distantiality," which Heidegger correctly (in my view) ascribed to inauthenticity.[17]

Thus it seems clear to me that the problem of identity should not be understood in the sense of numerical identity. In the final analysis this is also true for an aspect of the relation of oneself to oneself that Habermas correctly stresses—namely, the aspect of continuity in one's life history. I touched upon this briefly in the interpretation of Heidegger, but for the most part I have neglected it. I have not dealt with the dimension of the past in the relation of oneself to oneself at all, and I want to acknowledge this deficiency explicitly here; it also afflicts my treatment of epistemic self-consciousness. But the problem of one's own continuity is also a problem of qualitative identity. Of course, there are pathological cases that involve the loss of awareness of one's own numerical identity; and the fact that this problem is considered a part of the normal problem of identity in some of the literature is a further consequence of the lack of clarity in the concept of identity.[18] In the normal case numerical identity is the unproblematic presupposition of the question of continuity. The question concerns the relative extent of justification for the changes (and changes are *per definitionem* qualitative) in the way I understand myself, or more generally for the changes in my beliefs and purposes. I can only represent myself as an autonomous and responsible person through these changes if I can provide reasons (and not merely causes) for why I have changed in such and such a way. This is true in the same sense that I only relate autonomously to my life as it impends if I act reflectively, and this means acting on the basis of a justified choice.

It is possible that a part of the confusion that has prevailed in discussions of "identity" is to be explained by the absence of a concept of what it means to relate oneself to oneself. An essentially individualizing dimension is contained at the outset in the relation of oneself to oneself as understood by Heidegger; for one is confronted with one's own existence, which cannot be delegated (that is, "respectively mine"). The fact that I am present for myself as an individual rests upon the use of singular terms; but the fact that I am confronted with myself as an individual and am concerned about myself as an individual is based, in addition to the use of the singular term *I*, on the proposition that I have to be. Now the problem of identity seems to me to be involved in two respects. First, it arises because I can relate myself to myself only by understanding myself as such and such a person; thus the attainment of an identity is required. Here the word has an entirely ordinary use, and it is a qualitative one. Second, when it is claimed that the concept of identity is an "equivalent of the concept of the ego,"[19] the point is that I cannot allow the choice of this identity to be taken from me; that is, I choose myself, and this means that I attain an identity in the mode of *autonomy*. I cannot delegate the practical question to others; I can only either avoid it or raise it myself, and the same thing is true for deliberating and choosing. In deliberating and choosing each person is thrown back upon himself, and this applies even when one deliberates in concert with others. The peculiar individualizing of autonomous existence is contained in this relation, but this individualizing does not imply uniqueness. This state of being thrown back upon oneself also does not imply being thrown back upon an ego or a self; rather, as we have already seen, it represents a way to be, or a mode of relating to oneself.

Lecture 13

Concluding with Hegel, I

I indicated at the beginning of the semester that among the modern conceptions of self-consciousness that have broken away from the subject-object model only in Mead's case would we reach a position that could compete with Hegel's conception of self-consciousness. In Hegel's case we have a traditional theory of self-consciousness that relies on the subject-object model, but is distinguished from the traditional theories of self-consciousness because it understands self-consciousness as a practical relation of oneself to oneself while at the same time taking epistemic self-consciousness into account (as Fichte had also already done). Furthermore, it is characteristic for Hegel in particular (as for Mead) that the self-relation is constituted socially or intersubjectively.

There are two reasons why I want to contrapose the understanding of the relation of oneself to oneself as it has emerged in connection with Heidegger and Mead to Hegel's conception of self-consciousness. First, we can thereby deepen the critique of the traditional orientation of the problem of self-consciousness on the subject-object model, which I already developed at the beginning of the semester in connection with Fichte and the Heidelberg school. Second, I am also interested in comparing the conception that has emerged through Heidegger and Mead to the Hegelian conception from the point of view of their respective content, regardless of the formal-structural aspect. In this way I can answer the question that was posed at the beginning of the first lecture—namely, whether the topic of self-consciousness can still have the same relevance in a contemporary context for the idea of a rational form of life that it did for Fichte and Hegel. The whether is now no longer a question. But just for this reason it is even more important to recognize that the conception implied by Heidegger and Mead is fundamentally different from the Hegelian one; and this is true despite the fact that the same words are used. We have seen how the terms *freedom* and *truth* were constitutive for the conception of a reflective self-relation; although this conception is not precisely equivalent to either Heidegger's or Mead's account, it nonetheless resulted from the interpretation of both of them. Now Hegel also focuses upon the concepts of freedom and truth, and he does so far more explicitly than either Heidegger or Mead. This is evident in his elucidation of self-consciousness and spirit—and for Hegel it is only in spirit that self-consciousness is actualized. Thus we have a common denominator for the substantive problem at issue here: The concepts of freedom and truth are fundamental for understanding the relation of oneself to oneself, and they are especially crucial for the higher-level relation of oneself to oneself; for Heidegger and Mead this is the reflective self-relation, and for Hegel it is spirit. It will become clear, however, that these terms have a completely different meaning in the two respective cases.

Let me first summarize my view of the matter in connection with Heidegger and Mead. I will begin with freedom. Freedom is understood on two levels by both Heidegger and Mead. The first level represents, so to speak, the formal concept of freedom. In the preliminary treatment of Hegel's concept of self-determination that I presented earlier we already saw that Hegel also distinguishes two levels of freedom, and he explicitly calls the first level "formal." For Heidegger, the formal structure of freedom consists in the fact that the person always relates himself to possibilities of action in relating himself to his being; and for Mead, it consists essentially in the fact that the person as 'I' can respond in such or such a way to the normative expectations that are placed upon him or the offers of cooperation that are extended to him. By way of interpretation I have attempted to render both conceptions (which can be readily conceived in conjunction) intelligible on the basis of the yes/no polarity of practical sentences.

At the second level one does not relinquish the decision regarding the yes or no to any external or internal forces, but, as Heidegger says, one chooses oneself; thus freedom is implied here in the sense of self-determination. Or, as Mead sees it, one allows oneself to be determined rationally, and *rational* in this context means that which is capable of justification; and we have seen that justifiability in the practical sphere has an irreducibly intersubjective component. Heidegger's and Mead's conceptions of freedom are not in agreement with regard to this second level, and they both seem one-sided to me. They lose this one-sidedness and can positively complement one another, however, if both of them are understood in terms of what I have called the reflective self-relation; this implies that they both must be based upon the concept of deliberation. This concept is directly connected to what I termed the practical question, and we have seen that this question rests upon the yes/no polarity of practical sentences. Thus, according to our present characterization, we are free in the sense of self-determination if we act on the basis of an explicit or implicit process of deliberation in which the practical question is posed in its fundamental sense. In this way the aspect of reason stressed by Mead is included, since the concept of deliberation involves aiming for the good or the best, that is, for an objectively justified preference. On the other hand, we have seen that it is equally characteristic of the concept of deliberation that the process of adducing grounds must come to an end when decisions about one's life are at issue; thus the decision retains an irreducibly volitional or subjective aspect. This concept of freedom corresponds to what can be designated as responsibility in the narrow sense. For one says that someone acts or lives responsibly if he can provide a final or definitive account of his action; and this implies that he can justify his action to the full extent of its justifiability, and then bears the rest of the burden on himself. In contrast, someone is irresponsible or acts so if he either refuses to justify his actions altogether, or refuses to act because he cannot provide a complete chain of justification. The wider concept of responsibility must be distinguished from this narrow concept; the wider concept is roughly equivalent to accountability, and it implies that someone is merely capable of deliberating.

Now as to the concept of truth, the state of affairs appears initially confusing in Heidegger and Mead as long as we attend only to what can be found explicitly in their texts. In Mead the word *truth* does not appear at all, and in Heidegger we have seen that existence in the mode of authentic freedom (self-determination) is characterized directly as being "in the truth" (BT, p. 263). But Heidegger reinterprets the word *truth* in terms of "disclosure," so that something else takes the place of the question of truth and it thereby becomes superfluous to raise it at all. We will see that something similar happens in Hegel's case. On the other hand, the question of truth in Mead is basically contained in the question of reason, and the connection of the latter with the question of truth follows analytically from what I just said about freedom. Deliberation is essentially related to truth in a threefold sense; one raises questions about (a) what is actual (individual and social self-knowledge), (b) what is possible (knowledge of the situation of action), and (c) what is best among the possibilities that are given in the situation of action. This comprehensive meaning of the question of truth in its practical significance is easily overlooked because it is often insisted that truth only concerns matters of fact; in reality, however, the meaning of the question of truth is coextensive with the use of assertoric sentences. Whenever something is asserted—whether it be that something is such and such, that something is possible, that something is good or the best, or that something should be done— it is meaningful to raise the following question: Is what is asserted or believed only apparently the case, or is it actually or truly the case? And this question always means, Can it be objectively justified? The question of truth is identical with the question of reason. Now if my earlier thesis is correct that Heidegger's concept of self-determination permits and even requires supplementation by the concepts of deliberation and reason, then the following claim can be made, not directly for Heidegger, but for the conception that has resulted from the interpretation of Heidegger and Mead: Freedom in the sense of the narrower concept of responsibility (as just defined) analytically includes the question of truth in the threefold sense indicated above via the concept of deliberation. Thus the connection of freedom and truth (or more precisely, of freedom and the question of truth) follows from the connection of the two concepts of self-determination and the reflective self-relation. Of course, the domain of freedom extends beyond the question of truth precisely because, as indicated, the narrower concept of responsibility is not exhausted in the concept of the justifiability of one's own actions. This account of the connection of freedom and the question of truth delineates a form of the relation of oneself to oneself that meets the requirements of the narrower concept of responsibility. And it also represents an answer to the question that was posed at the beginning of the first lecture—namely, whether a concept of self-consciousness still exists today without which a form of life based upon reason does not seem conceivable. We will have to compare this conception of a relation of oneself to oneself that is understood from the perspective of freedom and truth with Hegel's concept of self-consciousness, since the latter is also centered upon freedom and truth.

Hegel addresses the problem of self-consciousness and its dialectic — and every topic that Hegel considers is dealt with in the context of its dialectic or else it would not merit philosophical recognition — at two points in his work. It is taken up first in the deservedly renowned second section of the *Phenomenology of Spirit* (PhG), and second in an extremely condensed version within the section on spirit in the *Encyclopedia* (§§424–437). This discussion of self-consciousness at two different points is of interest to us because in the *Phenomenology* Hegel is primarily oriented toward the concept of truth, whereas in the *Encyclopedia* he focuses primarily on the concept of freedom (cf. 424, 430, 436). The central position of the concept of freedom in the *Encyclopedia* is based upon the fact that in the *Encyclopedia* the entire discussion of spirit falls under this title, since spirit is understood here in terms of its contrast to nature (cf. 382). I will only go into this connection between self-consciousness and freedom later for supplementary purposes; it is to be found in the *Encyclopedia* and in the introduction to the *Philosophy of Right*, which falls within the same context and to which I referred earlier.

Let us first turn to the main text. In the *Phenomenology* Hegel treats self-consciousness as a distinct form of knowledge, but this does not prevent him from understanding it simultaneously in a practical sense. For Hegel, a specific concept of truth pertains to every form of knowledge or form of certainty. The chapter on self-consciousness is entitled "The Truth of Self-Certainty." Although this orientation toward the conceptual pair of knowledge (certainty) and truth has a general systematic meaning for Hegel, it has an especially pronounced importance in the *Phenomenology*. Therefore, I must make some general remarks about the topic and construction of this work. The manner and method in which any given phenomenon is discussed in Hegel's works is never simply descriptive, but always constructive; and this means that the discussion of this phenomenon cannot be understood at all without considering (1) the position that it has in the respective work, and (2) the method and objective of the work as a whole. The introduction to the *Phenomenology* provides us with an account of the central focus of this work, and also indicates the method to be followed in it.

The title page of the *Phenomenology* reads: "System of Science . . . First Part, The Phenomenology of Spirit." This work as a whole has the function of providing an introduction to the system. The problem that necessitates such an introduction, according to Hegel, is that a specific model of knowledge or a distinct mode of knowing is to be followed within the philosophical system; and this implies that a specific concept of truth must be presupposed. Indeed, a specific form of philosophical knowledge is alleged to be involved, and for Hegel this means a speculative form of knowledge; the latter is fundamentally different from the conception of knowledge and truth that is characteristic of common sense. Thus, before one can directly proceed to the philosophical system, the question arises as to the justification of this philosophical concept of knowledge and truth, which stands in contrast to our ordinary conceptions of knowledge and truth; these conceptions are also referred to by Hegel as those characteristic of "natural consciousness." Thus we (as natural consciousness) can apparently draw a deep and reassuring sigh of relief in the case of Hegel's first systematic step. In general Hegel begins precipitously and forgoes necessary preparation; thus, at the outset he confronts us in the system itself with concepts like being and nothing, which we have to regard as completely unintelligible if we are not deceiving ourselves. But here at the beginning of the entire inquiry Hegel has decided to condescend to us, that is, to natural consciousness, and to take us by the hand and lead us step by step, beginning with our ordinary understanding of knowledge and truth. We are to be led to knowledge that this ordinary understanding is untrue and one-sided, and we are ultimately to attain an adequate concept of truth that is no longer one-sided. Thus, Hegel's conception is that even natural consciousness or, as he also says, appearing consciousness (i.e., consciousness as it initially exists and appears) actually has a variety of conceptions of knowledge and truth. Therefore, the way that Hegel wants to guide us step by step assumes the form of leading us from one 'form of consciousness' (PhG 56)[1] to the next; and this is done in such a way that one can see that the next respective form has a more adequate concept of knowledge and truth than the preceding one, until finally the position of philosophical or absolute knowledge is attained. Since the book represents the path of appearing consciousness toward the true concept of truth, it is called the "Phenomenology of Spirit," and *spirit* is meant here in a broad sense that simply stands for consciousness (cf. *Logic*, pp. 781ff.). The unifying theme is the progressive experience of consciousness that every concept of truth is one-sided, and every case of one-sidedness contains a reference to another less one-sided conception of truth. For this reason Hegel also entitled the work the "Science of the Experience of Consciousness."* Now it is not self-evident that the forms of consciousness constitute such a comparative series in which the succeeding form is always 'truer' than the one preceding it, so that the process culminates in an absolute end point. Indeed, this is already a consequence of Hegel's philosophical conception of truth, as he concedes in the introduction (55ff.).

Now self-consciousness is supposed to be one of these forms of consciousness. If one approaches the issue in an unprejudiced way, this has to be somewhat surprising. And I must ask those among you who are already familiar with Hegel (and are surely more familiar with him than I) to make the effort to put yourselves back in the unprejudiced position that is a necessary condition for understanding an author. Understanding something does not mean empathizing and reiterating it; rather, we can only understand an author if we really engage ourselves with him but at the same time preserve every step of the way the freedom necessary to raise questions concerning the truth of his position. By this I mean two things; we must ask, first, What is he actually asserting? and, second, Is what he asserts true? It seems to me that a language-analytical method of interpretation is indispensable for this purpose. This contention could only be made good by actually carrying it out—that is, by providing a language-analytical interpretation of Hegel's dialectical method that simultaneously would be a language-analytical metacritique of Hegel's speculative critique of the understanding. But in the first place this would require a lecture course of its own, and in the second place I am not sufficiently well versed in Hegel for this task. In spite of this I venture to conclude this course of lectures with an interpretation and critical assessment of Hegel because his position seems to me too important in our context to be overlooked; and I also believe that at least the direction of my critique is correct.

---

*This title is not cited in Miller's translation of the *Phenomenology*, but it appears on page 61 of the German edition in the Philosophischen Bibliothek (Meiner) series (Trans.).

I noted that the fact that self-consciousness is supposed to be one of these forms of consciousness must be initially surprising. For it would be more plausible to conceive of "self-consciousness" as a specific phenomenon or a structure. But now is it supposed to represent a specific, one-sided conception of truth? We have to ask what the consequences of this account are for the topic of 'self-consciousness,' and which concept of truth is presupposed by it.

The first question can be answered quickly in a provisional way. Hegel *also* has the formal structure of self-consciousness in mind, but he is equally occupied with a specific conception of the relation of oneself to oneself in which a special importance is attached to the latter in contrast to the relation of oneself to something else and to others. Actually an aspect of self-consciousness pertains to every form of consciousness from sense certainty to absolute knowledge.

Now in order to be able to understand Hegel's perspective in elucidating the phenomenon that he considers in the section "Self-Consciousness," it is necessary to clarify his view of this comparative series of forms of consciousness; in particular, the justification for his conception of each succeeding form as 'truer' than the preceding one must be elaborated. Thus we must arrive at an understanding of what Hegel means by *truth*, and this must be pursued from two sides. First, what account does Hegel give of the understanding of truth of natural consciousness (and I am now not referring to a specific form of consciousness, but to natural consciousness as Hegel generally describes it in the introduction to the *Phenomenology*)? Second, what is the true, speculative concept of truth for Hegel?

Hegel immediately points out in the second paragraph of the introduction to the *Phenomenology* that what is characteristic for the natural understanding of knowledge and truth is the belief that truth stands on one side and knowledge on the other. He subsequently explains in the tenth paragraph how he understands this more precisely. I will examine this later. At the outset he employs this characterization as a foil in order to contrapose it sharply to his own view of the true concept of truth. This takes place in the third paragraph, where Hegel says "that the Absolute alone is true, or the truth alone is absolute" (PhG 47).

Thus, the true is supposed to be the absolute. How is this to be understood? One can easily become giddy when one hears of an absolute, but in Hegel's case this word has a well-circumscribed meaning. *Absolute* means the same thing as "unconditioned." Indeed, Kant had already designated the concepts of what is unconditioned as concepts of reason (*Vernunft*) and also as ideas (*Ideen*).[2] He thereby gave the talk of reason a significance that was crucial for German Idealism: It simply refers to the unconditioned; this contrasts sharply with the Western European tradition in which the word stands for justification and thus is associated entirely with an aspect of the understanding (*Verstand*). It is therefore not surprising that Hegel also designates the concept of the unconditioned or the unconditioned concept as the idea (*Idee*). And it is also for this reason that Hegel develops his proper concept of truth in that section of his *Logic* which deals with the idea; for the concept of truth is supposed to coincide with the absolute, and this signifies the unconditioned.

At the beginning of this section Hegel remarks, "The idea is the adequate concept, that which is objectively true or the true as such. When anything whatever possesses truth, it possesses it through its idea, or something possesses truth only insofar as it is idea" (*Logic* 755). The second sentence merely repeats the claim to totality that was already expressed in the sentence just cited from the introduction to the *Phenomenology*. The descriptively relevant statement is contained in the first sentence, which characterizes the idea and the truth as the "adequate concept." What does this mean? A concept is "adequate" if it agrees with reality (cf. *Logic* 614). Thus, the idea is "the unity of the concept and objectivity" (756). Hegel further explains that "being"— and here you must keep in mind that being is the concept with which the *Logic* begins and which underlies all subsequent, richer concepts— "has attained the significance of truth, since the idea is the unity of the concept and reality" (757). "However, the idea has not merely the more general meaning of the true being, of the unity of concept and reality, but the more specific one of the unity of subjective concept and objectivity" (758). He then says that "this identity has therefore rightly been defined as that of the subject-object" (758). According to Hegel, the true concept of truth implies the unity of subject and object, and this unity is understood at the same time as "identity." Since the subjective side is also conceived as knowledge or, as Hegel says in the *Phenomenology*, as certainty, we no longer have to deal here with a truth that stands opposed to knowledge—as is assumed within the natural conception of truth—rather, knowledge is incorporated as a moment within truth. The characterization that Hegel provides of absolute knowledge in the *Phenomenology* corresponds to this: "Truth is not only *in itself* completely identical with certainty, but it also has the shape of self-certainty" (485). This knowledge is absolute and the concept is unconditioned because "something only has conditions if it relates itself essentially to an objectivity that it has not itself determined, but which still confronts it in the form of indifference and externality" (*Logic* 455).

This thesis of the identity of subject and object, of knower and known, initially sounds like a characterization of self-consciousness. Or, more precisely, it recalls that Fichtean conception of self-consciousness according to which self-consciousness is envisaged as the knowledge of a subject that has itself as its object; thus, it is a case in which (as we heard earlier) knower and known are supposed to be identical. And Hegel in fact picks up the argument here; it is for this reason that he can say in the beginning of the discussion of self-consciousness in the *Phenomenology*: "With self-consciousness, then, we have therefore entered the native realm of truth" (104). Self-consciousness already belongs in the "native realm of truth" because here a subject-object unity is given for the first time, but it is still an abstract unity that has reality outside itself. And we have just heard that the real truth as idea is not the unity of the concept or subject with any given object (not even with itself), but with *reality as such (der Realität)*. Thus, the identity that Hegel envisions by means of the concept of truth is not the identity of the subject with that particular object that it itself is; rather, it is supposed to be an identity of this subject that is reflected into itself, that is, this being-for-self, with the being-in-itself of the reality that is confronting it. It is supposed to be an identity in which difference and opposition are incorporated and 'sublated' in that famous Hegelian sense (cf. *Logic* 107, 837ff.).

Thus the first constitutive feature of Hegel's concept of truth is that it is understood as correspondence (*Übereinstimmung*) of subject and object; second, it is crucial that this agreement is understood in terms of the concepts of identity and the negation of identity. I will return to the first point later. The second point presupposes concepts of identity and negation that are at variance with the ordinary understanding of identity and negation as contained in the use of the corresponding words of our language. Rather, these concepts are themselves derived from the subject-object model. The idea that identity and the relationship of the I to itself on the one hand and negation and the relationship of the I to other things on the other hand *reciprocally* shed light upon one another originated with Fichte; it involves the claim that identity and negation cannot be understood at all independently of the subject-subject and the subject-object relationship. We earlier encountered Fichte's puzzling and ultimately unintelligible conception that self-consciousness consists in positing oneself as identical with oneself; and there is a further conception corresponding to this that asserts that the subject-object relationship consists in the I positing the not-I in such a way that an opposition exists between the I and the not-I.[3] This conception poses as many difficulties for the concepts of identity and negation as it does for the elucidation of the subject-subject relationship (of self-consciousness) and the subject-object relationship. We have seen this for the subject-subject relationship. With regard to negation and the subject-object relationship, Fichte makes a mistake that is a consequence of the deficient knowledge of logic of his time: He understands not only the subject-object relationship but also negation as a relationship between two objects, and he thereby overlooks the propositional character of both the object and negation. Thus, the simplistic subject-object model has disastrous repercussions for the logical relationships. The talk of a "not-I" is an absurdity, since as Aristotle already pointed out singular terms cannot be negated.[4] Only predicates can be negated, and this itself refers back to the negation of sentences. Fichte's mode of procedure led to the possibility of speaking of an opposition or even a contradiction between two entities. And the application of this conception to the subject-object relationship yields the peculiar idea that the subject relates itself to something that stands in opposition to it in relating itself to other things. Finally, the view that one can elucidate what it means to have a conscious (intentional) relation to something by means of these abstract-ontological categories that are bound up with the unclarified concept of positing seems to be completely unjustified. Unfortunately this is also a view that is adopted by Hegel.

Hegel accepts the nonpropositional conception of negation or the negative (cf., for example, *Logic* 834ff., 835ff.), and the concepts of difference, opposition, and contradiction are closely connected for him on this basis; they are all understood as a negation of the concept of identity (cf. *Logic* 409ff.). In addition, Hegel accepts the dynamization of identity and negation that is contained in Fichte's concept of positing. This dynamization does not apply exclusively to the concept of the subject, but also applies to the concepts of identity and negation in general. For example, *something* (*das Etwas*) is "simple relation *to* itself in the form of being" (*Logic* 115, my emphasis) and *identity* is "simple negativity relating itself to itself" (412).

If one understands identity from the outset as a relation to oneself and difference as a relation to other things, the next step that Hegel takes no longer seems far-fetched. First, he emphasizes that even in abstract identity, and especially in that of self-consciousness, a negation is already contained. Second, he insists that only the "self-restoring sameness, or the reflection in otherness within itself" is a true identity; and on the basis of Hegel's concept of truth this means that it is "the true" (PhG 10).

This implies that identity and difference essentially belong together. The meaning of this sentence is ambiguous in Hegel. On the one hand, it has the harmless and, from a language-analytical perspective, self-evident significance that "$a = b$" (and "$a = a$" is obviously only a trivial special case of "$a = b$") only has a meaning against the background of "not ($a = b$)" and vice versa (cf. *Logic* 413–415). But on the other hand this principle also (and primarily) has another meaning, which is a consequence of Hegel's traditional, object-oriented way of thinking—namely, that what is identical with itself is also in the same respect different from itself and vice versa. It is only in this second way that the principle designates the structure that is intended by Hegel, and it is also only on this basis that it acquires the contradictory character that is necessary for Hegel.

Thus, you can see that from an analytical standpoint the scandal of the Hegelian conception does not lie so much in the thesis of real contradictions and in the 'dialectic' that results from it; rather, it is to be found in the way that the concepts of identity, negation, and so on are descriptively defined from the outset. Of course, I can only indicate the direction of the critique here; a thorough critical treatment of Hegel's conception of identity and negation would require an analytic interpretation of the entire relevant section in the "Logic of Essence" (*Logic* 409ff.). In any case, the usual critique of Hegel begins at a stage that is far too advanced. For the language analyst, the most astounding thing is the lack of care with which the logical categories were descriptively deployed in German Idealism, a lack of care oriented toward primitive models; indeed, they are still deployed in this way by those who philosophize in this specifically German tradition. In a certain sense this represents a regression to the level of logical development prior to Plato and Aristotle that was characteristic of the Eleatic school and the Sophists, who succeeded it. During this period when concepts such as being, change, identity, and predication were first reflected upon, the absence of linguistic reflection led to paradoxes; this lack of reflection was manifested in the object-oriented interpretation of determinations that are actually linguistic, and in the disregard for ambiguities. These same paradoxes recur in German Idealism, now to be sure deepened and apparently supported by the orientation toward the problem of subjectivity; still the difference is only that now they are affirmed, made objective and systematized. The enthusiasm for the idea of a philosophical system — a system that was essentially distinguished by the idea of a unified deduction of all logical-ontological categories from a single principle — had to reinforce the naiveté in descriptive approach even further, since every impartial examination of the descriptive meaning of these categories would have placed their subsumability under the principle of the system into question. Hegel contrasted his 'speculative' ('rational') conception of the concepts to that of the 'understanding,' that is, natural consciousness; but he correctly saw that his speculative conception merely makes explicit the contradictoriness that is already implicitly ('in itself') contained in the concepts of natural consciousness *as he* grasped them. From a language-analytical point of view this means that the speculative, dialectical conception of the logical-ontological categories is only a variant of the object-oriented conception of these categories that derives from a naive philosophical tradition. It is a systematic superstructure that consolidates this conception; it merely makes its latent paradoxes apparent and celebrates them as the truth.

The aspect of Hegel's account of the concepts of identity and difference that was just described can also be designated by means of a formulation of his own as the "identity of identity and non-identity" (*Logic* 74). But this is still not the concluding point of his analysis. The next (and for Hegel most crucial) step consists in not only conceiving of the fundamental concepts of identity and nonidentity as individually dynamic for themselves but also in viewing their interrelation as dynamic. Thus, the identity that exists between them is regarded dynamically; and this is now understood not only as an activity but also as a 'movement' (*Logic* 826, 835) in which this identity of the two sides is first established. It is only at this point that we arrive at what is meant by 'dialectic' (831). Thus, a movement is alleged to take place that starts from the "abstract relation to itself . . . which is being" (828), passes over into difference as "the negative" of this "immediacy" (834), and finally in the "sublation of difference . . . realizes itself by means of its otherness and by the sublation of this reality . . . restores its simple relation to itself" (837ff.). Since this identity that is realized through the assimilation and sublation of difference is the structure that Hegel designates as "truth," he immediately continues in the following way at the point last cited: "This result is therefore the truth" (837). But if this identity is essentially the result of a movement, it is also the case that (as Hegel insists in the preface to the *Phenomenology*, p. 11) the truth cannot be understood as anything but a result. And since the result is essentially a result of this movement and cannot be understood in separation from it, the truth is really "this whole movement" (28ff.).

The thesis that the identity of identity and nonidentity and consequently the truth is to be understood as such a movement is certainly a sublime idea. But the splendor of an idea is not the measure of its truth. And here I am obviously not using *truth* in the Hegelian sense, since this would lead us in a circle; rather, I am using it in the straightforward sense that is implied by the question of whether what is asserted is correct (can be justified). As far as I can see, Hegel did not justify this idea anywhere despite its centrality for him, and he never clarified the more precise meaning of this supposed movement. At best this movement seems comparable to the necessity of logical inference where one can say that if this proposition is true, then that other one is necessarily true. But in contrast to logical deduction, dialectical movement is not simply analytic but also synthetic (*Logic* 830). And Hegel's claim that the conclusion is truer than the premises in dialectical argumentation is closely connected to this; it contrasts with a formal-logical inference in which the conclusion is as true as the premises. But then the question arises as to where the additional synthetic moment originates. To be sure, Hegel still has an answer to this problem. Hegel's thesis is that each preceding stage already contains the additional moment of the next stage, but it is still in an undeveloped form or, as he says, it is still 'in itself' and not yet 'posited.' The philosophical unfolding of the respective concept demonstrates that it is not only what it seems to be at first, but that it is equally the succeeding moment 'in itself,' though of course it only contains the latter 'in itself.' This philosophical unfolding is still not the transition to the next stage, since at that point another concept emerges and what the previous concept only contains in itself is posited in the new concept. And since the previous concept always remains the concept that it is, it is still unclear what the thesis that one stage 'passes over' into the other is supposed to mean. It seems to me that the following explanation is the only one left: The structure of the next respective stage is truer than that of the preceding one; and in this context the comparative—the word *truer*—specifically means that the structure Hegel designates as truth, that is, the structure of the 'idea,' is more fully realized. But if this interpretation is correct, the alleged dialectic would not actually involve a movement at all, but would consist of a mere series that is defined by the terms of this comparative.

I will leave this point in this unsatisfactory interpretation in the hope that the Hegel experts among you will provide assistance in the discussion after the lecture. I now come to the last step that is important here. We have already seen that the dialectic of negation and identity does not merely apply to these concepts as such, but also pertains in a special way to the relation of the subject to reality. The last step we are concerned with consists in the further thesis that this dialectic is to apply to *all* logical-ontological categories, and ultimately to all conceptual relations of nature and of spirit. This means that they are all structurally equivalent to more or less complete realizations of that structure which Hegel designates as truth. Thus, the previously indicated movement is not only the movement between identity and nonidentity but also (insofar as it is this) *the one* movement of *the concept* (826); and this means the unified method that brings every subject matter to the level of the concept. Since the different contents are only the nodal points of this single dialectical movement, they constitute a system. There would be little point in commenting on this thesis abstractly. We will later examine it in relation to our substantive topic—self-consciousness—and the structural impoverishment that results from this sublime simplification will become apparent. I am merely concerned here with establishing the consequences for the concept of truth that result from this step. We now see why Hegel could say the following in characterizing the idea: "Something possesses truth only insofar as it is idea" (755). He supplements this at a later point: "The absolute idea . . . is all truth" (824). In addition, it now follows from the determination that the truth is essentially a "result" and that it is "this whole movement," that "the truth is . . . only actual as system" (PhG 14). "The true form in which the truth exists can only be the scientific system of such truth" (PhG 3). "The true is the whole. But the whole is only the essence consummating itself through its development" (PhG 11).

All of these additional characterizations of truth—that it is a result, that it is the whole movement, that it is only to be grasped as system or as the whole—are mere consequences of the definition of the truth as the idea, as the identity of the subject with reality. These are consequences that must follow if the identity (a) is conceived as a movement and if this movement (b) is all-embracing. But now the question of what this concept of truth has to do with our ordinary understanding of truth becomes even more pressing. In what sense can it be argued that when the subject identifies itself with reality, this and only this deserves the title of truth? You might reproach me here, since I have repeatedly emphasized that it is not meaningful to fight over words. Thus we should simply take into account here what Hegel understands by *truth*, completely irrespective of how this relates to our ordinary understanding of the word. You are right. In the end we will have to do precisely this. But our aim is to compare the way Hegel relates self-consciousness and its higher form, spirit, to truth with the reference to truth that emerges for the relation of oneself to oneself from the interpretations of Heidegger and Mead; it is therefore a matter of crucial importance for us to establish the relation between what Hegel means by *truth* and what one ordinarily understands by this word. While Hegel admits that his understanding of *truth* is something quite different from the one characteristic of natural consciousness, he claims in the *Phenomenology* that it can be shown step by step how natural consciousness experiences its own conception of truth as one-sided; hence, the speculative conception of truth is proven as the true, no longer one-sided form of truth for natural consciousness itself. Thus, I now come to the question of the point of departure of the *Phenomenology* after having provided an idea of the goal of its development. How does Hegel grasp natural consciousness and its concept of knowledge and truth? He elaborates this in the tenth paragraph of the introduction (PhG 52ff.), and I will now cite him extensively.

We must "first call to mind the abstract determinations of knowledge and truth as they occur in consciousness. Consciousness simultaneously *distinguishes* itself from something, and at the same time *relates* itself to it, or, as is said, this something exists *for consciousness*; and the determinate aspect of this *relating* or the *being* of something *for a consciousness* is *knowing*. But we distinguish this being-for-another from *being-in-itself*; whatever is related to knowledge is also distinguished from it and posited as also *existing* outside this relationship; the aspect of this being-in-itself is called *truth*." Hegel further adds: "Just what might be involved in these determinations is of no further concern to us here. Since our object is appearing knowledge, its determinations too will at first be taken directly as they present themselves; and they do present themselves very much as we have already apprehended them."

Is this correct? Does Hegel's description here conform to what we normally understand by knowledge and truth? Let us first examine more closely how Hegel describes knowledge. He says that consciousness "distinguishes itself from something, and at the same time relates itself to it." What kind of a phenomenon is thereby described? It is obviously not the special conscious relation of knowing at all, but a conscious relation in general; that is, the description pertains to what Husserl calls intentional consciousness, that is, consciousness of an object. It should be noted incidentally that the conceptual term by means of which Hegel describes the conscious relation to an object here is the dynamized concept of difference: Consciousness "distinguishes [*unterschiedet*] itself from something." The following remark that the object is "for" consciousness is obviously meant to emphasize again that the relation is not of any given type, but is a conscious one. And in the next sentence Hegel claims that the relation as characterized corresponds to what natural consciousness understands by knowledge. This assertion can only be termed a monumental error, although it is usually passed over by the ever-sympathetic Hegel interpreters as if it were self-evident. It demonstrates in a concrete case the carelessness with which the philosophers of German Idealism descriptively define the concepts that they later feed into the dialectical machinery.

It will suffice to recall some simple facts that stand contrary to this definition of knowledge. (1) Not every conscious relation to an object is a form of knowledge. (2) We can only know those objects that are states of affairs, that is, propositional objects. (3) Knowledge is a species of that intentional relation which is called belief, and belief involves a claim to truth in contrast to other intentional relations. (4) We say that someone not only believes but knows that something is the case if he not only claims that it is true, but (1) it also is true, and (2) he also can justify that it is true.

This last characterization, which constitutes the *differentia specifica* of knowledge, was first elaborated by Plato in his dialogue *Theaetetus* (201c), and it has not been seriously contested since that time. One might justifiably claim for Plato's account what Hegel unjustifiably claimed for his own: namely, this is how this determination presents itself. I leave it to you to make this clear to yourselves in connection with our actual use of the word *to know*. There are only a few philosophically relevant concepts that can be assumed to have been elucidated once and for all by a single philosopher. The relative ease with which this was done in the case of knowledge rests upon the fact that we have the generic concept of belief here, and for this reason only the correct *differentia specifica* had to be found. The concept of belief itself is not so easy to clarify; indeed, there is still no one who has succeeded in clarifying this concept or the use of this word up to the present day. It is that much more appalling that German Idealism was not even able to hold on to correct and uncontroversial results of preceding philosophical efforts in their descriptive complexity. For it would be absurd to contend that Hegel had corrected the traditional understanding with his account, which is both scanty and incorrect; he also never made such a claim.

Of course, I do not want to insist that Hegel is simply talking nonsense here. Rather, he means something quite specific—that is, the conscious relation of the subject to an object, the subject-object relationship. But it is not insignificant that he imposes the word *knowledge* on this structure, which he has positively in mind; for in this way he puts it *in the place* of knowledge, and thereby obscures the real phenomenon of knowledge from view. In the first place, the subject-object relationship is itself underdetermined, since its propositional structure is disregarded; and this is true irrespective of its questionable characterization by means of the dynamized concept of difference. Second, if something like knowledge is intended here, the discrepancy between knowledge and mere belief that is characteristic for the reference to truth is overlooked; and this is connected to the fact that the *differentia specifica* of knowledge is overlooked, that is, the relation to justification that is fundamental for the reference to truth. This is an omission that cannot be remedied later. Since the word *knowledge* is not related to justification from the outset, it is hard to see how this aspect could be reintroduced in the following dialectical development; and as far as I know, the phenomenon of justification and the question of justifying what is considered true is actually nowhere to be found in Hegel. Indeed, the phenomenon of the *question*, which belongs essentially to justification and to the relation to knowledge, does not appear at all in Hegel. This entire structural framework that characterizes the relation between belief and knowledge is constituted (a) by the question of truth that extends through this relation and (b) by the justification that is intended by this question; it is a structural framework that as a whole presupposes the propositional structure. At this point it has become clear that this structure presents a descriptive level of complexity that Hegel cannot attain with his logical-ontological model. Perhaps you will laugh and reply in this way: Hegel, who attains such sublimely complicated structures by means of his dialectical method, is supposed to be unable to apprehend in his concept these primitive structures of the mere understanding? Now I may be mistaken, but I fear that this is the case. Hegel's method of the "negation of the negation" is essentially bipolar and thus resembles the subject-object model from which it proceeds; and you cannot approach a phenomenon that from the outset has a multipolar and multidimensional descriptive structure by merely reiterating this structure. To be sure, the fact that Hegel could not have done justice to this phenomenon structurally does not prove that it cannot appear in his work; indeed, much more complicated phenomena appear, which he squeezes into the corset of his method. It is consequently even more noteworthy that the question of truth still does not appear in his work. And in any case the fact that it could not appear at this point, at the beginning of his exposition, is an indication of Hegel's inability to address this phenomenon.

It can already be expected in light of the foregoing that what Hegel says in the tenth paragraph of the *Phenomenology* about natural consciousness' conception of truth is no better than what he claims regarding its conception of knowledge. "But we distinguish this being-for-another from *being-in-itself*; whatever is related to knowledge is also distinguished from it, and posited as also *existing* outside this relationship; the aspect of this being-in-itself is called *truth*." Hence, *truth* would be defined as the independence of an object from the conscious relation to it, and it is assumed that such independence is intended in the conscious relation. But what we understand by *truth* does not consist in this. In the first place truth is obviously also propositional. We do not say that tables and chairs are true because they exist independently of our conscious relation to them. And it is also obvious that not every propositional object that exists independently of a conscious relation is true. It is perfectly meaningful to say that every state of affairs—whether it is true or false—is what it is independently of whether someone is referring to it.

What Hegel designates here as truth corresponds precisely to what he said about knowledge. Just as *knowledge* for him really meant the relationship of the subject to an object, *truth* stands simply for the object's independence in contrast to the subject's relation to it. Thus, what Hegel calls the relationship between knowledge and certainty on the one hand and truth on the other hand actually represents the so-called subject-object relationship in general. One might contest the harshness of my interpretation of this paragraph by citing Hegel's own remark at the end of the paragraph: "What actually might be involved in these determinations is of no further concern to us here." He characterizes them himself as obviously crude determinations. But this does not alter the fact that in his view they are determinations that correspond to the conception of natural consciousness; and in reality they are the determinations that constitute the foundation of the entire development of the experience of consciousness. My intention here is not only critical; rather, the point is to understand what is actually going on in the *Phenomenology*, and this requires understanding what the different forms of consciousness are really forms of. And we can now see that Hegel's concern is not knowledge and truth in the ordinary sense of these words at all but the far more general phenomenon of the subject-object relationship.

Hegel himself confirms this interpretation when he writes in the *Logic* (48): "In the *Phenomenology of Spirit* I have exhibited consciousness in its movement onwards from the first immediate opposition of itself and the object to absolute knowing. The path of this movement goes through every form of the relation of consciousness to the object and has the concept of science for its result." Thus Hegel can readily replace the characterization of the forms of the relation of knowledge (certainty) to truth with the characterization of the forms of the relation of consciousness to the object. These different forms and shapes are to be distinguished according to (1) the extent to which they preserve and deepen the independence of the objective side, (2) the extent to which they also develop an independence of the subjective side, and (3) the extent to which they simultaneously attain a unity (identity) of both sides while maintaining the independence of each side of the relation. But in this case the sequence of stages of forms of consciousness appears to be nothing more than a particular form of the movement of the concept, which we encountered a little while ago in considering Hegel's speculative concept of truth.[5] Hegel also seems to confirm this himself in the *Logic* (28): "It is in this way that I have tried to expound consciousness in the *Phenomenology of Spirit*. Consciousness is spirit as a concrete knowing, a knowing in which externality is also involved; but the development of this object, like the development of all natural and spiritual life, rests solely on the nature of the *pure essentialities* which constitute the content of logic." We can now understand the basis of Hegel's view that these forms constitute a series in which each succeeding form can be designated as 'truer' than the preceding one. This comparative—the word *truer*—does not concern truth in the ordinary sense at all, but has precisely the meaning that we already encountered in the case of the movement of the concept. It implies that the succeeding form in each case more fully realizes the structure of truth in the speculative sense—that is, the identity of the subject who is nonetheless independent with reality.

Thus, Hegel's claim in the *Phenomenology* to justify this speculative concept of truth in the face of natural consciousness through the development of the conceptions of the meaning of *truth* that natural consciousness itself adopts proves to be invalid. Hegel does not address what we ordinarily understand by *truth* at all, and what he proposes in the introduction to the *Phenomenology* as the conceptions that natural consciousness forms of its relationship to the object is already itself a philosophical construction. The formal structure of what Hegel introduces as knowledge and truth for natural consciousness and what turns out to be knowledge and truth for absolute knowledge is one and the same; the only difference is that in absolute knowledge what is divided in natural consciousness achieves an identity.

The hope that through the *Phenomenology* Hegel might furnish us as natural consciousness with a mode of access into his system (assuming we do not already understand ourselves as a construct of his system) has proven deceptive. Thus, the question of justifying the philosophical procedure that Hegel recommends is again completely open, and so is the question of how Hegel comes to use the word *truth* in precisely the way that he does.

At least the second question can be readily answered. Before doing this it must be noted that actually two modes of use of the word *true* are at issue here. On the one hand, the conception that Hegel develops in the introduction to the *Phenomenology* as natural consciousness' view of itself and its object corresponds to the conception of the speculative standpoint insofar as the subject-object relationship is involved in both cases. On the other hand, what Hegel designates as natural consciousness' concept of truth cannot be subsumed under the concept of truth that we have found in the *Logic*; in the *Logic* the word *truth* is reserved for the unity of the subject with the object (reality), whereas in the introduction to the *Phenomenology* it stands for the independence or being-in-itself of the object. There is no path that leads from one meaning to the other. In fact this divergence is not to be explained on the basis of the difference between natural consciousness and absolute knowledge, but in terms of the differing uses of language in the *Phenomenology* and the *Logic*. When Hegel reaches absolute knowledge in the *Phenomenology*, he states that truth has become fully identical with certainty (485). Thus, he adheres in the *Phenomenology* to the view that the word *truth* stands for the independence of reality, and therefore speaks of the identity of certainty with truth; in contrast, he speaks in the *Logic* of the identity of the concept with reality, and designates this identity as truth. In substance both views amount to the same thing, but this demonstrates in itself that we are dealing with two modes of use of the word *truth*. The version in the *Phenomenology* presents fewer difficulties. The way Hegel employs the word *truth* here indicates (as was shown in the interpretation of the tenth paragraph of the introduction) that it stands for an abstract aspect of what we normally mean by the word; and in the same sense what Hegel designates as knowledge stands for an abstract aspect of what we normally mean by this word. Knowing is in fact an intentional relation, but this alone does not make it knowledge; and something true is in fact something independent vis-à-vis the subject, but this alone does not make it a truth.

But what is the status of the concept of truth that is most crucial for Hegel, namely, the one that is formulated in the *Logic*? In my view this mode of use of the word *truth* can only be understood in a historical light. In the Middle Ages a definition came into fashion according to which truth was supposed to consist in the correspondence of thought with the thing, *adaequatio intellectus et rei*. This formulation can be understood to contain a correct though preliminary definition of the word *true*; but it can just as easily be interpreted in a way that results in nonsense. It is only meaningful (1) if both sides are understood propositionally, and (2) if the side of thinking is also interpreted objectively in the sense of what is thought, believed, or asserted. The formula would then have roughly the following meaning: Something that is believed is true if the facts really stand as they are believed to stand. You will recall that both of the above-mentioned aspects—that of propositionality and the contrast with belief—were missing in Hegel's characterization of knowledge; and they are obviously also missing in the way that the traditional correspondence formula was understood in German Idealism.

As an example I will read you the preliminary reflection from Schelling's *System of Transcendental Idealism*: "All knowledge rests upon the correspondence of an objective side with a subjective side. For one only knows what is true; but truth is generally posited in the agreement of the idea with its objects. We can call the totality of everything that is merely objective in our knowledge nature; in contrast, the totality of everything subjective is called the I or intelligence. Both concepts are opposed to one another. . . . But in every form of knowledge a reciprocal concurrence of both . . . is necessary; the task is to explain this concurrence."[6]

This formulation of the problem is incredibly primitive. Schelling proceeds from Fichte's concept of the positing of opposition, and constructs a subject that has no relation to an object and an object that is not yet the object of a subject. And now the "primary task of philosophy"[7] is supposed to be the explanation of how subject and object concur, and this means how truth as the correspondence of the subjective and objective dimensions is possible. Hegel is far removed from such nonsense. He correctly proceeds from the assumption that the subject is always already related to an object, and the question for him is not whether the two sides concur at all, but whether the way they are connected is a genuine unity in the sense of his dialectical concept of identity. Nonetheless, Schelling's formulation of the problem is instructive for understanding something of the background of Hegel's posing of the problem. They both have the subject-object relationship in view, and the word *truth* stands for the unity of subject and object for both of them. In both cases this use of the word results from a misunderstanding of the traditional *adaequatio* formula, and in both cases what is designated as truth has nothing to do with the ordinary meaning of *truth*.

At least the question of words is now settled. I said earlier that Hegel's assigning the word *truth* with a different meaning from the one it ordinarily has is not inconsequential; neither is the fact that he gives the word *reason* a different meaning (following Kant) inconsequential. It is not unimportant because in this way something else — a different type of relation — takes the place of the questions of truth and reason; and since the word is retained and its meaning is apparently only deepened, it seems as if nothing has been lost. We encountered a completely analogous structural phenomenon in Heidegger. But the situation in his case is more innocuous because his concept of truth as 'disclosure' merely vacillates between the more general phenomenon of disclosure and the question of truth; for this reason the relation to truth can be reestablished by means of mere supplementation and specification.[8] In Hegel's case something analogous might be envisioned for that concept of truth which stands for the 'independence' of the object. For the latter represents something that is simply more general than truth, and in this respect it is comparable in the abstract to Heidegger's concept of disclosure. It is clear, however, that very extensive supplementation would be necessary here. On the other hand, the same situation does not apply for Hegel's proper, speculative concept of truth. Hegel's account of the relation of truth here seems to represent a *different* relation to reality, one that positively excludes the question of truth. I say "seems" at first because we will have to see whether this is really the case; and this will require an examination of how Hegel's account of spirit is to be understood in its relation to truth or as truth.

I conceded earlier that every philosopher obviously is at liberty to define a word differently from the way it is ordinarily understood. But this is only legitimate if he provides an account of how the new meaning is to be distinguished from the usual one. Both Hegel and Heidegger neglected to do this, and the difficulty that was just indicated in both cases could only arise on this basis. The concession that anyone can define a word in the way he prefers obviously stands under the further restriction that he is only entitled to do so if he gives the word a clear, identifiable meaning. The mere fact that a definition is put forward—such as the claim that truth consists in the identity of the subject with reality—means nothing in itself as long as we cannot associate a clear meaning with the defining expression. And the matter becomes even more difficult when a philosopher not only cannot give a word a clear meaning (as happened to me in the case of the word *consciousness*) but also provides a definition in which words are connected in logically absurd ways. The question of whether the word *truth* has a clear meaning or any meaning at all as defined by Hegel is obviously equivalent to the question of whether the phenomenon or structure exists that Hegel intends by this word. And, of course, in this particular case the meaning of Hegel's method and system simultaneously stands and falls with this question.

I can only make the assessment that now follows with the qualification that was previously indicated (p. 274); nonetheless, it must be made, since otherwise we would not be able to proceed further. The structure that Hegel wants to designate by means of the word *truth* does not exist; the unity of identity and nonidentity that is intended by Hegel is logically absurd. It violates the meaning of negation as well as that of identity. If Hegel had introduced these words in a new way that was independent of their ordinary meaning, this critique would be precipitous. But Hegel did not introduce them in a new way (and it is obviously questionable whether words that possess such fundamental significance can be employed in a new way at all). He relies on our preunderstanding of these words, but he then employs them in misleading ways.

But even if the *structure* that Hegel intends to describe cannot exist, it still does not follow that there is not a *phenomenon* that corresponds to what Hegel has in mind. It would then simply have to be described in a structurally different way. I can elucidate what I mean as follows.

Hegel begins the section "Spirit" in the *Phenomenology* with the sentence "Reason is spirit when its certainty . . . is conscious of itself as its own world, and of the world as itself" (263). The structure of truth in Hegel's speculative sense is already attained with this step. Now it is logically absurd in my view to say that the subject is identical with reality, or that certainty is identical with its world. One can reply that it is only logically absurd if one understands the word *identical* in its strict sense. But Hegel intended the word in its strict sense. Still, it might be argued that what Hegel means by the sentence just cited is that the individual finds himself in an affirmative relation to his social-normative world, and only attains a relation to himself in this affirmative relation to his social world. Now this one can understand; however, the word *identity* is no longer contained in the explanation just offered. But one might also express the same point in this way: The individual only attains his own identity in identifying himself with his social-normative world. On this interpretation we would suddenly be very close to Mead's position. In the last sentence the word *identity* has been used again, but it is now employed in its social-psychological sense; and we have seen that this usage does not involve numerical identity, and is certainly not Hegel's mode of use. If the phenomenon that Hegel really had in mind when he talked about the identity of identity and nonidentity lies roughly in this direction, then Hegel's *Logic* would be nothing but a grandiose self-misunderstanding. There is no structure corresponding to what Hegel describes by means of the word *truth*, but this does not mean there is not a phenomenon that he had in view. Nevertheless, the latter can only be inferred from the concrete accounts of self-consciousness and spirit, and this also demands that one detach these accounts from their speculative formulation. The crucial idea here is that the individual only really relates himself to himself insofar as he is aware of himself in an affirmative relation to his community. When the phenomenon that Hegel intended has been disentangled from the speculative conceptual framework, we will be in a position to see whether it represents a productive contribution to the problem of a rational and self-determined relation of oneself to oneself and to others.

Lecture 14

Concluding with Hegel, II

In the discussion after the last lecture someone objected that in my exposition of the concepts of knowledge and truth in the introduction to the *Phenomenology* I focused exclusively on their initial characterization in the tenth paragraph and did not consider their more complex elaboration in paragraphs 12–15 (PhG 53–57). In fact, the additional remarks in the concluding paragraphs of the introduction are fundamental for understanding the method of the *Phenomenology*, and they make it necessary to qualify two of the claims that I made last time. First, the ordinary concept of truth does play a role here, at least for the method of the *Phenomenology*; second, this implies that the method of the *Phenomenology* cannot be as readily subsumed under the method of the *Logic* as I suggested. Nonetheless, I do not regret having represented things so one-sidedly at first, because the ordinary ('genuine') concept of truth remains subordinated to the speculative ('spurious') conception despite the fact that it comes into play here. And the same thing holds for the special character of the method of the *Phenomenology* in comparison to that of the *Logic*.

The problem that I overlooked in the last lecture is the fundamental problem of the *Phenomenology*—namely, that Hegel has consciousness undergo an 'experience' at every stage. I denied and continue to deny that this experience relates to a concept of truth in the sense of our ordinary understanding of truth. Rather, it involves the conception that consciousness forms in each case of the relation that exists between it and the object (reality). But this means that it involves its incomplete realization of that structure which in its complete realization corresponds to Hegel's speculative concept of truth. Or, to put it another way, this conception concerns the relation of knowledge and truth as these concepts are used in the tenth paragraph of the introduction.

Now we have already seen in connection with the abstract (or, if you wish, pure) dialectic of the *Logic* that at every level of conceptual development the moment pertaining to the next level is implicitly present; in this respect, every level in a certain sense already is (implicitly) more than it is (explicitly). On the level of the pure, conceptual dialectic this state of affairs leads to specious modes of expression such as the formulation that a concept already is something 'in itself' that is not yet 'posited' in it. But as soon as the dialectic of the concept takes place in the medium of *consciousness*, this state of affairs acquires quite a natural meaning that does not require such specious modes of expression. This is a consequence of the fact that in the case of a form of consciousness it is meaningful to say not only (1) that consciousness *is* characterized by a specific relation to its object but also (2) that consciousness *has* a specific *conception of* this relation of itself (of knowledge) to its object (to truth). Such a conception can be inadequate; in this case, this relation would not be comprehended as it really is, as it is in truth (and here *truth* has its ordinary meaning). Thus, it is now also meaningful to say that consciousness can have the *experience* that the conception it has formed of this relation is incorrect or even contradictory.

The abstract determinations that Hegel provides in the introduction do not clarify how such an 'experience' must be envisioned. Rather, this can only be inferred from the way that this experience is described in each case in the actual development of the *Phenomenology*. It should first be clear that the objective reason why consciousness at any given point has an incorrect or insufficient conception of itself (and from now on this means conception of itself and the object, and especially of the relation between the two) is that it always involves an incomplete realization of truth in the speculative sense. And this means that it always contains in itself implicit moments that are still not 'for it,' and these moments therefore are not yet explicit in the conception that it has of itself. In contrast to the case of a concept, it is entirely meaningful to say that the conception that we have of our relationship to the world contains implicit moments that are not explicit in it.

The experience in which it becomes apparent to consciousness that the conception it has of itself is incorrect—one-sided or contradictory—might be construed as a philosophical reflection upon the concepts that are contained in this conception. The experience of the incorrect, one-sided, and contradictory character of the conception would on this interpretation be somewhat comparable to the experience that Socrates' interlocutors have in a Platonic dialogue.[1] Hegel himself indicates that the conception of such a *possibility* is not out of place here, since at the beginning of every form of consciousness he outlines its concept from a philosophical standpoint before unfolding its 'experience.' In so doing he always discloses the one-sided and contradictory character of its conception in an anticipatory way.

Hegel does not mean, however, that the experience that consciousness has of itself—of its conception—is such an explicit process of philosophical clarification. Rather, it is important to note here that every form of consciousness, as a relation of consciousness to itself and to the world, consists in a concrete form of practice (*praxis*). This may be a cognitive practice—as in section A—or it may be a life practice in the narrower sense in those cases (such as self-consciousness) that involve a practical relation of oneself to oneself and to the world. Such a practice is always guided by the conception that consciousness has of itself and of reality. Hegel's thesis is that consciousness has the experience *in* this practice that the conception that it has developed of itself and of reality is inadequate. When consciousness seeks to realize its theoretical or practical conception concretely in the respective practice, the nonexplicit moments of the conception become apparent. Through this process consciousness experiences the untruth of its original conception, and here the word *untruth* has its ordinary meaning.

Now that I have clarified matters this far I can attempt to put the issue back into the terminology of the (quite inadequate) description that Hegel provides in the concluding paragraphs of the introduction. I have intentionally used a word up to now that Hegel himself does not employ—the word *conception*. Consciousness has the experience that the conception it has of itself and its object—and this means (according to the tenth paragraph) its conception of what knowledge and truth are for it—is incorrect. This can now be readily formulated in the words that Hegel uses in the twelfth paragraph: Consciousness has the experience that its concept does not correspond to the object (PhG 53). And I have no objection to this formulation. Then why haven't I expressed this directly in Hegel's words? It is because Hegel assumes at this point that by means of the expressions *concept* and *object* he is merely taking up the expressions *knowledge* and *truth* as he introduced them in the tenth paragraph. He writes, "If we designate *knowledge* as the *concept* . . . but the *truth* as what exists or the *object*, then the examination consists in seeing whether the concept corresponds to the object" (53). In view of the way knowledge and truth were introduced in the tenth paragraph, however, it is completely unintelligible how either one could be examined in light of the other; for, as Hegel himself notes in the thirteenth paragraph, "the knowledge that was present was essentially a knowledge of the object" (54). Hegel considers this objection in paragraph thirteen himself, but it seems to me that he answers it in a completely implausible way.

Nonetheless, the crucial objection lies elsewhere. It does not emerge from an immanent interpretation of the introduction, but from a consideration of what actually happens in the *Phenomenology*. If one wanted to understand *concept* and *object* (as Hegel implies) in the sense of knowledge and truth as characterized in the tenth paragraph—and this would mean in the sense of subject and object—this would imply that the subject would always somehow be assessed in light of the object. This difficulty cannot be resolved by Hegel's remark—which is itself introduced without supporting argument—that the experience of consciousness discloses that "what it previously took to be the in-itself" proves to be "only an in-itself for it" (54), and that this "being-for-consciousness of the first in-itself" is the object at the next stage (55ff.). If the expressions *in-itself* and *for it* are understood in the sense of the tenth paragraph, this remark applies at best to the transition from the stage of consciousness to that of self-consciousness, and is in no sense suitable for all of the transitions.

But it is precisely in the transition to self-consciousness that we find a different account in the text itself of how the talk of the examination of the concept in relation to the object is to be understood; in my view, this also represents the only adequate formulation. Hegel writes here, "The concept of the object is superseded in the actual object, or the *first, immediate conception (Vorstellung)* is superseded *in the experience*" (104, my emphasis). This explanation corresponds exactly to the description that I provided earlier: The concept stands for the 'first conception' that consciousness develops, what I termed the 'conception' that it forms; and the 'actual object' by which it is superseded is not the object, but the experience that consciousness has with this conception.

At this point at which Hegel concludes the section "Consciousness," it suffices to designate the concept as a concept of the object since what is essential for consciousness is still exclusively the object. Even so, the more complex formulation that I employed earlier is absolutely necessary for a characterization that applies to all stages (and especially to those of self-consciousness that concern us). The following principle thereby emerges and can be fully expressed in Hegel's terminology: The concept that consciousness develops of itself (certainty) and its object (the in-itself) is superseded by the "actual object," by the experience that consciousness undergoes concerning itself and its object. This formulation irreducibly contains four concepts. First, we have the tension between concept (first conception) and actual object (experience); second, each member of this conceptual pair is related to the concepts of certainty (subject) and reality (object), or to their interconnection. A reduction of one conceptual pair to the other is out of the question; thus, Hegel's attempt in the introduction to develop the entire problem on the basis of the two concepts, knowledge and object, had to fail.

It should now also be clear that the objection raised against me— namely, that I should have interpreted the concepts of knowledge and truth in the tenth paragraph in light of the following paragraphs—is not sound. The opposite is the case: What is meant in the following paragraphs can only be understood if the concepts of knowledge and truth are grasped in the way they were introduced in the tenth paragraph; and this is clearly indicated by the formulation just presented with the two pairs of concepts. Moreover, this is true for the entire work: Wherever the conceptual pair of certainty and truth is used, it retains the meaning of subject and object that was intended in the tenth paragraph (cf., for example, 104, 139, 211, 263, 485). The unity of subject and object in their independence (which implies the more or less complete realization of the speculative truth) consistently defines the topic in relation to which consciousness has its experience. This topic establishes the scenery in which every form of consciousness finds itself and the conception that it has of itself; for in each case this conception is essentially the conception that consciousness has of itself *in* its relation to reality. Now since each form of consciousness has an experience with its conception in which the latter proves to be incorrect, a movement develops on the basis of this scenery marked by the speculative conception of truth; and this movement is governed by the ordinary (genuine) concept of truth. The fact that what I have called the conception obviously can also be termed belief (and certainly not knowledge, as Hegel says in the concluding paragraphs of the introduction) indicates that truth in the ordinary sense is involved here. But as far as I know, Hegel himself never characterizes what I have called the conception as a form of belief.

At the risk of complicating matters still further, I must add that even in the pure dialectic of the *Logic* an *aspect* of the genuine concept of truth plays a role within the context of the scenery that is marked by the speculative (spurious) concept of truth. This aspect is the one according to which we can call a one-sided view of something untrue; and this aspect of the genuine concept of truth is also repeatedly deployed by Hegel when he claims that a higher stage represents 'the truth' of the preceding one, for example, "the truth of being is essence" (*Logic* 389). This legitimate mode of speaking, however, is always parasitic on the speculative mode here, just as in the *Phenomenology*; for the stage that is less one-sided is obviously the one that fulfills the speculative structure of truth more comprehensively. Nonetheless, if one wants to understand the confusing diversity in Hegel's use of the word *truth*, this use must be acknowledged as a distinctive one, since even on grammatical grounds it cannot be reduced to the speculative use. But in contrast to the use in the *Phenomenology*, this mode of use (which is typical for the *Logic* and can obviously be found in all the works) can only be seen to contain an *aspect* of the genuine concept of truth. For one can only really insist that a form of one-sidedness is untrue if it *claims* to comprehend the issue at hand in its entirety; thus, it must be a form of one-sidedness that is characteristic of consciousness or, more precisely, of belief.

Thus, in analyzing the role of the ordinary concept of truth in Hegel, we are confronted by a complicated state of affairs. Hegel has recourse to the ordinary use of the word *truth* in at least two systematic connections, but this must be qualified in several respects. First, this reference to truth is not relevant for the inner structure of any given form of consciousness. The 'experience' that the respective form of consciousness has is something that happens to it; that is, it does not raise a question of truth itself. And for this reason I still maintain that the phenomenon of posing the question of truth does not appear in Hegel's work. The reference to truth does not impress itself, so to speak, upon Hegel's image of man. Second, the partially genuine concept of truth of the *Logic* remains parasitic within Hegel's system upon his speculative concept of truth; and the real reference to truth that appears in the *Phenomenology* remains parasitic on the partially genuine concept of truth of the *Logic*. Third, Hegel merely returns *de facto* to the ordinary mode of use of the word *truth*, and never examines the structural presuppositions of this usage. In my view this is not an accident but is connected with Hegel's systematic approach. Thus, the more fundamental reason for Hegel's *immanent* conceptual carelessness in the introduction (which is generally not typical for him) is also to be sought here.

I can now return to the contention that I advanced at the outset of this lecture—namely, that the dialectic of the *Phenomenology* cannot simply be subsumed under the dialectic of the *Logic* because the genuine concept of truth partially enters into the former. I noted earlier with regard to the method of the *Logic* that I could not see how a movement could really be ascribed to it; the talk of a movement merely seems to be a metaphor for a series that is ordered according to a definite point of view. But as soon as this series appears in the medium of consciousness or, more precisely, in the context of an experience in which the conception that consciousness has of itself and its world changes, a real (and not merely metaphorical) movement is involved; and this consists in a change of consciousness. Thus, the important idea emerges of a transformation of consciousness that is motivated by internal consequences. To be sure, these internal consequences are restricted by Hegel to the conceptual connections that are predesignated in the *Logic*. Moreover, the extent to which a real movement—a movement of consciousness—can be ascribed to the dialectic of the *Phenomenology* is severely limited by Hegel's insistence that an experience of consciousness can only be assumed to take place within each form of consciousness; the transition to the next form is "our contribution" (PhG 55), that is, a speculative addition. In this respect, the succession of forms is only a 'movement' in fundamentally the same sense as the succession of concepts in the *Logic*.

Why did Hegel restrict the range of 'experience' so drastically? I can see two reasons. First, it would have been absurd in the case of the major transitions of the *Phenomenology* to speak of a corresponding experience and change of consciousness; these transformations involve different dimensions of consciousness, for example, the transition from consciousness to self-consciousness, and these transitions are artificial enough anyway. Second, Hegel wanted to regard the respective experience as restricted to its negative side: Consciousness merely experiences the contradictory character of its prevailing conception at each stage. We have seen that this experience takes place through consciousness' discovery of previously unnoticed aspects of this conception. According to Hegel, however, consciousness wants to adhere to its "first, original conception," and therefore it is merely caught in a contradiction. It is only "our contribution" to integrate those aspects into the conception that have negative consequences from the viewpoint of consciousness, and to bring the latter to a new, truer conception. This is the reason that Hegel himself specifies for why experience cannot extend beyond the limits of a particular form (PhG 56), but his justification for this claim is not readily apparent. Someone who regards a pure conceptual dialectic skeptically might say the thesis that one conception leads to another through its internal consequences can only be demonstrated by establishing that consciousness has this experience, that is, that it can itself recognize the latter conception as the truer one. But in this case the word *true* would have its ordinary meaning. Since Hegel must reject such an assertion of independence for the ordinary concept of truth as opposed to the speculative one, he may be compelled on this basis to concede only the negative side of the movement to natural consciousness.

In the chapter on self-consciousness to which I now turn we find examples of both types of dialectic. On the one hand, there is an artificially constructed dialectic in the introduction to this chapter in which the concept of self-consciousness is unfolded; and to those who are not committed to dialectic this can easily appear as mere jingle jangle. On the other hand, there are accounts in sections A and B of how a relation of oneself to oneself that starts from a specific conception of oneself changes by virtue of its internal consequences. The absurd way in which Hegel descriptively characterizes the phenomenon of self-consciousness in the introductory section reveals how entrapped he is from the outset by the subject-object model; and for an unbiased interpretation this appears as an additional impediment to the dialectical method. Nevertheless, we cannot simply disregard this section because (1) it constitutes the systematic point of departure, and (2) it is not possible to separate what Hegel was really concerned with from the unfortunate form in which he expressed it. Indeed, one of Hegel's central theses was that form and content constitute a unity. Nevertheless, as soon as we arrive at the more substantive content, I will attempt to indicate how it might be separated from the subject-object structure. For only in this way can the confrontation with the conception that emerged in connection with Heidegger and Mead become meaningful.

At the end of the preceding section, "Consciousness," Hegel arrived at a structure of the object of consciousness that he describes in the following way: "It is a self-identity that is also difference in itself. . . . This self-identical essence is therefore related only to itself; *to itself* here implies the relationship to an other, and the *relation-to-self* is rather a *self-sundering*; or, in other words, that very self-identicalness is an inner difference" (99ff.). A structure is thereby attained that first appears under the title "Life," but is really—in its 'truth' (102)—the structure of self-consciousness. I am not going to examine the question of the supposed genesis of this structure in the dialectic of consciousness, or the question of its provisional realization in the concept of life, since this would only lead us astray. Self-consciousness represents the most illustrative example for Hegel of this structure; and anyone who might question the meaning of this fantastic structure in its restricted application to life can immediately convince himself of its reality by attending to self-consciousness. "It is for itself, it is a distinguishing of what contains no difference, or self-consciousness." Please consider the remarkable assertion: When that which contains no difference is distinguished (assuming that this is conceivable), this *means* that it is "for itself," and *this means* self-consciousness. Hegel continues: "I distinguish myself from myself, and in doing so I am immediately aware that what is distinguished from myself is not different (from me). I, the identically named being (*Gleichnamige*), repel myself from myself; but what is posited as distinct from me, or as unlike me, is immediately not a distinction for me in being so distinguished" (102). Here we have a superb example of the dynamized concept of difference: The fact that I distinguish myself from myself means "I repel myself from myself." Hegel designates the I as the identically named being in an allusion to Fichte's "I = I."

Thus, Hegel accepts Fichte's concept of self-consciousness as a matter of course. This is only the first step for Hegel, but it is in his view a necessary first step. Of course, all of the objections that I marshaled earlier against Henrich's formulation of the problem also apply to this position, and it is unnecessary to repeat them here.

This first step contains the first realization of the identity of certainty and truth for Hegel, although it is still abstract. At the beginning of the chapter he writes: "But now there has arisen what did not emerge in these previous relationships, viz. a certainty which is identical with its truth; for the certainty is its own object to itself, and consciousness is to itself the truth" (104). My interpretation of the tenth paragraph of the introduction is thereby confirmed retrospectively. Hegel explicitly uses the words *certainty* and *consciousness* equivalently. And agreement with the objective side is not the identity of what is meant with what is actually the case, as the ordinary concept of truth would imply; rather, it is the identity of subject and object: "Consciousness is to itself the truth."

But this identity is still abstract: "Since what it distinguishes from itself is only itself as itself, the difference as an otherness is *immediately superseded* for it; the difference *is* not, and *it* is only the motionless tautology of: 'I am I'" (105). By "the difference *is* not" Hegel means a real identity would only be attained when difference has its own being or independence and is still superseded, although not in an immediate way.

Now the real form of identity is not supposed to be simply contraposed to the abstract one as a desideratum. Rather, dialectical method requires that abstract identity already contains the mome.it in itself that ultimately must lead to real identity. This is effected in the following way: All self-consciousness is in fact consciousness of other objects. Hegel sees in this an "opposition" or, as he characterizes it at a corresponding point in the *Encyclopedia*, a "contradiction": "Abstract self-consciousness is . . . the contradiction of itself as self-consciousness and as consciousness" (*Enc.* 425). The alleged existence of an opposition or contradiction here is not justified. It is again simply taken over from Fichte.

Thus, this second step in the dialectic of self-consciousness is as artificial and (if one takes it literally) as absurd as the first. But it gives Hegel the possibility of establishing a connection between the self-relation in self-consciousness and its relation to the objective world. We must grant Hegel the chance to extricate himself from the absurdities of his initial approach by introducing further absurdities; we thereby proceed roughly according to this formula: Absurdity multiplied by absurdity yields meaning. If someone begins with false premises and through a false inference draws a correct conclusion that he has really attained on the basis of descriptive insight, we would merely deprive ourselves of what we could learn from him by restricting our interest to analyzing his faulty logic. It is better simply to point out that the person is persistently inclined to present his ideas in a quasi-deductive manner. It would be even more absurd to insist that the procedure is reasonable because the results are interesting.

"Consciousness, as self-consciousness, henceforth has a double object: one is the immediate object, that of sense-certainty and perception . . . and the second, viz. *itself*, which . . . is present in the first instance only as opposed to the first object. In this sphere, self-consciousness exhibits itself as the movement in which this antithesis is superseded, and the identity of itself with itself becomes explicit for it" (105). This last sentence has far-reaching significance, since it defines not only the further development within the chapter "Self-Consciousness" but also the development of self-consciousness toward spirit and the further development of the *Phenomenology* as a whole. It contains the entire remaining program: The point is that self-consciousness must integrate the independent difference of the reality that opposes it into its original identity with itself; that is, it must realize the truth as Idea.

In order to understand how this movement is initiated, it must be noted that in Hegel's view the two sides of the opposition do not carry equal weight. For the truth of self-consciousness is it itself, and this is precisely because it is the identity of certainty and objectivity; it is itself now the in-itself, the independent moment (105ff.). When it still did not know itself as self-consciousness, the object was the in-itself for it, and the latter also always meant the independent and essential moment; it itself was the unessential moment for itself (cf. 59ff., 70). Since self-consciousness is now itself the essential moment for itself, the object is the unessential moment for it, a mere "appearance" (105), a "nullity" (109).

Even if we assume that this makes sense, it is still not clear for us as ordinary people how a movement is to begin on this basis. But it is clear for Hegel because self-consciousness cannot be satisfied in merely knowing that it is the essential moment. Rather, this certainty must become truth for it (109); but this implies that it must be reflected, so to speak, by the *object*—"in an objective manner" (ibid.). Now please don't be so dull as to say, indeed, the object *appears* as more unessential. For this will not suffice; rather, self-consciousness must demonstrate the object's lack of independence by *practically negating* it, or by "destroying" it (109).

Let us pause here and leave the question of the internal derivation of this dialectic out of account. We must first attend to what Hegel has actually accomplished in this first part of his dialectic of self-consciousness. He has accomplished the transition from theoretical self-consciousness to the practical relation of oneself to oneself. Even the talk of the 'essential moment' is ambiguous in this context. As initially introduced by Hegel, it has a purely theoretical meaning. But at the same time by its use Hegel wants to address that aspect of the relation of oneself to oneself which we express when we say "I am important to myself, I am concerned about myself." And since we always say this within a world in which others also may be important to us or represent the objects of our concern, this aspect can be immediately drawn into a sharp contrast by having the prospective agent say "I am concerned only about myself, only I am important to myself, and everyone else seems inessential to me, of no importance." If the point that Hegel has just reached is formulated in this way, it first becomes clear that we are dealing with a real possibility of the relationship of oneself to oneself. Second, the structure that is designated in this formulation ("I am concerned about myself") is no longer bound to the subject-object model. Third, a *conception* is expressed in the sentence "I am only concerned about myself," a conception that the relation of oneself to oneself forms regarding what it wants for itself in the world. It may be expected that an experience can emerge here that will compel the relation of oneself to oneself to change its conception as a result of its internal consequences. Thus a dialectic can be unfolded here in the unproblematic sense that was distinguished earlier.

To be sure, Hegel's claim to generate this practical, volitional relation of oneself to oneself out of theoretical self-consciousness is unfounded. But I find this less deplorable than the related fact that Hegel neglected to investigate the descriptive structure of (1) the volitional self-relation in general and (2) the volitional relation of oneself to oneself in particular. Instead of examining the descriptive structure of action, Hegel reduces the volitional as well as the theoretical modes of behavior to the subject-object model (as Fichte had already done before). The subject behaves theoretically when it allows itself to be determined by the object, and practically when in a reverse sense it determines the object. The propositional character of all volitional behavior is overlooked in this schema, irrespective of its different versions; and it continues to remain a mystery how a subject can relate itself volitionally to *itself*. I already pointed out earlier that the subject-object model had to obscure the structure that Aristotle had elaborated—namely, the structure that makes a volitional relation to one's own being possible; for there is no place for that structure in this model. And it is no accident that it was Heidegger who rediscovered the structure disclosed by Aristotle; for he broke away from the orientation toward the subject-object model but, in contrast to analytic philosophy, did not abandon the question raised by German Idealism concerning the relation of oneself to oneself.

Let us return to Hegel's train of argument. We have already seen that it has been characteristic of the entire tradition since Aristotle to distinguish between sensuous and rational (deliberative) volitional behavior. Only the latter, the 'higher faculty of desire,' was designated as the will, and its distinguishing feature is that it is free; on the other hand, sensuous appetite was designated as desire. This is important to keep in mind in order to understand why Hegel entitles the first stage of the practical relation of oneself to oneself "desire" (*Begierde*). The traditional distinguishing criteria between sensibility and understanding that are also accepted by Hegel involve the view that sensuously governed behavior is (a) passive and not active, (b) related to the particular without reference to something universal, and therefore (c) unstable. These characteristics were already definitive for Hegel's description of the first stage of theoretical consciousness—"sense certainty"—and they are equally definitive for the first, sensuous stage of volitional consciousness. The first criterion that I specified—passive and not active—certainly does not seem to fit well with Hegel's characterization of desire as "satisfaction" through the "destruction" of the object. Nevertheless, it is part of the general meaning of volitional behavior as such that it must be active; and this is especially true *insofar* as it is conceived within the subject-object model as a determining of the object. For Hegel, the contrast to the negation of the object in desire is the negation in work that molds the object, which appears later on; the mere destruction and appropriation of things in desire is passive in contrast to the active behavior toward things in molding them.

We should not make too much out of this first stage of the practical relation of oneself to oneself, and we certainly cannot associate it with a dialectic of 'aesthetic existence' in the sense of Kierkegaard's *Either-Or*; for Hegel, this would belong at a higher stage in the development of Spirit (cf. PhG 217ff.). It remains particularly unclear what the relation to *oneself* is in desire: Hegel talks about a "feeling of self" (PhG 118ff., *Enc.* 429); and in this case this lack of clarity seems to be intended by Hegel himself. Since for Hegel the character of universality and freedom pertains essentially to self-consciousness, he does not seem to want to consider desire as a form of self-consciousness at all, although he allows it to have an "experience" (109). This is confirmed by the fact that he only deals with it in the introduction to the chapter, and designates it at the end of this introduction as the second of the three "moments" in the "concept of self-consciousness" (110ff.). The first moment is the "pure, undifferentiated I," that is, "certainty," which only turns into truth in desire; but the third moment, which is again "the truth of the latter" (namely, of desire), is "the doubling of self-consciousness" (110). This is supposed to mean that the object of self-consciousness is not just any object, but is another self-consciousness. Thus it is claimed to be part of the *concept* of self-consciousness that the object confronting it is another self-consciousness; in other words, self-consciousness is essentially intersubjective. It thus appears that Hegel did not really intend desire as a form of self-consciousness, but needed it for two steps of the preliminary construction of the full concept of self-consciousness. It is used first as *terminus ad quem* of the overcoming of theoretical self-consciousness in a practical relation of oneself to oneself; second, it functions as *terminus a quo* of the conception of the practical relation of oneself to oneself as a relation of oneself to another self-consciousness.

How does this dialectic that drives desire beyond itself work? I will limit myself here to the crucial point at which the experience of desire, which Hegel outlines on page 110, culminates. We have just seen that self-consciousness destroys the object in order to let its certainty of being the essential moment acquire "an objective form" for it, that is, turn into truth; in this way this certainty is reflected back to it by the object. But this is implicitly a contradictory 'conception.' For if self-consciousness destroys the object, it can no longer confirm the certainty of its own essentiality through its relation to the latter. The fundamental idea that informs the entire dialectic of the following section A is thereby already formulated. Self-consciousness wants to know itself as the essential moment, but it can only achieve this to the extent that this is confirmed for it by the object confronting it; the object confronting it must confirm (1) its (self-consciousness') essentiality, and (2) its own (the object's) lack of essentiality. But this is an implicitly contradictory objective; for if self-consciousness regards its opposing object as inessential, the confirmation that this object is capable of providing for it also becomes inessential. Thus it will gradually have the experience that it must change its conception; in particular, it comes to see that it can only experience itself as essential in relation to the object confronting it to the extent that it itself recognizes the latter as essential.

The first step in this direction consists in the fact that self-consciousness cannot be satisfied when *it itself* confirms its essentiality *in relation* to its opposing object; rather, the latter must itself confirm its essentiality for it. This presupposes, however, that the opposing object is as independent as self-consciousness itself, and this implies that it also must be a self-consciousness: "Self-consciousness achieves its satisfaction only in another self-consciousness" (110). The certainty of being the essential moment can only now really turn into truth for it insofar as it is *recognized* by others. And the following is now clear here: Self-consciousness will have the experience that there is a dialectic in recognition that only reaches its goal when it recognizes the others in the same way it would like to be recognized by them. A situation is thereby attained that Hegel describes in this way: "They recognise themselves as mutually recognising one another" (112). With this structure, however, "we already have before us the concept of spirit" (110).

Let me pause again at this juncture, since we have now reached a point at which we can bring Hegel's concept of self-consciousness into connection with the conception of the relation of oneself to oneself that emerged through our analysis of Mead. At present the higher-level relation of oneself to oneself—that of 'responsibility' or of 'spirit'—is not yet the main issue; rather, the point of focus is the way that the relation of oneself to oneself is characterized in general. I indicated earlier that the positions of Mead and Hegel are comparable, since in both cases not only is self-consciousness understood as practical, but also the relation of oneself to oneself is conceived as intersubjectively constituted. But now we see that the connection is much closer in light of the fact that in Mead's case as well recognition occupies a central position. Since at this point we are not yet concerned with the higher possibility but with the general structure, it seems possible and more productive to examine the extent to which the two positions complement each other rather than confronting them with one another. What is missing in Hegel's account, and on the other hand what does it contribute positively? Both aspects—the positive and negative—are a result of the peculiarity of his approach.

We have to count both Hegel's proof and his descriptive elucidation of the alleged structure on the negative side of the ledger. If the desire to be recognized—that is, the need for 'self-consciousness' in the sense that this word has in ordinary language*—pertains essentially to the relation of oneself to oneself, it is because this is a phenomenological fact. And we can only regard the result of Hegel's supposed deduction as relevant and justified because we can detach it from the latter and place it back into the context of phenomenological facts. Our ability to do this rests upon the fact that Hegel has recourse to a word within ordinary language in dealing with the topic of recognition; and this distinguishes his treatment of recognition from that structure of self-consciousness from which he proceeded. He thereby has recourse to a phenomenon that also can be subsumed abstractly within his conceptual framework—mutual recognition of one another is a reciprocal subject-object relationship—but the precise descriptive meaning of this phenomenon can never be extracted from this conceptual framework. Rather, the desire to be recognized presupposes first the structure in which a person's self is at issue, that is, his being; second, an act of appreciation or a value statement (*Fürguthalten*) is contained in recognition. Thus, a multilevel propositional structure is involved. Hegel merely smuggled in the practical relation to oneself and the evaluative reference with the aid of his ambiguous claim that self-consciousness is itself the "essential moment." In this way he spared himself the trouble of examining the descriptive peculiarities and presuppositions of this structure.

In the preceding analysis we have only criticized the speculative concept of truth immanently, but now we can also evaluate it in light of the claim that there are phenomena that can only be understood

*That is, the sense of *Selbstbewusstsein* in German (Trans.).

with its assistance. Hegel regards reciprocal recognition as such a type of phenomenon: In it "the unity of itself in its otherness," the "I that is We and the We that is I," is supposed to emerge for self-consciousness (110). Hegel wants to say: Self-consciousness only becomes itself insofar as it recognizes the others as recognizing it. The phrase "it only becomes itself insofar as" sounds like saying that it only attains its identity insofar as. . . . But in the first place it is undoubtedly clear that the different subjects remain different; the talk of identity only obscures the positive descriptive sense of their behavior toward one another. Second, the expression "it only becomes itself insofar as"—which I admit is also used in ordinary language—is a misleading one. For its meaning is not that I fail to be identical with myself if this condition is not met. Rather, it means that I only attain what I want *for myself*, that my action and my being are only fulfilled, if I relate myself to others in such and such a way.

Although the structure that is alleged by Hegel does not actually capture the phenomenon to which it refers, he still succeeds in decisively elaborating the peculiar foundation of the relation of oneself to oneself in reciprocity. And he was able to accomplish this precisely because he had a structure in mind that was essentially characterized by a relation of reciprocity. Nevertheless, I believe that the connection here must also be seen the other way around. Two views which are partly phenomenological and partly normative in character represent the initial points of departure of Hegel's thought. These are (1) the conception of man as being fundamentally a member of a social world, and thereby only fulfilling his being in reciprocity, and (2) the dismay at man's actual alienation from the social world, and the idea of a return from alienation to harmony. Hegel only subsequently unified these points of focus within the paradoxical structure of the identity of identity and nonidentity, and this was a result of his participation in a misguided philosophical tradition. These points of departure form the distinctly unparadoxical nucleus of Hegel's paradoxical concept of truth.

In indicating Hegel's contribution to the elaboration of the reciprocal character of recognition (which remained implicit in Mead's case), I have already made the transition to the positive side of the ledger for Hegel. In my view, there are two additional points on this side that are particularly worthy of mention, and they appear in section A of the chapter "Self-Consciousness."

The first point consists in the fact that for Hegel recognition is related neither to any given set of accomplishments nor to character. Rather, it is related to the eminent accomplishment, so to speak, of proving oneself to be free. Hegel's concept of recognition thereby discloses an affinity with the Kantian concept of respect (*Achtung*).[2] Recognition in this sense is related to the person as person, to the person as a rational, free being. The treatment of freedom as an accomplishment might seem surprising. Isn't freedom simply a property? But we have seen that freedom is a gradual phenomenon. This has become evident in different aspects, although I have admittedly neglected to bring these aspects into a systematic connection. I will now merely recall the aspect that is relevant here: We have seen that one can raise the practical question regarding one's action in differing degrees of narrowness and comprehensiveness. It is posed most fundamentally if one questions how one lives; and the preparedness to raise the question of whether one wants to live at all also pertains to this. Hegel treats this problem in a similar way. Freedom in its first, "formal" sense consists for him in the ability to be able to 'abstract' from all determinations; and the latter includes one's own life (*Enc.* 382). For this reason Hegel's dialectic of recognition begins with the "life-and-death struggle" (PhG 114). On the one hand, self-consciousness wants to destroy its opponent in this struggle — and the continuity with desire is thereby still apparent. On the other hand, self-consciousness can only be recognized as free by its opponent in "staking its life."

But what compels Hegel to relate recognition to freedom so strictly? As we already saw earlier, this rests upon the fact that for Hegel the "reflection of the I in itself" as the abstraction from all determination constitutes the formal essence of freedom. In the *Encyclopedia*, Hegel begins the account of self-consciousness with the statement "The formula of self-consciousness is I = I; *abstract freedom* . . ." (424). The absence of a mention of freedom in the context of the introduction of "I = I" in the *Phenomenology* is connected with the peculiar intermediate status of desire. Desire is volitional behavior that is governed by sensibility. The concept of freedom applies only to the will. Hegel's treatment of freedom at the end of the introduction to the chapter on self-consciousness and in section A is for the most part implicit; this concept provides the guiding thread for his exposition only in section B. Nonetheless, there cannot be any doubt that Hegel's intention is to conceive intersubjectivity and freedom together by means of the full concept of self-consciousness. Thus, the fact that the object confronting self-consciousness is no longer to be conceived as a thing but as another self-consciousness is explained by Hegel in the following way: The object must itself "carry out this negation of itself in itself." "Since the object is in its own self negation, and in being so is at the same time independent, it is consciousness" (109–110); according to Hegel's definition, however, it is also precisely in this way that it is free. Of course, it is completely consistent that what one self-consciousness can recognize in the other can only be its freedom, since this is the only determination that it has up to this point; and in recognizing the other as free, it recognizes it as self-consciousness.

Hegel's view that freedom is based upon or even consists in the "I = I" is obviously an error, since this so-called reflection of the I upon or in itself does not exist. The astonishing degree of descriptive carelessness that Hegel shares with the rest of the tradition of German Idealism is again revealed here. The claim that freedom rests upon reflection only has a clear meaning if one understands *reflection* in the sense of deliberation—that is, deliberation about one's own action. Hegel saw a direct connection between freedom, abstraction, concept formation, and the I. Almost everything about this combination is false. German Idealism inherited the thesis from Kant that the I is, as it were, the original concept.[3] For Hegel, the "I is the pure concept itself," because it is "unity relating itself to itself." "Thus it is universality ... abstraction ... " (*Logic* 583). It is not only the connection of concept and I that is false; the traditional theory that concepts are based upon abstraction is also invalid. It is furthermore to be noted that although the phenomenon of abstracting general concepts from specific instances undoubtedly occurs, this is not the meaning that can be attributed to the need for speaking of a process of abstraction in connection with freedom. One can figuratively represent free, rational behavior in both a theoretical and a practical context as an attempt to step back and distance oneself from what is given. But this 'reflection' does not imply that a concept is abstracted from a datum, since what is given is always propositional; and abstracting from a datum by stepping back from it means precisely that it is put in question. This is done theoretically by considering whether things might be otherwise than is assumed, and practically by considering whether one should act differently from what is prescribed. Hegel correctly saw that this abstraction is a "negative attitude" (ibid.), and this actually should have referred him to sentences or propositional structures. Instead, he makes the mistake of relocating negation in an *entity*, the I, as the supposed difference in this identity; and it now appears as if it is this I that steps back from its determinations. It is part of Hegel's greatness that he continually breaks through to descriptive insights in spite of such structurally misguided assumptions. Thus he is completely correct in his conclusion that the freedom of an individual becomes apparent in his "ability to abstract from his very existence" (*Enc.* 382). But this is not based upon the "I = I," that is, the reflection of the I into itself, but rests upon the fact that the individual can adopt a position toward himself, toward his to-be. He thereby adopts a position toward the proposition that he will also exist in the future, and this is something that is actually capable of being negated in contrast to the alleged I.

In my view, the relationship of recognition to freedom is Hegel's second positive contribution in contrast with that which became clear about recognition for Mead. The first and truly central contribution is the emphasis upon reciprocity. The third contribution is a direct consequence of the first. It consists in the following insight: Since reciprocity pertains analytically to the desire for recognition, a dialectic is to be found in every case in which recognition is understood one-sidedly; in this dialectic, consciousness has the experience that its conception is contradictory and that it must change it if it wants to attain its goal. Here we are dealing with *dialectic* in its legitimate sense, which is not associated with the absurd speculative structure. While Mead merely distinguishes genetic stages of the relation of oneself to oneself in relating oneself to others, Hegel indicates that an analytically complex structure is involved; and from a motivational standpoint, it is clear that an individual first enters into this structure in a one-sided way (e.g., desiring recognition without wanting to recognize). Thus, it is to be expected analytically that either he will be frustrated in his conception of happiness or he will abandon the one-sidedness of his conception. Hegel considers two such one-sided constellations in section A, which since Marx has been the most famous and frequently in-terpreted part of the *Phenomenology*. To be sure, the "life-and-death struggle" and "lordship and bondage" are not merely examples of one-sided forms of recognition for Hegel, but necessary stages in the singular development of spirit. In the concluding section B of the chapter "Self-Consciousness," the dialectic of another complex structure in the relation of oneself to oneself (or in any case the beginning of this dialectic) is elaborated; this is a dialectic that no longer concerns the aspect of recognition but involves the aspect of freedom. For Hegel, the two moments of indeterminacy and of determinacy, of abstraction and concretion, already belong essentially to the formal concept of freedom; or, as I would express it, these are the two moments of calling into question and deciding. This structure again makes characteristic forms of one-sidedness possible. The one-sidedness may consist in the individual's neglect of the side of indeterminacy, so that he does not choose at all but simply allows himself to be determined (thereby relinquishing his freedom). Or it may consist in his belief that he can only maintain himself and his freedom by not making a decision; in Hegel's words, he does not venture out into the finitude of the concrete, but clings to the absolute infinity of his being-for-self (cf. *Philosophy of Right*, §13 Addition). Both of these forms of one-sidedness are also independent of Hegel's speculative structure, and we have already encountered them earlier in the interpretation of Heidegger and in the account of the concept of responsibility. But Hegel's essential contribution here lies in demonstrating that the conception implied in the second form of one-sidedness is contradictory and that it cannot even attain what it wants to attain. Someone who wants to protect his abstract freedom still has no choice but to exist concretely (PhG 125); thus, he can only attain what he desires if he gives up this form of one-sidedness.

The entire further development within the *Phenomenology* can be regarded in a certain sense as the further development of self-consciousness, that is, of the relation of oneself to oneself in relating oneself to other things and other persons. Hence, the further task would consist in disengaging the other phenomenologically valid dialectical structures of experience that Hegel distinguishes from the absurd structures of the speculative dialectic and making them fruitful for understanding the relevant phenomena. In my view this fruitfulness lies in making easier the question of which way of existing is better; for, in view of the difficulty of justifying value judgments, it represents an advance if it can be shown that certain conceptions of the good point to other conceptions as better on analytic grounds. To the extent that such an account succeeds, the hiatus between "is" and "ought" can be overcome and so-called ethical naturalism also acquires its own terrain in this way. Otherwise put: This hiatus can be overcome to the extent that consciousness must look not toward a more or less well-justified insight into what it ought to be, but merely has the occasionally painful experience that what it (and this means its conception of the good) is points beyond it. Hegel's view that the orientation toward an ought is on the whole superfluous and merely represents a one-sided attitude has one of its roots here, although it is admittedly only one. In examining this view and the account of forms of one-sidedness in the *Phenomenology*, it is now our task to identify the one-sidedness of Hegel's own position. I have thus arrived at the aim of this entire reflection: namely, the critique of the substantial nucleus of Hegel's conception of self-consciousness and spirit, and the fundamental confrontation of the latter with the conception that was developed in connection with Heidegger and Mead.

This confrontation should not focus upon the general structure of the relation of oneself to oneself, since we have already dealt with the crucial aspects of this question. Rather, the pivotal issue now is the higher-level possibility of the relation of oneself to oneself. I was able to characterize this for the conception that emerged in connection with Heidegger and Mead by means of the 'narrower concept of responsibility.' In Hegel we can only look for something comparable to this higher-level possibility in the transition from self-consciousness to spirit. In the *Phenomenology* a direct transition from the stage of self-consciousness to that of spirit is not to be found — although this transition is anticipated at the end of the introduction to the chapter "Self-Consciousness," as we just saw. On the other hand, such a transition does occur at the end of the dialectic of self-consciousness in the *Encyclopedia* under the title "Universal Self-Consciousness" (436).

Hegel writes here: "Universal self-consciousness is the affirmative knowledge of self in another self: each self as a free individuality has absolute independence, but . . . does not distinguish itself from the other. Each self is universal and objective. It has real universality as reciprocity in such a way that it recognises and knows itself in the free other; and it knows this insofar as it recognises the other and knows it to be free." This paragraph scarcely seems to reveal anything new beyond what was anticipated as the goal of the dialectic of recognition. The structurally peculiar formulations in which Hegel expresses his fundamental ideas should no longer trouble us; his claim, for example, that the self "does not distinguish" itself from the other self insofar as it recognizes the latter represents such a type of formulation. The key phrase *affirmative knowledge*, however, is important. For this talk of affirmation can be extended from the affirmative relationship of one individual to another in the sense of recognition to the affirmative relationship of each individual to the community that is composed of individuals as its parts. This is a transition that is very easy for Hegel to make, because he can apply his talk of identity in difference to both forms. If one wants to understand what is now meant in a structurally adequate way, this affirmation must be comprehended as an endorsement of the universal imperatives or norms that are contained in the "laws and institutions" of the community (PR 144). Hegel's desire to have the concept of affirmation understood in such a broad sense at this point in the *Encyclopedia* emerges clearly in the sentence that immediately follows. For here it is related to 'objective spirit,' the so-called spiritual substance: "This universal reflection of self-consciousness—the concept that knows itself in its objectivity as a subjectivity identical with itself and for that reason universal—is the form of consciousness of the *substance* of every essential form of spiritual life, of the family, fatherland and state."

We have found a structure that is quite similar to this in Mead. According to Mead, the individual only acquires a relation to himself by integrating the normative expectations of his community within himself through the adoption of roles. But for Mead this was only one aspect—namely, that of the "me." The other aspect—that of the "I"—concerned the freedom to be able to respond in such and such a way to the norms; and this included the possibility of being able to adopt a rational position against the existent norms in the name of a better society. Of course, this possibility is nothing other than the position of responsibility in the narrower sense.

How is this dealt with in Hegel? Doesn't he rule out this possibility by conceiving of the individual's relation to objective spirit as affirmative? In this case Hegel would not even reach what I called the higher-level relation of oneself to oneself in relating oneself to others. But in paragraph 436, which was just quoted, Hegel emphasizes not only the affirmative relation but also the freedom and "absolute independence" of the individual *in* this affirmative relation. *If* Hegel envisioned the speculative idea of truth that is realized in spirit—that is, the identity of the individual with the reality of objective spirit—in such a way that *in* this identity a space is left open or even demanded for the individual's own responsible adoption of a position, we will only be able to find this possibility in his concept of freedom. Thus we must seek the confrontation between the respective conceptions of the higher-level relation of oneself to oneself that are characteristic of the Heidegger–Mead and Hegelian positions in connection with the concept of freedom. The suitability of this approach is also evidenced by the fact that Hegel himself distinguishes two levels in the concept of freedom, as we noted earlier.

The most extensive discussion of the general concept of freedom is to be found in the introduction to the *Philosophy of Right* (PR), to which I have also previously alluded. A similar, briefer account of the general determinations occurs in the *Encyclopedia* in paragraphs 469–482. The entire PR itself, as well as the whole section on "objective Spirit" in the *Encyclopedia*, represents the further development of this concept, and in both cases the section "Ethical Life" (*Sittlichkeit*) is the most fundamental one.

The comparison of the two concepts of freedom is facilitated by the fact that the first level is characterized in a similar way by Hegel and by Mead or Heidegger—namely, as arbitrary choice (*Willkür*, PR 17). According to Hegel, this will is only formally free (14, 21), because it merely decides (12) and chooses (14) between contents that are given to it externally (or internally). "They are the impulses, desires, and inclinations through which the will finds itself determined in the course of nature" (11), without having a standard for the decision within itself (17). But this implies that it is actually dependent upon its contents (15), and therefore it is not truly, but only formally free.

The concept of responsibility in the broad sense corresponds to this formal concept of the will in Hegel. Someone has acted freely in this sense if one can say (a) he did it because he wanted to do it, and (b) he was accountable (i.e., capable of deliberating). The determining factor of his having acted in such a way was the simple fact that he wanted to do so.

If the formal concept of freedom in both instances is characterized by arbitrary choice, that is, by the absence of a standard, then the two conceptions of the higher level of freedom must be distinguished (if they are to be distinguished) on the basis of how they define the standard. Hegel says the formal will is still dependent. He thereby accepts Kant's concept of heteronomy. Thus, the higher level of freedom is understood as autonomy; the standard is self-determination. The two conceptions are also not different in this respect. But now the question arises: What does self-determination mean?

For the conception that is implied by the concept of responsibility in the narrower sense we have seen that autonomy consists in a specific way of choosing that is not exhausted in the reflective self-relation, but is essentially determined by it. This means that it is governed by the question of truth in the threefold sense of the question concerning what is actual (with reference to one's own being and that of society), what is possible, and what is best. Thus, the standard consists centrally in this question of truth. Someone who acts in this way acts autonomously. He does not allow himself to be determined, but acts in accordance with the standards that result from his own adoption of a reflective position.

It is clear that Hegel's answer to the question of what is self-determination must lie elsewhere in light of the fact that the phenomenon of the question of truth does not even arise for him. His answer is developed in two steps. In the first step "the abstract concept" of the truly free will—of self-determination—is specified: It is "the free will that wills the free will" (PR 27). Thus, Hegel takes the concept of self-determination quite literally: The will that determines itself is not determined by arbitrary contents, but by its very self. If one can imagine anything by this, the following additional statement will also seem plausible: "Only in freedom of this kind is the will by itself without qualification, because it is related to nothing except itself and so is released from every tie of dependence on anything else" (23).

But what is to be envisioned concretely by a free will that only "wills the free will"? Hegel provides a first answer in paragraph 21: It "is self-determining universality." This formulation strongly recalls Kant. According to Kant, the will is autonomous if and only if it acts exclusively in accordance with a maxim that it at the same time can will to be a universal law. And for Hegel the Kantian conception of freedom—that of *Moralität*—is a conception of the free will that is also legitimate within its limits, although it is one-sided and in this respect untrue. First, it is untrue because in Hegel's view the Kantian principle represents a mere tautology, an "identity emptied of content"; this universality is allegedly an abstraction from which everything and nothing can be derived (PR 135). Second, it is untrue because the Kantian principle is a principle of how things *ought* to be. For Hegel, the ought is something essentially subjective that sets itself against reality, and it has no truth because it does not know itself as identical with reality (*Enc.* 60, 511ff.). The partial 'truth' of *Moralität* is that within it the will does not oppose itself in its mere particularity to reality; rather, it is already a form of the "universal will existing in and for itself" (507), since it claims to know what "the good in and for itself" is (ibid.). Nevertheless, the *latter* is *contraposed* to reality as something that *ought to be*, and this constitutes the peculiarly abysmal untruth of this conception. In the ought, reflection "puffs itself up" against actuality (38). In those cases in which subjectivity assumes this form it inevitably receives the qualification of "self-conceit" (*Eitelkeit*) from Hegel as a consequence of its claim "to know better" (e.g., *Enc.* 512, PR, p. 10).

Thus, this is not what Hegel means when he talks about "self-determining universality." The real meaning of this expression obviously derives from Hegel's speculative conceptual framework. Universality as such is abstract identity or subjectivity. If it determines itself instead of adopting foreign contents within itself (as the formal will does), this implies that it assimilates the difference of being-in-itself within itself. This structure only attains its truth insofar as the being-in-itself (which is now understood as spiritual) attains the independence of a spiritual substance, that is, of objective spirit; and the subjective will must know itself as identical with the objectivity confronting it that fulfills this characterization. Thus "the free will which wills the free will" is by itself and is not dependent upon anything other than itself, not because it is not related to anything else, but because it knows itself to be identical with that to which it is related. And for this reason it is "*true* or rather *truth* itself, because its self-determination consists in a correspondence between what it is in its existence (i.e., what it is as objective to itself) and its concept" (PR 23).

You can now see that for Hegel freedom in the true sense of self-determination is nothing other than the realization of the structure of the speculative concept of truth. Self-consciousness reaches its fulfillment or, in Hegel's words, its truth as freedom existing in and for itself; and this *is* truth existing in and for itself. We have only encountered this speculative concept of truth up to this point from its theoretical side. How is it to be understood when it is employed in a practical sense, that is, as freedom? We can find the answer to this in the chapters on "ethical life" in *The Philosophy of Right* and the *Encyclopedia*.

In the *Encyclopedia* we read the following description at the beginning of this chapter (514): "The free substance that knows itself, in which the absolute *ought* is no less an *is*, has actuality as the spirit of a people . . . but the person as a thinking intelligence knows the substance as its own essence. . . . Thus, the person performs his duty as *his own* and as something which *is*, without the reflection of choosing; and in this necessity he has himself and his actual freedom."

Let us briefly review the fundamental statements of this paragraph. The ought, says Hegel, is "no less an is": What ought to be is no longer set against objectivity by subjectivity, as occurs in *Moralität*. Rather, it has being in "the laws and institutions existing in and for themselves" of the prevailing communal life, as Hegel explains in *The Philosophy of Right* (144). These laws and institutions have "an absolute authority and power infinitely more firmly established than the being of nature" (146). As Hegel further elaborates in the parallel section of the *Encyclopedia*, these laws and institutions represent "duty" for the individual; indeed, they represent a form of duty that the individual performs "without the reflection of choosing," without freedom in the subjective sense of reflectively choosing. This subjective reflection is not necessary because, as Hegel notes in the PR (148), the duties are "binding on the will of the individual." "In an ethical community, it is easy to say what man must do, what are the duties he has to fulfill in order to be virtuous: he has simply to follow the well-known and explicit rules that are marked out in his relationships" (PR 150). In paragraph 515 of the *Encyclopedia* Hegel explains that "*trust*—the genuine ethical frame of mind"—takes the place of "reflective choice." "In this way the substantial ethical order has attained its right, and its right its validity. That is to say, the self-will of the individual has vanished together with his private conscience" (PR 152).

I noted earlier that perhaps Hegel's affirmative characterization of the relation of the individual to objective spirit in the transition from self-consciousness to spirit in the *Encyclopedia* requires a qualification, since the individuals are conceived as independent and free. This presumption, however, has proven to be misleading. The possibility of an independent and critical relation to the community or the state is not admitted by Hegel. Rather, we hear the following set of claims: The existing laws have an absolute authority; what the individual has to do is firmly established in a community; the private conscience of the individual must disappear; trust takes the place of reflection. This is what Hegel means by the overcoming of *Moralität* in ethical life.

But in what sense, then, can Hegel still talk about freedom at all here? The last sentence of the section of the *Encyclopedia* with which I began (514) contains the answer: "Actual freedom" is understood as "necessity." This is expressed even more explicitly in paragraph 484: "Freedom, shaped into the actuality of a world, receives the *form of necessity*; the substantial connection of the latter is the system of determinations of freedom, and the connection of the latter in appearance is *power*, the state of being acknowledged, i.e. their effective validity in consciousness." This reversal of freedom into something that is normally considered its opposite means that the individual is to feel free precisely by fulfilling the duties originating from the power of the existing order; this follows both from the context of the remarks in paragraph 484 and particularly from the claims in paragraph 514, which were just cited. With this reversal, a level of perversity is reached that even Hegel cannot surpass; it is a perversity that is certainly no longer merely conceptual but also moral, so that it is difficult to consider it only from its conceptual side. This perversion is made possible conceptually by Hegel's definition of authentic freedom—self-determination—as being by one's self (*Beisichselbstsein*), and by his elaboration of the latter in terms of his speculative concept of truth. This makes it possible for Hegel to say (in the same paragraph, 484) that insofar as the will relates itself affirmatively to the social world or to the community, it is "at home with itself in it and united with itself"; and he adds that "the concept is thereby perfected into the idea."

I can now compare the conception of the authentic relation of oneself to oneself that was developed in connection with Heidegger and Mead to the corresponding Hegelian conception. In both cases a relation of oneself to oneself in relating oneself to others and to the community is involved (if we leave Heidegger out of account for a moment). In both cases the relation of oneself to oneself in the mode of self-determination is defined by freedom and related to truth. But while freedom consists in being reflectively *directed* toward truth for the conception of self-determination as responsibility in the narrower sense, for Hegel freedom is "the truth itself" (PR 23).[4] Of course, this can only be the case because Hegel does not really mean truth at all in employing the term *truth*, but something completely different— namely, the unity of subject and reality. And we can now see what this means concretely: the affirmative relationship of individuals to their community. Hegel reached the conclusion that this is precisely the true meaning of freedom by recasting the meaning of the word *freedom* as well, although he did this in a different way from what he did in the case of the word *truth*. Whereas he defined the meaning of the word *truth* from the outset differently from the way it is ordinarily understood, he initially grasped the word *freedom* roughly as it is ordinarily understood. But he subsequently introduced a change in its meaning; and the consequence of this change was that the word stands for exactly the opposite meaning. The result of both the perversion of the meaning of truth and the inversion of the meaning of freedom is that it no longer appears necessary to raise the question of truth and to demand freedom. For as long as we remain within the bounds of Hegel's terminology, we cannot have any idea of what it might mean to raise the question of truth. And a demand for freedom can no longer arise, for two reasons: (1) every demand would represent a regression back to the self-conceit of subjectivity, and (2) since un-freedom is designated as freedom, freedom already seems to be con-summately realized in the state of unfreedom, and there is therefore nothing more to be demanded.

Thus I arrive at the following conclusion. It is no accident that Hegel uses the same expressions that are employed by the conception of responsibility—that is, the expressions *freedom* and *truth*—for a different type of conception of the relation of oneself to oneself. In reversing the meaning of these words, he advances not only a *different* conception but one that is precisely the *opposite*. The real meaning of his conception consists in superseding the idea of responsibility; and exactly for this reason he cannot do it openly, but must use the same words. This makes Hegel's conception as relevant from a contemporary standpoint as the conception of responsibility itself. Hegel's philosophy is con-sciously and explicitly the philosophy of the justification of the existing order (cf. PR, pp. 4–6, 10–12), quite irrespective of how this existing order may be constituted. It is also for this reason that Hegel's political philosophy is appealed to by those contemporary German philosophers who still pursue the same intention. The justification of the existing order, however, is the precise opposite of the practical question of truth.

This outcome of my interpretation must seem so fatal that I would like briefly to consider some objections. First, I might be criticized for interpreting Hegel's conception of ethical life in too sinister a fashion. Second, the following question arises: To what extent does this view necessarily follow from Hegel's fundamental conception? In this context, a distinction must be made between his original intuition of a restoration of harmony and his structural presuppositions, that is, the subject-object model and the speculative dialectic that emerges from that model.

First, have I interpreted Hegel's conception of ethical life in a way that is too sinister? In my view, the texts that were cited speak for themselves. But I might be criticized for overlooking the fact that when ethical life appears as a higher stage in contrast to *Moralität* in the *Encyclopedia* and *The Philosophy of Right*, it is not the simpler form of ethical life that is involved. In the corresponding section of the *Phenomenology* this simpler form is the object of analysis, and it is treated as a stage that precedes that of *Moralität*. At this stage, the individuals still have not developed their own independence, and for this reason Hegel treats the community here as one that is characteristic of antiquity. On the other hand, when Hegel treats ethical life as a higher stage than *Moralität* in the *Encyclopedia* and *The Philosophy of Right*, it might be argued that the moral-critical stance in relation to the state is superseded in the positive sense in ethical life. It must be noted, however, that Hegel was not able to understand the structure of morality and the ought any better than he was able to grasp the structure of the question of truth. His subject-object model is too simple for both structures. Thus he could not see that when the ought is opposed to reality — "how it would be better" — the former itself discloses an *objective* dimension. It is an objective dimension that is itself differentiated into various levels in precisely the same way as the dimension of truth regarding states of affairs; thus, one can ask whether what is claimed to be better actually also is better, that is, whether it is justifiable as such. Hegel could no longer integrate these connections into his model, and he therefore adopted the view that the ought is something subjective, since it is contraposed by subjects to what exists. In locating all modes of conduct in the Procrustean bed of the subject-object relationship, Hegel could not grasp the structure of critique at all, whether it be theoretical or moral. On his account, the sole differentiations consisted in the greater or lesser independence of the two sides, and the greater or lesser unity between the sides. Since morality for him could only mean a form of subjectivity that insists upon its independence, it could not be integrated *as such* into ethical life or the state.

Hence, it is not surprising that one can find only the following account of how the independence of individuals is taken into consideration in *The Philosophy of Right*: "The state is the actuality of concrete freedom. But concrete freedom consists in this, that personal individuality and its particular interests not only achieve their complete development and gain explicit recognition for their right (as they do in the sphere of the family and civil society), but, for one thing, they also pass over of their own accord into the interest of the universal, and for another thing, they know and will the universal; they even recognise it as their own substantive spirit and actively pursue it as their final end" (260).

You might still argue that Hegel certainly does not claim that this relation of duty, trust, and so on, and the elimination of reflection and conscience, are required for any arbitrary state; rather, they are only commanded for a state that is, in the words of *The Philosophy of Right* (258), "rational in and for itself." First, I have not found any explanation in *The Philosophy of Right* of how the individual should relate to a state that is otherwise constituted. And Hegel also could not have provided such an explanation, since this type of an ought in the face of an existing order would again only be a regression into the "self-conceit" of subjectivity. Second, Hegel declares in the same paragraph (258 Addition): "On some principle or other, any state may be shown to be bad, this or that defect may be found in it; yet, at any rate if one of the mature states of our epoch is in question, it has in it the moments essential to the existence of the state.... The affirmative ... subsists in spite of its defects, and it is this affirmative factor that is our topic here." Third, what constitutes the rationality of the state in Hegel's view? I do not want to insist on this point, since even the most enthusiastic apologists of Hegel's political philosophy do not like to identify themselves with his concrete conception of the state. But this is not the issue here, and it is therefore unnecessary for me to examine this conception. Let us assume that Hegel had developed a conception of a state that is as good and just as one could imagine. Would it then be justified to demand unconditional obedience to the state and to require the surrender of responsibility on the part of the citizens? This idea is reminiscent of an argument that is frequently heard today in the Federal Republic of Germany; it is claimed that while criticism of the state may well be justified elsewhere, it certainly has no place with us because we live in the most liberal state that one car. imagine. In both instances there is a disregard for the fact that a state cannot be good or rational, much less liberal, if it demands an unconditionally affirmative relation from its citizens. In contrast, it follows from the conception of responsibility that a community only deserves to be designated as rational if its highest end is the responsibility of all citizens; and this also applies precisely in the relation of the citizens to the community itself.

To what extent is this Hegelian conception of ethical life as the truth of self-consciousness a necessary consequence of his initial approach? At least two levels must be distinguished in answering this question. The first level lies on the surface, so to speak, and consists in the affirmation of the existing conditions. This aspect follows from Hegel's fundamental conception of truth as the unity of concept with reality only if one equates reality, the 'actual,' with *what is actually present*. Hegel himself does this explicitly (PR, p. 10); and this occurs precisely at the point at which the notorious sentence "what is rational is actual and what is actual is rational" is also to be found. It is therefore absurd when the significance of this sentence is repeatedly minimized (as Hegel himself already did, *Enc.* 6) by alluding to the fact that *actuality* in the Hegelian system does not simply stand for what factually exists. In the context in which this sentence occurs, it does stand for what currently exists; and this is the only point that is at issue here.

It becomes clear in Marxism that Hegel's conception of overcoming the alienation between subject and reality can be distinguished from the equation of reality with what currently exists. But here the deeper reason as to why Hegel had to regard his conception as one that is realized in the present becomes apparent. For if one envisions this conception as a practical idea for the future, it seems to stand for something that ought to be; and we have already seen that Hegel misinterprets and rejects the ought as something subjective. Such a practical idea also would have required recourse to a specifically practical form of justification, that is, the justification of practical propositions. Hegel does not recognize this form of justification, and it would have been difficult for him to apprehend it within his systematic framework. Nonetheless, Fichte's example indicates that this was possible within the horizon of German Idealism. On the other hand, Marx and the tradition of Marxism accepted from Hegel both the repudiation of the ought and the lack of understanding for the independent justification of practical propositions. Thus, Marxism could also adopt the thesis that only the actual is rational, although it added the qualification that the actual is still developing. In his own way, Hegel prepared the foundation for the belief in the miracle that the real course of history would lead by itself to the good—that is, to the overcoming of alienation. This belief made it possible to project the ideal into the future while at the same time avoiding the issue of its practical justification. Recent experience, however, has led to the inevitable conclusion that history is not so miraculous, and thus even within Marxism there seems to be some recognition of the irreducibility of normative questions and of the independent status of the justification of practical propositions vis-à-vis the justification of theoretical propositions.

The deeper question is whether it would have been possible from Hegel's original standpoint to incorporate the freedom and responsibility of individuals into his conception of a good society. This question can be raised irrespective of whether this conception is viewed as a present reality or as a practical ideal.

Is the totalitarian character of Hegel's philosophy of objective spirit a necessary consequence of his original approach, or is it only a function of his personal ideological intentions and his idolization of power? Could the infelicities be corrected within Hegel's model? I have repeatedly made a distinction within Hegel's framework between (1) his specifically philosophical or conceptual-structural approach, which is to be grasped in his dialectic culminating in the truth as idea, and (2) the original intuition from which he proceeded. But this distinction does not play any role at the present stage of our reflections. It makes no difference whether we adhere to Hegel's explicit conceptual terminology and speak of an *identity* of the individual with the objectivity confronting him, or with less paradox speak simply of a *harmony*; in either case the implication is that for Hegel, negativity must always be overcome in the affirmative relation. On the other hand, if we conceive of the individuals of a society as responsible, that is, as placing themselves, each other (reciprocally), and their society into question, they must certainly reciprocally recognize one another; and they are mutually directed toward harmony as a regulative idea in the same sense that they are directed toward truth as a regulative idea. Nevertheless, they do not *find* themselves in a harmony, much less in an identity. Hegel has an essentially closed model, and the idea of re-sponsibility requires an essentially open model.

In his early writings prior to 1800, Hegel started perhaps from something like an idea of brotherhood or fraternity. He certainly did not realize this idea in his later conception of objective spirit, and he also no longer had this intention. But I now want to entertain this idea, because it is the most promising conception that I personally can extract from the intrinsically vague idea of a harmony. Further-more, I can only clarify the specific significance of the idea of re-sponsibility by making Hegel's point of departure as strong as it possibly can be in my view; and the extent to which I am still dealing with the real Hegel is not important here. It is also not necessary for my present purposes to define the idea of brotherhood more precisely. I can proceed from the assumption that we all have a rough idea of what this idea implies. Mead also was directed toward this idea, and it functioned for him as the regulative idea in terms of which the existing society can be criticized and improved. The concept of broth-erhood represents a specific idea of the good life—perhaps the best that we have. The idea of ethical life that Hegel develops in his doctrine of objective spirit is also a specific (and in his view realized) idea of the good life. In contrast, the idea of responsibility in what I termed its narrow meaning is not directly an idea of the good life. Rather, it represents a way of appropriating that which one regards as the good life: That is, one adopts it in the mode of the question of its truth and self-determination. The following question might now be raised: How can one justify that it is better to adopt an idea of the good life in the mode of self-determination rather than unreflectively? But in the same sense the following question can also be raised: How can one justify that one idea of the good life, such as that of brotherhood, is better than another? It is thereby clear that if one becomes engaged in justifying an idea of the good life, one already raises the practical question of truth; and this means that one already relates oneself to oneself in the mode of the reflective self-relation. Thus the idea of responsibility is the condition of the possibility of a rational relation of oneself to oneself, to others, and to society, irrespective of how this relation may be determined in content. Since the idea of responsibility is the formal condition of the rationality and autonomy of that for which we concretely strive, it also must always be a preeminent part of our idea of the good life in both its personal and its social dimension, however this may be more closely determined (even in the mode of responsibility). Every conception of one's own life and social life that does not give preeminent consideration to one's own responsibility and the responsibility of everyone is irrational.

Most past epochs thought that they knew what is good, and the philosophical systems that arose within them thought that they could directly specify what the idea of the truly good life is. This was still the case with Hegel. We have lost this certainty today. But the loss can also be a gain. Since we no longer believe that we are in possession of the truth, we can renew the Socratic experience that we can attain an outlook upon the good in the knowledge of our ignorance. In this process of being thrown back upon ourselves, we can learn to value the fact that we can *raise the question* of what is truly good.

Notes

Lecture 1

1. *Hegel's Lectures on the History of Philosophy*, trans. E. S. Haldane and F. H. Simpson, New York, 1955, vol. III, p. 217.

2. At the time these lectures were given, Ulrich Pothast was no longer in Heidelberg, but the relevant book first appeared as his Heidelberg dissertation.

3. *New Introductory Lectures on Psychoanalysis*, trans. J. Strachey, New York, 1964, p. 70.

4. Cf. my *Traditional and Analytical Philosophy: Lectures on the Philosophy of Language*, trans. P. A. Gorner, Cambridge, 1982, pp. 70–74.

5. Cf. ibid., p. 416, n.ll, and p. 300.

Lecture 2

1. "Anmerkungen zu Karl Jaspers 'Psychologie der Weltanschauungen," in H. Saner, ed., *Karl Jaspers in der Diskussion*, Munich, 1973, pp. 89ff.

2. Ibid., p. 93.

3. *Being and Time*, trans. J. Macquarrie and E. Robinson, New York, 1962, p. 67.

4. "Anmerkungen," pp. 85, 96.

5. *Being and Time*, p. 67.

6. Cf. my *Traditional and Analytical Philosophy*, pp. 8, 35.

7. *Critique of Pure Reason*, trans. N. K. Smith, London, 1963, B edition, 18.

8. Cf. *Being and Time*, p. 32.

9. Cf. note 2 and *Being and Time*, 41.

Lecture 3

1. Pothast, *Über einige Fragen der Selbstbeziehung*, Frankfurt, 1971, p. 9.

2. Chapter 1 of Investigation V.

3. Cf. especially Cramer's detailed critique of the conceptions of Husserl and the Kantian Natorp.

4. *Psychology from an Empirical Standpoint*, trans. Rancurello, Terrell, and McAlister, New York, 1973, book II, chapter 1, and in this connection, Pothast, *Über einige Fragen*, pp. 74–76, and Cramer, "Erlebnis," in H. G. Gadamer, ed., *Stuttgarter Hegel-Tage 1970*, Bonn, 1974, pp. 579ff.

5. Cf. Henrich, "Selbstbewusstsein: Kritische Einleitung in eine Theorie," in R. Bubner, ed., *Hermeneutik und Dialektik*, Tübingen, 1970, vol. I, p. 261, and the passages by Pothast and Cramer cited in note 4.

6. Henrich, "Selbstbewusstsein," p. 278.

7. J. G. Fichte, *Nachgelassene Schriften*, ed. H. Jacob, Berlin, 1937, vol. II, p. 357. Cited by Pothast, *Über einige Fragen*, p. 41.

8. *The One Possible Basis for a Demonstration of the Existence of God*, trans. G. Treash, New York, 1979, p. 59.

9. Cf. also Henrich, "Selbstbewusstsein," pp. 260, 278.

Lecture 4

1. Cf. also Pothast, *Über einige Fragen*, p. 18.

2. H. N. Castañeda, "Indicators and Quasi-Indicators," *American Philosophical Quarterly* 4 (1967): 85–100.

3. Ibid., p. 86.

4. Ibid., p. 87.

5. Cf. my *Traditional and Analytical Philosophy*, lectures 21 through 27.

6. For a more precise sense of this *definitively*, cf. ibid., lecture 24.

7. For a more detailed account of the following, cf. ibid., pp. 357–371.

8. Wittgenstein did not advance the thesis of veridical symmetry for reasons that remain to be discussed. But this thesis has been advanced by other analytic philosophers who stand in his tradition. Cf. P. F. Strawson, *Individuals*, London, 1959, chapter 3, 4, and S. Shoemaker, *Self-Knowledge and Self-Identity*, Ithaca, 1963, p. 170.

Lecture 5

1. Cf. P. M. S. Hacker, *Insight and Illusion*, Oxford, 1972, p. 185.

2. All citations from the *Blue Book* refer to the English edition: *The Blue and Brown Books*, Oxford, 1964.

3. Cf. Hacker, *Insight and Illusion*, chapter 7, §2.

4. Cf. ibid., chapter 7, §4.

5. A. Kenny, "The Verification Principle and the Private Language Argument," in O. R. Jones, ed., *The Private Language Argument*, London, 1971, p. 205.

6. Cf. W. V. O. Quine, *Ontological Relativity and Other Essays*, New York, 1969, p. 31.

7. Kenny, "Verification," pp. 216–220. Kenny incorporated this passage word for word in his book; see his *Wittgenstein*, London, 1973, pp. 190–195.

8. Thus, Kenny, "Verification," p. 218.

9. The reference to a "useful result" in paragraph 270 must be understood in the same sense.

Lecture 6

1. Cf. Hacker, *Insight and Illusion*, chapter 10.

2. "For we have a definite concept of what it means to learn to know a process better" (308).

3. Cf. especially N. Malcolm, "Wittgenstein's Philosophical Investigations," *Philosophical Review* 63 (1954): 530–559.

4. Hacker, *Insight and Illusion*, p. 274.

5. Cf. Shoemaker, *Self-knowledge*, chapter 6, 7. The entire chapter, as well as the whole book, is extremely instructive.

Lecture 7

1. Cf. A. MacIntyre, *The Unconscious*, London, 1958, especially chapter 4.

2. S. Hampshire, "Sincerity and Single-Mindedness," p. 244.

3. Or, in any case, the objective state of affairs that is remembered implies a "ϕ" state. If I remember that someone was standing here, this means that I remember having seen him standing here.

4. *Complete Works*, trans. J. Strachey and ed. A. Freud, London, 1953–74, vol. II, p. 270.

5. M. Bartels, *Selbstbewusstsein und Unbewusstes: Studien zu Freud und Heidegger*, Berlin, 1976, pp. 37ff.

6. S. Hampshire, *Thought and Action*, London, 1959, pp. 177ff. Cf. also Bartels, *Selbstbewusstsein*, pp. 108ff.

7. This is the title of a book edited by R. Dörbert, J. Habermas, and G. Nunner-Winkler. Cf. also J. Loevinger, *Ego Development*, San Francisco, 1976.

8. Cf. Loevinger, *Ego Development*, pp. 391-393.

9. Published in *Complete Works*, vol. I, pp. 282-397.

10. Cf. in this connection H. Hartmann, "The Development of the Ego Concept in Freud's Work," in Hartmann, *Essays on Ego Psychology*, London, 1964, pp. 268-296, Loevinger, *Ego Development*, chapters 13-15, and Bartels, *Selbstbewusstsein*, pp. 37ff.

11. Cf., for example, *The Ego and the Id*, trans. J. Strachey, New York, 1960, p. 27, and the survey by J. Laplanche and J. B. Pontalis, *Das Vokabular der Psychoanalyse*, Frankfurt, 1973, pp. 184ff.

12. *The Ego and the Id*, p. 45.

13. Cf. Hartmann, *Essays on Ego Psychology*, p. 127. It was certainly a step in the wrong direction to try to resolve the ambiguity in Freud's terminology in this way, because the talk of the ego (*das Ich*) is thereby definitively severed from its connection with the ordinary use of the word *I*. Loevinger tends toward a resolution in the opposite direction; cf. note 8, above.

14. *Complete Works*, vol. XX, p. 98, *New Introductory Lectures on Psychoanalysis*, p. 76.

15. *New Introductory Lectures on Psychoanalysis*, p. 73.

16. *The Ego and the Id*, p. 75.

17. *New Introductory Lectures on Psychoanalysis*, p. 88.

18. Ibid., p. 77.

19. Ibid., p. 76.

20. Ibid., p. 77, Plato, *Phaedrus*, 253cff.

21. *Republic*, 439c-d.

22. For Kant's terminology, cf. especially the first section of the introduction to the *Metaphysics of Morals* (*Doctrine of Virtue*, trans. M. Gregor, Philadephia, 1964, p. 10). The word *Wille* is sometimes employed ambiguously by Kant, so that it is also used synonymously with *Willkür*. Cf., for example, *Groundwork of the Metaphysic of Morals*, trans. H. J. Paton, New York, 1963, p. 80.

23. *Groundwork*, p. 100.

Lecture 8

1. This ambiguity is elaborated in detail by D. L. Greenier, "Meaning and Being in Heidegger's Sein und Zeit," Ph.D. diss. University of Heidelberg, 1975, 1.1.

2. Heidegger, *The Essence of Reasons*, trans. T. Malick, Evanston, 1969, p. 51.

3. Cf., among others, W. V. O. Quine, *From a Logical Point of View*, Cambridge, 1953, pp. 1–8, and E. K. Specht, *Sprache und Sein*, Berlin, 1967, pp. 42ff.

4. I have presented the following line of argument more extensively in "Existence in Space and Time," *Neue Heft f. Philosophie* 8 (1975): 14–33.

5. Cf. my *Traditional and Analytical Philosophy*, p. 370.

6. Ibid.

7. In the essay cited in note 4.

8. *De Anima*, II, 4, 415bl.

9. Ibid., 415bl3.

10. For Aristotle the preservation of the species is a special case of self-preservation. Cf. ibid., 415b6ff., and F. Ricken, *Der Lustbegriff in der Nikomachischen Ethik des Aristoteles*, Göttingen, 1976, p. 36.

11. Cf. Ricken, *Der Lustbegriff*, pp. 37–39, 126ff., and the references cited there.

12. Cf. *Politics*, I, 2, 1253a 9ff.

13. Cf. *De Anima*, III, 11–12.

14. Cf. *Nicomachean Ethics*, VI, 2, 1139a20.

15. Ibid., I, 6.

16. Cf. *Sickness unto Death*, in *"Fear and Trembling" and "The Sickness unto Death,"* trans., W. Lowrie, Princeton, 1941, pp. 168ff.

17. On veridical being and the assertion moment, cf. my *Traditional and Analytical Philosophy*, pp. 41–48.

Lecture 9

1. Cf. my *Traditional and Analytical Philosophy*, lecture 25.

2. Kenny's talk of "objectless emotions" appears to derive from the fact that in the English translation of *Zettel* Wittgenstein's expression *Gemütsbewegungen* is rendered as "emotions."

3. Cf. *Action, Emotion, and Will*, London, 1963, chapter 3.

4. What Heidegger calls the "burdensome character" (173) of Dasein, which becomes manifest in moods, even in the "mood of elation," cannot be regarded as 'negative.' This burdensome character simply stands for the unavoidability of having to exist. But Heidegger facilitated possible misunderstandings by not examining the specifically negative features of the negative moods or the positive features of the positive ones.

5. Cf. Aristotle, *Metaphysics*, IX, 6, *Nicomachean Ethics*, 1173a33, 1174b8, G. H. von Wright, *Norm and Action*, London, 1963, p. 41, and Kenny, *Action, Emotion, and Will*, chapter 8.

6. For the distinction between different concepts of possibility, cf. expecially U. Wolf, *Möglichkeit und Notwendigkeit bei Aristoteles und heute*, Munich, 1979.

7. Ibid., 24d, 25c, and Kenny, *Will, Freedom, and Power*, Oxford, 1975, chapter 7.

8. Kenny, *Will, Freedom, and Power*, p. 129.

9. Cf. J. L. Austin, "Ifs and Cans," in *Philosophical Papers*, Oxford, 1961, and P. H. Nowell-Smith, "Ifs and Cans," *Theoria*, 1960. The most recent interpretation comes from Kenny (*Will, Freedom, and Power*, p. 141). According to Kenny, the "if I will" is to be understood as a qualification of the "I can" and the latter is to be understood in the sense of the "can" of abilities. This conception, however, is contradicted by the fact that we do not use such sentences in order to ascribe a type of ability to someone, but in order to express a concrete possibility of action.

10. Kenny, *Will, Freedom, and Power*, p. 129.

11. Wolf, Möglichkeit, 256.

12. Kenny, *Will, Freedom, and Power*, pp. 129, 143.

13. Cf. Hampshire, *Thought and Action*, chapter 3.

14. Here I am indebted to Charles Taylor.

15. Hampshire, *Thought and Action*, p. 126.

Lecture 10

1. I have only briefly referred to this aspect, last mentioned on pages 173-174. I have dealt with it extensively in *Der Wahrheitsbegriff bei Husserl und Heidegger*, Berlin, 1967, pp. 310-326.

2. The most comprehensive discussion to date can be found in G. H. von Wright, *The Varieties of Goodness*, London, 1963.

3. G. Schneeberger, *Nachlese zu Heidegger*, Bern, 1962, pp. 148ff.

Lecture 11

1. *Politics*, I, 2, 1253a9ff.

2. Mead's statements on this topic are definitely clearer in the third supplementary essay, pp. 354ff., which is part of an original manuscript, than they are in paragraphs 8-9 of the compilation of lectures.

3. *Selected Writings*, ed. A. J. Reck, New York, 1964, p. 244 (my emphasis).

4. Cf. my *Traditional and Analytical Philosophy*, especially, pp. 223ff.

Lecture 12

1. *Politics*, I, 1-2.

2. H. L. A. Hart, *The Concept of Law*, Oxford, 1961, pp. 54ff.

3. *Nicomachean Ethics*, I, 6.

4. Cf. von Wright, *The Varieties of Goodness*, chapter 2, which deals with this sense of *good* under the title "technical goodness."

5. *Nicomachean Ethics*, I, 6.

6. Ibid., III, 6.

7. Ibid., II, 4–5.

8. There are good reasons here to suspect a mistake in the lecture notes. Mead probably simply said "adjusting oneself."

9. E. Erikson, "Identity and the Life-Cycle," *Psychological Issues* 1 (1959): 102.

10. J. Habermas, "Können komplexe Gesellschaften eine vernünftige Identität ausbilden?" in *Zur Rekonstruktion des Historischen Materialismus*, Frankfurt, 1976, pp. 94ff. The three levels are described similarly (and in part identically) by Habermas in "Moral Development and Ego Identity," in *Communication and the Evolution of Society*, trans. T. McCarthy, Boston, 1979, p. 85, as well as in the introduction to R. Dörbert, J. Habermas, and G. Nunner-Winkler, eds., *Entwicklung des Ichs*, Cologne, 1977, pp. 10ff.

11. D. Henrich, "Identität," in O. Marquard and K. Stierle, eds., *Poetik und Hermeneutik*, Munich, 1979, vol. VIII, p. 136.

12. Habermas, *Kultur und Kritik*, Frankfurt, 1973, pp. 226, 228.

13. For these formulations cf. also ibid., p. 230.

14. This is no less clear in this text than in the "Notizen zum Begriff der Rollenkompetenz." Cf. *Kultur und Kritik*, pp. 226, 229ff.

15. Cf. *Kultur und Kritik*, p. 229: "How is . . . the problem of self-identification to be resolved?"

16. Ibid., p. 230 (my emphasis).

17. I am indebted here to Karl-Heinz Breuer.

18. Cf., for example, D. J. Levita, *Der Begriff der Identität*, Frankfurt, 1971, pp. 56ff.

19. *Entwicklung des Ichs*, p. 9.

Lecture 13

1. Hegel's *Phenomenology of Spirit* is cited according to the Miller translation, Oxford, 1977, the *Science of Logic* (referred to in the text as the *Logic*) according to the Miller translation, London, 1969, and the *Philosophy of Right* according to the Knox translation, Oxford, 1952.

2. Cf. *Critique of Pure Reason*, B 382ff.

3. Cf. Fichte, *Grundlage der gesamten Wissenschaftlehre*, Jena and Leipzig, 1794, 2.

4. *Categories*, 3b24. More precisely, P. F. Strawson, *Logioco-Linguistic Papers*, London, 1971, pp. 96ff.

5. Cf., in this connection, H. F. Fulda, "Zur Logik der Phänomenologie von 1807," *Hegel-Studien*, Supplement 3 (1966): 75ff.

6. F. W. S. Schelling, *System of Transcendental Idealism*, trans. P. Heath, Charlottesville, VA, 1978, p. 5.

7. Ibid., p. 7.

8. Cf. my *Der Wahrheitsbegriff bei Husserl und Heidegger*, 15.

Lecture 14

1. C. Taylor, *Hegel*, Cambridge, 1975, pp. 133ff. I have also benefited in other ways from Taylor's unconventional interpretation of the method of the *Phenomenology* in the fourth chapter of his book.

2. Cf. *Groundwork of the Metaphysic of Morals*, pp. 103ff.

3. *Critique of Pure Reason*, B 134n.

4. A similar move could also be found in Heidegger. It is also the case for Heidegger that resoluteness (freedom) *is* the truth, and this is based too on the fact that he understands the meaning of truth in a misleading way; and this also has the consequence that the possibility of being directed toward truth (posing the question of truth) is obscured in Heidegger. Since I repeatedly refer to "the conception" that has emerged "in connection with Heidegger and Mead," this may give rise to a false impression that is overly favorable to Heidegger. But I have already pointed out that Heidegger's position at least leaves open the possibility of the question of truth, whereas Hegel positively obstructs it. This is essentially connected to the fact that Hegel also inverts the meaning of the concept of freedom and thereby thoroughly excludes the possibility of an 'open,' nonaffirmative relation of the individual to the world confronting him.

Bibliography

Alston, W. P. "Expressing," in M. Black, ed., *Philosophy in America*, London, 1965, pp. 15–34.

Anscombe, G. E. M. "The First Person," in S. D. Guttenplan, ed., *Mind and Language*, Oxford, 1975, pp. 45–65.

Aristotle. *Werke* (cited according to the standard pagination of the Prussian Academy).

Austin, J. L. *Philosophical Papers*, Oxford, 1961.

Ayers, R. M. *The Refutation of Determinism*, London, 1968.

Bartels, M. *Selbstbewusstsein und Unbewusstes: Studien zu Freud und Heidegger*, Berlin, 1976.

Brentano, F. *Psychologie von empirischen Standpunkt* (1874), ed. O. Kraus, Leipzig, 1924–25. (*Psychology from an Emprirical Standpoint*, trans. Rancurello, Terrell, and McAlister, New York, 1973.)

Castañeda, H. N. "Indicators and Quasi-Indicators," *American Philosophical Quarterly* 4 (1967): 85–100.

Cramer, K. "Erlebnis," in H. G. Gadamer, ed., *Stuttgarter Hegel-Tage 1970*, Bonn, 1974.

Dörbert, R., Habermas, J., and Nunner-Winkler, G., eds. *Entwicklung des Ichs*, Cologne, 1977.

Erikson, E. H. "Identity and the Life-Cycle," *Psychological Issues* 1 (1959).

Fichte, J. G. *Grundlage der gesamten Wissenschaftlehre*, Jena and Leipzig, 1794.

Fichte, J. G. *Nachgelassene Schriften*, ed. H. Jacob, Berlin, 1937.

Freud, S. *Aus den Anfängen der Psychoanalyse*, Frankfurt, 1962.

Freud, S. *The Ego and the Id*, trans. J. Strachey, New York, 1960.

Freud, S. *Gesammelte Werke*, London and Frankfurt, 1940. (*Complete Works*, trans. J. Strachey and ed. A. Freud, London, 1953–74.)

Freud, S. *New Introductory Lectures on Psychoanalysis*, trans. J. Strachey, New York, 1964.

Fulda, H. F. "Zur Logik der Phänomenologie von 1807," *Hegel-Studien*, Supplement 3 (1966).

Greenier, D. L. "Meaning and Being in Heidegger's Sein und Zeit," Ph.D. diss., University of Heidelberg, 1975.

Habermas, J. *Communication and the Evolution of Society*, trans. T. McCarthy, Boston, 1979.

Habermas, J. *Kultur und Kritik*, Frankfurt, 1973.

Habermas, J. *Zur Rekonstruktion des Historischen Materialismus*, Frankfurt, 1976.

Hacker, P. M. S. *Insight and Illusion*, Oxford, 1972.

Hampshire, S. *Freedom of Mind*, Oxford, 1972.

Hampshire, S. *Thought and Action*, London, 1959.

Hart, H. L. A. *The Concept of Law*, Oxford, 1961.

Hartmann, H. *Essays on Ego Psychology*, London, 1964.

Hegel, G. W. F. *Logik*, 2 vols., ed. G. Lasson, Leipzig, 1948. (*Hegel's Science of Logic*, trans. A. V. Miller, London, 1969.)

Hegel, G. W. F. *Phänomenologie des Geistes*, ed. J. Hoffmeister, Leipzig, 1949. (*Hegel's Phenomenology of Spirit*, trans. A. V. Miller, Oxford, 1977.)

Hegel, G. W. F. *Sämtliche Werke*, ed. H. Glockner, Stuttgart, 1956.

Heidegger, M. "Anmerkungen zu Karl Jaspers 'Psychologie der Weltanschauungen,'" in H. Saner, ed., *Karl Jaspers in der Diskussion*, Munich, 1973, pp. 70–79.

Heidegger, M. *Sein und Zeit*, Halle, 1927. (*Being and Time*, trans. J. Macquarrie and E. Robinson, New York, 1962.)

Heidegger, M. *Vom Wesen des Grundes*, Frankfurt, 1949. (*The Essence of Reasons*, trans. T. Malick, Evanston, 1969.)

Heidegger, M. *Was ist Metaphysik?*, Bonn, 1929.

Henrich, D. *Fichtes ursprüngliche Einsicht*, Frankfurt, 1967.

Henrich, D. "Identität," in O. Marquard and K. Stierle, eds., *Poetik und Hermeneutik*, VIII, Munich, 1979.

Henrich, D. "Selbstbewusstsein: Kritische Einleitung in eine Theorie," in R. Bubner, ed., *Herneneutik und Dialektik*, I, Tübingen, 1970, pp. 257–284.

Husserl, E. *Logische Untersuchungen*, Halle, 1900–1901.

Kant, I. *Critique of Pure Reason*, trans. N. K. Smith, London, 1963.

Kant, I. *Groundwork of the Metaphysic of Morals*, trans. H. J. Paton, New York, 1963.

Kant, I. *The One Possible Basis for a Demonstration of the Existence of God*, trans. G. Treash, New York, 1979.

Kant, I. *Werke*, ed. the Prussian Academy of Sciences, Berlin, 1902.

Kenny, A. *Action, Emotion, and Will*, London, 1963.

Kenny, A. "The Verification Principle and the Private Language Argument," in O. R. Jones, ed., *The Private Language Argument*, London, 1971, pp. 204–228.

Kenny, A. *Will, Freedom, and Power*, Oxford, 1975.

Kenny, A. *Wittgenstein*, London, 1973.

Kierkegaard, S. *"Die Krankheit zum Tode" und anderes*, ed. H. Diem and W. Rest, Cologne and Olten, 1956. (*"Fear and Trembling" and "The Sickness unto Death,"* trans. W. Lowrie, Princeton, 1941.)

Krüger, G. "Die Herkunft des philosophischen Selbstbewusstseins," in G. Krüger, *Freiheit und Weltverwaltung*, Freiburg and Munich, 1958, pp. 11–69.

Laplanche, J., and Pontalis, J. B. *Das Vokabular der Psychoanalyse*, Frankfurt, 1973.

Levita, D. J. *Der Begriff der Identität*, Frankfurt, 1971.

Loevinger, J. *Ego Development*, San Francisco, 1976.

MacIntyre, A. *The Unconscious*, London, 1958.

Malcolm, N. "Wittgenstein's Philosophical Investigations," *Philosophical Review* 63 (1954): 530–559.

Mead, G. H. *Mind, Self, and Society*, Chicago, 1934.

Mead, G. H. *Selected Writings*, ed. A. J. Reck, New York, 1964.

Nowell-Smith, P. H. "Ifs and Cans," *Theoria*, 1960.

Plato, *Werke* (cited according to the standard pagination of the Stephanus edition).

Pothast, U. *Über einige Fragen der Selbstbeziehung*, Frankfurt, 1971.

Quine, W. V. O. *From a Logical Point of View*, Cambridge, 1953.

Quine, W. V. O. *Ontological Relativity and Other Essays*, New York, 1969.

Ricken, F. *Der Lustbegriff in der Nikomachischen Ethik des Aristoteles*, Göttingen, 1976.

Ryle, G. *The Concept of Mind*, London, 1948.

Schelling, F. W. S. *System of Transcendental Idealism*, trans. P. Heath, Charlottesville, VA, 1978.

Schelling, F. W. S. *Werke*, ed. M. Schröter, Munich, 1927.

Schneeberger, G. *Nachlese zu Heidegger*, Bern, 1962.

Shoemaker, S. *Self-Knowledge and Self-Identity*, Ithaca, 1963.

Specht, E. K. *Sprache und Sein*, Berlin, 1967.

Strawson, P. F. *Individuals*, London, 1959.

Bibliography

Strawson, P. F. *Logico-Linguistic Papers*, London, 1971.

Taylor, C. *Hegel*, Cambridge, 1975.

Tugendhat, E. "Existence in Space and Time," *Neue Heft f. Philosophie* 8 (1975): 14-33.

Tugendhat, E. "Die sprachanalytische Kritik der Ontologie," in H. G. Gadamer, ed., *Das Probleme der Sprache*, Munich, 1967, pp. 483-493.

Tugendhat, E. *Vorlesungen zur Einführung in die sprachanalytische Philosophie*, Frankfurt, 1976. (*Traditional and Analytical Philosophy: Lectures on the Philosophy of Language*, trans. P. A. Gorner, Cambridge, 1982.)

Tugendhat, E. *Der Wahrheitsbegriff bei Husserl und Heidegger*, Berlin, 1967.

Wittgenstein, L. *The Blue and Brown Books*, Oxford, 1964.

Wittgenstein, L. *Philosophische Untersuchungen*, in *Schriften*, vol. 1. (*Philosophical Investigations*, trans. G. E. M. Anscombe, New York, 1953.)

Wittgenstein, L. "Wittgenstein's Notes for Lectures on 'Private Experience' and 'Sense-Data,' " ed. R. Rhees, *Philosophical Review* 77 (1968): 271-320.

Wittgenstein, L. *Zettel*, in *Schriften*, vol. 5. (*Zettel*, ed. G. H. v. Wright and G. E. M. Anscombe and trans. G. E. M. Anscombe, Oxford, 1967.)

Wolf, U. *Möglichkeit und Notwendigkeit bei Aristoteles und heute*, Munich, 1979.

Wright, G. H. von. *Norm and Action*, London, 1963.

Wright, G. H. von. *The Varieties of Goodness*, London, 1963.

Index